THE HEIRS OF TOM BROWN

THE HEIRS OF TOM BROWN

The English School Story

by ISABEL QUIGLY

1982
CHATTO & WINDUS
LONDON

PUBLISHED BY
CHATTO & WINDUS LTD
40 WILLIAM IV STREET
LONDON WC2N 4DF

Clarke, Irwin & Co. Ltd
Toronto

BRITISH LIBRARY CATALOGUING
IN PUBLICATION DATA
Quigly, Isabel
The heirs of Tom Brown: the English school story.
1. English fiction – 19th century – History
2. English fiction – 20th century – History and criticism
3. Education in literature I. Title
823'.8'09355 PR830.S/

ISBN 0 7011 2615 9

Phototypeset by
Western Printing Services Ltd, Bristol

Printed in Great Britain by
Redwood Burn Ltd
Trowbridge, Wiltshire

Contents

To Angeles Legarreta

the only person I know who,
for love of her charges,
boarded as an adult in a girls' school,
with gratitude for it and much else,
and love in return.

CHAPTER I

The schools behind the school stories

Invisible compost C. Day-Lewis

The public school in its heyday lasted for about a century, from the middle of the nineteenth century to the middle of the twentieth. Of course it existed before that and it still exists today, but not in the form made familiar by school stories to many who had never been there. In the first half of the nineteenth century and the second half of the twentieth it was a different place – different in style and function, in atmosphere and methods, in ideas and motives, different above all in its effect and in the emotional response it aroused. When confidence was high, and a particular kind of training was needed to produce a particular kind of man, it was as functional and as energetic as a power-house. When this confidence waned, and the training it gave, the men it produced, almost suddenly seemed irrelevant to the world as it had become, its manner changed, its ethos faded, and it ceased to be the sort of place people understand (with approval or disapproval, affection or dislike) by the term 'public school'.

Today it has lost its eccentricity and particularity, its ferocious influence, its emotional importance, its denseness and isolation from the rest of the world, its consequent power for good or ill. Yet 'school' is still an emotive word in this country; less so than it used to be but still able to raise a degree of nostalgia, interest, love, hatred and antagonism unlikely, indeed incredible, almost anywhere else, School clings through later life, known and named in reference books, in the briefest biography, when jobs and appointments are made, and in everyday social life. It clings because the type of education it gives, in a country where education is anything but uniform, marks the mind and to a great extent conditions intellectual development for good; it clings because it conditions (much less than it used to, but still very noticeably) future occupation, place in the world, niche, manner, personality, tastes and attitudes. Perhaps it clings above all because people react emotionally to the fact of having been, or not been, to such-and-such a school or type of school. 'England is perhaps the only [country] where the first testing question, whether from prospective employer or potential mother-in-law, is more likely to be "Where did he go to school?" than "Where does he come from?" or "What did his father do?" ', Francis Hope wrote as recently as 1971.

As the subsoil of adult life, or what C. Day-Lewis called 'an invisible compost',[1] school feeds adult feeling of all kinds. This influence is not what used vaguely to be known as the old school tie or the old boy network, something exerted for practical ends. What I mean is a matter of feeling, of affections and resentments, of personality. It is connected with a person's sense of the kind of man he is, the kind of background he has or admits to, the niche he expects to occupy in the world or would like his children to have. It is something underground and unacknowledged or today acknowledged with a smile. Edward Mack*, the American delver into the spirit of the public schools, who has examined them with the fervour of an anthropologist revealing exotic customs, has called it romantic attachment.

It was socially important, of course, this attachment. Just how important, just how far the influence went, is a matter for the social historian. In the century when imperialism was at its height, the century before Britain's collapse as a great power, a large proportion of the ruling class (which, for much of that time, really did rule) was influenced by it and – more important from the point of view of literature – so was a large proportion of the whole literate class. From there, it spread downwards and outwards. 'The number of men who reached the very top was minutely small in relation to the whole population,' R. M. Ogilvie wrote of the Edwardians, 'but they represented the flowers of a plant whose roots stretched deep into the community'.[2] Even during the single century of its heyday, the public school altered enormously in its ideas, methods and effects, in the kind of man it sought to turn out. If Dr Arnold had turned up at a public school in 1900 he would hardly have recognised what had happened since his reforms at Rugby, and would certainly have failed to understand the ideas of the boys themselves. He had hoped to turn

* Author of the immensely useful and interesting *Public Schools and British Opinion 1780–1860* (1938).

out Christian gentlemen; the later Victorian public schools wanted able administrators. But, early or late in the century, in fiction or in fact, the public school kept its long-term effect. It was a brooding, all-important presence, a matrix, a pointer to the future. No amount of dislike or criticism could ever get rid of that. In his history of the Victorian public schools John Honey wrote:

> This phenomenon . . . is perhaps unique in modern history . . . the completeness of the transfer to an alternative community – a distinctive emotional milieu, capable of generating its own set of values – as the common practice of an influential section of society, probably has no parallel in advanced societies.[3]

It was all very well for Graham Greene, in the demolishing thirties, to write of the schoolboy (in *The Old School*):

> Why . . . he should feel more loyal to a school which is paid to teach him than to a butcher who is paid to feed him I cannot understand;[4]

and logically he may have been right enough. But nearly fifty years and much demolition later, he is still emotionally wrong. Few people even today equate their school with their butcher or regard the two with feelings that are similar in kind. In Greene's day, the sunset of public-school glory, this was even less likely. Few people dislike their butcher, or have personal and passionate feelings about what he sells. Whereas plenty look back on school with feelings of bitter antipathy, with resentment not just for what happened while they were there but for its effect on the rest of life.

Greene was writing about public schools (his father was headmaster of Berkhamsted) but his views on school feeling could be discussed, to some extent, in relation to all English schools. For it was not just the grammar schools and innumerable privately run schools that in their heyday consciously copied the public schools. *All* schools in Britain shared and still share an outlook and an attitude markedly different from those of most countries on the continent. There, school is more likely to be a desk where for a few hours a day you are taught academic subjects; whereas, as Royston Lambert put it:

> unlike those on the continent, all English schools profess . . . a concern with the 'whole man', with ethical and character building ends, which derives from the Arnoldian public school.

This humanity or intrusiveness (depending on your view of it), this dealing with character and conduct as well as mind-training and skill-learning, is none of its business, critics of our system say. If the butcher does not criticise your manners, morals, haircut and language, why should the school, particularly if you are paying it? But this merely shows that Greene's analogy, in practice, fails to ring true, because the nearest analogy with school in our sense of the word – with the public school in its heyday, at least – is not school in the impersonal continental sense but membership of some strongly-flavoured racial or religious group, some authoritarian political party. It is like being an old-style Catholic or an orthodox Jew, a Jehovah's Witness or a member of the Communist Party. To find the same mixture of obsession, resentment and love-hatred that you find in school memoirs you must look at Joyce or Fellini or Buñuel on the Catholic Church, at Silone on the Communist Party, at Philip Roth or Brian Glanville on Jewish family life. As recently as 1938 Cyril Connolly could write:

> Experience undergone by boys at the great public schools, their glories and disappointments, are so intense as to dominate their lives, and to arrest their development. From these it results that the greater part of the ruling class remains adolescent, school-minded, self-conscious, cowardly, sentimental, and, in the last analysis, homosexual.[5]

It shows how fast the public schools have changed that this, which would sound grotesque and incredible if said today, could be said and accepted then.

Throughout the heyday of the public school boys clung to, and men remembered, their schools with what now seems an incredible degree of affection and nostalgia, or of resentment and dislike. When this country was a pivot of the world, and the public school a pivot of the country, this was much less surprising than it would be today, when there is nothing pivotal about either. At this distance the self-importance of the public school and its products seems extraordinary; so does the wish to stay there as long as possible, and later to cling to the patterns of school life. A few gave these feelings artistic expression, and so perpetuated them. Alec Waugh called *The Loom of Youth*, probably the most disapproved school story of them all, 'a love letter to Sherborne'.[6] 'It was in such a mood that a man at the end of a long and intense love affair writes to the mistress whom he still adores, but nonetheless holds largely responsible for the rupture,' he said of his state of mind when he wrote the book.[7] It is this 'long and intense love affair', and its expression in fiction, that is the subject of this book.

I shall be dealing with all sorts of schools stories but I shall stick fairly firmly to a recognisable *genre*. In a single book it would be impossible to cover *all* fictional schools (where would *Villette* stand, for instance? Or *Frost in May*? Or *Olivia*? What about Dickens' or Thackeray's glimpses of school life?). So I shall keep to public schools which were thought similar, in books or schools considered to be 'school stories' and not merely adult novels set in schools. The choice is necessarily arbitrary because hundreds of such stories were published. I propose to take books from *Tom Brown's Schooldays* up to, and around, the Second World War, by the which time, my feeling is, both they and the world they reflected were in steep decline.

2 *Nurseries of nobility* Ben Jonson

Why, a stranger to it might ask, was the public-school system which the school stories reflected ever developed? In most countries, indeed in most classes in this country, boarding school has generally been considered a punishment, a place where the unmanageable are tamed or the unloved disposed of. That the privileged classes should pay heavily to send their children away from quite early childhood (7–8 years old) seems to argue a curious outlook in the parents, perhaps even a sort of mass hysteria. Why did they do it, then? The worldly, the over-occupied, the unloving, were no doubt glad of a respectable excuse to be rid of their young for two-thirds of the year and to shift the responsibility for their development almost entirely on to others; and those living abroad had no choice but to do so. But why did even the most loving families, suitably placed not to, take their sons from the nursery to separate them from home and parents, warmth, domesticity, shows of affection, everything they were used to, all the patterns and artefacts of everyday life?

One answer, perhaps too simplistic, might be that, for many who belonged to these families, adult life demanded it. The strengths and limitations which ten years of such schooling produced were exactly those needed by imperial functionaries; and not only by them but by the many British who, in the public-schools' century, went about the world as civil engineers, as businessmen, as openers-up of new places, administrators of old ones. A boy with ten years' training (five at preparatory, five at public school) could face things which would daunt the untrained: loneliness, isolation, tough living conditions, the lack of home comforts, above all removal from all that was familiar: his own home, country, culture, family and friends. If at eight such removal was thrust on him, at eighteen he would consider it normal.

The amazing abnormality of life for those who manned the empire (and other remote parts of the world) is often forgotten, simply because it was for so long accepted. If school, in which boys were immersed from childhood, was the opposite of home and of the ordinary world, so too was imperial life, in which they might be immersed from adolescence. For long periods a man might have the companionship only of other men like himself, if he was lucky; if he was unlucky, he had the mere presence – never the companionship – of servants and inferiors. A life of celibacy – or at least of bachelordom – was assumed to be normal for years on end. When he married (and marriage was often even chancier than usual, a case of hasty desperation on home leave or of the artificially quick decisions people make who meet outside their familiar cultural context) his domestic life was generally choppy, with seasonal or professional interruptions. When it was too hot or too wet he would be parted from his family for weeks or even months; when work demanded it, the same. As soon as his children were past infancy they were whisked away to England for years of separation. Plenty of people now only middle-aged were sent 'home' for those heartbreakingly long periods: four years, five years at a time, during which they never saw their parents.

Families accepted separations we should now think barbarous. The Decembrist nobleman exiled to Siberia might feel, understandably enough, that he must part with his children for years in order to give them a suitable education in St Petersburg. The middle-class Englishman working abroad until recently felt much the same about school in England. Greene wrote in the thirties:

> Family life for such children is always broken. The miseries recorded by Kipling and Munro must be experienced by many mute inglorious children born to the civil servant or the colonial officer in the East: the arrival of the cab at the strange relative's house, the unpacking of the boxes, the unfamiliar improvised nursery, the terrible departure of the parents, a four-years' absence from affection that in child-time can be as long as a generation (at four one is a small child, at eight a boy).[8]

School, in these cases, was the rock these children clung to; or else the hated stepmother; or both at once.

Paradoxically, at a time when families and their groupings and influence were so important, the importance of home was often under-valued, and the importance of school correspondingly stressed. With parents often far away, many children were quite literally homeless. (Of his schoolboy hero in *Stanton*, Desmond Coke remarks, in an offhand way as if it were not the least bit odd or pathetic: 'He had never been homesick for the excellent reason that he had no home.') The solidness and permanence of school then made it seem an unmoving centre in a shifting world, common ground in a literal as well as a metaphorical sense. It took on a sort of familial, even ancestral importance, with mystical overtones. 'Religion plays, and will play, a small part in a boy's life at school,' wrote Alec Waugh, admittedly generalising, as he often did without seeming to realise it, but expressing a view which was quite credible sixty years ago. '. . . His religion, if he has one, is an unswerving loyalty to his house and school.'[9]

So, in childhood, school cut family ties, making it forever possible to bear long separations. Similarly, it cut out all that was feminine in life: the presence and personality of women, their companionship and influence. A boy who boarded at school in the old isolating conditions could hardly, at least without suffering, have strong family ties, and, before he ever made them as an adult, had to be content with a non-domestic, masculine world in which the wish for a woman's presence, or for relationships with his own children, had little place. The young at school seldom saw the inside of a home, or domestic life of any sort, except, in the artificially exciting short spells of the holidays, their own. In other words, school life was made as similar as possible to the life which might later be expected by many schoolboys. In atmosphere above all. When Connolly called the ex-public schoolboy 'homosexual' he was clearly speaking in the broadest terms. The *pattern* was homosexual: masculine values and company were enough; women were irrelevant to it. If a boy was highly sexed he might turn to other boys, *faute de mieux*, even if in more normal circumstances he would not have done so. If not, he lived a neuter life until he was adult. Even the minor patterns of school life can be interpreted in a sexual way (though woe betide the school-story writer who hinted at it). How else can the fagging system appear? – the way in which the youngest and freshest did chores (wholly domestic chores, considered totally 'feminine' in a period when no male would ever, in other circumstances, make toast and tea or lay and light a fire) for the oldest, the grandest, the most powerful and most impressive, and the pair could be officially alone together, with an official relationship as masters and servants, patrons and patronised. No doubt this relationship was generally 'innocent' (i.e. not overtly sexual). But the pattern of the arrangement, however innocently established, was clear. So was the pattern of everything else: it presupposed an adult way of life, quite startlingly unlike the 'natural' life of people at most times, in most societies. It is therefore in all senses, when looked at from this distance, startlingly artificial.

The strange conditions of public-school life have few parallels in other societies. Boarding school has existed in other times and places, of course, but never and nowhere as monolithically, as all-embracingly, and (within its particular social band) as broadly as in Victorian and Edwardian England. Perhaps the nearest parallel is with the system, in medieval and Tudor England, of sending children from a very early age to live in 'great households' where, acting as servants but also as privileged pupils, young noblemen and the talented more humbly born forged links that might last a lifetime. As Mark Girouard puts it:

It was a way of acquiring social polish, administrative experience, and material and sporting accomplishments. It provided a form of education at a time when schools scarcely existed, except those for the clergy.'[10]

In these households boys learned not just academic subjects but 'how to live', all the complicated ropes of a highly elaborate society; found patronage and a way of climbing above their family's level (Thomas More in Cardinal Morton's household,for instance, or Roger Ascham in Sir Anthony Wingfield's), and exchanged the patterns of home and parents and their own class for those of another world. Like the fags at public schools, they did menial tasks in their early years, their social position outside being subservient to their (amorphous, servile) position in the household: young nobleman and yeoman's son, they were all apprenticed to life together. They too were conditioned to lose strong family ties and feelings, and this, in public servants who must be mobile and, if not celibate, at least free of reliance on home and family, was a lifelong advantage.

These households were enclosed worlds, like the public schools, miniature facsimiles of courts and other institutions; worlds of order, ritual and ceremony, where precedent ruled and everything was established and immutable. Within these worlds the young were rigidly, but perhaps affectionately, not unhappily, enclosed. Ben Jonson called these households and this system 'nurseries of nobility'. Not very dissimilar terms were used to describe the public schools.

3 *Isolated from the age of eight to that of eighteen from all human contact with nine-tenths of their fellow countrymen* . . . T. C. Worsley

Because of its similar function in so many dissimilar lives, because of its immensely strong atmosphere and presence, and its influence upon personality and ideas and attitudes, the public school in its heyday was one of the great connectors. Of course it connected only those who had been there, a narrow social band compared with the whole population though much wider, if the term public school is used broadly, than many people think. (Chesterton suggested neatly how it opened social doors: 'The public schools are not for the sons of gentlemen, they're for the fathers of gentlemen'; and the founder of Radley said in 1872: 'One of the many uses of our public schools [is] to confer an aristocracy on boys who do not inherit it.') In its fairly narrow field, it had a democratic influence, by mixing the upper and the professional classes in a way that would otherwise have been unlikely, and thus promoting the intermarriage and cross-fertilisation of cultures as well as genes which outsiders have long pointed out as a healthy feature of English life. The aristocracy of England was never closed to outsiders, never fussy about quarterings of nobility and the rest of it, as it was in some European countries, and no public school was ever aristocratic, ever socially exclusive in a narrow sense. 'The insistence of the public schools upon gentlemanly, rather than courtly, qualities and their success in transmitting them to the state schools and the poorer classes, rendered them factors in civilisation which should be much esteemed,' Harold Nicolson, no very fond admirer of them, wrote.[11]

Yet popularly they were thought the great dividers and excluders. In a book significantly called *The Decline of the Aristocracy* (1912), Arthur Ponsonby wrote that a boy left public school 'saturated with class feeling'. Nearly thirty years later T. C. Worsley was saying much the same thing, more fully and fiercely:

> Isolated from the age of eight to that of eighteen from all human contact with nine-tenths of their fellow countrymen, and indoctrinated there with the habits and feelings of their own class, the public school products can have no conception of England as a whole . . . It isolates them as a class – so that England has a caste system more rigid than any other civilised country – and the more successful it is, the more thoroughly does it isolate them.[12]

All this may be true, and many people at the time or since would probably agree. But the class system of which the public schools were a part was much wider, more amorphous, more indefinable than mere sniping at the system ever makes it appear.

'Defining the class system [of England] is rather like mapping a delta which is liable to change its shape from year to year,' wrote John Atkins nearly thirty years ago. 'It is also a complex of minor relationships and unspoken conventions.' He went on later:

> Any class opinion or attitude . . . is part of you, grafted on to your skin shortly after birth, and a surgical operation is needed to get rid of it. Even then there will be a scar.[13]

In other words, long before public or even preparatory school has had its way the child has had its grafts of class, attitude, opinion, outlook. The Jesuits said the same thing long ago: the first seven years are vital. Modern psychologists confirm it, with tests from earliest infancy. So it is only quite late in development by culture or class that the preparatory school takes over.

In the heyday of the public schools English life was in every way divisive and exclusive. As Atkins says, again: 'English education was the result of the class system and in turn the education fortified the system.' Public school was part of the class structure, but anyone who belonged quite firmly within the public school world did not even need to go (or perhaps in retrospect did not need to feel he should have gone) to a public school. The borderline cases, the insecure, the social climbers, cared passionately where they had been educated: whether it was at a public school or not and, within the system, which public school they had been to, and even which house in the school. Class was a fact of life and social history, taken so much for granted in the public schools' heyday that only unusual people could get outside it in their sympathies. To most people most of the time, even the most humane, 'people' meant those of their own class. Even the socialist Thomas Hughes made his Tom Brown say: 'All boys are sent to a public school in England', without adding, even to himself, 'all boys like me', and without for a moment considering the minute proportion of the boy population that was in fact like himself. The writer addressing his readers assumed that they shared his class. Dean Farrar at the beginning of *St Winifred's* writes:

> It is the old, old story. Mr Evson was taking his son to a large public school, and this was the first time that Walter had left home. Nearly every father who deigns to open this little book has gone through the scene himself; and he and his sons will know from personal experience the thoughts, and sensations, and memories . . .

But the public schools were not *merely* seedbeds of class feeling. They provided much more. Royston Lambert says that for boarders 'the school largely supersedes the home . . . socially, culturally and even psychologically assuming some of the home's more intimate and emotional functions.' In this lay the schools' strength and what some have seen as their tyranny. Elsewhere Lambert says that the influence of public schools

> extends over time – over whole generations of one family, for example; it permeates and often determines the other social units in which its pupils or former pupils move, their families, preparatory schools, universities, friendship groups and occupational groups.

At one time it was common for a man to retire near his old school. It is still common, as it has long been, for a man to send his sons to his, often in spite of unhappy memories. A number of people, distinguished or not, have been buried at their old schools (Wavell at Winchester, for instance), and in a world where so many live nowhere in particular, have no settled, permanent home and no long family connections anywhere they know of, there seems a circular suitability about it, a sense of stability and homecoming. The upper middle class which dominated the public schools is probably the most shifting class of all. The professions often, and the services nearly always, make a man move where his work is, and the administrative class of imperial days was particularly, often pathetically, rootless. The upper classes through property and the lower through poverty have traditionally belonged to a particular place. The lower middle and mid-middle classes too are likely to be settled, through involvement in trade or business. But the old-style professional man or public servant or officer in the army or navy, particularly in imperial times, often had nowhere he belonged to; and if *his* parents in turn had had no settled place, or had outgrown humbler beginnings and moved away from them, as so often happened in Victorian times, he had none to return to, even in retirement.

Today's young will never feel so strongly about their schooldays in later life. Why should they? School is no longer tyrannical, it does not involve high politics or grave responsibilities, it no longer gives them the feeling of adult importance, of mattering in the world. Even public school is now so much a part of everyday life that its influence merges with many others; its pressures are lighter, its glories almost forgotten, its flavour is immeasurably less strong. The public school was once a tightly closed community, for a single sex and a single class, without visits or outings for weeks on end. It is now part of the local community, open to the nearest town or the surrounding countryside, with frequent visits from the family or weekends at home, with women teachers, the possibility of girl friends, in many cases girl pupils. Air travel has put an end to those enormously long separations, parents are much more aware of the enormity of them, and influences from outside have made the boy himself see the littleness of his particular world, the absurdity of taking too seriously its claims and its self-importance.

If the public school once influenced the grammar school, the tables have now been turned. Much that distinguished the public school has gone, and in essence there is now little difference between it and the one-time grammar school. 'As the universities become more important as the testing ground,' says Anthony Sampson, 'so the public schools become more vulnerable . . . They have become more concerned with intellectual training, less with character building.'[14] The Second World War killed off the world they were made for, a world in which there was not just a ruling class but a sense that this was a ruling country where everyone, not just the ruling members of it, could share a little in the sense of regality and empire. And since then, realising sooner than most that change was inevitable, the public schools have with a quiet, pragmatic, suicidal competence been changing themselves to suit the times – changing in spirit and in substance, though their image has changed rather less. They are still known as public schools (though increasingly all non-state schools are being called 'independent', a term that abolishes the byzantine complexities of past labelling), they still occupy the same buildings and grounds, they are still expensive and growing yearly more so, they still arouse some affection within and some envy without, and some people still call them divisive. But they are no longer what was formerly meant by the term 'public school'.

4 *Historically accidental and romantically misleading* Robin Davis

About what a public school was or was not, few people are agreed.* Among themselves they knew that they were graded like apples, that their position altered from decade to decade as fashions and headmasters changed and measurable achievements varied. But to the world outside, their differences were blurred by distance, and the further from them you were, the smaller and smudgier these seemed. Time makes them smaller and smudgier than ever, as they recede into the past. Soon they may come to look like the minute distinctions of chivalric lore that once seemed important.

The dictionaries give meanings for them which vary a little, though not much. The *Shorter Oxford English Dictionary* says:

Public school, 1580. A school which is public. 1. In England, orig., A grammar-school, endowed for the use or benefit of the public, and carried on under some kind of public management or control; often contrasted with a 'private school'. In modern use, applied esp. to such of these as have developed into large boarding schools, drawing, from the well-to-do classes, pupils who are prepared mainly for the ancient universities or for the public services, and also to some large modern schools with similar aims.

Cassell's calls it:

a school under the control of a publicly elected body; a school whose headmaster is a member of the Headmasters' Conference, usu. endowed school providing a liberal education for such as can afford it.

Webster's defines it as:

an endowed secondary boarding school in Great Britain offering a classical curriculum and preparation for the universities and public services.

* For useful information on the various types of school, their origins, functions, status, etc., see Alicia C. Percival, *Very Superior Men* (1973) and *The Origins of the Headmasters' Conference* (1969).

All these definitions have dated; Royston Lambert supplements them, not always quite accurately:

They are Victorian or pre-Victorian in foundation, siting and tradition. They are independent of public authority and selective in intake. They serve principally the upper income groups of society. Many of the governors, staff and families of pupils (especially of boarders) are educated exclusively within the public school system. The vast majority of pupils in them are carefully prepared academically, socially, religiously and so on by the preparatory school system adjunct to the public school.

Vivian Ogilvie (in 1957) called the public school 'an independent, non-local, predominantly boarding school for the upper and upper-middle classes';[15] A. F. Leach (in 1899), 'an endowed Grammar School, which is wholly or almost wholly a boarding school for the wealthier classes'.[16] Brian Gardner (in 1973), who spreads the net wide enough to include most non-state secondary schools (which is not the dictionary definition or the popular idea of a public school), writes:

All pre-Victorian boys' secondary schools have a common history: monastic schools, choir schools, chantry schools, reformation schools, privately owned schools, city livery schools, religious schools. The term 'public school' evolved, quite legitimately, to distinguish these foundations from private schools that had sprung up by the late eighteenth century to offer a broader curriculum than the older foundations, tied by their statutes. The new, Victorian, schools sought the cachet of being a 'public school' while enjoying a greater freedom.[17]

But when Sir Joshua Fitch published his book on the educational influence of Thomas and Matthew Arnold in 1897, it was clear that a very restricted view of the public schools was still held. 'In England the common use of the name is limited to ten or fifteen schools of the highest rank and the closest relation to the Universities, and for the most part of ancient and historical foundation,' he wrote, then listed the Clarendon Nine as being 'the most famous'.[18] In the 1860s the Clarendon Commission examined seven public schools (Eton, Winchester, Westminster, Harrow, Rugby, Charterhouse and Shrewsbury) which were known as the 'Clarendon Seven' and for some time considered by many as the only 'real' public schools. Later, two day schools, St Paul's and Merchant Taylors', were added to them and they became 'The Nine'. All these were old schools (though not as old as some – the King's Schools at Canterbury and Rochester, for instance, or St Peter's at York); but the public school in its modern form, the place people think of when they say 'public school', had, by the 1860s, been in existence for only about thirty years, since Arnold's time at Rugby.

Yet the term 'public school' was a term so often used, so centrally placed in social mythology, so familiar to (even when misjudged by) outsiders, that it is simply inaccurate to pretend that it had no existence. Its existence was not logical or exactly definable, merely emotive. But language is often emotive rather than logical. And this existence depended a good deal on people's opinion of it – 'I am believed in, therefore I exist.' It existed as a symbol of much more than itself: of a system, social and political, and of particular attitudes, large or small.

In the broadest sense, though this sense has little meaning now, it was socially descriptive. When Orwell writes of the poet John Cornford: 'The young Communist who died heroically in the International Brigade was public school to the core,'[19] you do not wonder what school he was at, but simply understand what Orwell meant about his attitudes, his qualities, his feelings and limitations, social background and historical ideas. Like many others who had been through public school and thought they had got well away from it, Orwell (divided between approval and dislike) used school as one of his main sources of imagery and example.

Where but in England would someone (and particularly a socialist like Orwell) start an essay as he does: 'John Galsworthy was an Old Harrovian'?[20] Where but in England would a prime minister (Baldwin) determine to have an extra Harrovian in his cabinet, because he himself had been at Harrow? Or, in the post-war world, where else would a Labour prime minister (Attlee) choose a man from his old school, Haileybury, 'all other things being equal', to join his, because they had been to the same school? Where else, if peerages were given elsewhere, would two men at least take the names of their old schools on being given peerages? Where else would a book not long ago be subtitled 'Memoirs of an Old Etonian Trumpeter'? (*I Play As I Please* by Humphrey Lyttelton.) Where else is school mentioned so often that it is hard not to know where a friend or even an acquaintance, politician or public figure of any kind, went to school or at least the type of school it was? Even today, newspapers describe a man as Etonian so-and-so or Wykehamist such-and-such. Middle-aged, middle-class writers have nearly all used school as socially descriptive, as something which will place their characters. Robin Davis may write, in his book *The Grammar School*, 'The term "public school" is historically accidental and romantically misleading . . . For me these schools are independent grammar schools,'[21] and logically, like Greene writing of the butcher, he is right enough. But something that existed so powerfully in the imagination cannot be abolished simply by saying that, in law and logic, it was never there.

As the subsoil of adult life, the public school in its century fed adult feeling of every kind. The man who had been successful there would compensate for adult failures, the schoolboy who had failed could later feel he had redeemed his failure, avenged his past. Somerset Maugham, for instance, was wretchedly unhappy at the King's School, Canterbury, if the autobiographical early part of *Of Human Bondage* is to be believed. Yet he poured money into it during the last years of his life. It seems oddly like the Latin emigrant to America, whose whole ambition to succeed is centred on the wish to show those left behind how rich and powerful he has become, how he is now in a position to give and patronise, where once he was poor and powerless; and to rub everyone's nose in it, too. Perhaps few are pursued as relentlessly as Maugham's nephew, Robin Maugham, claimed (fictionally) that the Etonian is. He made one of his heroes express it thus:

> Eton was a way of life. For, in a sense, Etonians never left Eton; they merely changed into being Old Etonians . . . It was a club where your standing depended not on what you were doing in your life but on what you had done in your years as a boy at Eton. By that behaviour and by that reputation, rather than by any subsequent success or failure, you were judged.[22]

No wonder Orwell gnashed his teeth, while agreeing with the truth of this kind of remark:

> 'Cultured' middle-class life has reached a depth of softness at which a public-school education – five years in a lukewarm bath of snobbery – can actually be looked upon as an eventful period . . . It is the same pattern all the time: public school, university, a few trips abroad, then London. Hunger, hardship, solitude, exile, war, prison, persecution, manual labour – hardly even words.[23]

A look at what a really successful Etonian felt about school early in the century confirms what he says. On leaving Eton Ronald Knox 'felt he was going into exile', according to his biographer, Evelyn Waugh. Shortly before leaving school he was seriously ill. 'He would remark in later life that if he had died then,' Waugh says, 'it would have been at the apogee of his worldly glory.'[24] And not, one feels, with too much tongue-in-cheek.

Nor was it only the successful and approved who felt like this. Only a few years after being removed in shady circumstances from Sherborne,* and then struck off the Old Boys' register for publishing

* See *Early Years* (1962) by Alec Waugh, for the reasons.

The Loom of Youth, against which preachers ranted in the school chapel for years, Alec Waugh wrote:

The public school system is built round certain distinct traits in the British character. It is the expression of the national temperament. Nearly everyone is happy at a public school. It is the manner of life that we enjoy, that is in sympathy with our tastes and customs. The reformers may say what they will. You cannot turn a dog away from the food it loves.[25]

Even odder, to modern readers, is his belief in the intensity of people's feelings about school long after they have left it. The father, he says, will 'recover his youth, and live again his school days in his son, only more intensely'. The boy who has just left will 'at every vacant moment of the day . . . compute what he would be doing if he were at school instead of at an office'. Of his own situation in the First World War, when he went into the army straight from school, he wrote:

I could not help comparing my present life with that I had been leading ten, eighteen, thirty months ago. As I marched over Ashridge Park, I remembered that a year ago I had been bicycling down to the football field for a puntabout or an upper; as I listened to a lecture on the establishment of an infantry brigade, I pictured the sixth form sitting under Nowell Smith for a discussion on the Romantic Revival; in the evening, on my way to night operations, passing Berkhamsted School and looking at the lighted windows, I would think: 'At Sherborne now they are sitting round the games study waiting for the bell to ring for hall.' Day by day, hour by hour, I pictured myself back at school . . . I was homesick.[26]

Homesick, or rather schoolsick, many adults seemed to remain, and even when they had been unhappy there, they often paid their schools the compliment of too much retrospective attention, too much resentment, if not too much love. In the view of Francis Hope:

The most infuriating thing about the English public schools is neither cruelty nor stupidity but a doglike desire for gratitude. Against it, indifference is the best and cruellest weapon.

Few writers, when the public schools rode high, ever managed to achieve this indifference. On the one hand there is Ronald Knox's 'Leaving Eton I felt definitely as a tragedy'.[27] On the other, Orwell's ferocious:

For many years I could hardly have borne to look at it [his prep school] again. Except upon dire necessity I could not have set foot in Eastbourne. I even conceived a prejudice against Sussex, as the county that contained St Cyprian's.[28]

Or Jocelyn Brooke's 'the worst I had to fear from the War was that it would be as bad as going back to King's School [Canterbury] again; but it never was'.[29] Somewhere between these extremes of feeling comes Hannah More's:

Throwing boys headlong into these great public schools always puts me in mind of Scythian mothers, who threw their newborn infants into the river. The greater part perished, but the few who possessed great natural strength . . . came out with additional vigour from the experiment.

5 *An educational device for maintaining a public service élite*

Rupert Wilkinson

In the century in which they flourished there was no more a typical public school than there was a typical person. Each school tended to think its own way of doing things was the right one. This opinion became codified into rules and rituals, which in places linger today as picturesque reminders of the old days. Shared experiences and memories were solidified into traditions and language and often into all sorts of unwritten but important rules. As boys took over from masters more and more in running everyday affairs in the public schools, the rituals sometimes hardened into compulsory ceremonies. At their worst these might be painful, frightening or even dangerous; at best, they provided the excitement of communal experience, warmth, and a sense of belonging.

A glance at the way the public schools developed is needed if they are to make sense at all; but so many pressures of history, economics, politics and social life affected their development that it is impossible to sum up what happened with any neatness. The Industrial Revolution and the enormous new middle class it produced, eager for a broader curriculum to fit boys for the busier, more competitive world they would be entering; religious fervour and social change, urging a greater respectability and more high-mindedness upon the schools; a few now neglected innovators before Arnold's time, then Arnold himself and the men he influenced, several of them pupils or assistant masters of his who in turn became headmasters at other public schools; even the coming of the railways, which could carry parents and boys about the country in numbers and at speeds unimaginable in more lumbering, horse-drawn days – all these combined to produce the public schools in the form they took; broadly speaking, a Victorian, middle-class form as opposed to a more aristocratic, eighteenth-century one.

Christopher Hollis said of Eton[30] what is probably true of all schools, that there was a silent conspiracy between boys and masters to suggest that the general level of social grandeur was higher than in fact it was; that the social exceptions, the most noticeable boys and their families, were typical, and the amorphous, middling majority (middling at Eton, as at every other school) somehow scarcely existed. In England there have never been, as there were in Russia or Spain, schools for 'the nobility'. The fact that the old public schools had been founded for the education of the poor had been almost totally forgotten by the middle of the eighteenth century, when the few old, famous schools began to be fashionable with the aristocracy, as they had not been before. Their history varied, but this was common to them all. Of the famous schools only Christ's Hospital kept – still keeps – its founders' original intention and remained to some extent a charity school. The Victorian foundations and those that came after them never aimed to educate the poor.

The concept of the Christian gentleman, Arnold of Rugby's ideal, as the desirable product of public-school education, was a far more generally attainable, therefore even socially more attractive, object to aim at than anything more aristocratic. A generation, certainly two, could produce him, indistinguishable from his fellows. But the public school grew out of political, as well as religious or intellectual, ideas and necessities, and the rise, heyday and decline of their ethos runs parallel with the rise, heyday and decline of a number of ideas from the early nineteenth century until the present day. As the nineteenth century advanced, the pressures and demands of imperialism increased. Rupert Wilkinson commented:

> In the society of late Victorian and Edwardian England . . . the role of the public schools was predominantly political. Behind the aim of 'character-building' lay a political bent that was inseparable from the traditions of the English gentry. Whether he intended it or not, Thomas Arnold's formula for creating 'the Christian gentleman' became an educational device for maintaining a public service élite.[31]

The first three decades of the nineteenth century saw gradual changes, with the older schools settling into what was to become their modern form. Questions were asked which were answered by the reforms, moral and organisational rather than educational, of the thirties and forties. The system spread, with the establishing of new schools and the enlarging of old ones, in the forties, fifties and sixties; questioning of the old curriculum and the old methods of management reached its climax in the sixties; and by the seventies the cult of athleticism, particularly in the new schools, had reached its height. Arnold, by then, had been not so much discredited as traduced;

people had really come to believe that the public schools in their philistine, games-mad, anti-intellectual, muscularly Christian form were directly descended from his reformed Rugby. In fact, Arnold set the tone for only about twenty years, training an elite of unboyish prefects exquisitely (some thought unhealthily) concerned with matters of conscience. Then Thomas Hughes, author of *Tom Brown's Schooldays* and the more tellingly entitled *The Manliness of Christ,* seemed much more to embody their spirit.

The demand was no longer for scholars or even, in Arnold's sense of the term, for Christian gentlemen. It was for able administrators to run the vast empire that, as the century advanced, took over the lives of an increasingly large number of Englishmen: 'honest, patriotic, unthinking young men to man Britain's outposts around the world,' as Hughes's biographers put it.[32] In these, what was needed, apart from a moderate degree of intelligence, was the mysterious quality called 'character'. And this was exactly what the public-school system, in the later stages of its development, produced.

Of the eighteen-fifties, by which time Arnold's ethos was spreading fast and far, an article in *Blackwood's* in 1876 said:

> Before that time, except for a vague pride in our public schools, or an equally vague horror of them, the general public gave the institution but small attention; it has remained for the Arnoldian brotherhood to introduce a new deity into our mythology and a new ideal into our aspirations. The Headmaster is the god, and the Public Schoolboy is the ideal, of this new creed.

The Victorian foundations became part of this mythology, less eccentric and individual than the older places, more like the stereotyped idea of a public school. So were the old grammar schools which (a handful out of dozens) came to be called and considered public schools, generally through the efforts and personality of a single headmaster. By 1873 Leslie Stephen was able to write: 'Neither the British jury, nor the House of Lords, nor the Church of England, nay, scarcely the monarchy itself, seems so deeply enshrined in the bosoms of our countrymen as our public schools.' Finally came the twentieth-century foundations, some modelled on the old schools, some in various ways reacting against them, but all, without realising it, anachronistic, for the impetus that would give them life and meaning – the functional reason for their existence – had almost disappeared.

6 *There's many a man sleeping on the embankment because he forgot his tenses* Francis Hope

Summing up such a large, untidy subject is like trying to put feathers in a bag. T. W. Bamford, biographer of Arnold and author of a general history of the public schools up to 1967, has done so, I think, as well as anyone. The term 'public school', he says, was already in use, though vaguely, by the beginning of the nineteenth century; before which the main schools were known as Great Schools. In 1801, Dr W. Vincent, asking what these schools were, said: 'Are we to understand only Eton, Winchester and Westminster?'[33] And in the 1880s, when writing of public schools in a history of educational theory, Oscar Browning still dealt with only these three.[34] In 1810, the *Westminster Review* wrote of including in the term 'not only Eton, Winchester and Westminster but the Charter House, St Paul's School, Merchant Taylors', Rugby and every school in England at all conducted on the plan of the first three.' Bamford himself always treats the Clarendon Seven – or Nine – as a group, compact and understandable, the old foundations. To these, during the nineteenth century, were added the new schools: Bradfield, Brighton, Cheltenham, Clifton, Dover, Epsom, Haileybury, Lancing, Malvern, Marlborough, Radley, Rossall, Wellington and others; and old grammar schools like Bedford, Bromsgrove, Dulwich, Durham, Felsted, Oundle, Repton, St Peter's (York), Sherborne, Tonbridge and Uppingham. He explains:

> At one time the club was more or less limited to seven schools and from time to time others were added to the fold. Exactly when a particular school reached the necessary stature for it to be associated with others without question is difficult to determine. Looking back, it is easy to fall into the trap of assuming that famous schools were accepted by the others long before they in fact were because they are so well known to us now. It is even easier to ignore the many promising schools which succeeded for a time and then fell out of the race. Criteria have altered too.[35]

How things stood at Sandhurst in the 1890s, how exactly graded the public schools had come to be, this passage shows:

> The Etonian was . . . the aristocrat of the little college world. This pride of place may have been grudged by those from Harrow or Winchester, but the cadets who came from the Haileyburys, the Radleys, the Wellingtons and the Tonbridges had no illusions on the subject and were in consequence able to retain their balance of self-esteem only by assuming an air of lofty disdain towards the ignoble fry from the Brightons, the Lancings and the Epsoms.[36]

And outside the public-school world, all was unimaginable darkness, the pit. To become 'a little office boy at forty pounds a year'[37] was the only alternative to Eton, Orwell kept being told at his prep school; and at his, Summer Fields, Christopher Hollis felt that 'to return to the Grammar School would have been a fate worse than death.'[38] And as recently as 1952, said Francis Hope, an otherwise sensible classics master urged him to work hard for his public-school scholarship with the warning: 'There's many a man sleeping on the embankment because he forgot his tenses.'

Definition, then, is impossible – whether membership of the Headmasters' Conference by the headmaster qualifies a school or not, whether the term is technical or merely social. But from a literary point of view, as imaginative country, the public school had an emotional meaning, indefinable and ineffable, perhaps, but subjectively vivid and intense. All that can be defined or at least described is what I have called the public schools' 'imaginative country', the way it looked not so much to those who were there as to those who looked back on it, or, at one remove further, the country invented in fiction as a luxuriant extension of it for those who had never been there. More solidly, one can define the attitudes and outlooks of the mainstream public schools, those which flourished in the century of their heyday and whose influence and pervasiveness were much greater (one finds on reading round them) than today seems credible. It was not just Connolly concocting his Theory of Permanent Adolescence who claimed such inordinate influence for them. Wholly without irony, Alec Waugh could write in 1922: 'School life is so vast, so varied, so many coloured, that it would be difficult for a boy to relinquish his hold upon the ambition that lies close to him in favour of the shadowy ambitions of the life that lies beyond it. School life is too big a pedestal for the statue that is to be placed on it. It dwarfs what it should present.'[39] One of Arnold Lunn's characters in *The Harrovians* remarks, though with rather more irony, 'Rather a pity, I think, that life should reach its highest point at nineteen.' And in a discussion of the inevitably disappointing future of even the most favourably placed boy who has been a dazzling success at school, Cyril Connolly remarked that 'early laurels weigh like lead'.[40]

I have mentioned 'mainstream' schools, but mainstream does not mean 'main' here. In a sense it means middling, and the public school as Arnold envisaged it appealed, as I have said, to the gentry rather than the aristocracy (the term 'middle-class' then applied much lower). Yet Arnold never envisaged the way the most mainstream public schools, the harshest and most extreme, were to go. He was the last man to make the school 'too big a pedestal for the statue'. The most mainstream schools were not the oldest or those with most prestige; at these, eccentricity and cleverness could always flourish and the cult of games never took over entirely. From outside, the schools may seem much of a muchness, a familiar landscape full of obvious features. Seen more closely, it turns out to be a collection of miniature landscapes, each different from the rest, with its own potholes and ridges, outcrops and uplands.

Each school developed in its own way under its own headmasters, each one of whom had his own views on everything to do with the school, his own personality that, if it was a strong one, expressed itself in the place, in his choice of staff, in his effect on the boys and, in the long run, in the kind of boy who was sent there. Even the geographical differences between school and school shaped their development and atmosphere. The main public schools were never 'local' in the sense that they drew their boys from their immediate surroundings, but their siting obviously mattered. Some were entirely urban, like Westminster, whose school chapel is the Abbey; some in what has now become suburbia, like Eton and Harrow; some in deep country, like Ampleforth; many – probably the majority – in small towns, particularly cathedral towns. To read round a particular period or person, taking the same school and looking at it through several pairs of eyes, is an exercise in the subjective. Nowhere else, perhaps, is one man's heaven so clearly another man's hell.

7 *Please sir, yes sir* Anthony Buckeridge

This is particularly true of the preparatory (or private) school, that necessary adjunct of the public school. 'The function of the preparatory school is to remove and iron out the idiosyncrasies of the home so that a standardised pattern may be presented to the public school,' wrote Alec Waugh, again without too much tongue-in-cheek. Preparatory schools lend themselves to gnomic remarks of the kind, and to parody and passion. Perhaps this is because they really are so much more 'private', more personal, than public schools, often being the property of one man whose personality and spirit can make or break them. A boy who hates his public school hates an institution, something large, long-established and impersonal. A boy who hates his prep school is often reacting against one man (and his wife, home and family). A home is more lovable, therefore more dislikable, than an institution, with a greater power for happiness or misery. The personal atmosphere provides plenty of scope for favouritism and the clash of personalities, and, the prep school being so much more familial than the public school, its success or failure in each case is much more a matter of personal reaction and taste. It is this family atmosphere that often appeals to parents, and may appeal to a boy. But if *that* particular atmosphere, that particular family, happen not to appeal to a particular boy, then he has no redress or escape, no large varied community in which to find a place of his own.

Half a century ago Alec Waugh described prep schools as 'schools that will take a small boy almost from the nursery, and train him in the course of four or five years to take his place in a large public school.'[41] The description is still accurate. As the headmaster of one of them wrote not long ago, they are 'schools which boys join, as a rule, between 7½ and 8, to be prepared for entrance to their public schools soon after their thirteenth birthday.'[42] To those who believed (who still believe) in the system, this was psychologically right. From his studies of children at boarding schools Royston Lambert maintains what many have suspected, that their ethos fails to 'take' if the child has not boarded really young. But to those who dislike the system or disapprove of its total implementation, this early type of schooling seems absurd or actually evil.

To Osbert Sitwell, for instance, it was a matter of brutalising the child when its personality was still soft enough to be moulded into any shape:

> Suddenly, just when they have reached an age when their intelligence and sensitiveness . . . can respond to the stimuli of their surroundings, they are whisked off to places of dreary internment, called private – though now more widely known as prep – schools, where the most extraordinary tribal values and standards prevail . . . until such time as their characters have been formed into the same dense, hard and unpleasant mould as that of those who teach them.[43]

Orwell felt much the same:

> I've always held that the public schools aren't so bad but people are wrecked at those filthy private schools long before they get to public school age.[44]

More laconically and personally, there is James Lees-Milne:

> My parents arranged for me to go to school. It was, they decided, high time, for I was already well over eight years old. Convention demanded that little boys should be wrenched from home at this age and dumped among a hundred others in a grim institution as unlike home as could be devised.[45]

Or Edward Lucie-Smith:

> By this time I was eight, and it was time to send me to boarding school. It was not an event I looked forward to with much confidence . . . I was convinced that school would be a place of imprisonment and terror. By and large, my sombre expectations were fulfilled.[46]

There are plenty of examples of these kinds, for prep school arouses the most virulent – as well as the most affectionate – of retrospective feelings.

With all the notice taken of public-school life, it is often forgotten that it involves not just the five years from thirteen to eighteen but the five years before that, from eight to thirteen. 'Successive generations passed ten of the most imaginative and impressionable years of their lives under influences other than those of their family,' Lord Ernle wrote in 1938. T. C. Worsley is one of the few to make a point of this, and, having come to disapprove of the system, he makes it with some sternness:

> The public school system does not begin and end with the public schools themselves. In particular it embraces the whole network of preparatory schools which feed it. The objections which can be brought against the preparatory schools are every bit as strong as those which can be brought against the public. They are run as one-man businesses, and are answerable to no one.

Preparatory schools, he says, are 'the system's weakest link . . . which find few defenders now [in 1940], even among the staunchest of the Old Guard.'[47] Paradoxically, forty years on, it is the preparatory schools that have changed least in the system, and have continued longer than the public schools in the spirit of their founders. Far from being the system's weakest link, they are now its most authentic old-style representatives.

Today, what was once taken seriously by the teenage boy is taken seriously by the small one, and it is at the boarding prep schools, not at the public schools, that life is still enclosed enough to seem unchanged, and shorts, sandals and cropped hair may still make a boy look different from the boys outside it. School stories have slipped down to a younger age group (as so many children's books have), and it is significant that the only really popular school stories still being written, Anthony Buckeridge's Jennings books, are set in a prep school. Jennings is the middling schoolboy, direct descendant of Tom Brown, and Darbishire, a bespectacled, long winded clergyman's son, to provide comic contrast, is his friend and foil. The Jennings stories were first published soon after the Second World War and no one has since grown older; which shows not so much the anachronistic spirit of school stories as the agelessness of prep schools. No old-style public school could be used in a contemporary setting. The dimmest reader would know that teenage boys like that no longer existed. But Jennings, with his 'Please sir, yes sir', and the tireless routine of cricket matches and comic disaster, is still acceptable.

Public school country, then, can no longer be taken realistically. Yet as an imaginary landscape, ritualised but recognisable, bait for the nostalgic, raw material for the joker, it still has some vitality. No one, I think, could accept a contemporary Greyfriars, even if the prolific Frank Richards were still alive. But his stories continue to be read as a sort of folk-art, and in retrospect, at least, they are cherished by many adults. The grotesque Billy Bunter (particularly hideous in the original illustrations, as models for which the artist's normal-sized sons apparently stuffed their clothes out with cushions) has become a part of English kitsch, beloved while sneered at, like garden gnomes or plaster ducks on the wall. But the world Bunter represented at several removes still lingers in a pale, more juvenile form at preparatory schools, where life is still crowded and compressed enough, high-spirited and intense enough, to engender some of the same attitudes in a world that has no place for them. Thus the once ample, indeed almost all-embracing public-school world, its outlook and its atmosphere, has dwindled to the schools where little boys have not realised that, elsewhere, it has no meaning.

CHAPTER II

The headmaster of fact and fiction

. . . electric with energy . . . Lionel Trilling

Of the three Thomases who moulded the Victorian public school (two real and one fictional: Arnold, Hughes and Brown), two were known as Tom and the third seems to have no first name at all, certainly no abbreviation of it. A hint that domestically he was Tommy seems almost profane, for it is as Arnold of Rugby, a name with an imperial or at least imperious ring, that he is remembered. That his fame today rests entirely on his achievements as a schoolmaster is something that would probably have offended him, since in his lifetime and no doubt in his own opinion he was much more than a mere headmaster; his interests ranging far beyond Rugby, teaching, or reform in the public schools, and his views on these being formed by his views on wider subjects, on the great world.

Lionel Trilling called him a man 'so notable, so strong, so decided, so confused, so representative', whose 'educational goal was, in a wide sense, always political'.[1] 'The school whose destinies Arnold really hankered to direct was Christendom,' Hugh Kingsmill* wrote. 'His ambition was to Christianise politics, to make the Church, that is, not a subordinate but a sovereign society.'[2] So he ruled Rugby with a grand, commanding air, first asserting and winning his right to independence of the school governors, however eminent they might be, and then fiercely defending the schoolmaster's right to become in-

* Brother of Arnold Lunn, who wrote one of the best known of all school stories, *The Harrovians*.

volved in issues wider than those of his own patch. An impressive figure, controversial, handsome, 'committed', much criticised, he was anyone's social equal and raised the schoolmaster's position among other educated people (which of course included parents) more than anyone had done before him.

Because he was not only a real-life headmaster but a fictional one as well, given fictional life in *Tom Brown's Schooldays* and thus transformed into a 'character', Arnold became the prototype of the fictional headmaster. School stories, like real schools, favoured the imposing headmaster seen from a lower level (the boys'), remote, Olympian, the almost invisible apex of a steep hierarchical pyramid, and in art as in life Arnold seems to have provided an exactly suitable figure. Of course the real Arnold was far more complex than the alarming stereotype he became in the stories. He was the least schoolmasterly of schoolmasters, just as his sovereign was, in many ways, the least Victorian of Victorians. Like her, he was intensely emotional, quite unlike the august, unbending pedagogue who would urge his pupils to an unnatural toughness: indeed, in a sermon, he deplored the fact that boys should 'feel ashamed of indulging [their] natural affections and particularly of being attached to their mothers and sisters and fond of their society'. Clearly he had what today would be called 'charisma'. 'There was something Jovine in his demeanour,' wrote one of his biographers, who went on to describe 'the great personality keyed to its highest pitch' when he preached. 'The tall, gallant form, the kindling eye, the voice, now soft as the low notes of a flute, now clear and stirring as the call of the light infantry bugle': this was how Tom Brown first saw and heard him in Rugby Chapel, and even from this distance he still holds something of the same fascination. Today, with his striking presence and firmly held, wide-ranging views, he would appear on television and become familiar to millions.

What to some seemed Jovine to others might seem pompous or inflated, of course; and if his image has struck some people as oppressive, I think his pupil and first biographer, A. P. Stanley, may be largely to blame. A straight-faced worshipper of everything connected with Arnold, Stanley gave him a stately earnestness that quite wrongly suggests perpetual solemnity. He wrote of 'the rare, the unbroken, the almost awful happiness of his domestic life',[3] a hard thing to live down, and an easy one to smile at; but the 'awfulness' was felt by Stanley, not necessarily conjured by Arnold. James Fitzjames Stephen, whose views enraged Matthew Arnold, stressed the elder Arnold's lack of humour and its effect on his pupils. A Rugbeian, he said, 'never tied his shoes without asserting a principle'. Well, Cyril Connolly remarked that Orwell 'could not blow his nose without moralising about conditions in the handkerchief industry', showing an exactly similar view of a man few would dare to suggest lacked humour. Arnold said gloomy things like: 'My sense of the evils of the times, and to what prospects I am bringing up my children, is overwhelmingly bitter'; but in moments of depression anyone may say this kind of thing (expressing it rather differently today). Arnold was intense but not, I think, depressing. One has a feeling of exuberance, physical and mental, and even Stanley's solemn portrait quite lacks the sanctimoniousness, the formidable dreariness, of Farrar's in the biography by his son (who ought, if anyone could, to have suggested his lighter, more human side).[4]

We tend to forget the youthfulness of the Victorians, in fiction or in fact. Arnold was just over thirty when he took over at Rugby. Today we should call him a young man, and he had an air of youthfulness about him – immense vitality, physical energy, a love of walking and swimming, of outdoor life and the interests that go with it, flowers in particular. Trilling said of him:

> He was electric with energy, his conversation was mercurial. He was in love with the world and its history; he held it the duty of the schoolmaster to know the world.[5]

This is totally unlike the 'narrow bustling fanatic' James Fitzjames Stephen* made him out to be, or the booming oracle he dwindled to in the school stories, in most of which the headmaster seems based, though more and more remotely as time went on, on Hughes's portrait of Arnold.

The schoolmaster of fiction, and often of memoirs as well, has had a wizened image, petty and pedantic where it is not foolish or cruel, the image of a man obsessed with timetables and housematches and the peg for his gown, with habit and detail, the repeated joke and the dreary ritual. From Mr Squeers onwards – to Mr Perrin or Waugh's Scott-King or even the amiable Mr Chips – he is the sort of man you would avoid spending time with if you could. 'He is awkward and out of place in the society of his equals,' Lamb wrote of the real, not the fictional, schoolmaster. 'He comes like Gulliver among his little people, and he cannot fit the stature of his understanding to yours.'[6] 'If one were invited to dine with a company representing all trades and professions, the schoolmaster is the last person one would want to sit next to,' wrote Auden.[7] And in the words of Harold Nicolson:

* The words were Matthew Arnold's. He saw in Fitzjames Stephen's review of *Tom Brown's Schooldays* a suggestion that Dr Arnold had been such a man, and wrote 'Rugby Chapel' as a reply to it.

Consider the eternal falsity of his position, those successive insincerities in which, owing to his profession, he is obliged to indulge. Upon the face and fabric of an adult schoolmaster these alternatives have left their cruel mark. Authority manifests itself, not in the secure gestures of proconsular or ministerial dignity, but in a look at once costive, fleeting and sly; a look induced by constant preoccupation with the surface of that dignity rather than with its foundations . . . Well he knows that it is not for him to mingle with his fellows in terms of natural human companionship.[8]

None of this applies to Arnold, the very opposite of all it suggests. An outstanding example of the large new professional class emerging in England in his day, a class full of enterprise and, in his particular case and that of a number of much-intermarried families down the century, of intellectual distinction as well, he embodied in his own family what we should now call a good social mix. Two generations back his forebears had been small farmers; his mother was apprenticed to a milliner; his brother married a London prostitute; his father had a child by one; one of his sisters married an earl; he himself was at school at Winchester. In background at least he was the nearest thing to classless that a man of his time could be, and he never tried or wanted to make Rugby an aristocratic school, still less a 'smart' one. Indeed, he discouraged the aristocracy from sending its sons there as strongly as he discouraged tradesmen from trying to do the same. When the Duchess of Sutherland wanted to enter her son at Rugby, purely out of admiration for Arnold, he urged her to send him to Eton, where he would find himself more comfortably at home.

The odd thing about Arnold's difference from other schoolmasters – from the supposedly typical schoolmaster, at least – is that his circumstances were so ordinary, so similar to theirs; circumstances that in others were often criticised for the narrow outlook they produced, the blinkered attitudes and absurd ignorance of the world outside school. From public school to university, then straight into school-teaching: Arnold's whole life, like that of so many at the time, was spent within the system, with like-minded friends, the same sort of intellectual stimulus, the same religious beliefs, the same interests, even the same holidays and relaxations. Engrossing domesticity from his early twenties, with eleven children (two died in infancy) in quick succession, meant that he never left the circular pattern of home and school, and his private life seems to have been as blameless as he expected to find it in others. The private pupils of his early years, and the Rugby boys during the fourteen years he spent there, were all of his own class and kind; many, like him, would be going to Oxford and Cambridge, teaching, entering the Church.

Uneventful lives may produce unadventurous attitudes, narrow circumstances, narrow outlooks. But Arnold's adventures were all of the mind, a part of his temperament. The idea of 'adventure' has many meanings, after all, and 'voyaging through strange seas of thought Alone' is surely one of them. Arnold had no outward adventures that we know of. Yet, 'misunderstood in his own day, disliked and loved with equal violence,'[9] as an editor of his son's letters to Clough described him, he was so contradictory a figure that a century after his death critics and biographers were still puzzled not just by his achievements but by his reputation and his personality.

There is not room enough to weigh the opposing elements in him, or to measure exactly his achievement in this sphere or that in the school world. This often seems to contradict that, making total agreement or disagreement impossible. But that he was a hero to those closest to him, beloved, revered, looked up to with tenderness as well as admiration by his children (Matthew the best documented, of course), by his pupils, whom he treated very much as part of the family, by masters, close friends and wife, says much for his innate, deep-seated qualities, as opposed to the 'outer', more flamboyant gifts of presence and personality. A mere figurehead of greatness never gets this full-hearted admiration from his intimates.

Arnold's life went smoothly, almost effortlessly, in the sense that its prizes came to him as they sometimes do to an intensely ambitious man who refuses to climb the conventional ladders and so, if he goes up at all, is bound to go in at the top. *'Aut Caesar aut nullus'*, he said, and buried himself in private teaching at Laleham on the Thames for the first few years, emerging only to apply for the headmastership of Rugby, to which he was appointed out of about fifty applicants, many academically more distinguished than he was and with strings to pull with the governors. The Provost of Oriel's* testimonial, saying that if Arnold became headmaster he 'would change the face of education all through the public schools of England', has been quoted so often, and seems so prophetically inspired, that people have tended to accept that this was what happened and that the prophecy was fulfilled in a complete and dazzling way. In retrospect it may seem so: G. G. Coulton in 1923 called the Rugby tradition which spread to other public schools 'probably the greatest educational movement of 19th-century Europe'.[10]

* Edward Hawkins, of whom Newman wrote in his *Apologia pro vita sua*: 'I can say with a full heart that I love him, and have never ceased to love him.' He lived to a great age. Matthew Arnold's most recent biographer, Park Honan, says of him: 'Born before the storming of the Bastille, Edward Hawkins was still living in his nineties when Winston Churchill and Lenin and Stalin were infants.'

Changes there were, of course, but not so radical or so complete, above all not so single or unaided, as has popularly been thought. Bernard Darwin wrote:

When he died. . . he had done what Dr Hawkins of Oriel had prophesied of him . . . if not in education, technically so called, at any rate in morals and decency, or if we prefer a less generous word, in respectability. Even if we cannot quite see how he did it, nothing can take away the solid honour of that achievement.[11]

To most people, then and now, it has appeared that he took over a chaotic situation: that at Rugby and the other public schools all was hard drinking and riots, roasted fags, and floggings, but by the time he died things were orderly and well-behaved. The truth is, of course, more complex than the legend. As always, things happened more slowly than they seem, from this distance, to have done. The public schools *were* radically altered by Arnold's time at Rugby, but more because people's attitudes towards them changed and so the way was open for an enormous increase in their numbers and influence, than because he made any radical alterations in the curriculum or their organisation; and more because he influenced the next generation of educators – headmasters among them – who spread the Rugby tradition than because, in his own short lifetime, he changed the public schools which then existed. Indeed, he had mixed feelings about them and in a note left for his brother-in-law, to be opened if he should die young, he said that while he would send his sons to Harrow were he to live, if he died his wife should move near a suitable day-school and keep them at home with her.

The public-schools' barbarism before his day has been emphasised so often that one hesitates to remark on it again. Some boys, the tough and the quick-witted, enjoyed themselves, but the idea that 'public schools [were] the nurseries of all vice and immorality' was so widespread that it seemed unarguable. In his life of Addison Dr Johnson wrote of the 'savage licence' which prevailed in them, especially in the practice of 'barring out', which meant that the boys rioted, occupying buildings, barring doors and yelling defiance from the windows at their masters, who sometimes tried to force their way in. The boys' brutality merely reflected that of authority. Busby* at Westminster in the seventeenth century (an enormously long reign, from 1639–

* Richard Busby (1606–1695), a famous flogger yet much admired and even loved and respected headmaster. Although, according to the D.N.B., 'Busby's name has become proverbial as a type of the severest of severe pedagogues,' he was also, it says, 'the most pious and benevolent of men'.

1695), and Keate* at Eton in the nineteenth, were famous floggers, and not surprisingly they and their obscurer imitators produced in turn what Kingsmill called 'a pandemonium of youthful savages'.[12]

Arnold belonged to his age enough to believe that expulsion and beatings were a necessary means of discipline. But his whole attitude to the boys was unlike that of most of his contemporaries and predecessors in the public schools. When lying was the most ordinary part of schoolboy behaviour (Keate in fact was insulted if *not* lied to, thinking it showed a lack of healthy respect), he trusted them to tell the truth. Instead of taking them on as enemies, he cooperated with them in what he considered (even if they did not) the work of salvation. And he strengthened immensely the prefectorial system, so much so that it is often thought he invented it, although in fact it was already in use, less effectively and intensively, by his time. At first he took all his prefects from the sixth form, which they reached through intellectual merit; later, in keeping with his ideas on the pre-eminence of character, he made boys prefects not for their cleverness but for their virtues.

Disciples and friends among the boys, some of them ardent admirers, later spread his legend. Despite his awe-inspiring presence, he clearly aroused affection and a sense of his own humanity and kindliness. The two sides – the alarming and the friendly, the Jovine and the relaxed – often went together, in fact. He expelled George Hughes, Tom's brother, from Rugby,† then promptly invited him to stay with his own family in the Lake District – an odd way for a headmaster to behave, one feels today. Outside the school people might dislike him, but those within it – the staff whose prestige he raised and whose authority he upheld, and most of the boys whose development he watched with eager interest – nearly all became his loyal admirers. Prigs they might be called by some outside Rugby, but there was no contesting the fact, when Arnold died, that his pupils loved and admired him a great deal more than boys at the time were expected to love and admire their headmaster.

Other schools had made reforms before his arrival – Shrewsbury

* John Keate, headmaster of Eton from 1809 to 1834, another famous flogger, who once whacked more than 80 boys on a single day. When he was first appointed headmaster, he had to control 170 turbulent boys in one room, and put up with songs sung in chorus during lessons, fusillades of bad eggs, and having his desk smashed up. 'He was little more (if more at all) than five feet in height,' wrote A. W. Kinglake, 'and not very great in girth, but in this space was concentrated the pluck of ten battalions.'

† For refusing to name the boys who had broken some pottery. Park Honan in *Matthew Arnold* (1981) describes George as 'a warm-hearted, reticent, handsome and ill-starred rebel'.

under Samuel Butler*, for instance, or Charterhouse under John Russell. Even at Rugby Thomas James (headmaster from 1778–1794) had brought in some of the reforms Arnold was to be credited with, though in an embryonic form (Samuel Butler, the writer, not the headmaster, admittedly an eccentric in his admirations and dislikes, thought all Arnold's reforms could be traced back to James; indeed he maintained rather dottily that Arnold himself had had no effect at all, either at Rugby or elsewhere). But there had been no great centralising power like Arnold's, no irresistibly attractive – or electrifyingly dislikable – personality. Trilling wrote in the late thirties:

> Modernity has not been kind to [him]. Men who have had the ear of our time have made his name something of a mockery. Bertrand Russell has used him as a symbol of all that was repressive in the old education. Lytton Strachey has represented him as intellectually dishonest and emotionally warped.[13]

But today we should be better able to assess him, for the public schools as he envisaged them or as they became in the hands of his successors are part of history, whereas in the thirties they were still part (too heavy and too tyrannous a part) of English life. A sillier essay than Strachey's on Arnold[14] has seldom, I think, been taken seriously, and plenty of people who never read a word of Arnold's own writings must have believed Strachey on a subject he deeply mistrusted and misunderstood. His caricature was not just of Arnold but of everything he hated in Victorianism, and Arnold was part of what seemed the still living menace of his age's attitudes, a personal bogey, author of many wrongs.

But whatever the controversy that surrounded him, in his lifetime or years after it, Arnold was no innovator, certainly no revolutionary. His enemies sneered at his political radicalism, but educationally he was no reformer, and not even attracted to the idea of change. According to one of his biographers:

> He was strictly conservative in this sphere [education] and we do him no injustice by suggesting that the revolutionary changes which have taken place for good or ill in school and university education in this country owe nothing to his inspiration. He left the system exactly where he found it with one exception. The exception was the new stress which was placed on the importance of religion and morals.

'The business of a school-master,' Arnold himself wrote, '. . . is the cure of souls.'

* Not to be confused with either of his namesakes, one the author of *Hudibras* (1612–80), the other the author of *The Way of All Flesh* (1835–1902). The latter was the headmaster's grandson.

2 *When the Caliph Omar destroyed the libraries of Alexandria . . . great numbers of tragedies by Euripides and others are said to have perished . . . When I read about this as a boy it simply filled me with enthusiastic approval.* George Orwell

Arnold interpreted 'soul' in a broad sense, to include the mind and outlook, the whole intellect. 'In his hands education became deliberately "education for life,"' Rex Warner wrote of him.[15]

He has been much criticised (it was Strachey's bitterest complaint against him) for his order of priorities in dealing with the boys at Rugby. 'What we must look for here,' Arnold wrote, 'is, first, religious and moral principles; secondly, gentlemanly conduct; thirdly, intellectual ability.' Yet this order was hardly surprising at a Christian school where, *sub specie aeternitatis,* every boy was of equal value. The first two aims were, after all, both high and modest, and attainable by everyone who believed in their validity, whereas intellectual ability was a gift. According to Fitch, Arnold believed that the school

> should be first of all a place for the formulation of character, and next a place for learning and study, as a means for the attainment of this higher end. Discipline and guidance were in his view more prominently the business of a schoolmaster than the communication of knowledge . . . The community should be *au fond* a place of work, and . . . the proper business of a good school, the production of exact and accomplished scholars, should be thoroughly well fulfilled.[16]

Arnold *did* rank intellectual development high, in other words; but as a Christian he ranked moral development higher. This did not make him a philistine or, as Swinburne put it, 'the head-gardener of the main hotbed of philistine saplings now flourishing in England'.[17]

And he set his intellectual aims within a wider context. Trilling's remark that 'his educational goal was, in a wide sense, always political', was a shrewd comment on a man who had been criticised for keeping the teaching at Rugby just as it had always been, for failing to broaden the curriculum. Yet it was for their relevance to modern life and to what he called 'the great science of the nature of civilised man' that Arnold defended the teaching of the classics. Stanley wrote that:

> he was the first Englishman who drew attention in our public schools to the historical, political and philosophical value of philology and the ancient writers, as distinguished from the mere verbal criticism and elegant scholarship of the [previous] century.[18]

It was for what he considered its irrelevance to modern life and thought that Arnold disliked the idea of introducing science, which, he felt, had 'nothing to do with the knowledge which the Reform Bill calls for', in other words, the kind of judgement needed to deal with current questions, with the life around us. 'A man may be ever so good a chemist,' he wrote, 'or ever so good a mechanic, or ever so good an engineer, and yet not at all the fitter to enjoy the elective franchise.'

On the other hand, a study of the classics, Arnold asserted, made him that much fitter for it:

> Expel Greek and Latin from your schools, and you confine your views of the existing generation to themselves and their immediate predecessors, you will cut off so many centuries of the world's experience and place us in the same state as if the human race had first come into existence in the year 1500 . . . A large portion of the history which we are wont to call ancient, the later history of the Greek republic and that of the period of the Roman Empire, is practically modern – much more modern, say, than the age of Alfred, as it describes society in a state analogous to that which we have now reached in the history of England.

But he was surprisingly open to the idea of widening the curriculum in the case of the less able:

> I think if my own children gave promise of considerable power, and of a fondness for reading, I should send them to a good classical school because to such minds the classical seems to me to afford the best possible discipline . . . But if my boys were of ordinary talents, with no fondness for reading, or in other words of a feeble intellectual appetite, then I should think that another kind of treatment was best for them . . . While the mind is incapable of receiving the benefits of a classical education, precious time and opportunities would be wasted by obstinately forcing upon light soil a crop which requires the strongest and richest.

This was a far more liberal attitude than he is generally credited with. But the system was entrenched and made liberalising difficult:

> Public schools necessarily influence the system followed at private ones, and are themselves influenced by the universities, and with these last therefore the reform should properly begin, as they will act downwards even upon the smallest schools in the kingdom. But till this reform does take place, the question seems to be, how far other things can be taught at a preparatory school without putting a boy at a disadvantage when he goes to public school.

The same thing applies in a much modified form today. The various stages of school are still interlocked, though growing less so as the system disintegrates: the child at a state school from five to seven may not get into the preparatory school chosen for him, the child not sent to a prep school may not get into the chosen public school, inadequate secondary schooling may not get him to the university he wants, and so on.

Shane Leslie's *The Oppidan* shows that the classical curriculum and methods of teaching in use at Rugby in Arnold's day were still in force, to the exclusion of almost everything else, at Eton around 1900; and, at Eton fifteen years or so after that, Orwell seems to have scraped through the work much as Tom Brown did, with a minimum of pleasure or profit and, presumably, little memory of it later. Simon Raven described the public schoolboy some years after Orwell's schooldays: 'The poor little wretch is exhausted by syntactical disciplines, hampered by boring notes, cheated by bowdlerizers.' Orwell's main criticism was that it left boys without time or energy for more intellectually interesting pursuits. Educated Englishmen, he claimed, were on the whole ill-read in their own literature. More angrily and, to the reader, more sadly, he described how he felt about the whole system of school work:

> When the Caliph Omar destroyed the libraries of Alexandria he is supposed to have kept the public baths warm for eighteen days with burning manuscripts, and great numbers of tragedies by Euripides and others are said to have perished, quite irrevocably. I remember that when I read about this as a boy it simply filled me with enthusiastic approval. It was so many less words to look up in the dictionary – that was how I saw it.[19]

That was how, presumably, most schoolboys saw it and it explains both the widespread use of cribs and the general hatred of 'work' in school stories.

Winston Churchill was one of the few to set down (in *My Early Life*) the sort of comments a schoolboy might make, must often have made, when taken unimaginatively and without explanation through the first stages of Latin. What was the point of the vocative case? Why address a table as 'O table'? Why, indeed, address it at all? The whole question of 'work' – officially the main purpose of school – was dealt with so little and so lightly not just in school stories but in memoirs of school that it is hard to discover just what schoolboys were up to most of their working lives. Of all the school stories, *The Oppidan* gives what is probably the most detailed and intelligent description of school work, as well as the most vivid sense of the labour, satisfaction and triumph involved in it.

3 . . . *all that is real – virtue, merriment, and humanity.* A. H. Gilkes

So Arnold provided the idea of the great headmaster in fact and in fiction. Although his ideas were stimulating and forcefully expressed, the more one looks at what happened the clearer it seems that most of his achievement stemmed from personality rather than theory. It was his presence that made Rugby boys change, masters admire, parents believe in him; and later, it was the memory of that presence in those who had known it that made other schools follow. His fervour, his company, his preaching, his whole cast of mind – these were what made his ideas seem memorable and alive.

A 'great' headmaster in something like the same mould became almost a necessity in any school establishing itself, a man who could pull it up from nothing in particular, set a pattern, impose his ideas. (This did not apply so much to schools already established, which could coast along on what they already were without needing this new vitality.) A kindling presence, an impressive appearance, mattered enormously. And not only in the nineteenth century. As recently as the nineteen-twenties Roxburgh seems to have been picked as the first headmaster of Stowe largely for 'presence', and to have established the school almost entirely by means of it. Even today headmasters of independent schools often seem to be chosen for the same thing. Not surprisingly, or even wrongly: the headmaster is figurehead as well as chief executive and needs to embody the external as well as the inner qualities of leadership.

When presence was combined with ideas and intellect, and the inner qualities matched the outer, the effect might be enormous. But sometimes presence went with little else. The headmaster was then an actor, dressed and made up for the part, and it might seem more important than anything else for him to look right and play the part convincingly. Welldon of Harrow,* whom I discuss in Chapter 7, was clearly a 'personality'. As one of his assistant masters wrote:

> Put a toga on Dr Welldon and he might well have personified the greatest of the Romans. Immense power, vigour and unquestioned authority were stamped upon his whole person . . . His was a commanding personality, which one felt to be ill-fitted to brook opposition. He called to mind the picture of a Roman dictator or Cardinal Wolsey.

Yet he wrote one of the feeblest and most sentimental of all school stories as well as a totally unappreciative final report on one of his most gifted pupils, Galsworthy; under the masterful exterior he obviously lacked both moral weight and intellectual power; and indeed left Harrow in secret ignominy, kicked upstairs to a bishopric and thus able to avoid disgrace for involvement with one of his boys.

The impressive headmaster of real life – a Thring of Uppingham or, with a very different style, a Sanderson of Oundle, for instance, both of whom transformed obscure grammar schools into nationally known public schools – was transposed into popular fiction, as a rule,

* Not to be confused with James Ind Welldon, a famous headmaster of Tonbridge.

as The Doctor. Ian Hay described him as wearing cap and gown even when whacking offenders; adding laconically: 'For all we know he wears them in bed.'[20] Seen from boy-level he was, of course, remote and imposing. In the popular stories it seems natural for him to make knees tremble merely by appearing, but even in a book as adult in its way as *The Oppidan,* Warre – another real headmaster portrayed, like Arnold, in fiction – still appears at Eton as almost ludicrously Olympian. The headmaster as Great Panjandrum was part of school lore, and it is clear that he often played up his own position (and, almost incidentally, personality) to keep boys and even parents in awe of him. Busby of Westminster is said to have kept his hat on in Charles II's presence, explaining that his boys must never think anyone greater than himself. A similar story is told of a headmaster of Eton and one of the Georges.

But there were headmasters who did not conform to the pattern, who went against prevailing fashions of thought and moral trends. There were 'great' headmasters who were not necessarily great personalities, who disliked the whole idea of what we should now call the cult of personality. In life in general, as well as at school, there is always the clash between the outer and the inner qualities, between display and reticence, the grand exterior which delights and (possibly) disappoints, and the life of the spirit which may inspire fewer, but more deeply. Public-school life seemed made for peacocks, for prowess and extroversion, swank and display, the headmaster strutting above the rest and encouraging his boys to copy him. One of the most attractive exceptions, A. H. Gilkes, a 'great' headmaster if his own writings and the testimony of others are anything to go by, wrote a couple of school stories, and by the eighteen-eighties, when his first one appeared, was able to write: 'There are a great many school stories in existence.'[21] The genre was already established.

As Master of Dulwich College from 1886–1914, Gilkes spanned the 'hardest' period of the public schools. They were then at their most competitive, games-mad, snobbish and anti-intellectual. Gilkes disliked competitiveness, the cult of games, snobbery and philistinism. Not only did he disapprove strongly of the whole idea of boy rivalry, the central pillar of the system, but he disliked its necessary adjunct – the cult and cultivation of the bloods, the whole idea of schoolboy grandees: noticeable, outstanding boys remarkable for athletics and good looks, whom the system taught what he called 'advertising', in other words, self-aggrandisement and self-consciousness and conceit, pushing for popularity and prestige, all the flaunting, dramatic qualities encouraged in most school stories. He was a good athlete himself, having played cricket for his college at Oxford and soccer for the university, but he hated the worship of games in the public schools. More unusually, he saw through the social ideas of the time and disliked the thought of the public-school product as superior to all others, with manners and customs that were necessarily the standard by which all others must be judged. He even disliked the idea of boarding.

By writing about these things he 'burnt his boats', according to a colleague, while teaching at Shrewsbury, as far as the mainstream schools were concerned. A large day-school like Dulwich was clearly ideal for him and he made it an extraordinarily free, happy place with an atmosphere to lure the schoolboy P. G. Wodehouse (who chose it for himself) and to arouse lasting affection. Coming there when the dynamic Welldon was swept up to Harrow, Gilkes was at first compared unfavourably with him by the boys, seeming to lack (deliberately, one feels) the dramatic effectiveness so useful in public figures, and sometimes to play himself down on public occasions. If Welldon recalled a great Roman, Gilkes, according to one of his assistant masters

> might have stood for a Greek statue of a patriot statesman . . . His choice was to exercise power through persuasion and sweet reasonableness – to make his appeal to the inner spirit – for his conviction was that the majority of men and boys are reasonable.[22]

Boys and Masters (1887), his curiously forgotten, highly attractive school story, praised by Gladstone, was unusual in its refusal to side with this or that boy or faction, and uses many of the familiar themes of the already established school story – rivalries, cribbing, sports-mania, school illness and death – with delicacy and point. The less successful, unfortunately named *The Thing that Hath Been or A Young Man's Mistakes,* has greater originality and in a sense greater interest because its theme is central to Gilkes's outlook. It is the story of Socrates in modern dress. For Gilkes, whose own 'Socratic irony' was mentioned by a friend, Socrates must have embodied, in his life, ideas and person, much of what he wanted to put across; and although Socrates is nowhere mentioned in the novel, it was obviously intended for those who would recognise the parallels between ancient Greek and modern English life.

A modern Socrates, Gilkes says, acting as gadfly, moral arbiter and social misfit in a public school, would be hounded from it by the guardians of established values, just as surely as Socrates ended with his cup of hemlock. A brilliant, ugly young man, virtuously brought up by a clever but lowly-born mother, is brought into a public school to raise teaching standards, spurned by boys and masters for his 'ungentlemanly' looks and manner, disliked for attitudes which show up the laziness, ineffectiveness and snobbishness of others, even suspected of stealing because, as an outsider, he is morally suspect from the start, and finally dismissed because he cannot accept orthodox religion (Gilkes was in orders late in life, but always fairly unorthodox in his religious attitudes). His answer to a master who, jealous of his growing influence with the boys, tells him not to associate with them outside the classroom, sums up all Gilkes's attitudes. He asks the master:

> Do you know – you and you only – what is a good schoolboy? May not others also set up an ideal opposed to yours? This boy that you would raise here, is it the true type? – a boy who associates with those who wear a certain clothing, and have a certain income, whatever it may be, and may not associate with others, whoever they may be. This is to exalt into realities things that are not real – clothing, the outside of things – and to depress all that is real – virtue, merriment, and humanity. And these manners you teach your pupils, are they good manners? Good manners must spring from a heart of courtesy; but the manners you teach are manners which are good on the outside only, and cover a gross barbarous heart. Look at your own, the outcome of what you teach. You have spoken to me in a manner which should bring you shame to think on.

This was inflammatory stuff for an age and milieu which, in theory, knew all about Socrates and, in practice, rejected his ideas (his questioning of the orthodox, his determination to get at the truth, his way of drawing out the best from an unlikely source, not being satisfied with the surface talent of the obviously gifted). Lunn and others remarked on the same thing with regard to Christ, theoretically the inspiration of the public schools, in practice utterly rejected by their (later) spirit. Much earlier Gilkes had written of the 'senseless arrogance' of the public-school products; of the idea 'that men are divided into castes, of which they belong to a high caste, and need only be scornful towards all others'; above all, he had maintained that it was 'the mark of a gentleman to forego his own advantage, and to move without scornfulness among men.' Asked what he had learned at school, all the public schoolboy could answer, he said, was: 'I have learned to play [games], and to despise most of my species.'[23] These ideas were embodied, undidactically and obliquely, in his fiction. One of his masters wrote:

> He employed his literary powers, and they were not small, not as a pure creative artist, producing a picture of life as he saw it, but as a practical philosopher, trying to find an attractive way of instilling the ideas which his philosophy of life had formed.

This philosophy went not just into his fiction but into his whole way of life, his treatment of the school, his relationship with the boys. As with Arnold, theory and practice were one. Indeed his ideas were not unlike Arnold's, although they had gone further, in social matters particularly; and if Arnold had not been traduced, by the end of the century the schools might have been something like those Gilkes had in mind. As it was, it is impossible to measure his effect on the hundreds of boys who passed through his hands in nearly thirty years as a headmaster. Perhaps much of the sunniness of *Mike* and of Wodehouse's other school stories (St Asaph's* notwithstanding) was a result of his happy time at what seems to have been, under an untypical headmaster, yet one directly in the tradition of the untraduced Arnold, an untypical school.

* St Asaph's, Mafeking Road, Bramley-on-Sea, prep school of Bertie Wooster and many of his friends, ruled by the Rev Aubrey Updike; sometimes called Malvern House, Bramley-on-Sea, but still given the same headmaster.

CHAPTER III

The school story as moral tale: Hughes and Farrar

Thinking over what I should like to say to him before he went to school, I took to writing a story . . . Thomas Hughes

The school story was born with Thomas Hughes, whose *Tom Brown's Schooldays* (1857) unselfconsciously, indeed unconsciously, founded a new genre. The reason for writing it was simple. His son was going off to public school. 'Thinking over what I should like to say to him before he went to school,' Hughes wrote, 'I took to writing a story, as the easiest way of bringing out what I wanted.'

Although the book has generally been regarded as entertainment, he wrote it as a moral tale, advising his readers rather more vehemently than he would today. When reviewers said there was 'too much preaching' in it and hoped there would be less in future, they were sharply put down in Hughes' preface to the sixth edition:

> Why, my whole object in writing at all was to get the chance of preaching! When a man comes to my time of life and has his bread to make, and very little time to spare, is it likely that he will spend almost the whole of his yearly vacation in writing a story just to amuse people? I think not. At any rate, I wouldn't do so myself . . . My sole object in writing was to preach to boys: if ever I write again, it will be to preach to some other age. I can't see that a man has any business to write at all unless he has something which he thoroughly believes and wants to preach about. If he has this, and the chance of delivering himself of it, let him by all means put it in the shape in which it is most likely to get a hearing; but let him never be so carried away as to forget that preaching is his object.

The first school story, then, was didactic, a moral tale. So, very much so, was the second, F. W. Farrar's *Eric, or Little by Little*. But whereas Hughes occasionally goes in for deliberate sermonising and even apostrophises his readers in a Farrar-like way, as a rule his spiritual advice is filtered through a sense of cheerful, optimistic, pragmatic good nature, with plenty of fun to sugar the pious pills. Farrar's school stories are gloomy, doom-laden tales of adolescent saints and sinners, and among the central school-story writers had no important followers; although in a more general way, as part of evangelical writing, among adults rather than the young, their influence was pervasive enough to produce a number of boys called Eric surprisingly long after the book's original publication: Eric Gill and Eric Blair (George Orwell) were two acknowledgedly named after his hero.

The public school turned out to be a remarkably convenient setting for fiction. It was an enclosed community, self-contained, self-sufficient, concentrated, dramatic; a place where people could either be seen as 'humours' rather than individuals, acting out their roles in the way expected of them, arousing partisan feelings for or against; or else treated as fiercely individual, in contrast to their narrow surroundings and rule-ridden existence. Isolated communities have always attracted novelists, and in its isolation the public school was comparable only with prison or monastery, with both of which it had a good deal in common. Politics have always attracted novelists, too – the struggle for power and position, gerrymandering and one-upmanship, ambition naked or covert, the shifts and developments within groups, factions and parties. All this, on a small scale, the public school provided. Then human relations are the raw material of fiction and, again to a high degree, they matter particularly in small, self-contained groups; groups that, at a public school, were concentrated further by close proximity and adolescence.

The late Victorian and Edwardian public school provided fertile ground even for the adult novelist; or rather for the novelist who, in those days of extreme reticence, was poised, in a good deal of fiction, between the adult world and the child's, since women at least were kept in conditions of childish ignorance (then, more flatteringly, considered childlike innocence) officially all their lives, and certainly until marriage. Many books now considered to be for children were originally written for this adult, or semi-adult, public, and the school story became split into roughly two forms: the popular, which began with Hughes and flourished after Talbot Baines Reed developed it twenty-five years later, a story aimed specifically at boys and dealing with a recognisable, reassuring pattern of school life and behaviour; and the more adult, more individual novel in which school provided a setting for the clash of character in intensely concentrated conditions, or the background for a documentary portrayal of school life. The two forms overlapped a good deal, of course, and the more adult stories were widely read by the young, certainly by almost-adult boys in the upper forms of public schools. In general the popular, boy-centred stories (which in the end lapsed into the purely 'kitsch' stories involving Bunter and his cronies) dealt with schools of an unspecific sort, an amalgam of attitudes, characters and situations which soon hardened into unalterable conventions; whereas the more adult tended to deal with individual, even recognisable schools at particular periods. The 'serious' school story often used the conventions of the more popular, and had similar plots and scenes and even similar stereotypes; and very occasionally the two forms were found in the one book.

Since it dealt with a ceremonial world, one of order and ritual, the school story soon became ritualised too. At the real public school in its latter heyday everything down to the smallest detail (in language, clothes, behaviour, conversation, attitudes and so on) was controlled by rule and precedent, and the school story which reflected this soon became recognisable and repetitive. Derek Verschoyle wrote of Malvern in his day:

> Physique, intellect and religion are cultivated in the light of a prescribed formula . . . The Public Schoolboy abandons or suppresses the normal impulses and energies of childhood. Actions, thoughts and beliefs (and, after the preliminary conditioning, feelings) are standardised to suit the market.[1]

The major schools, as I have said, as a rule stood a little outside these conventions or interpreted them in their own way. But in the mass of the schools, and the mass of the stories, the rules were strict.

2 . . . *such diminutive insects* . . . Jonathan Swift

How was the writer of school stories, then, to deal with his material, this vigorous world of the feverishly active young, trained to behave with exact decorum in a world of Byzantine complexity, rule-ridden not so much by orders from above as by conventions and traditions enforced by the boys themselves? Was he to write as an adult, or as a boy? For adults, or for boys? Did he look back nostalgically, or from above, remotely, or did he squat, like Mr Bultitude of *Vice Versa,* who magically changed places with his schoolboy son, in order to see things at school level? Every school story has its particular eye level. The writer has to decide which is to be his.

As an adult, he cannot feel the excitements of adolescence as an adolescent does; cannot really care ('straight', on its own eye level, without irony) about the fate of house-match or school colours, who is or is not made a prefect, is or is not allowed to wear a coloured waistcoat or carry an umbrella. Yet irony is a difficult tool to use, especially in addressing the young. 'The past is a foreign country,' as L. P. Hartley put it in the first sentence of *The Go-between* (where schoolboys in the holidays become involved in adult deviousness and sexuality); a country most writers find it hard enough to enter, without having to stoop in order to do so. Of course, the problem is common to all writers for children. But the writer of school stories was in a more complicated position than the rest because he was not quite writing children's books; or at least not dealing entirely with children's lives or addressing himself exclusively to the young. Although his field might seem narrow, in fact it involved a whole world beyond the immediate one.

It was not a matter of microcosms, of exact, small-scale models of the world outside. I cannot believe that school ever faithfully reflected something as varied and far-flung as the 'real' world, or that success or failure there provided any reliable guide to success or failure in the future. Its image of the world was distorted, if only because the outside world was full of alternatives and choices and variety; whereas public school in the old days provided few choices and innumerable prohibitions. What made the school story psychologically complicated, too, was the fact that, although the two places, school and the outside world, differed from each other, they belonged together, were interlocked like pieces of the one jigsaw puzzle. In their heyday, public schools were a part (a distorted and distorting part, but a part nonetheless) of that world outside.

So the writer of school stories, knowing or at least sensing this, was in a strange position. He had to keep putting himself into the shoes of an age-group whose outlook and feelings were, or should have been, quite unlike his own, he had to be absorbed enough in what happened to make it interesting to himself, and so to others, he had to treat the relations between master and boy from the boy's point of view when he was in fact the age of the master, yet to keep enough detachment to make it all sound right, to hit the right note while bearing in mind all sorts of separate, even conflicting, responses and interests – his own, his young readers', his adult readers', even those of the characters in the book (adult or young, again at distinct levels). All too easily he might become too much involved in the school atmosphere to be taken seriously outside it, or too little involved to make it acceptable to anyone at all. Perhaps this is why the school story, although socially and historically of great interest, as a literary genre was a stunted growth which never achieved height or serious status. At its best it never produced a tree. Except perhaps for *Stalky & Co.*—that thick-leaved growth that dominates the rest, full of birds' nests and creepers and long, secret roots—only a few bushes appeared, as formless as *Tom Brown's Schooldays,* slips from which sprouted and resprouted until, by the turn of the century, the ground was thick with them; tiny, almost undifferentiated tufts of a peculiarly stylised fiction.

So there was always the problem of where the writer was to stand, what his eye level was to be. In everyday life there is a physical comparison. If as an adult you meet someone you knew as a child and have not met since, it is easy to recognise him, as a rule, if you were then, and still are, both the same height. Because it is *relative* differences that make things unrecognisable, and things that change subjectively because of the weather of our minds, the pathetic fallacy: the house that has shrunk, the forest that turns out to be a coppice, the master, once alarming or learned or sophisticated, grown comfortable or prosy or socially quite dull. Swift made the point more succinctly than anyone I can think of, in *Gulliver's Travels*. Of course, he was making it all the time in a literal way by setting his hero among people much smaller or much larger than himself. But when Gulliver is among the giants of Brobdingnag, and describes the reaction of their king to what he says about political life in England, he does just what I am trying to do. Swift writes:

> He could not forebear taking me up in his right hand, and stroking me gently with the other, after a hearty fit of laughter, asked me whether I were a Whig or a Tory. Then turning to his first minister, who waited behind him with a white staff, near as tall as the mainmast of the Royal Sovereign, he observed how contemptible a thing was human grandeur, which could be mimicked by such diminutive insects as I: and yet, said he, I dare engage, these creatures have their titles and distinctions of honour, they contrive little nests and burrows, which they call houses and cities; they make a figure in dress and equipage; they love, they fight, they dispute, they cheat, they betray. And thus he continued on, while my colour came and went several times with indignation to hear our noble country, the mistress of arts and arms, the scourge of France, the arbitress of Europe, the seat of virtue, piety, honour and truth, the pride and envy of the world, so contemptuously treated.

So, surely, must school politics have seemed to the adult writer. Without irony or comedy (both difficult, in the circumstances, to use) it must have been hard to deal with them at all. In the school story he was dealing not just with childhood and adolescence but with an institution that stretched into later life, that was formed by large external pressures of history and politics, class and custom. The patterns of public-school life were formed by, and then became part of, the life of all kinds of other institutions and places – army, empire, politics, social life; and the school story, unsatisfactory though it may have been, was an image (small-scale and inadequate but faithful) of much more in literature if not in life: of the political novel, the novel of adventure, the novel of social *mores,* and patriotic verse. It accepted every aspect of its age, good or bad, acceptable or unacceptable today, more frankly than more sophisticated adult fiction could afford to, so that it contained every adult attitude compressed and therefore concentrated: not just snobbery and jingoism, for instance, but uglier things like anti-semitism, racialism of all kinds. If there was a two-way process in life (the schools' effect on things in general, the pressure of things in general on the schools), there was obviously a two-way process in literature as well.

To show how attitudes from the school world affected the larger one would involve a study of the whole century's history – social, political, economic. That the public schools were deeply, often exaggeratedly, conscious of that history and their part in it is clear. At varying levels of seriousness or pretentiousness this is stressed, over and over again. Anthony Powell wrote half a century ago:

> The government of the country was somehow made an almost personal matter. It was as if, instead of saying 'If you don't learn to speak French properly, you will never be able to enjoy yourself in Paris,' our mentors said: 'If you don't learn some sort of civilised behaviour, England will become impossible for everybody!'[2]

That was at Eton, cradle of ministers and potentates, but even when he looked back on his less expectant Marlborough days Louis MacNeice could write:

> From the British public schools come the British ruling classes. Or came till very lately. It was from the public schools that our Governments caught the trick of infallibility. The public-school boy, after a few years of discomfort, has all the answers at his fingertips; he does not have to bother with the questions.[3]

A year earlier, Rupert Wilkinson wrote:

> The mechanics of the English public school, both as an education system and as a self-contained political community, throws a light on human society that can be extended to many different cultures.[4]

And H. J. Bruce wrote in 1947:

> Book learning could be acquired, even better acquired, without going to a public school. What could not be acquired . . . was the sense of independence and responsibility which made and still makes a British public-schoolboy fit to take his place in the world, fit, if called upon, to govern a province . . . The

fact that we have as a whole excelled as colonisers is probably due in large measure to the habit of government learnt early in life.[5]

So the politics of school overlapped with those of the world outside it, the training and expectations provided for the boys faithfully reflected their likely future, and through the years their system of government was adjusted to fit the larger system, which had similarly hierarchical patterns. Richard Usborne put it thus:

Young Johnny's parents pay large sums for young Johnny to live in this autocratic discipline, subdued until the time comes for him, as a prefect, to subdue.

Push that a stage further and you have the pattern of life for adult Johnnies in public affairs. Whether or not we think that it worked, that the system in fact produced boys adequately, even successfully, prepared for what lay beyond school, the fact remains that it aimed to do so, that consciously and deliberately the boys were fed with particular expectations, particular dreams, a sense of what might be called responsibility, or might be called self-importance. And much of this sense was boy-generated. As Noel Annan wrote of *Stalky & Co*:

Real education is what the boys teach each other in ways the masters cannot. The in-group teaches spontaneously the way society works.[6]

3 . . . *Spartan rather than Athenian* . . . Sir Joshua Fitch

Hughes never really solved the problem of whom he was addressing. He never seems to have wondered about it. It is hard to know whether we are to identify with the tireless ten- or eleven-year-old Tom who arrives at Rugby on what must be the longest and busiest day in schoolboy history; or with the author, who now and then grabs his (by the sound of it, often supposedly adult) reader by the lapels and makes some point or other; or with the melancholy adult Tom who, like Matthew Arnold in 'Rugby Chapel', watches with loving grief at Arnold's tombstone. Other school-story writers, more conscious of the problem, were often at a loss how to deal with it. Desmond Coke wrote in a preface to one of his novels:

If it is asked whether the book is meant for 'grown-ups' or for children, I can only say for either, but more especially for those lucky people, not so small a band, who by steadily refusing to grow old, have managed to be both.

Better writers than Coke have known this dilemma. And the young themselves may be suspicious of the attitudes it engenders, as they are suspicious (in school stories, almost invariably) of the over-matey master, the adult who tries to be one of them. 'Can't say I like the boy among boys,' one of Lunn's Harrovians growls about such a master. 'I like a ruddy beak to be a ruddy beak.'

Nor can Hughes have known what *Tom Brown's Schooldays* was to do. It was a clear case of art being overtaken by life. With it, he achieved more than he aimed at or deserved – more influence, more fame, a permanent niche in a specialised corner of English writing. Although written as fiction, it came to be regarded as fact. More oddly, it came to influence life in a way few novels have managed to do and, for all its lack of intellectual pretensions, patterns of thought as well. Unwittingly, it came to mean too much, and could not bear the weight of such importance; and although Hughes wrote it with a serious purpose, he could not have foreseen its effect, certainly not the sidelong, unexpected ways in which its influence would work. When he wrote for the edification of his readers he envisaged this edification as something personal and spiritual, a call to the individual heart. Certainly he never meant to write a blue-print for the public schools.

Yet his (joint) biographers tell us that 'it is no exaggeration to say that *Tom Brown's Schooldays* made the modern public school';[7] one of them is Edward C. Mack, whose research into public-school history has been both deep and wide. Sir Joshua Fitch said much the same, in greater detail:

> The Arnoldian tradition which has become slowly evolved and has fixed itself in the minds of most English people is based more upon Mr Thomas Hughes's romance than upon the actual life [of Arnold] as set forth in Stanley's volumes. *Tom Brown's Schooldays* is a manly, spirited book . . . but, as Matthew Arnold once said to me, it has been praised quite enough, for it gives only one side, and that not the best side, of Rugby school life, or of Arnold's character. It leaves out of view, almost entirely, the intellectual purpose of a school.[8]

Its inadequacy as an apology for Arnold and his system would not have mattered if it had been less successful and so less influential. Hughes can hardly be blamed for its effect. Towards the end of his life he actually came to dislike some of the things that were going on in the public schools, some of the attitudes being fostered there. Of the cult of games which grew up in his lifetime he wrote: 'Athleticism is a good thing if it is kept in its place, but it has become very much overpraised and overvalued among us.'[9] Yet although he came to dislike some of what he saw, the size of the part he had played in bringing it about probably never occurred to him. He was too modest a man to rate his effect very high.

What was this effect? First of all, it was (unwittingly) to diminish Arnold's influence, both religious and intellectual. Hughes's biographers wrote:

The middle-class public, indifferent or hostile to Arnold's intense spirituality, his almost heretical religious and social views and his deep respect for learning, responded readily to the more mundane idea of a group of self-reliant manly boys tamed into submission to Christian principles . . . With the decline of the religious and social liberalism that had inspired both Arnold and Hughes, and the rise of the new imperialism . . . the better discipline and *esprit de corps* that Arnold had helped establish in order to effect liberal moral aims became fetters binding the average public-school boy to that worst of idols, 'good form': a reverence for things established.[10]

By failing to understand Arnold's ideas, Hughes misrepresented and (as things turned out) betrayed him. His readers went further than he had ever meant to go, and in turn misrepresented and in the long run betrayed *him*. For gradually, as the spirit of Tom Brown took over from that of Arnold, diluting, simplifying and finally coarsening Arnold's message, attitudes and ideas which Arnold would never have approved, yet people believed and continue to believe were his, became codified and hardened. Self-reliance became competitiveness, manliness became, first, heartiness and later hardness, moral toughness; above all, intellectual interests were subordinated to the cult of games. The public-school hero was no longer the good or the clever, but the athletic.

It is almost impossible to exaggerate the degree to which athletic prowess was admired in the middle half-century or so of the public schools, or from about the 1870s until the First World War. Before that, other things counted; after it, dissenters were heard, a reaction set in. But in their toughest form and at their most 'characteristic', the public schools (especially the Victorian ones – that is, the new foundations or the enlarged grammar schools) worshipped games to a degree so remarkable that it is now hard to credit it. It seems to have been G. E. L. Cotton* (the original of the 'model young master' who pleads with Arnold on Tom and East's behalf in their early, uproarious days and gives Tom tea on his last day at Rugby) who established the cult of games deliberately when he became headmaster of Marlborough in 1852. From there the mania spread and almost every memoir of school life around the end of the century and after it, certainly every school story, remarks on the hysterical adulation of the good athlete.

The hero of *The Loom of Youth,* which was written in 1916, says:

* Once engaged to Arnold's daughter Jane, Matthew Arnold's favourite sister. She later married William Forster, who is mainly remembered for his work on the Elementary Education Bill of 1870. The four children the Forsters adopted, orphaned by the death of their mother in the Punjab in 1858, and their father, Jane's brother William, the following year, took the name of Arnold-Forster. For a study of William Arnold, see Frances J. Woodward, *The Doctor's Disciples,* OUP (1954).

For the last twenty years at least the only thing Public School boys have cared about is games . . . No one works at a Public School. People who do are despised. If they happen to be good at games as well, they are tolerated. It is a condemnation of the whole system.

C. Day-Lewis wrote of Sherborne in his day:

Theoretically, of course, we were based on *mens sana in corpore sano*. But in practice there was a conflict in which *mens* lost hands down every time . . . Sherborne, as I have said, was a games-mad school. The 'bloods', the boys with the highest prestige, were almost invariably athletes; if they had brains too nobody objected, but it was the blue-and-gold ties of the First XV or the First XI which made them demi-gods.[11]

Harold Nicolson wrote of his time at Wellington:

Had I had displayed with ball or bat the same promise as I displayed with Greek iambics, I should have been made to feel that with care and application some sort of future opened before me.[12]

Marlborough seems to have been even harsher. There, brains (intellectual or aesthetic interests, at any rate) were actually despised, thought objectionable. As T. C. Worsley wrote:

It is almost impossible to convey to anyone who hasn't experienced it the momentousness of such an event [being chosen for the school cricket team] in a school as athletics-worshipping as Marlborough was. Public approval among masters as well as boys was reserved for the athlete . . . It was made very clear to me, from the very first day of my first school trial, that any truck with the aesthetes, with whom I should otherwise have joined my sympathies, would be regarded as treason and punished by exclusion from the places of power . . . Cricket matches in those days occupied an inordinate amount of the cricket Eleven's days in the summer term, and one's form-master would show a shrugging, tolerant indulgence towards one's absences and deficiencies. Poetry, and all such things, were put firmly behind me.[13]

Even at day schools the same ideas prevailed. Leonard Woolf wrote of his time at St Paul's:

The only standard of human value against which the boy was measured was athleticism. Use of the mind, intellectual curiosity, mental originality, interest in 'work', enjoyment of books or anything connected with the arts, all such things, if detected, were violently condemned and persecuted . . . This attitude was not confined to the boys; it was shared and encouraged by nearly all the masters.[14]

At most of the Clarendon schools, athleticism was never so fiercely imposed. Games were not compulsory at Charterhouse when Max Beerbohm was there, and the eccentric, uncooperative boy got through his schooldays, not radiantly happy, but at least neither bullied nor bored. William Plomer could say: 'I do not remember ever having played a game of either cricket or football at Rugby.'[15] Although under Warre's headmastership Eton sounds as games-mad as anywhere, Ronald Knox in the early years of the century – under Warre – was famously popular there and blissfully happy, although clearly a rabbit at games. L. P. Hartley, similarly unathletic, found Harrow a place where eccentricity could flourish. 'The boys were as unlike each other as they well could be,' he wrote. 'and whatever personal peculiarities, pleasant or unpleasant, they started with, time and the influence of school seemed to foster.'[16] Westminster and Winchester were always known as clever schools with better things to think about, on the whole, than mere athletics.

So there were freer corners of the system; and since much that is written about the public schools comes from the intellectual and the unathletic, perhaps it is not surprising to find such vociferous denunciation of the cult of games. But even bearing this in mind it still seems clear that athleticism was ferociously upheld in the mainstream schools in their heyday, and that even in the twenties and thirties, when it had become respectable to sneer and suggest alternatives, the cult continued, even at supposedly progressive places. 'Art had a vaguely homosexual connotation,' John Gale wrote of Stowe in the thirties. 'Games were the thing. I have heard that in comparison with many other public schools Stowe was enlightened. The others must have been odd.'[17]

This kind of attitude was not, of course, Hughes's fault. He certainly did not despise (though he did not sufficiently prize) intellectual interests and intellectual effort. But his book, too popular and too easily assimilated, did suggest in an unaggressive way that the most thrilling thing about school life was sport; from which it is a small step to the idea that, if sport matters more than work, then work matters rather little; and from that the steps become progressively smaller to the idea that sport is everything, intellectual interest nothing, or even actively reprehensible and despicable. When, on Tom's first evening at Rugby, Old Brooke tells his house: 'I know I'd sooner win two School-house matches running than get the Balliol scholarship any day,' a remark that qualifies him as either a liar or an idiot, there are 'frantic cheers' for his lie or idiocy; and presumably (in the heat of the moment at least) approval from Hughes.

But in Arnold's day at Rugby things were free and casual in comparison with the rigidity and precision of later public-school life. After lessons boys were free to roam the countryside, for fishing, birdnesting, and all sorts of botanical interests or illicit but cheerful outdoor occupations. Exercise was of a general, unorganised kind (running, swimming and so on); hare-and-hounds and even games of football were muddy, crowded, unprofessional scuffles for which the boys simply took off their coats and pitched in, whatever they happened to be wearing. In any case, there was no uniform. Arnold himself liked physical exercise but cared nothing for organised games. At the end of *Tom Brown's Schooldays* he sets off for the Lake District on the day before the great cricket match of the year, obviously not interested enough to stay and cheer the Schoolhouse on. And nobody minds or criticises him for it.

In Joshua Fitch's view:

> He certainly did nothing to encourage that extravagant passion for athletics, that exaltation of physical prowess to the same level as intellectual distinction, which has in later years so seriously debased the ideal and hindered the usefulness of the public schools . . . Modern experience in [them] curiously reproduces that of Greece more than two thousand years ago. For the moment the type of schoolboy and of manhood most in favour with the British public is Spartan rather than Athenian; but there can be no doubt that Arnold, faithful to the teachings of his own master [Aristotle], would have sought to resist the prevailing fashion, and to confine athletic sports within narrower limits.[18]

Oscar Browning felt much the same:

> The most salient characteristic of modern public schools is the reception of games into the curriculum on an equality with work, if not into a superior position. Of this Arnold would have entirely disapproved. He would have seen that it ministered to a lower standard of effort, that it vulgarised intellectual labour, that it substituted self-indulgence for self-denial, and that it placed those boys in positions of command and influence who were frequently most unfit to exercise either the one or the other.

But Hughes's simple message went out, uninfluenced by Arnold's concern for things of the mind, or by his subtlety and originality. Even his political radicalism vanished into Hughes's spirit of pleasant, hearty democracy, in which the old squirearchy was to be allied with the rustic working class against the new industrialised city folk, proletarian or middle-class. Things went askew with Hughes's message, in more ways than one. He loved sport and believed in its good influence as a way of teaching courage, cooperation, and loyalty to a particular place, team, school-house or even country. What he did not foresee was that, because success in it demanded careful organisation and firm leadership, practice and professionalism, it would cease to be merely enjoyable and become a tyranny in the public schools. It would involve the tightening up of the time-table, the arrangement of the schoolboy's every free moment, the loss of every interest unconnected with it. The public schools in their heyday, particularly the 'hardest', most mainstream, had little time for hobbies, cultural interests, even wide reading, and certainly gave them little encouragement.

4 . . . *Tom Brown the potential pro-consul.* Mack and Armytage

More importantly, Hughes's social message turned sour. His biographers wrote:

> The Rugby Hughes extolled was misinterpreted by most of his middle-class readers. [He] hoped that public schools would nourish crusaders for the Christian life, Arnoldians who would fight for Saxon simplicity against Norman guile, the followers of Christ and King Alfred; but his middle-class readers saw only Tom Brown the potential pro-consul. It was so easy a message to misinterpret. Where Tom [Hughes] saw such schools as nurseries of social servants, his middle-class readers saw them as training grounds for sahibs. Unwittingly, he touched a vein of class sentiment, which erupted . . . into yet more public schools which were far from fulfilling the wishes of either Arnold or his disciples. Tom himself was worried about such consequences.[19]

Hughes had been at pains, indeed, to stress the middlingness of his hero, social as well as intellectual, and this must have given a wide range of readers a comfortable sense of involvement in his affairs. To many, in fact, Hughes must almost have seemed to be championing 'us' against 'them', the humble against the proud; certainly the rough-hewn against the polished. The first quarter of his book, which is not about school at all (though dramatised versions of it have generally ignored this), shows Tom in the context of his family and their way of life. 'The Browns' (a generic name for all people of their kind) embodied, for Hughes, all the unpretentious, median qualities he approved of. 'Noble families,' he says, 'would be somewhat astounded . . . to find how small their work for England has been by the side of that of the Browns.' You would think he was talking of peasants or, at most, yeomen farmers, rather than that well-to-do landowner and magistrate Squire Brown. Rural and rough Tom's family may have been, but in the corner of England they owned the Browns were kings. Certainly they belonged, numerically and by social acceptance, to the top tenth of English society at that time. But Hughes himself belonged to that top tenth, and so the fact that the Browns were in the lower, non-aristocratic part of it was what counted, as he dwelt almost smugly on their lowliness.

Hughes hated snobbery as he hated all affectation. Above all he would have thought it unmanly, trivial, unworthy of anyone serious.

'But, goodness, I can't stand a fellow who gives himself airs, and thinks himself a chalk above everybody who can't dress and do just as he can,' his hero bursts out in *The Scouring of the White Horse* (1859).* Part of the charm of *Tom Brown's Schooldays* lies in its breezy acceptance of all comers, the humanity of its feeling at every social level. On the other hand, Hughes belonged to his age and his social attitudes were complex and contradictory. Tom Brown plays with the village boys (to the scandal of neighbours of his own class), but once he gets to Rugby such boys can never again be considered as companions. For all Hughes's democratic beliefs and even instincts he never, in any recognisable, modern sense, bridged the gap between his own class and those below it; for all his efforts and his socialism he never lost what we should now call a scout-masterly air, unwittingly hearty and patronising.

For over a century Hughes's attitude to Tom Brown made writers point out, hands raised in admiration, how classless the public schools were. What they meant, of course, was that within certain classes the public schools were unsnobbish (though even this seems highly dubious). As recently as 1953, in an introduction to *Tom Brown's Schooldays*, Lord Elton could write that the post-Arnoldian public school was 'the only institution in Victorian England in which snobbery was unknown', where 'son of duke and son of banker rubbed shoulders on terms of complete familiarity'.[20] But to those outside the public-school world there can have seemed little difference between dukes and bankers, compared with the differences between them and the rest of the world.

Nor were dukes' sons found at most public schools, which were anything but socially homogeneous. They were layered like *mille feuilles*. Among the *Loom of Youth* papers at Sherborne (handed over to the school by Alec Waugh when they had made their peace) there is a Wodehousian-sounding letter to the author from a friend still at school, written soon after he left. 'Dear Wuffles,' it starts, 'How wags the world with you?' It then goes on to describe a match played against another school, not very different in status from Sherborne, whose effrontery ('awful little ticks') in playing Sherborne at all enrages the boy. This was during the First World War. By the Second, things seem to have changed little. In an essay on his schooldays Kingsley Amis described how, when his London day school, much older than its host school and of high standing academically, was sent to Marlborough to escape the bombing, no social contact, official or unofficial, took place between the two schools in the time he was there.

* A novel about the adventures of a country clerk seeing the festival of the Scouring of the White Horse of Uffington (where Hughes was brought up).

Quite simply, they were not on speaking terms. Examples of this sort of thing abound, too numerous to quote and all rather nasty: schools refusing to play schools they considered just that little bit beneath them, and so on. So much for the public schools' vaunted democracy, even in relation to other public schools. In relation to the rest of the world – well, at Hughes's Rugby boys in the non-public-school rest of the world are always referred to, without malice but also without embarrassment, as 'louts'; at Reed's St Dominic's and at Leslie's Eton they are 'cads'; today they are still often called 'oicks' or 'yobboes'.

Another reason for Hughes's wholehearted approval of the Browns was racial rather than social. They were English, like the Vale of the White Horse from which he and they came, a part of the country for which he felt an almost mystical attachment. I said 'racial' rather than 'national' deliberately because he seems to have thought of the Browns as he thought of the Berkshire countryside, as English in the sense of pre-Norman. 'How the whole countryside teems with Saxon names and memories!' he exclaims of Uffington. '. . . There's nothing like the old countryside for me, and no music like the twang of the real old Saxon tongue.' In the early part of the book, he is dealing with something wider than the public schools. He is trying to convey (almost as Kipling did in *Puck of Pook's Hill,* though he does it much less skilfully than Kipling) a sense of the past, the rural past and the essential Englishness of what was then almost untouched country; to show how historical events overlapped in the one place and the landscape bore signs of Saxon, Dane and Norman, medieval and Tudor and industrial, all of which formed the rich simplicity of the present (simple, at least, in his boyhood: against the increasing complexity of modern life he did not rail so much as humorously protest). The beauty, the rightness, the values of the English countryside and its life were things he never lost sight of or faith in, however often he knocked against the realities of Victorian urban, industrial life.

This was the attractive side of his immaturity, of his ability to feel and behave like a schoolboy, even in middle age. The first quarter of the book is his credo, part autobiography, part local history, part story-telling. In it he mixes fact and fiction, himself and the Browns, his views on almost anything and their pragmatic non-philosophy. Into the boy, Tom Brown, went all this – Hughes's own early happiness and security, and the faith it had given him in the essential goodness of others; his own simplicity and goodheartedness, as well as his limitations of mind and outlook. He might deny that Tom Brown was a self-portrait, but he was clearly identified with Tom by his readers and by the public in general, and, since he allowed the poster to say 'Vote for Tom Brown' when he stood for parliament, he cannot have minded. Clearly he had a romanticised view of the Browns and their Saxon forebears, the kind that reflects a passionate attachment to a particular mythology and culture as well as countryside and people. It was the sort of thing C. S. Lewis felt from boyhood for something he called 'Northernness',[21] to which, in his later fantasies, he was able to give life. Hughes was no fantasist, so his sense of 'Saxonness' tends to sound either absurd or inexpressible. But it gave a glow to his approval of the dogged, apparently unromantic Browns.

So Tom Brown became the ideal English schoolboy (and thus potentially the ideal Englishman) and for a century his deep-dyed ordinariness and its corollary, philistinism, helped to form the image of ideal young manhood. The later school-story heroes, lacking Tom's warmth and open-heartedness, became *merely* ordinary, thick-headed, philistine. To modern taste they seem unbearably dull, but clearly their contemporaries, particularly around the turn of the century, approved. The hero of Charles Turley's *The New Broom* (1911) is typical. When he visits another master and finds himself 'surrounded by Oriental pots and fans he [feels] inclined to smash them'. 'Hunter amused himself by pointing out some of the beauties of his room,' Turley goes on, 'and by watching the disgusted face of his guest. "I don't pretend to know anything about this sort of thing," John said,' and clearly has Turley's, and Turley's readers', approval.

In the later school stories, a reaction against 'decadence', a nervous rejection of all it might seem to suggest, was obviously part of this. But even if one discounts that, the hero of school stories and his extension, the hero of popular adult fiction, descends in an unbroken line from Tom Brown; unbroken because the development can be traced exactly, stage by stage, but sharply curved in a direction that might roughly be called from left to right. Characteristics which lay undeveloped and unexplored in Tom Brown grew into much more definite and dislikable qualities. The *persona* of the socialist Hughes became a fierce upholder of the establishment and a snob as well; the cheerful idler who skimped his homework became a ferocious hater of the intellect, an enemy of ideas, in the broadest sense of culture. The hearty became the tough, the tough became Bulldog Drummond. And the same sort of process took place in the public schools.

5 *Tom Hughes the 'blue' . . . the ideal hero of the British public . . .*

C. E. Raven

Hughes himself has always had a good press. The fact that his was an attractive personality, and that *Tom Brown's Schooldays* was an attractive book, made both him and his book more influential than they need or ought to have been. Greater literary talent, a more original mind, might have made the first school story a better one, but less likely to be copied, to set up a taste for school stories. Almost haphazardly Hughes found a literary formula that could be used in a variety of ways and at all kinds of levels; so in literary as well as social and educational terms the influence of his book was out of all proportion to its merits. A likable literary hack put down his memories for others to relive and enjoy with him. This made plenty of readers relive theirs, and other writers imitate him. For a century almost the whole of the literate class in England shared similar memories of at least one part of life, and school stories lapped their readers in a common nostalgia.

Hughes had powerful but pragmatic views, hit-or-miss ideas. Inclined as he was to simplify, he had the energetic, confident mind that makes narrow, limiting judgements seem wider and wiser than they are. In spite of much religious earnestness, he tended to bring out a bluff, hearty response to anything too complex or too taxing. 'I saw much of Maurice,' he wrote of F. D. Maurice,* admittedly a prolific writer of difficult works, 'but while loving him personally, as all did who came into contact with him, I am free to confess that I never could make head or tail of what he taught or what he meant.' Hughes's infectious laughter seems to burst off the page, but it was as inadequate for dealing with Maurice as Strachey's thin smile was later to be for dealing with Arnold. Hughes revered and even loved Arnold, but never really made head or tail of what he taught or what he meant, either.

Unlike Arnold, Hughes came of an old-fashioned, well-established layer of the country gentry; unsmart people whose children entered a comfortable niche in English life without great effort but who believed in effort on others' behalf. He lived a long life and spanned much social change: he could remember old ladies paying calls in sedan chairs (there is a sedan-chair man at Rugby in Tom Brown's time), while his daughter May, who spent a lifetime among the London poor, died during the Blitz in 1941. His life as barrister, judge, MP, leading figure in the cooperative movement and Principal of the Working Men's College which, with Maurice, he helped to found, was a full one, packed with schemes and infectiously enthusiastic plans, not always carefully considered. The last grand scheme of his life, a colony in Tennessee, known as Rugby, set up for landless Englishmen ('younger sons'), not surprisingly failed for lack of proper planning, with financially disastrous results for Hughes himself, who had even sent his aged mother to settle there.

* Frederick Denison Maurice (1805–72), influential divine and spiritual leader of the Christian Socialists, one of the founders of the Working Men's College.

Everyone liked Hughes, his colleagues and his equals, the students at the Working Men's College (with whom he boxed – though they were warned beforehand not to knock him down), the young and the old. His home life seems to have been charmingly informal for its time and his goodness, or at least an unforced 'niceness', apparent to all. Even when he has been dead too long for his personal charm to count directly, he comes attractively to life. 'A character so genial, lovable and manly,' says one book; 'a man of admirable character, tirelessly active in social reform; a muscular Christian and a broad churchman; a man without guile despite the fact that he was a lawyer,' says another; 'sane, simple, vigorous . . . large in every way,' says a third. 'There was a goodness about him,' this book goes on to say, 'that, combined with a joy in everyday living, was completely satisfying.' C. E. Raven called him 'Tom Hughes the "blue", with the healthy mind and the healthy body . . . the ideal hero of the British public and the sporting press'; and someone in the *Spectator* wrote that his presence made one feel that 'the air was lighter and the clouds were on the move'. Obituaries make the best of things, of course, but one by his friend J. M. Ludlow,* the first reader of *Tom Brown's Schooldays* and its initial encourager, sounds heartfelt. 'He cannot be called a great writer,' Ludlow wrote, 'least of all did he pretend to be great, either as a writer or as a man. Yet he was, in a sense, greater than a great man – a great-souled man. Nothing base, nothing small could be found in him. Moreover, his character and his writings were alike typically English – English of the best.'

This Englishness and likableness, this lack of side and affectation, this easily acceptable heartiness which made religion seem simple and goodness a straightforward habit, free of Arnold's scruples and soul-searching and of Farrar's hysteria; above all the manliness Hughes expounded and cultivated, all made *Tom Brown's Schooldays* irresistible in its early days. Manliness had none of the jingoistic, nationalistic, or plainly comical overtones it later acquired. ' "Manliness" and "manfulness" are synonymous, but they embrace more than we ordinarily mean by the word "courage",' Hughes wrote, 'for instance, tenderness, and thoughtfulness for others.' The words 'tender' and 'tenderness' were favourites of his, in fact, and the pages of his book are overflowing with feeling. Sixty years later a typical public-school hero is described by Desmond Coke as being 'accustomed from

* John Malcolm Forbes Ludlow, one of the founders of the Christian Socialist Movement and the Working Men's College, active in social reform, the cooperative movement and friendly societies. He and Hughes had a semi-communal house built for their two families in Wimbledon, and it was in the shared library there that he first read *Tom Brown's Schooldays*.

childhood to express even the tenderest emotions with reserve'. 'Reserve' never occurred to Hughes as anything but regrettable. 'Public schools cultivate reserve, and so strongly that I think one never quite gets rid of it, although one gets better in after-life,' he wrote. 'I wish it was not so; it is one of [their] disadvantages.'

Thus Hughes introduced his readers to a public-school world in which there was plenty of room for feeling and warmth; in which the sharp distinction between school and the rest of the world, between family and school friends, did not yet exist; in which a headmaster, however awesome, could cradle a weeping boy's head in his arms without embarrassment to either (as happens with Arnold and East) and loving friendships between boys aroused no uneasy feelings in themselves, their masters, or their readers. It was a world of innocent good nature, artlessly described, and to the schoolboy reader forty or fifty years later it must have seemed unimaginably distant.

6 . . . *the famous epithet of 'Barbarians'*. . .

Sir Joshua Fitch, quoting Matthew Arnold

The secret of Tom Brown's success, both psychologically and realistically – and artistically, too – is that he wants to go to Rugby, that he is delighted to be there and has no doubt that it is all quite splendid. 'Oh, don't stop!' he tells the guard on the Tally-ho coach as they bowl along in the cold on his way to Rugby for the first time, and the guard tells tales of battles with pea-shooters on that same route between Rugby boys and the Irish navvies who then swarmed about the countryside – road-building, canal-cutting, and a little later railway-making. 'Tell us something more . . .' If he had been sent unwillingly he would have found Rugby unbearable, harsh and rough as its conditions were, brutal as the bullies could be. Or the reluctant schoolboy of Tom's age might be merely homesick, cause enough for misery without any of the rest. But to Tom the pride and excitement of belonging to a group of boys of all ages between nine and nineteen (or a little more at either end) make everything acceptable, thrilling, friendly; and to a gregarious extrovert like Tom, friendliness is everything.

Because he joins enthusiastically in whatever happens, and is generous and goodhearted with it, he makes friends; not just with East, Arthur and Martin but, once things have settled down for him, with most of his house and form. He is the popular figure East never becomes and anyone who remembers from childhood scenes of communal enjoyment will warm to the descriptions of sing-songs and suppers and other such shared experiences, and Tom's response to them – his sense of belonging to a great community breathing as one.

The Tally-ho guard's tales stir Tom (on a small scale but authentically) in the way that the English army is stirred before Agincourt. They are few but lucky to be there, enviable to the rest of the world, a band of brothers among whom he is to take his place.

The book's enthusiasm is infectious and lacks the idiotic gush of some of the later school-story enthusiasms. It suits the intellectual level of the moment. At ten or so, a vessel filled to overflowing with any experience – except, alas, the intellectual – Tom is stirred by pretty well anything: sausages round the fire, Dr Arnold's sermons, Old Brooke's encouragement after his first football game. As he grows older he takes to other things: mischief and disorder at first, then what Hughes calls 'steadier' pursuits. His story, though not vapid, is a happy one. He has the sort of sunny strength that keeps him from despair, even from long-term gloom. Flashman's bullying he can stand: it leaves him spiritually undefeated. Towards the end of the book, when Arthur asks him: 'What do you want to do here, and to carry away?' Tom expresses his simple aims. 'I want to be A1 at cricket and football, and all the other games, and to make my hands keep my head against any fellow, lout or gentleman,' he says. 'I want to get into the sixth before I leave, and to please the Doctor; and I want to carry away just as much Latin and Greek as will take me through Oxford respectably.' Then he pauses. ' "I want to leave behind me," said Tom, speaking slow and looking much moved, 'the name of a fellow who never bullied a little boy or turned his back on a big one." ' Three aims, sporting, intellectual, and moral, in that order; the first aim ambitious, the second and third quite modest. They were just the aims, in just the order, to appeal to later generations of readers. Tom and East, for pleasure, read Captain Marryat; he is part of their evening life, like bottled beer and baked potatoes ('murphies'). The same sort of boy would later read Thomas Hughes.

What Hughes fails to suggest is that Rugby provides any interest in things of the mind, that intellectual pursuits have any place there. Lessons, for him, never seem to go beyond the sluggish routine of the lower fourth, where 'young gentlemen of all ages, from nine to fifteen, expended such part of their energies as were devoted to Latin and Greek over a book of Livy, the *Bucolics* of Virgil, and the *Hecuba* of Euripides, which was ground out in small daily portions.' Work seems to consist entirely of this painful drag through lines barely understood at all, with cribbing from 'copy books' handed down from each generation of boys to the next, without understanding or pleasure or, it would seem, profit. Tom must get something out of it, since he reaches the Sixth and eventually Oxford. But it seems an odd system that gives a moderately intelligent boy, not quite incorrigibly idle, so little in the way of intellectual stimulus and satisfaction. Hughes seems not to question this, and only in the case of Martin, Tom's friend the mad scientist, with his pet magpie and stuffed animals, his inventions and 'stinks', does he seem to wonder about the whole basis of public-school teaching. 'Martin . . . was one of those unfortunates who were at that time of day (and are, I fear, still) quite out of their place at a public school,' he writes. 'If we knew how to use our boys, Martin would have been seized upon and educated as a natural philosopher' (i.e., scientist).

Nor does he seem to have much idea of Arnold's intellectual interests and aims. He mentions him 'editing classics and writing histories', but that is about all. You would hardly suspect that Arnold had wide-ranging views on anything except religion and the classics, for it is his human and moral qualities that Hughes stresses, and Tom grows to love. Nor would you think Rugby a place of intellectual effort, where lessons are done and boys may acquire not only some learning but some culture and mental stimulus; for it is as a place of human relationships and moral growth that Hughes shows it. Tom is concerned with a good many things but hardly at all with work. What count, for him, are relationships, friendships, admirations; with East, Arthur and Arnold, first of all; then with more peripheral friends and masters, Diggs, Martin, Old Brooke, Cotton. Fiction is admittedly concerned most of all with humanity and feeling, but it is still strange how totally the intellectual life of Rugby is ignored.

Shrouded in clouds of awe and admiration, Arnold, like Tom, progresses through the book and, like Tom's, his status changes. It is disconcerting to find that when Tom arrives at Rugby, Arnold is 'looked upon with great fear and dislike by the great majority even of his own house'. Hughes explains:

> When he first came into collision with boys or customs there was nothing for them but to give in or take themselves off; because what he said had to be done, and no mistake about it. And this was beginning to be pretty clearly understood; the boys felt that there was a strong man over them who would have things his own way; and hadn't yet learned that he was a wise and loving man also. His personal character and influence had not had time to make itself felt, except directly in contact . . . He had found School, and Schoolhouse, in a state of monstrous licence and misrule, and was still employed in the necessary but unpopular work of setting up order with a strong hand.

Yet Arnold's weekly sermons stir his young audience deeply. 'What was it that moved and held us, the rest of the three hundred reckless, childish boys, who feared the Doctor with all our hearts, and very little besides in heaven or earth?' Hughes asks, trying to explain and interpret the 'great and solemn sight' of Arnold preaching.

It was not the cold, clear voice of one giving advice and warning from serene heights to those who were struggling and sinning below, but the warm, living voice of one who was fighting for us and by our sides and calling on us to help him and ourselves and one another.

In spite of the awe-inspiring presence, it is always Arnold's humanity that he stresses, and he makes Tom see through his alarming exterior quite early in his schooldays. 'It's all his look that frightens fellows,' he tells East consolingly, meaning that one must not take too much notice of that look.

One of Arnold's sons, another Thomas,* wrote: 'We were very much afraid, if we did wrong, of being found out and punished, and still worse, of witnessing the frown gather on his brow.'[22] Arnold's personality was clearly almost frighteningly strong, and a man's presence can seldom have been more directly influential, if we accept the immense effect of the schools that followed Rugby and if Arnold's presence is seen as the main factor in his influence. In Tom Brown's case, respect grows into reverence and finally into love, and when, at the book's end, a friend calls out to him: 'Your old master, Arnold of Rugby, is dead' (this is the first time he is named in the book: before that he is always 'the Doctor'; a good dramatic touch), Tom is overwhelmed with grief. Nor was this fictional overstatement. 'The abrupt tidings gave me a shock like a heavy blow,' a pupil of Arnold's wrote of his death. 'I simply staggered under it. I got to my room as soon as I could to give way, for I felt that . . . the first great grief of my life had fallen upon me.'

Apart from Arnold, the main characters were not taken directly from life. Like most novelists, Hughes mixed up 'various traits and incidents . . . recorded from memory', according to his wife. George Arthur was often thought to be a portrait of A. P. Stanley,† Arnold's first biographer, but probably only because his Christian name was Arthur; in any case, he and Hughes only just overlapped at Rugby and did not know each other until after the book's publication. The School-house servants – Mrs Wixie, Old Thos, Bogle and Sam – were all recognisable; and Flashman was said by a contemporary to be 'a painfully correct photograph of —; I won't recall his name.' Martin was a mixture of two boys, one known as Taxidermy Taylor, the other

* 1823–1900. Teacher and literary historian, converted to Roman Catholicism, taught at Birmingham Oratory School under Newman, then became Professor of English at University College, Dublin, where he knew Gerard Manley Hopkins. Father of Mrs Humphrey Ward and of Julia, who married Leonard Huxley and became the mother of Aldous and Julian Huxley.

† Arthur Penrhyn Stanley, 1815–1881, Dean of Westminster. *The Dictionary of National Biography* suggests that he was the model for Arthur, adding that 'his personal charm was a stronger influence than his books'.

an 'awfully clever' lad who 'used to make little steam engines, cast his own wheels, etc'; Crab Jones in the football match may have been a boy known as Crab Smyth, or possibly was suggested by Matthew Arnold's nickname of 'Crab' since Matthew and Hughes were school-friends; and the great fight in real life took place between boys called Orlebar* and Jones, with Hughes as one of the seconds. It seems to have been more ferociously fought than it was in the book, for Orlebar fainted and was unable to get up in time and Jones was so disfigured that Arnold, who stopped the fight, could not recognise him. Both boys were given two hundred lines of Virgil to recite as a punishment and they became, and remained, firm friends; thus confirming Hughes's belief that 'fighting with fists is the natural and English way for English boys to settle their quarrels'. Many years after the fight two elderly clergymen met at Rugby when Hughes's statue was unveiled there, and found themselves discussing the famous fight he had put into his book. Only halfway through the conversation did they find that they were the original fighters, Orlebar and Jones.

Small objects and incidents have achieved a sentimental importance through Hughes's use of them. Tom and East scratch their names on the minute-hand of the great clock at Rugby. A minute-hand of a clock kept at Rugby has Hughes's name scratched on it, although, as his son said he had never heard Hughes mention it, anachronistic piety may have been responsible for it. In the football match on the day of Tom's arrival no-one runs with the ball, although William Webb Ellis had picked it up at Rugby and run with it as early as 1823, thus officially creating Rugby football; but this was not accepted in the Rugby game until 1841–42, when Hughes himself was captain of Bigside. And so it goes on, detailed and eventful, but I have not the space to deal with it all and others have already discussed individual incidents at length.

The best known of these, showing the extent of public-school brutality at the time, appears in what Hughes calls 'the War of Independence', waged by Tom and East, with help from a kindly older boy called Diggs, against the bullies, led by Flashman. Tom is seized and 'roasted' over a fire. 'I trust and believe that such scenes are not possible now at school,' Hughes wrote of it. '. . . But I am writing of schools as they were in our time, and must give the evil with the good.' The official harshness of punishments (thrashings by masters and

* Dr Arnold's son Edward married a Caroline Orlebar (their son founded the publishing house of Edward Arnold). I have not discovered whether she was related to Augustus Orlebar of the fight but the unusual name and the Rugby connection suggest it.

prefects, endless physical assaults for what now seem minor offences) probably made bullying inevitable by tolerating an atmosphere of physical violence; and not just bullying of the person but bullying through another sort of assault – on possessions or privacy: the wrecking of a boy's books or clothes, ink poured into desks, things strewn about or 'borrowed'. Tom and East – and even Arthur, whom they lead high-spiritedly astray at times – are themselves involved in general uproariousness with keepers and farmers, locals of various sorts whose possessions (chickens and fish) they think little of taking. This more than anything shows the class differences of the time in the way the classes expected (and got) different treatment for similar offences. Not many years earlier stealing such things was punishable by death or transportation; whereas to boys like Tom and East it is just an amusing incident to be put right, if discovered, by a small tip. Ironically Hughes, who set out so determined to preach to his readers, was vehemently attacked by some of them for the sins he lightheartedly made his hero commit.

The *Christian Observer* of June 1858 said the book was likely to produce 'sensual, careless, book-hating men – low in morals, lower in religion, and destitute of those qualities which fit men, not merely for the occupation of heaven, but for the higher offices and duties of life'. This may sound fierce for so relatively lightweight a book, but even the friendlier Fitch remarks severely: 'It is to be feared that Hughes's own boyhood was not spent with the best set at Rugby.' To Stanley, *Tom Brown's Schooldays* was 'an absolute revelation'. 'It opens up a world of which, though so near to me, I was utterly ignorant,' he wrote. Men like Stanley and Fitch were shocked not just by the behaviour of boys like Tom ('delighting in wanton mischief, in sport, in a fight, and even in theft from a farm-yard, distinguished frequently by insolence to inferiors, and even by coarseness and brutality, and not by love of work or any strong interest in intellectual pursuits,' as Fitch put it), but by the wider implications of their attitudes; in other words, Hughes's attitudes.

His book, Fitch said,

> gives the reader the impression that it is the chief business of a public school to produce a healthy animal, to supply him with pleasant companions and faithful friends, to foster in him courage and truthfulness, and for the rest to teach as much as the regulations of the school enforce, but no more . . . This picture of a public school . . . will probably be quoted in future years as illustrating the low standard of civilisation, the false idea of manliness, and the deep-seated indifference to learning for its own sake which characterised the upper classes of our youth in the early half of the nineteenth century. In short the book will be held to explain and justify the famous epithet of 'Barbarians'

which Matthew Arnold* was wont to apply to the English aristocracy and to that section of society which was most nearly influenced by the great public schools.[23]

Fitch was right: the book *was* 'quoted in future years', but not always, or even often, with disapproval. Probably the most widely quoted sentences, the most central in tone, are those of Squire Brown as he muses on what to tell Tom when he goes off to Rugby for the first time.

> Shall I tell him to mind his work, and say he's sent to school to make himself a good scholar? Well, but he isn't sent to school for that – at any rate, not for that mainly. I don't care a straw for Greek particles, or the digamma, no more does his mother. What is he sent to school for? . . . If he'll only turn out a brave, helpful, truth-telling Englishman, and a Christian, that's all I want.

This, we have often been told, was the attitude of the typical English parent of his time and class – no-nonsense, pragmatic, practical, good-hearted. Lytton Strachey, who should have known better if he had read even the seven books in the bibliography at the end of his essay on Arnold, makes it appear to be *Arnold*'s attitude as well. 'That was all,' he says, 'and it was that that Dr Arnold set himself out to accomplish.'[24] Of course it was not. Far from not caring 'a straw for Greek particles', as far as the school curriculum was concerned Arnold cared for little else. And again and again he stressed the importance of the intellect, of mental stimulus. 'If the mind becomes stagnant it can give no fresh draught to another mind,' he wrote. 'It is drinking out of a pond instead of a stream.' But Hughes was read much more widely and attentively than Arnold, with far-reaching and grave results.

If Hughes shocked some readers, he bored others with his preaching, and much of it has probably been skipped, ever since the book first appeared. Towards the end of it preaching grows more frequent; Hughes finds a good excuse for it in something which was to figure, not unrealistically, in school stories down the century. This was the school illness. To modern readers it may seem just an excuse for weepy drama of an unacceptable sort; but it was a fact that epidemics swept regularly through the schools and illness could carry off the young in terrible numbers. Death was one of the main preoccupations of the Victorian public schools (quite apart from the *idea* of death – in war, in school stories generally – which I shall deal with later), and it would have been unrealistic to ignore the untreatable diseases which insanitary buildings and unhygienic domestic arrangements made likely; while the crowded conditions and sheer harshness

* In *Culture and Anarchy*.

of cold and hunger, especially among the small fry, must have dangerously weakened the delicate. Tom himself seems not to suffer from these conditions and to have enough pocket money to supplement the school food; but the frail, the timid, and those poorer than the rest must have shivered and starved a good deal, like hospital patients or prisoners without family or friends in places where outsiders are expected to supplement the official rations. Arthur without Tom to guide him would certainly have suffered. As it is, he succumbs to the fever that has already killed a boy at the school.

The crisis passes, and Tom visits him. Hughes writes:

> Never till that moment had he felt how his little chum had twined himself round his heartstrings; and as he stole gently across the room and knelt down, and put his arm round Arthur's head on the pillow, he felt ashamed and half-angry at his own red and brown face . . . Arthur laid his thin white hand, on which the blue veins stood out so plainly, on Tom's great brown fist . . .

Hugh Kingsmill suggested[25] that this was like a Victorian husband's tiptoe visit to his wife after childbirth, and all it needed was for Arthur to hand over the baby; but this seems an exaggerated fantasy when Hughes is just indulging in a little post-crisis sentimentality of a familiar Victorian kind. After that there is a great deal of preaching; much talk about cribbing and honesty, about East's confirmation, about belief; but perhaps even in its early days readers skipped it and hurried on to the final cricket match. At tea with the young master immediately after it, Tom learns that his turnabout in behaviour some years earlier was the result not of his own strength of will, as he has always thought it, but of Arnold's insight in getting him to care for Arthur, the shy, virtuous new boy likely to be lost and bullied. On hearing this, Tom recognises Arnold's amazing care of him and the others at Rugby; however full his life may be, he still has time for the problems of the individual boy. 'The Doctor's victory was complete from that moment,' Hughes says, 'over Tom Brown at any rate . . . It had taken eight years to do it, but now it was done thoroughly, and there wasn't a corner of him left which didn't believe in the Doctor.' Tom's grief at Arnold's death is made the more poignant by the thought that he never said this, never managed to express his gratitude or show his feelings. Hughes said it and showed them posthumously, dedicating the book to Mrs Arnold.

In innumerable editions and formats, *Tom Brown's Schooldays* went round the world and up and down the social scale. About halfway between its day and ours, in 1913, Lord Kilbracken, in an introduction to a new edition, told how the cricketer, Sir Pelham

Warner, who had been at Rugby, described Tom Brown's fame in the most unlikely places.

In those distant lands, [lands where he went to play cricket] it was a common topic of conversation to ask the English players about their places of education, and whenever this happened, the names of other schools . . . were received with comparative indifference; but the name of Rugby was generally hailed with the exclamation, 'Oh, how interesting!' and a series of questions, founded for the most part on 'Tom Brown', usually followed.

Nearly seventy years later, Tom Brown is probably still just as well-known, films and television having taken his story round the world again and into homes where public-school life is unknown. And he keeps being revived. His image changes from one generation to the next, and so does Arnold's (which is harder to put across credibly or attractively). Charles Kingsley believed in the book from the start, but even he might have been amazed to know that nearly a hundred and thirty years later Tom Brown is still a household name. He wrote to its publisher, Daniel Macmillan:*

It will be a great hit. It is an extraordinary book. Take it all in all, you won't see such smart writing, such knowledge of slang and all manner of odds and ends, combined with the actual knowledge of boys, with the really lofty tone of religion and the broad humanity in any living writer. Besides, it is the only book of its kind.

7 *The story of 'Eric' was written with but one single object – the vivid inculcation of inward purity and moral purpose.* F. W. Farrar

It was not the only book of its kind for long. A year after its publication *Eric or Little by Little* appeared. Though very different in tone from Hughes's book, it was written with exactly the same purpose: to 'preach to boys'. But Hughes got in first with his cheerful, attractive preaching, which reconciled his readers to the didactic approach. Had *Eric* been the first school story it might, as founder of a genre, have been stillborn. From a literary point of view, it was rather better than its predecessor, but it was unappealing. And with the years it became progressively more unappealing until today, the anti-Victorian, looking for an example of Victorian attitudes at their remotest from modern taste, might well pick on Frederick William Farrar, head-

* Daniel Macmillan, 1813–1857, bookseller and, from 1844, publisher; with his brother Alexander, founder of the firm of Macmillan; friend of F. D. Maurice, Charles Kingsley, Hughes and others connected with Christian Socialism and influential in steering a number of – later distinguished – young men towards it. He published Kingsley's *Westward Ho!* (1855) and *Tom Brown's Schooldays* (1857) and Hughes wrote a 'Memoir' of him in 1882.

master of Marlborough, Canon of Westminster, chaplain-in-ordinary to Queen Victoria, grandfather of Field Marshal Montgomery, and author of *Eric* and other works cordially hated by his grandchildren.

Eric has been mocked so often that people quote it at one remove, without having read it. Like *East Lynne*, another highly readable Victorian example of excess, equally often misquoted, it lingered on as a piece of folklore long after it had ceased to be taken to heart by the average reader. Not that Farrar's work has ever quite died away. Reprinted many times, *Eric* was brought out in 1971 with a reappraising and even admiring foreword.* Nonsense it may largely be, but it is still something of a spellbinder, because Farrar had certain qualities at a much higher level than many more sensible and credible writers of school stories: a strong sense of the dramatic, a power to conjure conflict, spiritual as well as physical, an ability to involve the reader in his characters' lives. Above all, he had a burning belief in the importance of what he was saying.

And 'importance' is the key word. The trouble with school stories, on the whole, is triviality. 'The worst of school life, from the point of view of a writer,' wrote P. G. Wodehouse 'is that nothing happens.'[26] Ian Hay remarked on 'the humdrum daily life [of school] – and,' he went on, 'no one who has not lived through it for weeks at a time knows how humdrum it can be . . .'[27] A Wodehouse or a Kipling could make much out of little, but many school-story writers, among them the best known and therefore the most influential (Hughes and Vachell are obvious examples) refused to accept the uneventful image and dramatised it so much that the 'adventurous' picture (bullying, drinking, literal cliff-hanging) has been a familiar one since public schools were used as a setting for fiction. It takes a very good writer to deal with non-events, or what seem to the outsider very small events, and most school-story writers either cheated, by making life more eventful than it was or could be, or else inflated the trivial, thus giving whole thing an air of triviality.

But nothing is trivial from the strictly moral point of view, and to Farrar his boys' actions were not schoolboy trifles but events of (literally) everlasting importance, the shapers of their eternity. The scratches on the schoolboy soul were, to him, like those on a vegetable marrow which, as it grows, grow enormous with it; and if everything a child does leads irrevocably to salvation or damnation, as Farrar believed it did, then what he showed his readers was not everyday life in the ordinary sense but events of extreme danger and drama, a tightrope existence balanced precariously above catastrophe, in which a single unwary step might be fatal. The Four Last Things (death,

* by John Rowe Townsend. The publisher was Hamish Hamilton.

judgement, hell and heaven) loom over every page and so, to a man as intense as Farrar, everyday events, even at school, have an intense importance. And with a personality as strong as his, this intensity could become almost hypnotic, especially to those (the majority of his readers, presumably) with beliefs like his.

As a teller of improving tales Farrar scores over Hughes mainly because of this ardent, concentrated belief in the importance of what he is saying. Both wrote with an identical object, a purpose they both acknowledged. 'The story of "Eric" was written with but one single object – the vivid inculcation of inward purity and moral purpose,' Farrar wrote in the preface to the twenty-fourth edition, in 1889. '. . . I trust that the book may continue to live so long – and only so long – as it may prove to be a source of moral benefit to those who read it.' Hughes kept being distracted from his directly didactic aim by adventure and high-spirited boyishness and a diffused interest in life in general, which made him wander off the point in a journalistic way. But Farrar stuck closely to his purpose, produced tracts, and in time joined the more-or-less unread.

So genial is Hughes's reputation and, at least at popular level, through Hughes's school story, Arnold's that it is easy to forget how close in atmosphere and even in opinion Farrar was to both Hughes and Arnold. Temperamentally he was closer to Arnold (Hugh Kingsmill described *Eric* as 'the sort of book Arnold might have written had he taken to drink').[28] Arnold never wrote a novel but, to judge from his sermons and miscellaneous writings, he matched Farrar in ardour and earnestness. All three believed in the importance of a boy's moral attitudes at an early age, and treated him as mature enough to make choices which would affect the rest of his life. Hughes took a rosier view of his boys' future than the other two did. Arnold, grimmer than Hughes and intellectually more distinguished than Farrar, believed in the unregenerate nature of boys but in the improving possibilities of maturity. The earnestness which in him seemed noble, however, in Farrar seemed priggish.

It is Farrar's manner, rather than his matter (which, if one accepts his original religious premisses, is not the least bit silly), which chiefly makes *Eric* seem absurd. The purple passages are more quotably ridiculous than others, even in school stories: the rebuke to Eric for 'swearing' when he calls a master a 'surly devil' (though fashions in language change fast: Orwell at prep school evidently thought 'dashed' a rather daring word); the famous apostrophe to him when dirty talk is going on in the dormitory; Russell's saintly deathbed. But this is because Farrar, as always, *goes too far.* It is what he is famous for, ridiculed for, in a sense admired for.

Unlike Tom Brown, who manages to lark about and, for pages at a time, to forget eternal values, Eric is never allowed out of sight of them. And they are strict, a narrowly interpreted set of rules outside which there is no hope of moral safety or final salvation. Farrar links every thought, word and deed directly to a psychic thermometer which tells us exactly what stage of virtue or depravity his hero has reached. A burning concern, not just for Eric but for the readers Eric is teaching how or how not to live, makes the story both dreadful and exciting. With Hughes one skips the preaching. With Farrar – so hypnotic is he – one scarcely dares to. The urge to laugh fights with the urge to listen. The spell is never quite broken.

The same spell-binding manner was used, to simpler, more immediate effect, in Farrar's *Life of Christ*, famous in its day and still highly readable. His description of the Crucifixion is an extraordinary evocation of an event passionately participated in, evoked in highly-coloured yet moving detail and with what is, for Victorian taste, an almost ferocious realism. For all his absurdities, Farrar is in a different class from Hughes as a writer. Yet Hughes, across the years, is lovable and remembered and Farrar is not. This may be partly because Hughes was lucky in his biographers, whereas Farrar was early embalmed in pious dreariness by his son Reginald's biography.

That popularity may go with excess, that there is something fascinating in itself about psychological and artistic exaggeration, is shown in Farrar's case by the relative popularity of his two school stories, *Eric* and *St Winifred's, or The World of School*. *Eric* was born from Farrar's own experiences as a schoolboy, *St Winifred's* from his experiences as a schoolmaster, and, when used artistically, early memories are nearly always more powerful than adult experience. Both books are shrill and overwrought but *Eric* goes further than *St Winifred's* and is therefore, in a curious way, the more dramatic. Farrar's son commented:

> *Eric* was written from reminiscences of a school in the Isle of Man [King William's] and of an epoch where alike the virtues and the vices of boys were more primitive and less sophisticated than is the case in our large public schools. *St Winifred's*, which came six years later, and was influenced by both Marlborough and Harrow experiences, though it has had less effect, perhaps, is truer to the real life of boys and has been far less open to criticism.

Less open to criticism but in both senses less amusing; less memorable, quotable, absurd and gripping. *Eric*'s intensity is missing, as well as its quaintness: the dramatic conflict, the emotional tension.

The boys in both books, most boys have since agreed, are remarkable prigs. But it was Farrar's limitations as a writer that made them seem so. Extraordinary boys – saintly, scholarly, promising an amazing future, precociously serious – were produced in Victorian times, when the circumstances of childhood, particularly in clerical and/or scholastic families (often the same thing), seem to have favoured the mixture of temperamental docility and intellectual liveliness which sometimes turns up prodigies. Martin Benson, who died at Winchester at the age of seventeen and was buried there, one of the gifted sons of E. W. Benson, first headmaster of Wellington and later Archbishop of Canterbury, seems to have been one of those who combined piety with brilliance, lovableness with gravity, from a very early age. One does not laugh, or find him odiously priggish in his letters, any more than one laughs at the precocious talents of John Evelyn's son two centuries earlier, who died at the age of four able to read in several languages including Hebrew and Greek; or, near our own time, of the seven-year-old Ronald Knox punning in Greek and English.

It is not that Farrar's boys are too good or too gifted to believe in but that they are not credible as people, good or bad. Sometimes, as is often the case in Victorian fiction, they are like miniature adults, with their elders' sedateness and verbosity, or else a wickedness too dreadful and contemptible for their age. And sometimes, by contrast, Farrar treats them as if they were quite small children. ' "Hurrah! hurrah! hurrah!" cried a young boy, as he capered vigorously about and clapped his hands . . . "Hurrah! hurrah!" and he again began his capering – jumping over the chairs, trying to vault the tables, singing and dancing with an exuberance of delight . . . Fanny [his cousin] still heard his clear, ringing, silvery laughter as he continued his games in the summer air.' This gambolling child turns out to be Eric, aged twelve; yet Fanny, brooding over the possible ill effects of school, thinks: 'Those baby lips, that pure young heart . . .'

His theme, in *Eric* wholly and in *St Winifred's* partly, being the corruption of innocence, Farrar exaggerates the initial innocence and seems to find nothing ludicrous in expressions like these. Uneasiness with adolescence was common among the Victorians, and although Farrar's two school stories deal almost entirely with teenagers, he seems to see them either as young children or else as adults, skipping puberty and its aftermath almost entirely. Eric is a headstrong, proud, gifted boy ('full of life and spirits, brave, bright, impetuous, tingling with hope, in the very flush of boyhood'), with everything seemingly in his favour, who is gradually sucked into the viciousness of school life, runs away, suffers hardships and finally dies of them. It is often said (by people who cannot have read the book carefully) that at school he is exposed to every sort of vice, including drunkenness, evil talk, and homosexuality. In fact, of these, only drunkenness gets explicit treatment. Other sins are wrapped in so much verbiage that it is almost impossible to tell just what Farrar means to say. Beer-, wine- and (in those days, the cheapest) brandy-drinking are described in some detail, small boys creeping out at night to fetch drinks at the inn for their elders, and bigger boys staggering back to shock their sober companions at school prayers. Pipes and cigars are smoked, and pigeons stolen from a master's garden, then cooked for a birthday party.

Of homosexuality, there is no overt mention. A chapter called 'Dormitory life' is concerned entirely with pillow-fights, leap-frog and amateur theatricals, although by the headmaster's reaction when he walks into the dormitory you would think he had stumbled on an orgy. The boys are effusively affectionate in the early Victorian manner, but Farrar neither finds nor suggests that there is anything sinister in this. They link arms, hold hands, fling an arm round a friend's shoulder; the cover of my copy of *St Winifred's* shows two boys thus intertwined, one holding a cricket bat, the other a book, and indicating, in the simplest way, the division between brain and brawn which was later to become so important. Generally they use Christian names unless on distant, or at least cool, terms. Eric realises that he is under a cloud, for instance, when addressed as 'Williams' by a friend.

The use of first names was another obvious difference between the early and the later school stories. Half a century later, and beyond, they were a give-away, something from the world of home and parents, and therefore a secret, since they laid a boy open to ridicule. 'Had I been addressed by my Christian name at my private or even my public school, I should have blushed scarlet,' Harold Nicolson wrote, 'feeling that my privacy had been outraged and some secret manliness purloined from me.'[29] In one of Barrie's plays* a boy at Osborne lives in terror of anyone there discovering that his first name is Cosmo. Until not long ago schoolboys would ask to be addressed on envelopes by surname and initials; on no account must the first name be used. This, like many of the ultra-tough attitudes, was a middle- rather than an upper-class phenomenon, and it belonged to the later rather than the mid-nineteenth century. Perhaps some of the dislike and disapproval Farrar's boys aroused was not so much because they were prigs as because they showed their feelings, and were not ashamed to be seen with their families, weep in public, or confess to the usual domestic affections.

The chapter in which Eric listens to evil talk in the dormitory is long but nowhere explicit. It is called 'Ye shall be as gods', which suggests that the talk is not merely 'dirty' but informative. Farrar's idea of suitable talk among the young may have been very different

* *Alice-sit-by-the-fire*.

from ours, of course. Ball, the speaker, is 'cursed with a degraded and corrupting mind' and has 'tasted more largely of the tree of the knowledge of evil than any other boy' (significantly, Farrar misquotes here: the tree is 'of the knowledge of *good and* evil'). But what subjects he actually speaks about, we are never told. Farrar says:

> The first time that Eric heard indecent words in dormitory No. 7 he was shocked beyond bound or measure. Dark though it was, he found himself blushing to the roots of his hair, and then growing pale again, while a hot dew was left upon his forehead . . . For half an hour, in an agony of struggle with himself, Eric lay silent . . . the moment had passed forever; Eric had listened without objection to foul words, and irreparable harm was done.

'I hurry over a part of my subject inconceivably painful,' Farrar writes, then lingers over it for several pages, saying little to help us discover what is happening. His famous call to Eric has long been a favourite with his mockers:

> Now, Eric, now or never! Life and death, ruin and salvation, corruption and purity, are perhaps in the balance together, and the scale of your destiny may hang on a single word of yours. Speak out, boy! Tell these fellows that unseemly words wound your conscience; tell them that they are ruinous, sinful, damnable; speak out and save yourself and the rest. Virtue is strong and beautiful, Eric, and vice is downcast in her awful presence. Lose your purity of heart, Eric, and you have lost a jewel which the whole world, if it were 'one entire and perfect chrysolite', cannot replace.
>
> Good spirits guard that young boy, and give him grace in this his hour of trial! Open his eyes that he may see the fiery horses and the fiery chariots of the angels who would defend him, and the dark array of spiritual foes who throng around his head. Point a pitying finger to the yawning abyss of shame, ruin and despair that even now perhaps is being cleft under his feet. Show him the garlands of the present and the past, withering at the touch of the Erinnys (*sic*) in the future. In pity, in pity, show him the canker which he is introducing into the sap of the tree of life, which shall cause its root to be hereafter as bitterness, and its blossom to go up as dust.

These two paragraphs, with their biblical echoes (so much more forceful then than now), in which Farrar seems to snatch the reader, as well as Eric, by the wrist and harangue him, give the book's fervent, tremulous atmosphere as well as any. But Eric fails to respond to all this retrospective advice. 'His curiosity was awakened; he no longer feigned indifference, and the poison of evil flowed deep into his veins.' Yet what this poison is we are never told. Sexual information? Smutty stories? Profanity? All these are hinted at. 'Oh, young boys, if your eyes ever read these pages, pause and beware,' Farrar says at this point. 'The knowledge of evil is ruin, and the continuance of it is moral death.'

This is oddly contrary to what he says elsewhere. Mr Rose, a master who seems to be Farrar's mouthpiece, says that

> the innocence of ignorance is a poor thing; it *cannot*, under any circumstances, be permanent, nor is it at all valuable as a foundation of character. The true preparation for life, the true basis of a manly character, is not to have been ignorant of evil, but to have known it and avoided it.

This much saner view explains why Farrar and others like him thought public school, despite its horrors, a suitable training-place for the young. Its dual influence, its seesaw pattern of good and evil, is stressed again and again. 'What *noble* histories . . . of honour and success, of baffled temptations and hard-won triumphs; what *awful* histories of hopes blighted and habits learned, of wasted talents and ruined lives!' Farrar cries, the choice being always between extremes of sanctity and wickedness. There seem to be few middling boys or middling fates, although, as Mr Rose says, 'it is quite possible to be *in* the little world of school life, and yet not *of* it.' Yet Eric and his brother Vernon, promising candidates for success and goodness, end up almost totally depraved (by Farrar's standards) and, incidentally, dead.

In *St Winifred's* the same sort of problems arise, though Farrar by then sounds a good deal less hysterical. There is talk of 'vice' and 'evil', of 'wickedness' and 'the unclean' and 'all that is vile and base'. Kenrick, the secondary hero, is like Eric in that he falls from grace and high promise, gets in with bad companions and alters completely. But instead of dying to atone for it, he is saved on the brink of disaster. This, while more credible than Eric's fate, is obviously less dramatic. Then interest – therefore anguish and drama – is shared between two boys, and thus fatally weakened in both; and when one saves the other from drowning, the climax is lost. The taste for death had an artistic justification and many Victorian stories, even for children, had numerous deaths in them. *Froggie's Little Brother* (1875) by 'Brenda' or Mrs G. Castle Smith is the best known of many. Farrar's boys in particular, being too good or at least too earnestly envisaged for this world, were artistically propelled towards the next. So *Eric,* which took them there, is the more effective book, if realistically the more absurd.

In *St Winifred's,* as in *Eric,* it is hard to tell just what Farrar's hints of evil mean. He makes much of the practice of 'taking up' at public schools, for instance; the older boy making friends with an attractive younger one, giving him the run of his study, protecting and pampering him, going for solitary walks with him and in general behaving in a romantically emotional way, with quarrels and reconciliations, heights and depths of feeling. Clearly he thinks these friendships are bad for the boys, spoiling the younger, flattering the elder, causing emotional storms and preventing both from making friends in their own age groups. But it is never clear whether he disapproves on sexual grounds or simply on grounds of common sense and convention.

In many cases, Farrar's books had the effect he hoped for. 'I really can say that I have never gained so much from all that I have ever heard or read, or that has happened to me, as I have from that book,' a reader, one of many fans, wrote of *Eric*. 'In the hour of weakness I have found them [Farrar's books] a source of strength,' wrote another. 'I wish that the Captain of every school in England could read what you say,' wrote a third. In a way Farrar's reticence, or vagueness, was a part of his appeal, because readers could read into his book as much or as little as they liked. The confusion of young readers when they met so much darkly inflammatory stuff can be imagined, though, uninstructed as they were in sexual and even physiological matters.

Farrar and Hughes, moralists both but on different levels of commitment, had their effect on didactic children's writing, Farrar more than Hughes. But neither had close followers. Farrar in fact was an early exponent of a method, and of attitudes, that spread up and down between children's fiction and books for adults and was perhaps found most obviously in the steamy readability, the sententious moralising, of Mrs Henry Wood, an enormously popular writer in her day, whose characters often came to similarly sticky ends after similarly explicit warnings. After Hughes and Farrar the school story seemed to *reculer pour mieux sauter*. The jump into real popularity and widespread approval came twenty-five years later, with Talbot Baines Reed.

CHAPTER IV

The central school story: Talbot Baines Reed and his followers

. . . cheerful puritanism . . .

The man who spread and popularised the genre was Talbot Baines Reed, one of those Victorians whose energy and drive make the rest of us, a century later, feel a little limp. Yet, like Hughes, he was popular both alive and posthumously, with an attractive presence which came across in his writing and the sort of dynamic personality that makes and keeps friends. His intellectual gifts were greater than Hughes's, though, and he has a lasting reputation based on more than his school stories, as a leading figure in the world of typography, whose biography was written by no less a figure in that world than Stanley Morison. Reed's life's work, his *History of the Old English Letter Foundries,* was, according to Morison, 'the first attempt to present a documented, consecutive account of the art of typefounding in England and Scotland . . . a masterpiece of its kind.' 'The pioneer value of Reed's work is as conspicuous today', he wrote in 1960, 'as it was then for its originality, range of reading and depth of research . . . An astonishing achievement.'[1] And A. F. Johnson, editing a reprint of it brought out for the centenary of Reed's birth in 1952, called it 'a classic of typographical history'. Admirers of Reed as the author of agreeable but lightweight school stories may be disconcerted to find his life dealt with from quite another angle, his reputation assessed at a very different level of seriousness.

Reed embodied many Victorian qualities – industry, high principles, courage – but all of them laced with good humour. A modern admirer, Brian Alderson, has called him 'a man who knew how to be both serious and humorous, and who was strong, but at the same time innocent and affectionate.'[2] Some of this mixture of strength and gentleness comes across in an address he gave to a new boys' club in Manchester. 'The strong fellows should look after the weak,' he told his audience, 'the active must look after the lazy, the merry must cheer up the dull, the sharp must lend a helping hand to the duffer. Pull together in all your learning, playing and praying.' He might be strong, active, merry and sharp himself, but unlike many of his contemporaries he had time for those who were not.

Yet he was described as having a 'cheerful puritanism' about him, and his standards of industriousness, that primary Victorian quality, were high. The man he called the 'loafer', who worked from nine till seven and 'absolutely [let] the rest of the day go by', earned his contempt. He took it for granted that an office lunch hour would be spent on something intellectually more rewarding than food, and that when a man got home he would take out microscope or books and pursue some regular, strenuous course of study. Yet he married young, led a full social life, was a good sportsman and amazingly energetic in everyday life (twice he walked from London to Cambridge for fun). Then there was what he cheerfully called his 'drudgery' in the family firm, a type foundry near the Barbican, which he entered at seventeen; an enormous amount of reviewing and miscellaneous journalism, and the school stories and other fiction; all this as well as his main work – the research into printing and typography. The 1870s and '80s were years of growing interest in all aspects of printing, and pioneering studies appeared, first among them William Blades's *Caxton*. Encouraged by Blades, Reed went ahead with his research into a subject about which almost nothing was known, and in 1887 produced his *magnum opus*. Later he became secretary of the newly-formed Bibliographical Society, and, characteristically, he used his knowledge of printing as a background for some of his fiction. He was only forty-one when he died.

It was with the founding of the *Boy's Own Paper* in 1879 that his fiction really took off. From the start he was closely associated with the magazine. His elder brother was on the committee of the Religious Tract Society which launched it, and he himself appeared on the first page of the first issue, with a lively piece called 'My First Football Match', signed 'An Old Boy'. Later he wrote on cricket, rowing, and other sports and, more importantly, produced the serial stories which were later collected into books; first *The Adventures of a Three-Guinea Watch,* and after it the most famous of them all, *The Fifth Form at St Dominic's*. Some of the stories are about a school called

Parkhurst, which at once became popular; but St Dominic's overtook it in fame and success.

The Religious Tract Society believed that crime among the young was encouraged by the 'pernicious' reading which was all many boys could find, and that it was part of its task to promote healthy reading which would entertain and therefore sell. 'Its editors understand boyhood well, enter heartily into its pursuits and pleasures,' the Prospectus for the *Boy's Own Paper* said. 'True religion, in their view, is a spirit pervading all life, in work, in play; and in this conviction, rather than any purpose of direct doctrinal teaching, this tone was given to the paper.' Reed disliked directly didactic stories, thought Farrar knew nothing about boys and considered *Eric* 'a religious tract thinly disguised as a school story'. Stanley Morison wrote that *Eric*:

> sickened . . . especially those sturdy, commercial, manufacturing men who came forward after the Crimean War to lead the new age of administrative efficiency which the military muddles had inspired . . . They wanted their offspring to have something 'manly' to read . . . The middle classes, especially the manufacturers and their counterparts in the City, had money, brains and pride. Self-respect would not allow them to send their sons to the elementary schools, state or voluntary, established for the shopkeeping and lower orders. New schools, therefore, were founded for boys from the homes of well-to-do men of business.[3]

It was perhaps boys like these who were considered the *Boy's Own Paper's* 'central' readers, but the magazine spread far beyond them. Within four years it had a circulation of 250,000. It filled an obvious social gap, and writers like Reed were needed to provide serials for it, week after week.

Reed wrote a great many stories for boys, some of them 'sketches' (of particular occasions, or particular types of boy), a couple of them historical novels, and most of them school stories. *The Willoughby Captains, The Master of the Shell, The Cock House at Fellsgarth*: these are all rousing, readable books, but the favourite and most famous, right from the start, was *The Fifth Form at St Dominic's*. As it first appeared in serial form, the thirty-eight chapters were all much the same length, and ingenuity was needed to keep the plot going; because, as with all serials, each incident had to be self-contained and satisfying as a piece on its own. And it was a serial, not a series, with a continuous plot running through it; not, like *Stalky & Co.*, a series of incidents connected only by their characters and situation.

It was immediately popular and has remained so for a hundred years. Why has it lasted so long without dating in the wrong way?

Probably because, as Brian Alderson put it, 'it is much less a book about "school" than a book about "people", and what Talbot Baines Reed has to say about people is still worth reading today.' One of the reasons for its wide popularity, perhaps, is the fact that it appeals to a wide range of ages. Readers tend to identify with characters their own age, and Reed has two heroes, separated in age by a little over five years. Stephen Greenfield is only ten when he arrives, very green and nervous, at St Dominic's; Oliver, his brother, is sixteen, an important person in the Fifth Form. So while two thirds or so of the action deals with the sharp adolescents of the Fifth – Wraysford, Oliver's best friend and rival, who is to become a don; Pembury, a waspish, brilliant cripple who edits 'The Dominican' and is later to edit a national newspaper; and Oliver himself, with a bright future at the bar – the rest is concerned with the rowdy small fry in the Fourth Junior, fags divided into two fiercely inimical packs, the Tadpoles and the Guinea-pigs. Among these, Stephen soon becomes prominent, and the rivalries between the shrill, aggressive bands of little fellows (noisy Bramble and his chum Padger on the one hand, Stephen and his friend Paul on the other) take one into a more rumbustious area of school life.

Public- and prep-school ages were less sharply divided then than they later became and the troubles of quite small boys could thus be brought realistically into public-school life. Not that Stephen's troubles are very serious. He is teased for his greenness when he arrives, and given a joke exam paper which of course he cannot answer, but tries desperately hard to deal with. But there is little noticeable bullying or unedifying behaviour. In any case, Oliver is always at hand to save Stephen from trouble and temptation.

Temptation – indeed, all the story's viciousness – is found at the Cockchafer Inn, where card-playing, drinking, gambling, and above all an evil landlord called Cripps, lure the innocent and the not-so-innocent into parting with pocket-money and signing promissory notes. Loman of the Sixth (a suitably-named boy, as so often in school stories) is in trouble at the Cockchafer, where he owes £35 to Cripps, a vast sum for a schoolboy in those days. Meantime, back at school, while the Guinea-pigs and Tadpoles keep up their unending rivalry at the bottom, the Fifth are locked at the top in permanent conflict with the Sixth, a conflict that reaches its height when both forms enter for the Nightingale Scholarship, worth £50 in prize money and much glory. Excitement mounts as the Nightingale day looms up, and when the results are announced Oliver has won, closely followed by Wraysford. But an exam paper has been stolen, suspicion falls on Oliver, and he is too proud to declare his innocence. The entire Fifth, including the reluctant Wraysford, sends him to Coventry, the only boy convinced of his innocence being his younger brother. At the prize-giving, when the results are given, Wraysford gets wild applause and Oliver is hissed.

Loman, relying on the Nightingale money to pay his debt to Cripps, is now up to his neck in trouble, and finally runs away, pursued and rescued by Oliver. After hanging between life and death for four weeks he is shipped off to that convenient Victorian dustbin, Australia, where, we later learn, he becomes a reformed character. The final chapter takes us five years ahead, with Stephen at the top of the school, Oliver and Wraysford down for a visit, Loman expected from Australia, and an atmosphere of great friendliness all round. One of the chapters is set outside the school: the Greenfields and Wraysford take a canoeing holiday on the Thames and at one point are swept over a weir. Wraysford saves Stephen's life (as in real life Reed saved a cousin from drowning). Saving lives became part of the familiar school-story plot, with every minor school story having its bolting horse or breaking ice, cliff-top fall or incoming tide. Farrar, too, had had his dramatic rescues. A boy saves another's life, cementing a friendship or, if they are enemies, completely changing the relationship. Both sorts of life-saving take place in *The Fifth Form at St Dominic's*.

Reed makes much of the importance, social and moral, of school friendships. So intertwined are the boys' lives, so interdependent their attitudes and even feelings, so much do they learn from one another, that the closest sharers of these lives and attitudes and feelings matter immensely (their quality, their influence). This belief he manages to put across less sentimentally than Hughes or Farrar. The lonely, dishonourable, but pathetic rather than wicked Loman talks wistfully of the sadness of school without friends – particularly without one special friend – and when he confesses to Oliver how deeply he has wronged him (because it was Loman who stole the exam paper, of course, and let Oliver be blamed) one feels Reed's sympathy for the lost and friendless rather than his condemnation of the wrongdoer. He says:

> I *must* tell you the rest, Greenfield, please. You're the only fellow I can tell it to. Somehow I think if I'd had a friend like you all last year I shouldn't have gone wrong as I have. How I used to envy you and Wraysford, always together, and telling one another your troubles!

To outsiders, the close friendships of public-school life were perhaps the most wistfully regarded thing about it: not so much the general jollity of communal life (though that too was stressed, particularly by Reed) as the jollity-plus-sentiment of friendships like Oliver and Wraysford's, or Tom Brown and Arthur's. 'Pairing' was an acknowledged part of school life, encouraged by all sorts of school arrangements – the sharing of studies, the need to have a regular companion for walks – and having a 'best friend' was socially, emotionally, even practically necessary. Not having someone to share things with was socially disastrous, the officially unloved being herded together in humiliating proximity, a comradeship of outcasts. So the school stories, particularly the more serious, often make much of this – the worldly temptation of being befriended by someone grander, more popular, socially smarter than oneself, the pangs and embarrassments of rejection, the wish to swap partners, the loneliness of having no-one. Its patterns were so much like those of courtship and marriage that, in their innocence, they make one smile: there is nest-building and domesticity, fidelity and betrayal, attraction and rejection and jilting; there are emotional storms, divorces, new partners and new domestic arrangements; there are even servant problems, with the fags.

2 . . . *a perfection of unreality from which there was no escape*

Frank Eyre

To many, *The Fifth Form at St Dominic's* seems the ideal school story, literary enough to please adults, lively enough to please boys; cheerful, unobsessed, highly readable and enormous fun. It was, indeed, the kind of book many later school-story writers would have liked to write and consciously or unconsciously imitated or actually copied. It is easy to belittle it, because we seem to have been there before. And so we have – but in inferior versions. Reed was a better writer than his followers and has been diminished by their imitations.

The vivacity, the overflowing high spirits, the sense of crowded exuberance, of staircases crammed and pillow-fight nights and the rest of it – all this has been used again and again by writers less good than Reed and less enjoyable. When Frank Eyre wrote that Reed 'brought the school story to a perfection of unreality from which there was no escape'[4] or Thomas Seccombe in his preface to *The Loom of Youth* spoke of 'the calculated falsity of Talbot Baines Reed', they were probably considering his effect rather more than his achievement. His effect was to set up the genre of school story within particular conventions, to give it a rigid framework inside which writers could repeat themselves almost indefinitely; it was also to split the school story fairly sharply into the 'serious' and the 'popular'.

On the one hand were the respectably considered minor school stories, which ran into hundreds, perhaps thousands; and later, the disapproved-of stories of the Bunter type, which I shall call the 'pop' school stories (both types descended directly, although, as time went on, more and more remotely, from Reed). On the other hand were the 'serious' stories in which the conventions played a minor part (although still occasionally observed), the school was often recognisable, the audience was envisaged as an adult as well as a young one and on the whole as belonging to the public-school class, and the intention was to make a more literary work than was generally found in the genre.

Every genre, every type of fiction, even, has a central work that lasts and copies of it that are forgotten. It may not be a great work and the copies may not be any worse than their prototype but it has a strong presence, it is the first to catch a particular atmosphere or mood or outlook, and above all it is imitable. To take examples among children's books: *Little Lord Fauntleroy* is one; *Little Women* another; *Anne of Green Gables* another. None of these is a great work, or so original that it stands alone forever. But each was the first or the most noticeable of its kind, the stereotype or cliché (in the literal sense of both words) from which many others, weaker, more extreme and less talented, were taken. At the opposite end of the pole, the true originals set up no new genres and have no direct imitators: *A High Wind in Jamaica* set no fashion for ten-year-old murderesses or *Lord of the Flies* for marooned schoolboys, and Kipling might have killed the school story stone dead as a genre if *Stalky & Co.* had been the first of its kind.

But Reed, whose high-spirited accounts of public-school life spread the word, among those who had never been there as well as many who had, that boarding in such places was the jolliest thing imaginable, was just the man to set up an imitable original. (He himself had never experienced boarding, incidentally, having been a day-boy at the City of London school.) He liked generalising from the particular, which made him easy to imitate, and although his main characters were spirited and individual, his minor ones were types. And that was the start of the typecasting which took place in the typical (not the literary) school story from then onwards. Reed altered the shapeless, long-winded, garrulous and moralistic school story and gave it a usable form, the first of its iron conventions.

The plot of *The Fifth Form at St Dominic's* shows how many of the incidents and patterns became standard in school stories. The stolen exam paper, the innocent wrongly accused, his suffering, proud loneliness and final triumph, the boating accident, the runaway lost in a storm, rescued by the boy he has wronged and brought back to the school half-dead; even small incidents like Mrs Greenfield calling out advice about flannel vests through the train window as Stephen goes off to school (to his scarlet embarrassment in front of the other passengers) and the larger patterns of rivalry between Fifth and Sixth forms, Tadpoles and Guinea-pigs – all these were used and re-used for the next half-century or more. Some of Reed's incidents echo *Eric* but Reed, who was acceptable to boys, never went as far as Farrar, who was (as time proved) unacceptable. The drinking and gambling in the Cockchafer are not unlike the general dissipation in *Eric*, Loman's escape from his unbearable troubles and guilt at school is not unlike Eric's flight, and the two brothers, one tender and vulnerable, the other old enough to look after him, are directly comparable.

But Reed's message was hopeful, his (implied, not direct) moralising therefore palatable: evil deeds are redeemed, no-one is utterly depraved (except the innkeeper Cripps, a being from another world and not particularly credible); the bully is not taken seriously, the headmaster is kindly and human, and the cavortings of the small fry are watched with humour. With plenty of sentiment but not too much sentimentality, Reed's school is a friendly place and what 'preaching' there is is pleasantly disguised. But the school story contained all kinds of ill-matched elements (the spontaneous with the artificial, for instance; the ebullience of young life with the conventionality of school customs), and in order to cope with it Reed gave it a form carefully tailored for its purpose. Writers who came after him used this form more strictly, less imaginatively, making it more unvarying and repetitive.

Of course conventions, in a conventional form, are part of its charm and purpose: without them, audience or reader may feel cheated. Things foreseeable and unalterable and used a hundred times over are part of the pleasure, in which surprise and novelty have no part. A sort of double amusement is aroused, a kitsch response. Only the young child or the childish adult will take it to heart. The older or more knowing may take it, though, with equal pleasure, in quite another way – as reassurance, as repetitive fun that drums nostalgically on the past, in every complex emotional way that pop art is taken in the modern world. The same sort of thing happens with science fiction, with westerns, with detective stories, even (recently) with the romantic novel.

Reed himself enjoyed the naming of types, which some might call, more grandly, the making of symbols (though between type and symbol there is a gap, narrow but crucial). In his book of collected sketches, *Parkhurst Boys*, there is a long section entitled 'Boys we have known'. There they are: the Sneak, the Bully, the Duffer, the

Dandy and many more. This was all very well for Reed, who was inventive enough to get away with typing his characters while giving them a vigorous presence, and who probably never meant to suggest that everyone else should do the same. But it had a very limiting effect on his followers. In *The Fifth Form at St Dominic's* there are already signs of it. There is Simon, 'the donkey of the Form', and Braddy, 'that big hulking youth . . . the bully, the terror of the Guinea-pigs and the laughing stock of his own classmates'. In the last chapter the pair of them return, adult but unaltered:

> There was Tom Braddy, for instance, smoking a big cigar the size of a pencil case, looking the picture of a snob. And with him, a vacant-looking but apparently self-satisfied young man with puffy cheeks. His name is Simon . . .

The child is father of the man, Reed is saying all too clearly. And so it came to be said in the later school stories. As the boys became, more and more, types rather than individuals, there was no chance of growth or development for them (as there is in a serious school story like *Boys and Masters*, in which growth and development are the book's main theme; or even in *Stalky & Co.*, where people in some ways expand and extend themselves between the early pages and the end). At Greyfriars, and even at other more seriously intentioned places in school stories, each boy embodied a particular characteristic, never varying, always using the same catch-phrases, always coming up to expectation. As the stories became more stylised, the identifying characteristic became more obvious and absurd – the toff with his lisp and monocle, the Chinese boy with his pigtail. Of course there are 'characters' in real life, eccentrics who quite naturally seem to embody particular attitudes or casts of mind. Hughes has his mad scientist in *Tom Brown's Schooldays*, Martin; but with his chronic lack of money, his odd ways of raising the wind and his need to work by firelight when he cannot afford even candle-stubs, he has a very recognisable life-style and presence. Later, such characters in school stories were reduced to single types. In western films the hero, the villain and their allies can be clearly distinguished by the colour of their shirts – dark for villainy and light for virtue. In the school story, with everyone wearing uniform, distinctions were as sharp but conveyed in other ways. They were distinctions of character, almost invariably conveyed through appearance, stance and presence.

3 *It's a way we have in the Public Schools,*
Which nobody can deny! Rudyard Kipling

Reed himself showed distinctions of character through appearance from the very beginning. 'Was ever such a radiant young hero turned loose into the world?' he asks in *The Adventures of a Three-Guinea Watch*, having described the most conventionally envisaged youngster imaginable just off to his public school. Tom Brown looks much the same: 'a boy to be proud of,' says Hughes, 'with his curly brown hair, keen grey eyes, straight active figure'. Lord Baden-Powell, hero of many schoolboys, seems to have fitted the part when he was a schoolboy: 'a boy of medium size with curly red hair, decidedly freckled, with a pair of twinkling eyes' was how a contemporary at Charterhouse described him. Twinkling eyes were a necessity, red hair, freckles and curls a bonus; medium size was suitable, too, because the hero was never outstanding, just rather more likably medium than the rest. Sometimes he would be described as if he were quite a child ('an impudent little face full of brightness and mirth, and everything about him suggested frolic and fun'[5] – Gillian Avery has called boys of this kind, much loved by the late Victorians, 'sinless pickles'), while the illustrations made him look very much a young man. This central schoolboy would 'grin' rather than smile; he was mischievous in his early days, lordly yet democratic later on and adored by the small fry; and a sportsman rather than an intellectual, of course. By the early years of this century he was hackneyed enough for Rupert Brooke to be irritated by his invariable 'wiriness'.[6]

The Bully was the opposite of all this, either fat, unkempt, greasy, scurfy and out of condition, a certain candidate for the bath of ink, glue and feathers that awaited the unpopular and unwashed, or else lynx-eyed and sinister, 'foreign', in some way an outsider. This latter sort of bully gave the always lurking xenophobia of the time an excuse to emerge. Hughes's bully, Flashman, the first of his kind, was nothing in particular as a personality, merely 'big and strong for his age' with 'a bluff, off-hand manner, which passed for heartiness, and considerable powers of being pleasant, when he liked'; although someone remembers him as being, a few years back, 'a dirty little snivelling, sneaking fellow'. George Macdonald Fraser has resurrected him in his Flashman novels and given him a posthumous reputation for looks and dash, but this was merely recreating a character that was never there.

Farrar's boys, handsome rather than healthy, fine-boned rather than wiry, were soon to be swept away. They began school life with a natural nobility and beauty. Of Eric and Vernon Farrar writes: 'The small shining flower-like faces, with their fair hair – the trustful loving arms folded round each brother's neck – the closed lids and parted lips – made an exquisite picture' (though they sound like two infants intertwined in the one cot they are in fact Eric aged twelve and his younger brother); of Evson in *St Winifred's*: 'It was impossible to see him and not be struck by his fine open face, and the look of fearless and noble innocence in his deep blue eyes.' The lower a boy was to sink, the higher his early promise must be, and all these lovely lads were obvious candidates for temptation, if not ruin.

As schoolboy heroes these were soon rejected, but a variation on the theme of noble, defenceless innocence was continued in the feminine boy, a foil for the manly, protective hero. Innocent and defenceless, though not necessarily noble, he was Fluff in *The Hill*, with 'the delicately tinted face, the small, regular, girlish features, the red quivering mouth'; or Arthur in *Tom Brown's Schooldays*, 'a slight, pale boy, with large blue eyes and light fair hair, who seemed ready to sink through the floor'; or the Dormouse in *Jeremy at Crale*, 'round and plump, fluffy-haired, wide-eyed and rosy-cheeked', with 'exactly that helpless immature look of a young bird fallen from its nest'. Hughes has the nastier version of such a boy:

> one of the miserable, little, pretty, white-handed, curly-headed boys, petted and pampered by some of the big fellows, who wrote their verses for them, taught them to drink and use bad language, and did all they could to spoil them for everything in this world and the next.

After someone protested that things were no longer like that at Rugby, Hughes said in a footnote: 'There were many noble friendships between big boys and little boys but I can't strike out the passage; many boys,' he went on meaningly, 'will know why it is left in.' The sexual role of such a boy and such relationships in a one-sex community is plain enough, but it is part of the larger subject of adolescent sexuality in conditions that were sexually askew.

Even in the best school stories other characters tend to be recognisable because they are seen from a particular angle which distorts them into familiar shapes. At the lowbrow end of the genre they are frank caricatures, often with the exuberance of comic postcards, which their illustrations closely resemble. Nearly all headmasters, as I have said, are distantly descended from Arnold; and assistant masters are equally familiar. The hearty, popular one is contrasted with the dry old stick, all droopy moustache and chalky gown; the huge, hairy games master with the nonconformist who lends the boys his books, and is thought a radical. Then there is the jabbering French master (pointed beard and two-tone shoes), the professional pedant, the sadistic whacker, the kindly dodderer, and so on down to the brisk matron, comic parlourmaid and cheeky 'boots'.

Then there is the place, instantly appealing and recognisable, with large trees and quadrangles, playing fields, huge chapel, unspoiled surrounding countryside. To many people space meant both luxury and romance, the country as opposed to the town, the English idea of the patrician. No matter that the original three 'Great Schools', and Harrow with them, were now in towns or suburbia; the picturesque idea of the public school, and therefore its fictional image, was in deep country, often with an old abbey as part of its buildings, bringing shades of an ancient monkish past and instant historical atmosphere.

The more memorable school stories, based on particular schools, often escape the undifferentiated air of the rest, topographically and architecturally. *Stalky & Co.* is set in bleak, ugly buildings which match its unconforming realism; *The Hill* is set so carefully and exclusively in Harrow that its position and its buildings, like its slang, apply nowhere else. But most school stories – the mainstream and the popular – are a compendium of familiar qualities and places and situations. The fictional public school is not only remote from the rest of the world but quite deliberately maintains an air of austerity that is the opposite of the suburban comfort most of its readers would either know or aspire to in real life. Dadoes, passages, brown or dark green paint, iron bedsteads, scratched desks, chill dormitories and cosy, shabby studies are as much a part of the image as the free, enormous exteriors, all elms and limes and copper beeches; indeed in some places in real life they still survive (the tin baths at Winchester, for instance), half-loved, half-hated, familiar and anachronistic props for the dramatic background of much of childhood and adolescence. Even the smaller props, tuck-boxes and toasting forks and games vests, never change.

Unalterable, too, are the ritual occasions in school stories, set pieces which test the writer's skill because they have been used so often before. The central ritual occasion is generally a match – cricket or football, house against house or school against another school in what is often seen as Homeric contest, grand and cosmic. The Eton and Harrow match in *The Hill*, the cricket match between Wrykyn and Sedleigh in *Mike*, the furiously played football game on the day Tom Brown arrives at school or the cricket match he captains on his last day there: it is on these that school drama depends. 'England owed her Empire far more to her sports than to her studies,' the *Public School Magazine* commented in 1898, and although it may be mentioned with approval that this or that scholarship has been won it means little compared with athletic glory. *Stalky & Co.* is one of the few books to mock sports-mania, and its heroes refuse to be brain-washed into thinking a house-match the most important thing in school life. Generations of the young *were* brain-washed, though, if not by school itself then by school stories and the images of heroism they set up.

Over and over again the almost mystical meaning attached to games – certainly to their moral worth and purpose – is made clear. Newbolt's 'Vitaï Lampada' – 'There's a breathless hush in the Close tonight' – is probably the best known example of this: school heroism in the sports field is transmuted into heroism on the battlefield, the 'voice of a schoolboy rallies the ranks' of seasoned soldiers, and 'play the game' becomes a motto for every occasion. And less explicit cases abound: the school sermon with its cricketing analogies, the supposed equivalence of athletic ability and moral worth, the implicit suggestion that 'manliness' (however interpreted) is found only in sport, and that with it go all kinds of other qualities, including physical beauty. The very fact that matches, though so often described that they are almost impossible to describe again with much liveliness, are set down in detail in most school stories, suggests that the reader is expected to be interested enough to take them, stroke by stroke.

Ritual scenes of danger, rescue and adventure cement or create friendships, as I have said; and in a sub-section of this category come ritual brushes with the law. This may be embodied in masters, again subdivided into young ones, green enough to rag, ancient custodians of the school folklore, full of waggish wisdom, housemasters respected or despised, sarcastic masters one learns, like the boys, to hate. Final arbiter of everything, benign dictator who may not know the outrages perpetrated in his name, is the headmaster. The boys (and readers) may know he has an ordinary life of some sort, a wife and children may even be mentioned, but it is impossible to imagine it or them because there is something profane about the thought of his domestic life, like the idea of a parent's sexuality. This is where monks and nuns score as schoolteachers: they have no known private life, no embarrassing domesticity.

Nearer home, the law takes the form of prefects, those centurions of the school empire, often more dreadful, or at least more immediately dreaded, than masters. In the public-schools' heyday they had more naked power, and could wield it more directly, than they were ever likely to have or to wield in later life; not quite the power of life and death but that of happiness and misery, of good and ill for many around them, and with it went the sort of personal prestige that comes to few but national heroes in later life. Hughes wrote in *Tom Brown's Schooldays*:

> In no place in the world has individual character more weight than at a public school. Remember this, I beseech you, all you boys who are getting into the upper forms. Now is the time in all your lives when you may have more influence for good or evil on the society you live in than you ever can have again.

'Prefectship is the coping-stone of a public-school education,'[7] wrote S. P. B. Mais, and those who did not achieve it missed the central experience, as day boys did.

Significantly, though, few school stories are written from the standpoint of a prefect. The hero may end in a position of authority, like Tom Brown, but this is seldom the level from which the action is seen and judged. Perhaps the oddness of such absolute power, the artificial prestige which seniority could give, made it embarrassing to write from that level. Perhaps it was uncomfortably close to the writer's own, the prefect's position being a shade too adult yet without the checks upon it that adult life makes upon everyone, however eminent. For within the sphere of school life the prefect was a dictator (less rational, therefore in a sense almost less approachable, than head- or housemaster), against whom there was no appeal; or if not a dictator on his own at least part of an oligarchy, none of whose members would diminish his power or prestige.

Nearly every boy arrived at his public school prepared by his prep school to be awed by authority, which in its most immediate form meant the prefects. A variation on the theme of the stammering, blushing, much-impressed new boy is sometimes the outsider – foreign or colonial – with none of the right responses. The hero of Charles Turley's *A Scout's Son* comes from a life of total freedom (mental as well as physical) in Canada and other unschooled places. 'Coming here is like going to prison,' he says, and is totally unimpressed by the head of house, a boy of almost imperial eminence in the opinion of the small fry. 'I haven't seen anyone funnier since my father and I bumped against a mad chief in Zululand,' the new boy remarks of him, a curiously subversive statement from a writer generally as conventional as Turley. Because humour – even a sense of proportion – is the only weapon that may succeed against the hierarchical system, and so, in the conventional school story, which supports the system, there is little room for it – except in special cases like those of Wodehouse or Kipling, whose rules are all their own.

Another embodiment of the law is the local landowner, on whose property it is easy to trespass, deliberately or by accident. As a rule he comes round to the trespassers. In *Stalky & Co.*, M'Turk and Colonel Dabney, on whose land he and his friends have trespassed, are social equals because M'Turk is 'viceroy of four thousand naked acres, only son of a three-hundred-year-old house, lord of a crazy fishing boat, and the idol of his father's shiftless tenantry'. In *A Scout's Son* the local landowner, Sir Vivian, turns out to be the schoolboy poacher's godfather and his parents' dearest friend, just when the poacher's social status, and whether his father is quite a gentleman, is being discussed at school. In Angela Brazil's *For the Sake of the School*, the same sort of thing: he turns out to be the heroine's long-lost grandfather, and since he is a peer and she a girl from the Australian outback, socially much despised, this at once puts things right.

Familiar in all public-school children's lives until a generation or two ago in the form of nannies and others is the adult who may officially be in a position of authority but is socially an inferior. Like the NCO in relation to the green young officer, he can bully, badger, taunt, punish and generally make life miserable for anyone under him, but while doing so will never fail to address him as Sir and will himself be addressed by the smallest child by his surname or perhaps his first name. Although not quite a servant, he is in a servile position in the sense that everyone, in a carefully layered society, is in a servile position in relation to those in the layer above him. When this social pattern is shifted, the reality of school life is lost. In Hylton Cleaver's *Return to St Benedict's*, for instance, the old school porter is almost the book's hero. He addresses the boys by their surnames and therefore the Old Boys by theirs; so that there is the situation (absurd in the context of the public schools) of a school servant addressing returning cabinet ministers and other suchlike grandees (since in school stories visiting Old Boys are always cabinet ministers and suchlike) as Smith and Jones. The school sergeant in *Stalky & Co.*, the gamekeeper in *Tom Brown's Schooldays* (whom Tom, for all his democratic background, rudely addresses as Velveteens), the policeman shoved into the pond in *Mike*, the shopkeeper in *The Hill* who lends money on a forged letter, Cripps at the Cockchafer who gets St Dominic's boys to run up bills, any number of tuck-shop keepers, matrons, porters and the like, all represent authority in the sense that they can make things awkward, can report misdeeds and so produce punishments, but also represent the outsider, the whole non-public-school world in which the public-school product is, *ipso facto*, in a position of *social* authority.

This is most noticeable in the case of the police, because here, more than in any other category, legal rights seem to have been subordinated to social custom in a way that would be unthinkable today. In the school story, in fact in popular fiction of all kinds until the Second World War, the policeman is a lowly comic, big-footed, slow-witted, ponderous and pedantic, a foil for any quick-thinking public-schoolboy who knows (given the social code) that he need show no particular respect; and he can be relied upon to keep to the social rules, to acknowledge the relationship between authority and those he would consider, in a non-legal situation, his social superiors. What schoolboy today, faced with an inquiring policeman in the middle of a fight, would have the nerve to say, as Wodehouse's Wyatt in *Mike* coolly does: 'This is quite a private matter. You run along on your beat?'

Within the school, there are other rituals, occasions on which behaviour is standardised, reaction foreseeable and unvarying. At the lowbrow end, evasions of punishment, ingenious or absurd: lines written with three pens lashed together, whackings received through three layers of blotting paper; at a less lowbrow level, sessions with housemaster or, occasionally, headmaster, often occasions for embarrassment if the master tries to be human; visits from bishops or politicians or soldiers, sometimes taken admiringly straight, like the explorer who comes to sing the Harrow songs (as Churchill used to, in real life) in *The Hill*, sometimes treated with contempt, like the 'Jelly-bellied Flag-flapper' in *Stalky & Co.* Then there are joyful scenes of triumph – winning the match, scoring the vital goal, fielding the vital catch, house supper, school songs, end of term; the grimly dramatic – expulsion senses, reconciliation scenes, deathbed scenes; and, in the more seriously intentioned, often scenes in which a master, treated warily by his colleagues and authority in general, introduces the hero to modern poetry and political ideas with coffee and cake.

Scenes of corporal punishment, though frequent, are generally skimmed over in some embarrassment. Today, beatings seem one of the oddest aspects of public-school life, one of the most plainly askew; and perhaps even at the time a straightforward writer of school stories, while failing to analyse what he felt, obscurely scented something embarrassing somewhere – a sexual significance, a powerful sense of outrage in physical assault. This was all the more so (all the odder and more perverted) when relations between authority (masters or prefects) and boys were in other ways, at least officially, formal, non-familial, non-physical, so that punishment was not a case of a quick slap or a clip over the ear (the corollary, sometimes, of physical warmth) but a stately, ritualised performance. Except in adult books gunning for the system rather late in the day – like David Benedictus's *The Fourth of June* – where the outrage of such performances is emphasised, they are played down so much that it is hard to know whether the weapon of chastisement is slipper or birch.

Much, much more could be written about chastisement, since

every school story has instances of it and betrays attitudes towards it, even if they are only negative attitudes of uneasiness and evasiveness. To most people now it is probably the most distinctive and 'distancing' of all the practices which make public schools in their heyday seem so far away in time and feeling. For it is not their social divisiveness, isolation and peculiar disciplines that set them so far from modern ideas, so much as the violence underlying their life, the use of force, not reason or persuasion, to achieve results, the physical hurt and humiliation involved (officially, as part of the code of practice) in upholding it. Even the most enlightened, 'modern' and much-praised of masters went in for a deal of violence we should now think incredible. Sanderson of Oundle, for instance, the subject of a biography by H. G. Wells, according to an admiring Old Boy,

> exercised his punitive functions at a white heat of passion, possibly because then and then only could he trust himself to operate effectively . . . a hail of swishing strokes that seemed almost to envelop one . . . The expiatory strokes were liable to fall on one's back or legs, one's hands or forearms.

Can one possibly imagine, today, a man whom Wells could call 'beyond question the greatest man I have ever known with any degree of intimacy . . . a very delightful mixture of subtlety and simplicity, generosity, adventurousness, imagination and steadfast purpose',[8] behaving in such a way? Or there is General Sir Ian Hamilton's memory of Benson at Wellington:

> He had a violent temper. He would turn perfectly white sometimes when flogging a boy . . . When I went to the bathing lake and stripped I became the cynosure and stupor of the crowd. The blues of the previous week had changed to green and yellow, whilst along the ribs under my arm – where the point of the cane curled – the stripes were dark purple.[9]

The future archbishop caned him every morning, for lateness.

In much public-school writing, chastisement seems to be regarded almost as a matter of pride, a toughener of bodies, not a hardener of hearts.

> Corporal punishment brings with it its own consolations of martyrdom – an almost comfortable glow of exaltation, pride in one's fortitude, a consciousness of being the object of general sympathy and interest, and a feeling that one has expiated one's crime, that bygones are bygones,

Sanderson's pupil, after this alarming account of his headmaster in action, goes on to explain. Indeed, a famous flogger in charge seems often to have aroused admiration, the psychological implications of which may seem obvious to our psychologically more sophisticated age. The headmaster of *Stalky & Co.* (to the real-life model of whom

Kipling dedicated the book) canes for no provable offence, from a sense of rough justice the boys enormously admire. 'Among the – lower orders this would lay me open to a charge of – assault.' he says, swishing wherever a dash comes in the sentence. 'You should be more grateful for your – privileges than you are.' When he canes the entire Upper School at the end of term ('I can connive at immorality, but I can't stand impudence'):

> the boys awaiting their turn cheered . . . and . . . flung themselves upon him to shake hands. Then they seriously devoted themselves to cheering till the brakes were hustled off the premises.

As Stalky puts it, full of delighted excitement:

> It's a way we have in the Public Schools,
> Which nobody can deny!

The subject of sex in the public schools, to which the same couplet might be applied, gets even less explicit treatment. As Richard Usborne puts it of Wodehouse's adult heroes (public schoolboys all, a few years on),

> There is no suggestion that [they] would recognise a double bed except as so much extra work to make an apple-pie of.

4 . . . *a new kind of English in which words like cads and rotters and expressions like bally bounders and beastly fellows played a large part*

H. E. Bates

So the framework of the central school story was set up, and the split between the 'serious' school story and the one within the framework became clear. As the central school story grew more popular and knowledge of its conventions became more widespread, it acted on schoolboys – and perhaps, a very little, even on schools – rather as television (much more powerfully) acts today on everyday life, making people think that this or that is done or not done, is frequent, acceptable, socially desirable. It gave a certain self-consciousness to boys in real life, making them feel – just a little – that they were playing roles, taking part in some dramatic, almost dramatised event; rather as the knowledge that there are television cameras about makes people overact in public events today. That the stories influenced boys, at least in their early years and in their expectations of school, and that their conventions were familiar to everyone, is clear from plenty of school stories.

'The Doctor? I suppose he'll be called the Doctor? Like they are in the stories,' young Martin, in Eric Parker's *Playing Fields*, says when he first goes to see his future prep school. 'The *Boy's Own Paper* was right,' he finds when he gets there. 'There was the big, bald forehead. There was the commanding nose. There was the black tail coat, the white tie, the grey trousers, the portly waistcoat.' And when he sets off for his first term, it is with the self-consciousness of a school-story hero: 'Here he was driving with his father to the station, as boys drove in school stories, with his new portmanteau and his tuckbox and his hamper.' Peter in *The Harrovians* knows just what to expect (though it hardly comes up to expectation) when he first goes to school, and the whole of *The Bending of a Twig* is about the absurd romanticism fostered by school stories, and the disillusions of real life.

Even when boys were not going – quite – to public schools, the stories shaped their expectations. When H. E. Bates won a scholarship to Kettering Grammar School, he knew just how things would be:

> I knew very well that the masters would wear black gowns and possibly mortar-boards too. The prefects would have studies in which they fried sausages and drank beer on the quiet in the middle of the night and those boys whose parents were a little better off would wear Eton collars and the little black jackets my grandfather used to call bum-freezers. I should have to learn Latin and French and a new kind of English in which words like cads and rotters and expressions like bally bounders and beastly fellows played a large part. Life was going to be on a higher plane altogether.[10]

At the lowbrow end of it all, in the Greyfriars stories and others like them, although most of their readers were never going to see the inside of a real public school, expectations like these were raised and the romantic idea of public-school life was spread.

After Reed came the flood of minor school stories by late Victorians and Edwardians and, finally, Georgians. To look up the work of a single-minded, prolific school-story writer is a sobering business, because, like today's romantic novelists, these writers turned their books out by the dozen, the score, even the hundred. And apart from all these, many who wrote books of other kinds for the young (Tom Bevan, for instance, who wrote adventure stories as a rule) had a school story or two to their credit. Men like Walter Rhoades, Hylton Cleaver, Alfred Judd, R. A. H. Goodyear, Gunby Hadath or Harold Avery turned out quite seriously intentioned and, in their day, quite well considered school stories; while below them flourished a more fantastical undergrowth of stories, generally disapproved of by authority; in this century, largely the work of a single man, Charles Hamilton (alias Frank Richards and many other names). The well-considered books were often given as prizes, at school or Sunday school, and old copies of them often have an attractive prize-winner's plate in the front.

Harold Avery's stories were typical of those in this category, and very much in the Reed tradition. They were lively, cheerful, warm-hearted, fairly unsnobbish, full of the familiar events of school fiction and with everything that happened apparently lifted from an earlier story or likely to be used in a later one. They perpetuate the main-stream ideas, above all the idea that, as Reed put it, 'a pair of well-trained athletic schoolboys with a plucky youngster to help them, are a match any day for twice the number of half-tipsy cads.'[11] All of them mention Bible-reading, gentlemanly behaviour, flannel vests, and the importance of loyalty to friends and not sneaking about anyone, even enemies. Most have a stolen exam paper, a false accusation, a fatal or near-fatal accident, a spectacular rescue, several matches and several 'rags'. Most are long-winded; many, at least, are long. On average, Avery's books are two or three inches thick or more. The next-to-last paragraph in one of them, *The Triple Alliance*, gives the flavour of post-Reed high spirits:

> Diggory and 'Rats' promptly fell into each other's arms, and all four coming into violent collision, tumbled down amidst the debris of the overturned coal-box; and after rolling over one another like a lot of young dogs, scrambled to their feet, turned out the gas, and rushed away to complete their packing.

The Dormitory Flag, The Chartered Company, A Boy All Over, Through Thick and Thin, one called simply *A School Story*, and many more by Avery: these were the approved books, better written and closer to life than the later 'pop' stories but not really very different in atmosphere. All the fun of juvenile life, they suggest, is to be found at school.

Although the 'serious' school stories often concentrate on the pair of friends, and on romantic friendships, the more middling concentrate on the gang. Perhaps there was some self-consciousness about 'exclusive' friendships, and the group made too-passionate attachments unlikely. Avery's 'triple alliance' is like Tom Bevan's 'mixed quartet' in *The Lower Fourth at Underhill*, or indeed (at a very different level) like Stalky and Co; and even when the gang has no special name the fact of being in the same house, form or study gives the boys a strong sense of cohesion and unity. Reed's *Parkhurst Boys* is echoed in G. Forsyth Grant's *Beresford Boys* and others with similar titles – *The Boys of Blair House*, *The Boys of Penrohn*. G. Forsyth Grant was unusual among writers of boys' school stories because she was a woman; she wrote steamy sentimental books in the Farrar tradition: *The Hero of Crampton School*, *Chums at Last*, some of them illustrated by 'her son (a schoolboy)', clearly a lad as untalented with his pencil as she was with her pen.

Occasionally things are varied by the use of attitudes we now find offensive. Popular fiction of all kinds has always contained them, of course. Class feeling appears constantly, in some more officiously than in others. Sometimes the story is on the side of democratic attitudes, as in *The Lame Dog* by Walter Rhoades, in which a cockney boy called Herbert Crump, whose father has made a fortune in America, is sent to a public school, Tollemache's, and there first bullied and finally accepted, mainly because the hero, Dick Trescott, befriends him, and the villain who has bullied him is caught stealing and expelled. The moral of this is clearly that kind hearts are more than coronets but the general attitude is, by present-day standards, highly patronising even towards acceptable kind hearts. The Reed/Avery school of cheerful manliness suggests that although outright cads (it is never clear how far this word applied to social, how far to moral, outsiders) cannot be tolerated inside a public school, all cheerful manly fellows are much of a muchness there and you are decent and friendly towards the outside world when you happen to strike it.

But sometimes a school story is obsessed with class, which makes for sad reading because it blots out all other interests and pleasures. In Robert Leighton's *The Cleverest Chap in the School* it is not just a part of the general fabric of things (as it is in, say, Angela Brazil) but something the young brood endlessly about, feel small on account of, toadying to others or at least feeling thoroughly prickly. Like *Tom Brown's Schooldays* and no doubt others, it was written for the author's son, to whom it is rather touchingly dedicated; and one wonders what the boy made of his father's repetitive use of the class theme. 'He's a ripping cricketer, even if he isn't a born gentleman,' someone says of the hero, Pinkney, on the second page. Pinkney is a sort of Admirable Crichton, at once brilliant and athletic. 'But who expects any of us to be born gentlemen, I'd like to know. We're not a public school, or even a preparatory; we're only a Grammar School, and there's a heap of difference.' Up turns an Etonian, hiding behind the unlikely name of Snooks, to play in the vital cricket match in place of Tony Mumford, who has been arrested on a trumped-up charge. 'I should hardly have expected an Etonian, who is necessarily a gentleman, to call himself a friend of a fellow who has just been arrested,' Pinkney says in his stately way. Snooks turns out to be Maurice Wrinklebury, son (or is he?) of Sir Charles Wrinklebury of Wrinklebury Hall. 'I believe it's the grief of his life,' one of Pinkney's schoolfellows says of him, 'that he's no more than the son [or is he?] of an insignificant shipping agent, and that he hasn't been sent to a public school.' The plot is preposterous but it becomes less preposterous to imagine a village wet-nurse swapping babies to give her own son the advantages of Wrinklebury Hall, when you see everyone so conscious of his social superiority or inferiority to everyone else; a somehow melancholy sight in a school story.

Racialism turns up too. Anti-semitism appears in some of the 'serious' stories, as it does in much fiction of the time, and, in the more light-hearted, what now seems racialistic is just the crude expression of widely-held popular ideas of the time. Walter Rhoades' *The Boy from Cuba* starts with:

> 'Just think of it! A nigger! A genuine nigger! Woolly head, flat nose – '
>
> 'Banjo and bones and the rest of it.' . . .
>
> 'Well, we'll hope he isn't a cannibal . . . or there'll be nothing left of you but shirt-buttons. I'll write your epitaph for you:
>
> Here lies Franky Holland, who never grew bigger,
> Because he was eaten, when young, by a nigger.'
>
> . . . 'What's the chap's name?'
>
> 'I don't know. Sambo, I suppose. If it isn't, it ought to be. Oh, it's a sickening business.'
>
> . . . 'Why doesn't he go to a native school, with the other blackamoors?'

And so it goes on. When the boy turns out to have an English father, a Spanish mother, and Mr Rackburn, a local grandee, as a grandfather, all is well. When a boy calls him 'nigger' the new boy thrashes him, but the word becomes his nickname, worn with pride. The racial or social outcast who makes himself accepted at school is a variant of the psychological misfit, and occasionally he is used in a school story. Later, in the pop stories, black, brown and yellow boys (and, in the girls' schools, girls) appeared regularly at English schools. The best known of them was Hurree Jamset Ram Singh of Greyfriars, whose speech seems taken straight from F. Anstey's Baboo Bannerjee B.A. These exotic foreigners were generally highborn – African princesses, maharajah's sons, the offspring of robber barons in the Far East or Central America; money and pedigree apparently removing much youthful prejudice over colour.

It would be tedious to go through the many minor writers of school stories in the tradition of Reed, to list their names or discuss their books. They seem, though they cannot be, innumerable. It is the major books that differ: the minor overlap with one another. People interested in school stories often have one obscure writer they value above the other obscure ones, think neglected and would like to see reappraised. I have found what I think are unfairly forgotten names among the 'serious' writers of school stories, but not among the central, the Reed-followers, who seem to me, with small variations in quality, to be much of a muchness in interest. The school story had everything to attract the hack and the humdrum (as well as the occasional Kipling, who presumably took a hack, humdrum subject to see what he could do with it). No one can claim to have read all the mainstream school stories, nor, perhaps, should anyone want to. As the proverb (Italian, I think) says: 'You don't have to eat the whole ox to know that the meat is bad.' Not that they are so very bad, but you don't have to read these hundreds, perhaps thousands, of school stories to know the atmosphere, the attitudes, the limitations of the genre; although it helps to be a fast enough reader to devour a good many.

CHAPTER V

Vice Versa

Places of dreary internment Osbert Sitwell

At almost the same time, in 1882, a school story appeared so different from the others in form that it cannot be pigeon-holed with any of them. It is based on magic; thus fantasy enters for the first and (as far as I know) the only time this very solid genre. Yet readers accepted it and its curious arrangement of reality from the start and, when school stories are discussed, its name often comes up. Apart from Angela Brazil's books, it was the first school story I myself came across and I remember well the eery pleasure of finding it, when I was six, in my father's study. F. Anstey's *Vice Versa: or A Lesson to Fathers* is still read and loved, and perhaps more properly than *Tom Brown's Schooldays* or any of the rest can be called a classic.

School fiction, unlike school memoirs, is generally cheerful, if intense. The atmosphere of most school stories suggests that on the whole the experience of school was well worth having, or at least (in retrospect) having had. At the more lowbrow level a mindless delight is actually part of the school spirit: one wonders how the Greyfriars boys ever get through the holidays. In other words, the joys, excitements, intensities, 'politics' and in general the rewarding experiences of public-school life were all familiar from fiction, if not from experience, to many by the early years of the century; while its horrors began to become almost equally familiar from memoirs in the twenties and thirties, although only today's permissible frankness has made it possible to reveal such things as the overt sexuality often found there.

Vice Versa is a remarkable exception to the cheerful, mindless school story, the more remarkable because its framework is entirely non-realistic. It describes a plunge into the world of school by an adult who finds it pure nightmare. The time covered is a week: it is a measure of the book's success that it feels like months. Here, the question of eye-level really comes into its own.

Strictly speaking *Vice Versa* is not a public-school story at all. In fact, when the hero's wish to go to a public school is granted, his troubles are over. Crichton House, where he languishes, seems to be one of the 'academies for young gentlemen' that aped the manners of the public schools and flourished until the Second World War (some indeed still exist, in a modified form). But it seems a piece of social unreality to suggest, as Anstey does, that it is a short step, and one often taken, from such a school to the most famous public schools. 'I'd like to go to Marlborough, or Harrow, or somewhere,' Dick tells his father. 'Jolland [his friend at Crichton House] is going to Harrow at Easter.' In the end Dick is sent to Harrow by a chastened father and all ends well. But the point about places like Crichton House is that they were not prep schools, preparing boys for higher things. They were copies of both prep and public schools, small, family-based establishments with a few masters (in this case only two), catering for boys all the way up to eighteen or so; and the point about the boys who went there is that they generally had not the smallest chance of going anywhere else – certainly not to Harrow.

Why Dick is at Crichton House is something of a mystery. Like many parents, his father seems to have chosen it for rather thin reasons. 'It's an excellent school,' he tells the unhappy Dick, '– never saw a better expressed prospectus in my life. And my old friend Bangle, Sir Benjamin Bangle, who's a member of the School Board, and ought to know something about schools, strongly recommended it – would have sent his own son there, if he hadn't entered him at Eton.' (A likely tale, one feels, and so, clearly, does Dick.) However that may be, Dr Grimstone's Crichton House seems to be considered an alternative to public school, small-scale but imitative, a compendium of school attitudes and customs, into which are packed all possible variations on the theme of school – privations, whackings, snobberies, raggings, chilblains, tall stories, inedible food and even occasional larks. Technically it may not be a public school but behaviourally it is exactly the same.

Vice Versa is fantasy, with magic pretty crudely introduced. C. S. Lewis, who called it 'the only truthful school story in existence', saw the magic as an advantage:

> The machinery of the Garuda Stone really serves to bring out in their true colours (which would otherwise seem exaggerated) the sensations which every boy had on passing from the warmth and softness and dignity of his home life to the privations, the raw and sordid ugliness, of school.[1]

In fact, within the fantastic framework it is one of the most realistic of the school stories, realistic in tone and spirit and, one feels, in physical detail; realistic above all in taking the lid off the familiar preconceptions about school life and boy nature. Mr Paul Bultitude, city businessman and the portly, elderly parent so often found in those days of late middle-class marriage and early stoutness, expresses a jovial wish that he, like his larky son Dick, might return to the fun and frolics of Dr Grimstone's, those 'happiest days' of ghoulish memory to many. As he says this, he happens to be holding the magical Garuda Stone, brought home from India by his scapegrace brother-in-law and lying about ever since. Instantly he shrinks to the size, appearance and even clothes of his fourteen-year-old son who, seeing the possibilities of the situation, seizes the stone and wishes to be given his father's looks. Mr Bultitude is thus whisked off to Crichton House and Dick is left at home to do what he likes, spend what he will, and generally enjoy himself (practical jokes in the office and children's parties at home) as seems proper to a child let loose in the adult world (when fourteen was younger than it is now) and determined to make the most of it.

Dr Grimstone's school is one of those described by Osbert Sitwell as 'places of dreary internment', in spite of a motherly Mrs Grimstone and a pretty daughter called Dulcie who turns out to be what would now be called Dick's girl-friend. Mr Bultitude (perhaps more suitably called Paul, in the circumstances) at first imagines it will be easy to escape from his peculiar situation, imprisoned as he is not just in a foreign milieu but in a foreign body. If he explains things to Dr Grimstone – man to man – they will quickly be sorted out. He will then return home, a further swapping of appearances will somehow take place, and all will go back to where it was. But things are more complicated than he expects. Not only is it impossible to persuade anyone that a fourteen-year-old boy is in fact a middle-aged man: the fourteen-year-old body actually inhibits Paul in his relations with others. At first he tries to treat Dr Grimstone as an equal and assert his rights. But gradually, as Dr Grimstone grows more and more annoyed with what seems to him impertinence, Paul finds himself awed by the man's dreadful headmasterliness or headmasterly dreadfulness. The Doctor, as he is called, is indignant to find Paul, whom he naturally thinks is Dick, using what seems inappropriate language in addressing him, and a tone that, he feels, must surely be ironically intended.

For it never crosses Paul's mind to pretend he is Dick or to behave like a boy of fourteen. He insists on speaking, reacting and behaving exactly as an adult of his age and kind would do in normal circumstances: pompously, priggishly, long-windedly and (of course, things being as they are) disastrously, since neither the boys (who at first think he is teasing but later, resentfully, decide that he means it) nor the Doctor (who takes it as plain impudence) will stand for it. Anstey is asking, in other words: 'What is "rational" behaviour at school? How does an ordinary person – not a schoolboy – react when kicked, punched, teased, tormented night and day, fed on disgusting food, forced to play pointless games by the hour, unable to order the smallest detail of his own life, or to have money, rights, principles, feelings or privacy? What does he do when even letters home are censored, when the misery looks like going on for another four or five years and imprisonment, during term time, is total?' Boys, he seems to be saying, are made to bear what no adult would tolerate for a moment, and not just made to bear it but told they are enjoying it, told that never again will they find themselves as happy. 'All the – hum, the innocent games and delights of boyhood, and that sort of thing, you know,' Mr Bultitude mutters, trying to cheer his snuffling son when the time comes to go back to school; and that same evening, in the guise of Dick, he creeps 'sore and trembling with rage and fright into his cold hard bed', after a cheerful bout of bullying from the others in his dormitory.

This, at the deepest level, is what *Vice Versa* is about. But Anstey does not go into it deeply. At times his book seems potentially as full of irony and bitterness as *The Way of All Flesh*; but he sheers away from the implications of the story, which he seems to have lighted upon almost by accident, and asks questions about endurance and suffering almost by the way. He stresses the fact that you cannot apply the same standards to boy and adult ('to an ordinary boy life there [at Crichton House] would not have had any intolerable hardships, if it held out no exceptional attractions,' he says at one point), and suggests that most of his troubles are Paul Bultitude's own fault for failing to fit in and accept the boys' code of conduct. This he refuses to do. Instead of imitating, as best he can, the way his son would be likely to behave, he sticks to his adult eye-level: addressing the boys as if they were his juniors and the masters as if he were at least their equal. Whatever happens, he behaves as an adult of a humourless, unbending kind would behave. When he sees – or rather smells – a boy sucking peppermints on the train back to school, he complains to the Doctor as an intolerant traveller disturbed on a journey might do and the boy is punished. When physically attacked (for this and other reasons, later on) it seems perfectly reasonable to him to complain again, as an assaulted adult would go to the police.

When challenged to fight, Paul reacts with horror. When approached by Dulcie Grimstone, who, thinking he is Dick, flirtatiously recalls their past friendship, he is embarrassed and shocked.

Since sneaking is the worst sin in the schoolboy's code, his actions, rational though they appear to him, lay him open to violent attack and forfeit him sympathy from everyone, even those who think themselves old friends. He comes to realise, too, the way in which arbitrary adult action may affect a child's life in ways undreamed of by the unimaginative parent. His son Dick, for instance, had the previous term promised to bring some rabbits and mice back to school that term for a number of customers who had paid him for them in advance. Paul (in his Mr Bultitude days) drowned all these animals in a pail of water, refusing to listen to Dick's explanation and thinking they merely polluted the house. Back at school, he finds himself pursued by his (or rather Dick's) creditors, and forced by a fair-minded master to hand over his pocket money, which exactly covers the debts. Paul, as parent, told Dick how ample this allowance would be. As boy, he discovers how little it amounts to, and how powerless he is to escape from school without a penny left for train fares, after paying the rabbit- and mice-buyers back.

Life is unbearable in almost every way. The awfulness of lessons he cannot follow seems the least of Paul's worries, since cribbing is easy and the masters, two doubtless underpaid drudges, are not too demanding. The awfulness of games is more obvious, games consisting mainly of a version of prisoner's base which Dr Grimstone thinks good for the young. Even the masters loaf about the yard while this is played, unless he actually comes out to watch. The awfulness of food is the most immediate and obvious of the troubles. Back at school on the first evening. Paul finds that supper consists of 'small pieces of thinly buttered bread . . . with tumblers of water', and refuses it, only to be rebuked by the Doctor for faddiness, called a pig by the boys and forced to eat two 'moist and thick' slices of bread which, still delicate in his eating habits, he can scarcely swallow.

At breakfast next morning, he was disgusted to find, not a couple of plump poached eggs, with their appetising contrast of ruddy gold and silvery white . . . a crisp and crackling sausage or a mottled omelette . . . even the homely but luscious rasher, but a brace of chill forbidding sardines lying grim and headless in bilious green oil. It was a fish he positively loathed . . . He roused himself, however, to swallow them, together with the thin and tin-flavoured coffee. But the meal as a whole was so different from the plentiful well-cooked breakfast he had sat down before for years as a matter of course, that it made him feel extremely unwell.

To make things worse, the Doctor is gobbling kidneys on toast, 'at which envious glances were occasionally cast'. Dinner that day consists of:

a thick ragged section of boiled mutton, which had been carved and helped so long before he sat down to it, that the stagnant gravy was chilled and congealed into patches of greasy white [and] a solid slab of pale brown suet pudding, sparsely bedewed with unctuous black treacle.

Anstey spreads his causes for gloom and scarcely mentions food again, but in a rather different context we hear of 'a particularly unpopular pudding . . . a pallid preparation of suet, with an infrequent currant or two embalmed in it'.

But privations are only part of a more general horror, physical, aesthetic, moral, affective. Largely because of his sneaking, Paul is beaten and bullied. We are told of his first night:

They at once proceeded to form a circle round him and, judging their distance with great accuracy, jerked towels at his person with such diabolical dexterity that the wet corners cut him at all points like so many fine thongs, and he spun round like a top, dancing.

This kind of thing goes on without a break. 'He had come down to breakfast, after being knocked about as usual in the dormitory overnight,' Anstey says, 'with a dull wonder how long this horrible state of things could possibly be going to last.' Another time he is made to 'run the gauntlet':

He had a confused sense of flying madly along the double line of avengers under a hail of blows which caught him in every part of his head, shoulders and back till he reached the end, where he was dexterously turned and sent spinning up . . . again . . . Never had Mr Bultitude felt so sore and insulted. But they kept it up long after the thing had lost its first freshness – until at last exhaustion made them lean to mercy, and they cuffed him ignominiously into a corner.

Then there are the minor pains and humiliations of every day, the 'sly jog or pinch', the 'sharp jog below his back, which jarred his spine and caused him infinite agony', the 'abusive epithet hissed viciously into his ears'.

With all this goes a sense of injury, loss and loneliness that is almost, though not quite, pathetic and moving. Not quite because Mr Bultitude is never really human and because Anstey is never sure what to do with pathos, a quality that seems to embarrass him. Again and again he succeeds in describing Paul's sufferings with eloquence and truth; then, reverting to comedy, he trips up our sympathy, makes light of it, alters the atmosphere. Still, there are moments in which the essence of deprivation is caught, moments when everything combines into a complex pattern of wretchedness: the ugly surroundings, the unsympathetic atmosphere, the personal affronts and miseries:

> As he took in all the detail of his surroundings – the warm close room; the raw-toned desks and tables at which a rabble of unsympathetic boys were noisily whispering and chattering, with occasional glances in his direction, from which, taught by experience, he augured no good; the high uncurtained windows, blurred by little stars of half-frozen rain, and the bare, bleak branches of trees outside tossing drearily against a low leaden sky – he tried in vain to cheat himself into a dreamy persuasion that all this misery could not be real, but would fade away as suddenly and mysteriously as it had stolen upon him.

This could come from many school memoirs, though from few school stories: with its sense of forlornness, its mixture of physical and spiritual ills, of a particular *concentration* of misery perhaps experienced only in youth, when things seem incomparably bad because there is no means of comparison, no other badness against which to measure them. The cosy school evenings of fiction, the high-spirited, crowded communal life, is shown here bare and unromanticised, from an adult eye-level.

It is this crowdedness, this total lack of privacy, that in retrospect probably seems worse than anything about school life. Few adults can accept it, or the institutionalising that goes with it. It is perhaps the central misery of prison, certainly in its fiercer forms such as the concentration camp: the reduction of personality, the loss of selfhood, the denial of the right to be quiet, self-contained, alone. Yet it is often assumed that children not only accept but enjoy it – as some of them do. Louis MacNeice, for instance, at school felt that there was a kind of power, a secret importance, inherent in the communal expressions and actions: 'at school one was a person, at home one was just a child.' Of his first days at prep school, he wrote:

> Very soon, I preferred school to home, felt I had everything in hand . . . At the beginning of term, if I got there early, the pegs in the passage would be naked, then, as they flowered with hats, my excitement would rise and bubble and soon all would be parrot-house. I welcomed even the smells – boots and gas and antiseptic – and found even the changing-room more romantic than the bathroom at home.[2]

The institution, the communal life, made him feel distinct and important and powerful. But as a rule it seems to have worked the other way round – the new boy was depersonalised, lost in a common identity.

This loss of selfhood is what the adult generally cannot bear and what makes adult memories of school life more bitter in retrospect than the writer probably felt at the time. Partly it is the normal adult's revulsion against the artefacts, the physical surroundings, of communal life – their smells and atmosphere as well as their appearance – that makes school so often seem worse at a distance than it probably was at the time: aesthetically more displeasing, emotionally more distressing.

All this, Anstey does not really face in *Vice Versa*. His analysis of the ills of both Mr Bultitude and Dick at Crichton House (a typical school of its kind, he seems to suggest; and not wholly disagreeable, with at least a pleasant female side to the Grimstone family) is superficial and confused. The reasons given for Paul's misery are all immediate and understandable – things like the food and the unfriendliness, the boredom and bullying, the dreary games in the yard, misunderstandings and a sense of captivity. Anstey does not say, or even seem to consider, that such things (all the circumstances of such a school together) are intolerable to human dignity – partly because Paul is so pompously 'on his dignity' that they seem almost to serve him right. Nor does he suggest that personality is lost under such conditions; again, partly because Paul's personality is so unattractive that one scarcely cares whether it is lost or found. Anstey seems to feel that Dick, or any other ordinary schoolboy, must feel a lot less wretched than his father does in the same circumstances, because, by fitting in with the other boys' code, he makes friends and has a place in their world and this compensates for more external miseries. Mr Bultitude is miserable, he appears to suggest, mainly because he does not belong, because he has no place at school like the place he has at home or at the office – a recognised role and function, a part to play. If he were the right age, or even if he tried to behave as if he were the right age, if he reacted as the other boys expect him to, then he might feel a good deal happier.

Admittedly it is possible to be happy with bad food and in ugly surroundings, and friendship, the sense of belonging, is probably the best antidote to such ills. Yet Dick, who is popular and lively, his dormitory's official story-teller, leader in all rags and mischief and therefore looked up to by the others, is still miserable at school, still begs to leave, still weeps (at fourteen, an age when public tears are a humiliation) as the cab approaches to take him away from a home that is anything but ideal – indeed, that sounds a pretty unhappy alternative to school. Crichton House, Anstey seems to be saying, though with some confusion, is a poor school which, because of its bad conditions, produces misery. Send a boy to a better one and all will be well. All is, in fact, more or less well by the end of *Vice Versa*, with

Dick set for Harrow. Yet Crichton House is modelled directly on the public school Dick longs to go to. It is a public school in miniature, and one wonders where the difference lies. (In the mind? In Dick's?)

It is not the system, then (Anstey contends); only the individual school that is wrong. But, since the school directly reflects the system, it is hard to see just what he is saying. Perhaps not so much that the school or the system is at fault as that adults are often hypocritical and foolish and can make the young suffer through their lack of understanding. It seems as if, in spite of himself, Anstey was writing a psychological novel about parents and children rather than a straightforward school story, a novel about redemption of a kind; as if, in some subterranean way he did not quite intend to use, he was saying that it was not so much the school as all the circumstances of Dick's life that were at fault: the motherless household without a centre, the stiff, indifferent, hollow father, a parent almost as dreadful, if taken to heart, as Butler's Mr Pontifex (only much more lightly drawn, therefore less directly criticised). A week of strenuous suffering at Crichton House improves him enormously, while a week with Dick in the guise of his father at home improves relations with the others in the family – particularly the daughter Barbara, who feels at last a little closer to him and writes a happy letter to her supposed brother at school, telling him how much her supposed father at home has changed for the better.

Back at home in his normal role again (the magic having worked once more), Mr Bultitude profits from this new warmth and understanding, and, since human relations are all circular and self-perpetuating, discovers a charm he has never yet known in his children's company, and becomes more indulgent, more interested in them, and in general more human. He forgives Dick for the trick he and the Garuda Stone have played on him and magnanimously decides to send him to Harrow. Dick, all gratitude, keeps the secret of the swapped roles. At once their relationship is on a new footing. In spite of the trouble his father had made for him, things are happier for Dick at Crichton House when he returns for the current term because more hopeful. This, Anstey seems to feel, on the surface of his feelings at least, is what counts: Crichton House is nearly behind him, Harrow before him, and all is well. But, perhaps more importantly, there is the new relationship with his father; and perhaps Anstey (undeliberately, I think) was writing not so much about the sorrows of school life (in a system he seems to approve of) as about the sorrows of coldness and misunderstanding between parents and children. Only he was too busy being jokey, fantastical and highly realistic, all at once, to notice that this was what in fact most concerned him.

CHAPTER VI

The school story as imperial manual: *Stalky & Co.*

Mucky little sadists H. G. Wells

Kipling, being incomparable, must also have a chapter to himself. If other writers and their material sometimes seem a little thin, he seems the opposite – too complex and contradictory for brief treatment and likely to overflow the pages with the richness and oddity that were all his own. In life, though reserved, even secretive, about his private self, he was a joiner, gregarious though not, in either sense of the word, really popular; in literature a loner, so much unlike his contemporaries, so utterly unclassifiable, that even as the writer of a school story he has almost nothing in common with other writers of school stories.

There is no story, no consecutive narrative, in *Stalky & Co.* This is a strength, as Kipling must have known when he began to write, not a single school story, but a series of sketches set in a single school community. Most school stories sag because their action is not interesting enough and you cannot keep up enthusiasm for it across many chapters. Kipling's stories first appeared in the *Windsor Magazine* in England and in *McClure's* magazine in America, and were published as a book in 1899; but others were added, and the complete *Stalky & Co.* did not appear until 1929.* In any case, although he

* Bibliographically, the complete *Stalky & Co.* is too complicated to be dealt with here. Roger Lancelyn Green's *Kipling and the Children* (1965) throws light on some of its complexities, at a fairly amateur level. Those interested in its exact history will have to consult more scholarly bibliographical works.

'toughened' the United Services College into something much closer than it was in fact to the central public schools of the time, Kipling had no interest in the usual stuff of school stories. No one in *Stalky & Co.* cares a rap for house matches or indeed for sport of any kind. No one steals an exam paper, falls over a cliff, or is cut off by the tide. The small-scale moral problems of cribbing, the larger sexual dilemmas, do not exist. There are no rivalries over who shall or shall not be a prefect. Stalky despises the official authority of the prefects, and his followers never dispute his rule. None of the usual school-story preoccupations is found there, in other words.

Stalky & Co. aroused, sometimes still arouses, a frenzy of indignation, of moral, social, even literary outrage. 'Mucky little sadists' was H. G. Wells's comment on Stalky and his friends; 'little beasts', A. C. Benson's. 'A more odious picture of school life has never been drawn,' said Somerset Maugham; adding characteristically: 'Westward Ho! was a third-rate school.' 'An unpleasant book about unpleasant boys at an unpleasant school,' wrote one of its reviewers. 'Mr Kipling obviously aims at verisimilitude,' wrote another; 'the picture he draws is at any rate repulsive and disgusting enough to be true.' 'Only the spoiled child of an utterly brutalised public could possibly have written *Stalky & Co.*' wrote a third. '. . . the vulgarity, the brutality, the savagery . . . reeks on every page . . . it is simply impossible to show by mere quotation the horrible vileness of the book describing the lives of these three small fiends in human likeness; only a perusal of the whole work would convey to the reader its truly repulsive character.' Nearer our own time Edmund Wilson, who loathed the book with perhaps a peculiarly American edge of feeling, described it as 'a hair-raising picture of the sadism of the English public school system',[1] and called it 'from the artistic point of view, the worst of Kipling's books: crude in writing, trashy in feeling, implausible in a series of contrivances that resemble motion-picture 'gags' . . . an hysterical outpouring of emotion kept over from schooldays.' Yet, whatever other people's feelings about it, Richard Usborne maintains that 'Kipling was teaching, in a sense, all the time. He was saying: "What a great school, what a great headmaster, what clever and interesting boys! That's the way other schools, headmasters and boys ought to be."[2] Kipling himself would have agreed: he claimed to be teaching (and preaching) in *Stalky & Co.* Louis L. Cornell says that Kipling shows 'a world of wild, coarse humour, in which beatings and practical jokes are as empty of real pain as the smack of slapstick in a farce'.[3] And, in spite of these totally contradictory, even confusing views of it, boys often loved it and still do. *Pace* Edmund Wilson, it contains some marvellous pieces of writing.

Among all the 'serious' school-story writers only Kipling and Wodehouse really count, and Wodehouse's school stories, even *Mike*, were early work he himself valued little. Other school stories are read for interest – sociological, historical, educational, all sorts; for nostalgia, amusement, the reliving of old times, for any number of non-literary reasons. *Stalky & Co.* can be read for its writing. The first striking thing about it is its opening sentence:

> In summer all right-minded boys built huts in the furze-hills behind the College – little lairs whittled out of the heart of the prickly bushes, full of stumps, old root ends, and spikes, but, since they were strictly forbidden, palaces of delight.

What other school-story writer could put forty-odd words together like that?

A little later, sandwiched between approving grunts and expressions like 'Whew!', 'By gum!' and 'Isn't it scrumptious?' is this magnificent description, cinematically introduced when Stalky pulls aside the curtain of undergrowth where the three boys are sitting:

> He parted the tough stems before him, and it was as a window opened on a far view of Lundy, and the deep sea sluggishly nosing the pebbles a couple of hundred feet below. They could hear young jackdaws squawking in the ledges, the hiss and jabber of a nest of hawks somewhere out of sight and, with great deliberation, Stalky spat on to the back of a young rabbit sunning itself far down where only a cliff-rabbit could have found foothold. Great grey and black gulls screamed against the jackdaws; the heavy-scented acres of bloom round them were alive with low-nesting birds, singing or silent as the shadow of the wheeling hawks passed and returned; and on the baked turf across the combe rabbits thumped and frolicked . . . The sea snored and gurgled, the birds, scattered for the moment by these new animals, returned to their businesses, and the boys read on in the rich, warm, sleepy silence.

Is this trashy or crude? Whatever one's feelings about *Stalky & Co.*, a description like that puts it in a totally different category from the work of Hughes, Farrar, Reed, even Anstey, or indeed anyone else who had turned up on the school-story scene so far.

'The more one reads Kipling, the more complex and baffling he becomes,' wrote Bonamy Dobrée.[4] Complex, almost baffling, is the background of *Stalky & Co.* as well, particularly if one considers Kipling's general reputation. On the one hand, views like Orwell's, which have found general acceptance, at least among Orwellians:

> It is no use pretending that [his] view of life, as a whole, can be accepted or even forgiven by any civilised person . . . Kipling *is* a jingo imperialist, he *is* morally insensitive and aesthetically disgusting;[5]

on the other, the way he became, in a curiously roundabout fashion, almost a part of the public-school ethos, certainly an official part of the scout movement, which took over some of his characters at wolf-cub level and generally promoted many of his ideas. Lionel Trilling perhaps comes somewhere in the middle:

Kipling was an honest man and he loved the national virtues. But I suppose no one ever did more harm to the national virtues than [he] did. He mixed them up with swagger and swank, with bullying, ruthlessness, and self-righteousness, and he set them up as necessarily antagonistic to intellect. He made them stink in the nostrils of youth.[6]

Kipling's schooldays were like no one else's. He was an oddity among schoolboys at a school that, compared with others at the time, was itself an oddity, the newly established United Services College, ruled by a headmaster remarkably untypical for the time. There, the swarthy boy who was 'Ruddy' to his family became 'Gigger' (from Gig-lamps, because he wore spectacles) to his schoolmates; and, embarrassed for some reason at the Joseph that was his first name, claimed, when pressed, to be John. Also, importantly, he was the Punch of 'Baa! baa! Black Sheep', that terrible tale of childhood misery that may seem to have little to do with the frolics of *Stalky & Co.* but lurks behind it to explain some of the things that are, if not entirely inexplicable, at least hard to explain. And so, because one of its early pupils happened to be a writer of genius, a school that was almost a sport among public schools of its time became established in many people's minds as the prototype, the central, recognisable, true-blue school of them all, delightful or horrific, depending on their view of it.

In real life it was like nowhere else, as the boys themselves knew, a cut-price place for parents who could hardly afford public school, an offspring of the smarter Haileybury, housed not in rolling parkland or monastic calm but in what Kipling called, in his introductory verses to the book, 'ten bleak houses on the shore' – in other words, a row of seaside boarding houses in North Devon. 'Even by the standards of those days, it was primitive in its appointments,' he wrote half a century later, 'and our food would now raise a mutiny in Dartmoor.'[7] When he arrived there in 1878 it was certainly raw – only five years old and with boys who, he later said slyly, 'were perhaps a shade rough'. On this he expanded with what seems like some pride:

The boys said that those with whom Cheltenham could do nothing, whom Sherborne found too tough, and whom even Marlborough had politely asked to leave, had been sent to the school at the beginning of things and turned into men.[8]

Apart from this initial toughness, it differed from other public schools in a number of ways. Kipling's biographer Charles Carrington has listed them: 'No parades, no uniforms, no bands or flags, no patriotic propaganda.' Although Anglo-Indian in tradition, it was, he says, not military in tone. Nor was it particularly religious. 'It differed from the general run of mid-Victorian public schools,' Carrington goes on, 'in its secular tone; there was no school chapel; Price [the headmaster] was not in holy orders and was not a strong churchman.'[9] There was no fagging, either; and according to the man who was the model for one of the main characters, 'the brutish, uncivil, outsiderish recourse to the cane was unthinkable' where Kipling was concerned. In other words, Kipling coarsened and toughened the reality he had known. Also, Price was a close friend of the Kipling family, known to its younger members as 'Uncle Crom'. Although this family connection is not mentioned in the book (Kipling's schoolboy self, Beetle, has no outside-school relationship with the headmaster) in real life it must have affected his status and feelings. Graham Greene* and, more recently, Thomas Hinde* have described what it was like to be the headmaster's son, with a foot in either camp. Kipling's position must have had a pinch of that feeling about it.

More importantly, it differed from other schools in that it allowed a boy like Kipling, so short-sighted that he was hopeless at games and in other ways quite unlike the object of schoolboy veneration at the time, not merely to be admired for his early brilliance, but even to become something of a hero for it, a source of interest and pride not just to the masters but to the other boys. Intellectually he was given every encouragement. Price gave him the run of his own library, where he read widely in French as well as English, and two other masters had an important influence on his development as a writer. Above all, as *Stalky & Co.* for all its gags and high spirits makes clear, there was room for intellectual interests, for reading and discussion. It was not shameful to admit to reading or writing poetry or anything else. G. C. Beresford, the model for M'Turk, wrote:

> Our school-fellows bore no resentment with regard to aestheticism, as anything that Gigger did 'went' . . . At Westwood Ho during the Gigger regime games or athletics were not placed above brains in the estimation of many of the boys. It was necessary, indeed, to be a little apologetic about sports and repetitions of *mens sana in corpore sano* or whatever it is and to be constantly aware that in the large world outside the school, there were very different standards.

* See, respectively, Greene's *A Sort of Life* (1971) and Thomas Hinde's *Sir Henry and Sons* (1980).

This makes for a very different atmosphere from that of many school stories, in which the intellectual as dissident is a common feature, and any intellectual interests are subterranean, unadmitted, a source of embarrassment. The image of Kipling as a boy is very different, too, from most people's idea of him as an adult. Carrington writes:

> No one then regarded 'Gigger' as a writer of 'patriotic' verse. He was a rebel and a progressive, which is to say, in 1882 – paradoxically – that he was a decadent. His friends, his teachers, were liberals, his tastes were 'aesthetic', the writers he most admired were the fashionable pessimists.[10]

Price would nowadays be called left-wing. In the words of Beresford:

> The picture in *Stalky & Co.* of the Head as a nursing mother of jingoes, a trainer, a guide and an inspirer of Imperial fuglemen and a stimulator of prancing frontier officers wants some accounting for when one discovers that during a summer holiday in the days of the Russo-Turkish war, Price organised, hand in hand with Burne-Jones, a 'Workmen's Neutrality Demonstration' in denunciation of our Imperial Beaconsfield in the blameless district of Islington.

Add to this the fact that Kipling knew something of literary and artistic London, spending the school holidays with cultivated friends in Warwick Gardens, who knew Christina Rossetti, Jean Ingelow, and the de Morgans; that he had two famous painter uncles, one of his mother's sisters being married to Sir Edward Burne-Jones, the other to Sir Edward Poynter; that he was physically precocious (with a noticeable moustache when barely twelve and a big bushy one in a school photograph at fifteen) and sexually forward, having fallen in love at fourteen, and considering himself engaged to the girl when he left school at sixteen – an engagement to which he felt bound for six more years at least – and it would be hard to find a more outlandish schoolboy, if the straight, central schoolboy is thought to be someone like Tom Brown.

And yet, as always with Kipling, one has to qualify and almost to contradict each statement, for everything about him was several-sided and can be interpreted in several ways. He may have been brilliant and well-read, he may have been intellectually, physically and even emotionally precocious; he may have admired the aesthetes and even the decadents of his time, and enjoyed immensely a cultural spree in Paris in his mid-teens and the company of his pre-Raphaelite relations in London. But his attitudes in *Stalky & Co.* often seem those of a tough young thug. Perhaps largely to compensate for his difference from the rest, he assumed a tone that was not merely vehement and noisy but often aggressive, even violent. 'A sophisticated philistinism, a deliberate brutality of speech, is one of the most unpleasant features of *Stalky & Co.*,' writes Andrew Rutherford.[11]

Kipling's position at school – at that particular school – may to some extent explain this. For he was an outsider there, subjected to a training that had nothing to do with his prospects and talents. Like many parents, Kipling's had, with the best intentions, chosen their son's school for the wrong reasons. Its cheapness was no small advantage (later, they were unable to consider university even for so gifted a boy, their only son); but their main, most obvious reason seems to have been their friendship with the headmaster, Price. Of course it was reassuring to have a friend in charge, and one their son respected and liked; especially when they were to be thousands of miles away in India during his later schooldays, and when their earlier arrangements, leaving him and his sister with strangers, had been disastrous. Price seems to have come up to expectation, to have done all he could for the boy's expanding mind and interests, to have appreciated his gifts and aroused in him a lasting sense of gratitude and warmth. Kipling's time at the school was memorable, vigorous, generally cheerful, intellectually stimulating and a source of close (though not, it seems, lasting) friendships; someone has suggested the study-sharers were 'cronies' rather than friends. But the United Services College was the wrong school because it had been founded for a specific purpose which had nothing to do with him, his future plans, his family tradition or his physical capacity.

This purpose was the training of imperial administrators and army officers, something that Kipling, with his extremely short sight, could never become and for which, with his obvious, early-exhibited talent as a writer, he would clearly have been unsuitable anyway. So everything the school was doing excluded him – by implication, at least – and with one side of him he resented that exclusion. Philip Mason has described him as 'trained as an officer who could never have a regiment, a ruler with no one to rule, an artist who must on no account betray his emotions.'[12] In a sense he admired intensely the straightforward, physically competent, courageous, prefect-like young men his school was aiming to turn out; in another he sneered at the good boys, the prigs and conformers, certainly the flag-waggers, the patriots who cheered at house matches.

How much his appearance affected him at that age we cannot know. That he was heterosexually inclined, even in his early teens, we do know. But the fact remains, as almost every school story in some way reminds us, that in the all-male community of school certain patterns of homosexuality existed, and that, as part of the pattern, looks – the complement of athletic prowess – undoubtedly counted. Kipling was certainly a very strange-looking boy, if photographs and descriptions can be trusted: plump, peering, very dark, very mature-looking for his years, furred like a monkey even in adolescence. The dark and slightly repulsive name of Beetle, which he gave himself in the story, seems to suggest he sensed something squashable and insect-like about his presence. Perhaps this added to his sense of exclusion, and the almost hysterical exuberance of *Stalky & Co.* was surely an effort to assert himself as belonging with the others, as being one of them. That he became what he was and stood for what he came to stand for seems odd if you consider his heritage, his immediate family, his own gifts and physique; but it seems a good deal less odd if you look at the divided loyalties and – presumably – longings of his adolescence, given voice with defiant eloquence in *Stalky & Co.*

2 *Stalky stalked . . .*

It is the only school story, I think, in which life at school is shown as *directly* parallel with life in the Empire; a training directly related to the life that lay ahead for many public schoolboys at the end of the nineteenth century, particularly boys from Kipling's school. 'Eighty per cent of the boys had been born abroad, in camp, cantonment, or upon the high seas . . . Seventy-five per cent were sons of officers in one or other of the services, looking to follow their father's profession,' Kipling writes. That school life was a narrow version of later life and that the patterns of prefect-rule were similar to those of the Empire was often implied, of course, but no book went as far as *Stalky & Co.* in making exact comparisons. 'Slaves of the Lamp', set about fifteen years after the main story, says quite explicitly: Look what happens! Send them to a school like that and see how they turn out! The ruses Stalky employs so effectively with his Sikhs and Pathans are exactly those which he and M'Turk and Beetle used to defeat the hated master, King, at school. Even the song in the house pantomime of Aladdin – 'Arrah, Patsy, mind the baby' – is played on Stalky's bugle to rally his troops and identify his allies. And Stalky's qualities, Kipling claims, are not unique. 'India's full of Stalkies – Cheltenham and Haileybury and Marlborough chaps – that we don't know anything about,' he says in the final chapter (Beetle has at last become 'I'). Thus Stalky is made generally applicable, an image of much more than himself. 'The Stalky ethos was raw, practical and unsentimental, and it shocked a good many patriots and Old Boys,' Janet Adam Smith wrote; adding that while Newbolt

> celebrates the solitary hero, honourable and brave . . . Kipling celebrates the ingenious and crafty hero, working with others in a vividly realised situation.

Newbolt's poetical heroes tend to die, nobly; Kipling's prose ones to survive, craftily. Kipling's were more use to the Empire.[13]

Kipling's schoolboy hero is one of his most interesting characters, not so much in himself as for his effect on others. 'That – is – entirely – Stalky,' someone says admiringly in the last chapter, after hearing how, in Egypt in '84,

> Stalky got embroiled with Fuzzies five miles in the interior. He conducted a masterly retreat and wiped up eight of 'em. He knew jolly well he'd no right to go out so far, so he took the initiative and pitched in a letter to his colonel, who was frothing at the mouth, complaining of the 'paucity of support accorded to him in his operation'.

The Infant, who has been telling the others this, concludes: 'Gad, it might have been one fat brigadier slanging another!' Exactly, exactly how he behaved at school, everyone feels, including the reader: always taking the initiative and getting in first, so that the opposition feels guilty or inadequate, the enemy is not merely routed but apologetic as well. The word 'stalky' in U.S.C. slang at the time, meant crafty and cunning and effective. 'Stalky stalked,' someone else says. 'That's all there is to it.' Man and boy, Stalky is involved not just in defeating the enemy but in winning 'face', confusing the opposition and, most importantly, coming out on top. If a good pinch of luck is needed for all this, so too are cunning and unshakable confidence. Stalky has them all.

Resourcefulness and ruthlessness are his two main qualities. A loner, in that he can be self-sufficient, he is very much a leader nonetheless, demanding obedience, knowing just what he wants and getting it. In India he becomes 'an invulnerable *Guru* of sorts' to his Sikhs. Like Kim – and quite unlike the idea of the stand-offish Englishman – he becomes very much a part of India, of his men's lives and customs. 'Stalky *is* a Sikh,' says someone else. 'He takes his men to pray at the Durbar Sahib at Amritzar, regularly as clockwork, when he can.' With the wily intelligence that at school makes him find eyries on forbidden cliff-tops and generate smells in the rival house, that allows him to improvise all along and see at once the possibilities for mayhem in a drunken villager or an attic opened up for plumbing, he uses the same tactics in India to stir up enmity between allies, setting Khye-Kheens against their rival Malôts. And thus, with a mixture of toughness, intelligence and luck, he becomes a hero to his men and to his friends at home, who listen to other Old Boys' tales of his exploits with admiring whistles. Everything is exactly in keeping with schoolboy patterns, everything has worked out just as it should. And, incidentally, the real-life model for Stalky ended up a general.

But where would Stalky be today? There would be no legally respectable place for him, no scope for his talents. Except, if you can call it legal, in some kind of intelligence work, the secret service and whatever that entails in the way of Stalky-like action. Significantly, the best-known Kim today is not Kipling's hero but the man named after him by a very Stalky-like father, 'Arabian' Philby. It took an Empire to harness Stalky's volcanic energy and restlessness. The conditions of the time, the available followers, even the political climate – all had to be right. Probably the last Stalky figure, on a large scale, was T. E. Lawrence. But there must have been many lesser-known Stalkies in the Second World War, given scope as commandoes and agents and infiltrators, all sorts of freelance adventurers and escapers for whom the more modern world no longer has room or, more importantly, taste. The only undoubted Stalky I have known committed suicide, unable to find a role or even a place in today's world. For one thing, the Stalky figure requires dedicated followers, blind admirers, and these no longer exist. The love that asks no question is no longer admired, or even possible, nationally or personally. In fiction, he declined into the ugly right-wing toughs admired by Sapper; in life, today, probably into the pathetic mercenaries who turn their high spirits to dubious causes.

3 *In the moral life of history there are apparently no gains without losses. Few books urge us to confront this contradiction more barely and boldly than* Stalky & Co. Steven Marcus

One of the book's haters said that Stalky and his friends were 'not like boys at all, but like hideous little men'. They might have taken that as a compliment. Certainly they would have liked Carrington's remark that the book shows 'a world of work like manhood, not a world of play like childhood'.[14] Beetle and M'Turk are less important to the myth than Stalky, although Beetle, being Kipling, expresses and sustains it. They provide Stalky with support and an audience; an inferior though affectionately regarded following, like his later Sikhs. To them he is 'Uncle Stalky', the one they trust, who never lets them down, who can always engineer escape and victory. Beetle is literary, dim-sighted, the school poet, full of quotations in French and Latin, yet always wholly if anarchically involved in the doings at school and the running battle of wits with authority, mostly in the person of King.

M'Turk, known as Turkey, is Irish, flamboyant, the 'arty' one of the three. He reads Ruskin and, when they get a study, sees to its decoration, with scornful remarks about the others' taste. In the first chapter he is given a prominence he never gets again, leaving Stalky and Beetle gazing admiringly and incredulously at him. Technically this is curious – promoting him and therefore demoting Stalky the first time we meet them. Presumably Kipling felt confident enough of Stalky's role. What happens is this. While trespassing on the local landowner's property, the boys see a keeper trying to shoot a fox. M'Turk is convulsed with rage: 'An' a vixen, too – at this time o' year!' Instantly he is transformed into 'a new Turkey – a haughty, angular, nose-lifted Turkey' who takes his intense indignation to the landowner, Colonel Dabney, and almost assaults him for having such a keeper. 'It was the landed man speaking to his equal – deep calling to deep – and the old gentleman acknowledged the cry,' Kipling says. Colonel Dabney apologises, promises to demote the keeper that same day, gives the boys beer, sends them to the Lodge with messages that will assure them future welcomes and strawberry teas, and altogether behaves as he should. Later the story comes full circle when he behaves even more as he should by flinging King and other lesser enemies off his land when they have been chasing about on it, hoping to catch Stalky and Co., who, from the Lodge parlour, hear the Colonel's bellows as he berates the supposed poachers. Never again does Turkey achieve such eminence.

Other boys flit in and out of the action, friendly presences rather than close friends. The prefects are fair game for Stalky and Co., but pulled down less ferociously and gleefully than the hated King, being lower on the school ladder and less hateful. King, classics master and housemaster of the rival house to theirs, is the arch-enemy, sarcastic, clever, but humanly inept; and, significantly, hating Beetle in particular. Prout, their own housemaster, is dull and inadequate rather than actively vile. The chaplain is a friend, humorous and respected. And the headmaster, like Uncle Crom, though much more of a swashbuckler and a beater, is clearly a great man and father-figure to them all. Even as Old Boys they tell him their troubles and ask his advice; and then he shows them 'in language quite unfit for little boys, a quiet and safe way round, out or under'. 'The Coll.', as Kipling calls it, is turning out its quota of administrators and officers. Although the country is not at war, nine Old Boys have been killed in India over the past three years, and from border skirmishes and local upheavals news of deaths and heroism trickles in all the time.

And yet, for all this sense of glory and adventure only just off-stage, and for most of the boys just ahead in the future, a healthy realism pervades the place. More than most public schoolboys at the time, they know why they are there. 'We've got to get into the army or get out, haven't we?' says one of them. 'King's hired by Council to teach us. All the rest's flumdiddle. Can't you see?' King may be hateful but he is 'the best classical cram' and so must be tolerated. The same boy deflates King's snobbish insistence on public-school behaviour. 'Besides, as I told King, we aren't a public school,' he says. 'We're a limited liability company paying four per cent.' At times the public-school ethos is strong, at others the boys recognise themselves as something much more recognisable today than then: as exam fodder, to whom cramming is more important than football, and who accept that 'extra-tu' must come before a match against the Old Boys, even if the Old Boys will have to be played by a scratch school team. Not many school stories were as realistic as that. It is a far cry from Old Brooke preferring house-match victories to Balliol scholarships. Kipling's boys are poorer than Hughes's on the whole, and know their parents cannot afford school and 'extra-tu' for too long.

In this realistic framework Stalky acts like an avenging angel, invisibly powerful. Whenever the authorities crack down on him and his friends something happens to avenge them. Nothing that can be traced back to them, nothing provable or obviously boy-engendered. It is just that things, as it were, cosmically happen, out of the blue, as if some wrathful spirit were on their side. Sometimes these things are amusing, sometimes not. When King is thrown out by Colonel Dabney as a poacher, it is acceptable vengeance, and one shares, a little, the boys' gleeful 'gloats' of triumph. Then a drunken carter throws stones through King's study window and Beetle, who is in the study legitimately at the time, adds horribly to the damage while King is out of the room. No master, even King, would seriously think a boy had done what Beetle does, so he gets away with it; but this is not funny at all, and one begins to understand some of the outrage that greeted *Stalky & Co.*

Beetle is ruthlessly, sickeningly efficient. Kipling writes:

> Then did Beetle, alone with the wreckage, return good for evil. How, in that office, a complete set of 'Gibbon' was scarred all along the back as by a flint; how so much black and copying ink chanced to mingle with Mander's gore on the tablecloth; why the big gum-bottle, unstoppered, had rolled semi-circularly across the floor; and in what manner the white china door-knob grew to be painted with yet more of Manders's young blood, were matters which Beetle did not explain when the rabid King returned to find him standing politely over the reeking hearth-rug . . . But it was to a boot-cupboard under the staircase on the ground floor that he hastened, to loose the mirth that was destroying him.

Mirthful is the last thing most readers feel at this tale of vandalism. There is something peculiarly nasty about the writer Kipling making his fictional *persona* deface a set of books.

Two pages later he is doing the same sort of thing on a smaller scale among the boys of the Lower Third, who need to be taught a lesson. The small fry are

> busy with their Saturday evening businesses [some of which, incidentally, make a modern reader shudder] – cooking sparrows over the gas with rusty nibs; brewing unholy drinks in gallipots; skinning moles with pocket-knives; attending to paper trays full of silk-worms, or discussing the iniquities of their elders . . .

In walk Stalky and Co. Kipling goes on:

> The blow fell without warning. Stalky upset a crowded form of small boys among their own cooking utensils; M'Turk raided untidy lockers as a terrier digs at a rabbit-hole; while Beetle poured ink upon such heads as he could not appeal to with a Smith's *Classical Dictionary*. Three brisk minutes accounted for many silk-worms, pet larvae, French exercises, school caps, half-prepared bones and skulls, and a dozen pots of home-made sloe jam. It was a great wreckage, and the form-room looked as though three conflicting tempests had smitten it.

Most famously nasty of all is the chapter called 'The Moral Reformers', described by Wells 'the key to the ugliest, most retrogressive, and finally fatal idea of modern imperialism' which 'lights up the political psychology of the British Empire at the close of the nineteenth century very vividly'.[15] The friendly chaplain has asked Stalky and Co. to stop the bullying of a small boy by two 'precocious hairy youths between seventeen and eighteen, sent to the school in despair by parents who hoped that six months steady cram might, perhaps, jockey them into Sandhurst'. By a trick, Stalky and Co. manage to get the two culprits tied up, and suddenly the atmosphere changes. 'Stalky took the armchair and contemplated the scene with his blandest smile. The man trussed for cock-fighting is, perhaps, the most helpless thing in the world,' Kipling says. The boys are then tortured. What this involves we are never exactly told, but Kipling's skill in suggesting what is done is creepily effective, and we have a vivid sense, not just of the victims' pain and humiliation, but of their torturers' pleasure in inflicting it:

> They were corkscrewed, and the torture of the Corkscrew – this has nothing to do with corkscrews – is keener than the torture of the Key.
>
> The method and silence of the attacks was breaking their nerves. Between each new torture came the pitiless, dazing rain of questions . . . Sefton was 'rocked' till his eyes set in his head and he gasped and crowed for breath, sick and dizzy.
>
> 'My Aunt!' said Campbell, appalled, from his corner, and turned white.
>
> 'Put him away,' said Stalky. 'Bring on Campbell. Now this *is* bullyin' . . .

Set him up, Beetle. Give me the glove an' put in the gag.'

In silence Campbell was 'rocked' sixty-four times . . .

Then came the tears . . . appeals for mercy and abject promises of peace.

They are then forced to say humiliating things, to repeat whatever they are told to say.

When Sefton calls Beetle a 'blind beast', Beetle takes violent vengeance: 'Blind, am I,' said Beetle, 'and a beast? Shut up, Stalky. I'm goin' to jape a bit with our friend . . .' He then beats him with a cricket stump.

'Aren't my eyes lovely?' The stump rose and fell steadily throughout this catechism.

'Yes.'

'A gentle hazel, aren't they?'

'Yes – oh yes!'

'What a liar you are! They're sky-blue. Ain't they sky-blue?'

'Yes – oh yes!'

'You don't know your mind from one minute to another. You must learn – you must learn.'

At this point even Stalky intervenes.

'What a bait you're in!' said Stalky. 'Keep your hair on, Beetle.'

'*I've had it done to me*,' said Beetle [my italics].

In the story, Beetle is meant to refer merely to earlier school bullying of himself. But Beetle is Kipling, and Kipling had plenty more to remember. 'I've had it done to me' surely refers, though perhaps indirectly and unconsciously, to earlier sufferings and blows of fate: to what happened in 'Baa! baa! Black Sheep', to the House of Desolation where he languished as a child, to the humiliation of having a placard with 'Liar' written on it hung on his back, even to the fact that others could call him a 'blind beast'.

The two victims have elaborate moustaches and whiskers of which they are immensely proud. Stalky and Co. shave and burn them off:

The thin-haired first moustache of youth fluffed off in flame to the lather-line in the centre of the lip, and Stalky rubbed away the burnt stumpage with his thumb. It was not a very gentle shave, but it abundantly accomplished its purpose.

'Now the whiskers on the other side. Turn him over!' Between match and razor this, too, was removed. 'Give him his shaving-glass. Take the gag out. I want to hear what he'll say.'

. . . Two fat tears rolled down his cheek . . . Sefton cried like a twelve-year-old with pain, shame, wounded vanity, and utter helplessness.

Finally the victims are made to sing 'Kitty of Coleraine' for their torturers' amusement.

Admittedly these victims are bullies themselves, who have tormented a much younger boy, but nothing excuses the ugliness of Stalky & Co. at this point. Later the headmaster and the chaplain, after a letter of complaint from Sefton's mother, discuss what may have happened. The chaplain has a fair idea: '– they either educate the school,' he says, 'or the school, as in this case, educates them'. In a roundabout way he talks to Stalky and Co. about it:

> 'Boys educate each other, they say, more than we can or dare. If I had used one half of the moral suasion you may or may not have employed . . . I suppose I should now be languishing in Bideford jail, shouldn't I? . . . What are you laughing at, you young sinners? . . . What I looked into this den of iniquity for was to find out if any one cared to come down for a bathe off the Ridge . . .'

'You young sinners' is the chaplain's cheerful compliment. Campbell's 'You are devils, you know, ' comes closer to the reader's feeling. Add to this chapter the odd reference to casual mistreatment of younger boys and equally casual 'borrowing' of their property, and one has an uneasy sense of generalised – not necessarily individual – bullying. For all its high spirits, it is not a pretty picture.

Prettiness, of course, was not what Kipling was after. In his way he was out to preach as much as Hughes had been; but his preaching had a different moral to point, his teaching a different lesson. He wrote, in *Something of Myself*:

> There came to me the idea of beginning some tracts or parables on the education of the young. These, for reasons honestly beyond my control, turned themselves into a series of tales called *Stalky & Co.*

'Tracts' and 'parables' are words with religious overtones. The first suggests lessons to be preached, the second, moral truths in disguise. Applied to much of *Stalky & Co.* they sound grotesque. But Steven Marcus, examining the modern reader's dilemma in reading Kipling, has put it well. I have heard much the same argument used in defence of Henry Williamson, a more extreme and attractive (and therefore beguiling) example of an outlook in some ways not unlike Kipling's.

Marcus writes:

> The point to be grasped is that among and alongside all these bad attitudes which seem calculated to outrage the values that most educated persons today affirm – values which can be roughly summed up in the term liberal democracy – there exist other attitudes and values whose absence from contemporary life we all feel and are probably the worse for. The values are described by obsolete words like honour, truthfulness, loyalty, manliness, pride, straightforwardness, courage, self-sacrifice and heroism. That these virtues exist as active and credible possibilities in *Stalky & Co.*, and that they seem not to in

ours – or, if they do, appear almost solely in corrupted forms – must give us pause. Such a fact may serve to remind us that the moral benefits, conveniences and superiorities of modern democratic societies have not been acquired without cost. Part of this cost seems pretty clearly to have been paid by a diminution of the older masculine virtues . . . In the moral life of history there are apparently no gains without losses. Few books urge us to confront this contradiction more barely and boldly than *Stalky & Co.*[16]

Not all of *Stalky & Co.* is on this stern level of morality (however one takes it). There are tales of more light-hearted vengeance which read more agreeably. Yet even these involve what we would now think a strange callousness; towards animals, for instance. To get his own back for an insult from King, Stalky shoots a cat, with characteristic sang-froid, merely to make a smell when he hides the cat's corpse under the roof, behind the top-floor ceiling, in King's house. (Cats, admittedly, were then considered rather as vermin are today: there were too many of them, wandering uncared for, and the average boy's instinctive reaction, I have myself been assured by an elderly gentleman, was to reach for his catapult when he saw one out of doors.) Other chapters are not directly vengeful. Old Boys return and tell great tales. A dreadful man comes to lecture the school on patriotism, and Stalky, followed by the rest of the school, leaves the recently-formed school corps in protest. A pinch of class feeling appears here. Foxy, the school sergeant who drills the corps, is delighted with the lecture and thinks it should inspire the boys. The lower orders, Kipling seems to be saying, are taken in by such phony sentiments; public schoolboys are not. Elsewhere the lower orders are more attractively portrayed, and so is the boys' relationship with them. They seem almost part of the landscape, a fact of nature to be enjoyed simply and affectionately, like rabbits in fine weather or a view of Lundy. Stalky, who has Kim's chameleon qualities and suits himself to his ambience, falls into a broad Devon accent when talking to them.

With all these facets, no wonder *Stalky & Co.* is the most memorable as well as in places the most horrible of all school stories: it has more force and presence than most of the rest put together.

The boys are teaching each other to live in a society that will be an enlarged version of school. They have their heroes – the headmaster, for one – but their true mentors are their peers. That these peers are sometimes vicious and violent makes one feel, perhaps smugly, that society today is 'better' – certainly that its official ideas are kinder, more sensitive, less aggressive. Small boys today do not roast sparrows on pen nibs, and older boys might hesitate to shoot a cat just to produce a stench. Or is it just that a Kipling today, if such an anachronism were possible, would be embarrassed to write a chapter like 'The Moral Reformers'? Sometimes one feels with Orwell that Kipling is morally insensitive and (therefore) aesthetically disgusting; at others that he makes every other writer of school stories except Wodehouse seem trivial or pedantic, simply because he can write, and has the vision and the irony to see beyond trivialities and detail and to make much out of little.

Of course he has his limitations. Like his characters, he stays on a single plane of feeling, a particular level of life. The school in its heyday was fiercely selective; it used and approved only certain parts of the boy's spirit. The school story, similarly, touched on only a part of his experience, his possibilities, his psyche. *Stalky & Co.,* for all that it implies a great deal, is even more selective, more school-centred, than most school stories. But because Kipling was the man who made the selection, his pin-hole view of school opened on to an immense world beyond. His boys seem to keep their school selves into adult life, or perhaps are simply adults in school dress. Whichever it is, we remember their public faces and names, their non-familial persons, and it comes as a shock to be reminded that, by close and careful reading, it can be discovered that Stalky, M'Turk and Beetle are known to their families as Artie, Willie and Reggie. It is almost as shocking as it is to recall, in a very different context, that Colette's glamorous Chéri really answers to the name of Fred.

If Kipling, for all his apparent suitability and liking for it, was to some extent a misfit in the school system, this may have been due not just to his originality of mind and inability to fit the pattern of his particular school but (perhaps, at least partly) to his own lack of the homosexual ingredient necessary for success anywhere in the system. It was not just that he seems to have lacked a taste for it (though some have found a pinch in *Stalky & Co.*) but that, for all his liking for male pursuits and company, he lacked the ability to charm others – at school, this of course meant other males – and was therefore a misfit socially, and, even more, aesthetically. The aesthetic factor was enormously important, not just in overtly homosexual relationships but, more generally, in the whole pattern of school behaviour and school success and therefore in the school story; and the matter of sexual preference became so tangled (at the obscurest, least conscious level) that the modern reader who tries to disentangle it may find his head spinning.

CHAPTER VII

The school story as love story: Sturgis, Welldon and Vachell

. . . What earthquakes of the heart and whirlwinds of the soul are confined in that simple phrase, a schoolboy's friendship!

Benjamin Disraeli

In the nineties and the early years of the new century, before readers or writers had heard of Freud or begun worrying about the underlying aspects of adolescent behaviour, the sexual side of school life was still dealt with in so unsexual a way in the school stories that readers accepted them easily as tales of noble friendship; which indeed, if looked at in a particular way, they were. Parents who, a few years later, in *The Loom of Youth,* were to be horrified at the merest hint (often so dark that it is hard to catch it) of physical manifestations of homosexuality, were ready to accept the most ardent degree of affection between boys if it involved no physical expression (except a chaste deathbed kiss, if things had grown as mortal). The whole subject of sexuality at school was undiscussable, at least openly, in the context of the school story: the word used for it, characteristically, was 'beastliness', which inhibited further enquiry. Yet the patterns of school life, as I have said, were homosexual (in the literal if not the accepted meaning of the word), or inclined to encourage homosexual feelings; and success or failure seems often to have depended on the lure or lack of overtly sexual qualities: physical beauty, sensual awareness, femininity or masculinity. The age, on the other hand, demanded an indefinable, even ambiguous something called 'manliness'. Were tough, undomestic conditions likely to produce it, or was the lack of female influence more likely to stimulate homosexual feelings by creating an emotional vacuum? About so simple a question, no one seems even to have wondered. The taboos surrounding all such discussion, except among the exceptionally 'advanced', were so strict that, even if anyone *had* wondered, there would have been little chance of saying so – at least in print.

The three books I have chosen as examples of the school love story are H. O. Sturgis's *Tim* (1891), J. E. C. Welldon's *Gerald Eversley's Friendship* (1895) and Horace Annesley Vachell's *The Hill* (1905). All three writers seem to have been ingenuous, and clearly felt no self-consciousness about admitting the pre-eminence of physical attraction in their stories, the object of love always being dazzlingly beautiful as well as dazzlingly athletic (the body thus being emphasised, as well as the face). In each case it is love at first sight, the *coup de foudre*, and in each case it is the beloved's beauty, rather than his character or attainments, that matters. In each of the three the beloved is wayward, casual, easily swayed and drawn away, lacking emotional constancy and intensity, less loving than the lover, less worthy in every way except in the all-important matter of appearances. Beauty is basic to the school love story. Yet in spite of a deeply romanticised sensuality, things remain 'pure' in the sense that 'nothing happens', physically or (as far as we are told) in the lover's imagination. The relationship is high-minded, uplifting, 'spiritual'; it dominates the lover's (though not the beloved's) life.

And so the love story in a school setting was a romantic genre born of psychological naivety. Friendship between boys, including romantic love and sensual attraction, could be described, in those unselfconscious days, in terms that today would raise, if not smiles or sniggers, at least self-consciousness, an awareness of what was involved. Some may deplore the smiles or sniggers, the loss of innocence (as well as ignorance), and the fact that friendship between those of the same sex, in our cautious age, has been demoted from its one-time eminence or at least devalued. In the early period of the public schools' heyday the pleasant innocence of their elders may have had its effect on the boys. Sin, vice and other inflammatory words could mean rebelliousness, lying, cribbing, bullying, stealing. Only much later – three or four decades after Arnold – did they come to have a specifically sexual meaning, and by the nineties, in spite of what we should now think a general unawareness of such things, the ease with which close relationships and physical effusiveness were treated in the early days was giving way to a more suspicious attitude from above, a more 'knowing' and therefore sniggery one among the boys. The idea of warm, ennobling friendships even between older and younger boys was common in Arnold's days and even later; the whole tradition of Greece, embodied in the public schools' emphasis on the classics, encouraged it.

Hughes shows Arnold deliberately 'planting' Arthur, a younger boy and an attractive one, in Tom Brown's study as a steadying influence, a power for good in the life of a giddy, mischievous boy in his mid-teens. Admittedly he also shows the other side of the older–younger boy friendship, and with some disgust: the pretty, flirtatious youngster known in some schools as a 'tart' (see Robert Graves on Charterhouse)[1] getting protection and prestige from his relationship with a powerful elder. Arnold may have been well aware of the dangers of this sort of thing, since he hoped to limit public schools to boys of twelve and over, and thus encouraged the movement for preparatory schools. But there seems to have been little watching and snooping in his day; above all little sense that friendships between boys of different ages or between boys and masters were necessarily suspect or undesirable. Suspiciousness in adults often plays a part in suggesting to the young what their elders fear may happen, and the young are often – or at least used to be – less knowledgeable than adults think them. In school memoirs there are often references to puzzlement over the dire warnings of a father when the boy left home, a housemaster when he arrived at school, even a clergyman later, when he was confirmed; an almost total inability to understand what was meant by terms like 'filth' or even 'self-abuse'. Filth might very well refer to ear-washing, after all, or the regular changing of socks.

I know that when I boarded it took me years to discover – and then with shock and disapproval at the nasty-mindedness of adults – why we were allowed to wander about in threes but not in pairs; above all why it was the gravest sin in the calendar – punishable, I could not for the life of me see why, by instant expulsion – to get into someone else's bed. In the nineteenth century suspiciousness of such things and physical shyness came quite late. Arnold strokes East's head when he breaks down and weeps; boys in real life – not in fiction – were known to fling their arms round a master's neck (often after a beating or a severe reprimand); Tom quite unguiltily cradles Arthur's head in his arm when he visits him after his illness; and so on and so on. But by the nineties (after the Wilde trial with all the prickly awareness it brought in its wake), suspicion was beginning to lower over the school scene, and it is surprising to find that all three of the school stories I have chosen to illustrate the love story in a school setting were written as late as they were with no apparent thought of it. All three were of course written from memory about things as they were in the writers' own schooldays, and so, like all school stories, at least slightly anachronistic. Today, a less chaste view of the effect of male beauty on other males can be expressed. John Lehmann gives an example in a novel:

> Sometimes, at a school like Eton, a boy appears of such exceptional beauty and sexual fascination that he becomes a legend. This phenomenon seems to appear at almost regular intervals, like the reappearance of a comet progressing across the heavens with its mysterious illumination. It happened while I was there. The boy's name in this case was Sandy Rogers. During my last two years, everyone was talking about him, and most were lusting after him . . . Besides his unearthly beauty, he also had a great gift as a footballer, and, when he was on the field with his house eleven, older boys from other houses would often gather round just to watch his exquisite flying figure, groaning with longing as he tossed the tarnished gold of his hair back from his forehead, or charged into the scrum with arms flying . . . He appeared to have the unconscious power to uncover a hidden vein of pederasty in the breasts of the most normal seeming male.[2]

What is the difference between this and the ardours (quite as intense) of *Tim, Gerald Eversley's Friendship*, or *The Hill*? The description of the glorious-looking footballer fits almost weirdly the object of love in all three of them. But the *explicit* sexuality of the attraction, the *admission* of sexual feeling in writers, readers and fictional characters, is missing from the earlier books. Only today is it possible to recall, in memoirs as well as fiction, the overt and conscious, admitted and even tolerated sexuality of much public-school life.

There was plenty of schoolboy effusiveness and ardent friendship in Hughes and Farrar, of course; but this was truly 'innocent', and characteristic of early Victorian attitudes and manners (among adults as well as boys) rather than seriously homosexual. What I have called the love stories are different in that they deal with a relationship between two boys and nothing else. Love is the books' whole reason for existing and provides their plot, action and interest. The plots are in fact like those of other love stories, conventional except for the fact that the lovers are male and the action takes place at school. In each case there is rivalry and jealousy in love; and, significantly, since the love described can go no further without expression, in all three the last-chapter death of lover or beloved. As in *Mr Perrin and Mr Traill* Hugh Walpole made his heroine look like an attractive boy – indeed, heroines of the time were often, and again significantly, described as 'boyish' – so the romantic feelings of the boys in these stories are transferred rather abruptly to girls who, in two cases being sisters of the original beloved, may remind the lover tantalisingly of him. Gerald Eversley falls unconvincingly in love with his schoolfriend's sister. John Verney, in the sequel to *The Hill*, loves the sister of his school friend killed in the Boer War, and once again his rival in love is the fascinating Scaife who was his school rival in love years before. There is a hint of such feeling in *The Oppidan*, when Socston, having shamefully deserted the schoolfriend who loves him dearly, meets the sister of this friend, finds her enticingly familiar, and falls in love with her. And nearer our own time, the same pattern appears in *Brideshead Revisited*, where Charles Ryder's love for Sebastian is echoed in his later love for Sebastian's sister Julia, something of the same intense sexuality colouring both relationships.

Sturgis, Welldon and Vachell all write of schoolboy love as a permanent passion, stamping a lifetime. The far from ingenuous Disraeli, describing its passionate aspects without suggesting that permanence, conjures its flaming, concentrated intensity in *Coningsby*, the early chapters of which take place at Eton.

> At school, friendship is a passion. It entrances the being; it tears the soul. All loves of after-life can never bring its rapture or its wretchedness; no bliss so absorbing, no pangs of jealousy or despair so crushing or so keen! What tenderness and devotion; what illimitable confidence; what infinite revelations of inmost thoughts; what ecstatic present and romantic future; what bitter estrangements and what melting reconciliations; what scenes of wild recrimination, agitating explanations, passionate correspondence; what insane sensitiveness, and what frantic sensitivity; what earthquakes of the heart and whirlwinds of the soul are confined in that simple phrase, a schoolboy's friendship! 'Tis some indefinite recollection of these mystic passages of their young emotion that makes grey-haired men mourn over the memory of their schoolboy days.

2 *What woman could love him as I do?* H. O. Sturgis

Tim, the first of the three love stories, is the only English school story I can think of by an American; but he was an expatriate, settled, like many a good Old Boy, near his old school. Howard Overing Sturgis, 'Howdie' to his friends, who included Henry James, Edith Wharton, Percy Lubbock and A. C. Benson, was an Etonian who lived on the edge of Windsor Park in a Georgian house called Queen's Acre (always known as Qu'Acre), where, being rich and companionable, he entertained. James's biographer, Leon Edel, describes him as 'witty, poetic, sociable, gentle, and not at all intellectual,' his 'most characteristic eccentricity' being 'his addiction to embroidery and knitting'. Percy Lubbock wrote of him:

> He sat at home, wound his wool and stitched at his work; he took a turn in the road with his infirmary of dogs; with head inclined in sympathy and suavity he poured out tea for the local dowager who called on him.

George Santayana called him snidely 'a perfect young lady of the Victorian type'.

Tim, the hero of his school story, is the child of separated parents, brought up till the age of seven by a loving nurse, without companions but 'hatless, lean, brown and happy'. To a modern reader this sounds attractive and healthy but it does not satisfy his father, who writes from India that he expects to find a 'true, sturdy little pink-and-white Briton' – hatless, lean, brown boys being associated in his mind with natives, no doubt. Before his father's arrival home, Tim has been accidentally shot at by a thirteen-year-old neighbour, Carol Darley, grandson of Squire Darley, the owner of Darley Court, which Tim's father has rented throughout his childhood. When, after his not very serious injury, Tim opens his eyes to see a golden-haired, blue-eyed Carol bending over him, he thinks him an angel from heaven. From that moment, Tim is possessed by Carol; for the rest of his life he worships him, and every other feeling is subordinated to this love.

When Tim's father arrives home he finds Carol at the house and, in spite of the difference between his age and Tim's, thinks him his son and clasps him excitedly in his arms. The tall, strapping, manly, gloriously handsome boy looks exactly like the son he has dreamed of, and when Carol disgustedly pushes him away and he sees his real child – a puny, dark little fellow, totally unlike Carol – he is bitterly disappointed. Tim, sensing this, is frightened, and the relationship, off to a bad start, takes years to recover. Things are further complicated by the fact that Tim wants Carol constantly at the house whereas his father, embarrassed by his original upsurge of feeling for Carol and obscurely offended by its rejection, wants never to see him again.

Carol goes off to Eton and Tim works hard at his lessons so that he will be able, first, to communicate with him and, later, to join him. At twelve, delighted to do so because he thinks he will be joining Carol, he goes off to Eton himself, in every way unprepared for the realities of school life. Carol has no idea how to treat him, either, and although they are in the same house the friendship languishes. 'The typical "swell" or successful public-school boy,' Carol has been adaptable and happy from the start. Sturgis writes:

> With his frank, boyish manner, good looks, an inborn knack of games and the experience of a private school, [he] soon found his level . . . whereas Tim, unused to the society of boys, forbidden by the doctor to play violent games on account of his health, too weak to withstand bullying, yet too simple-minded to lie or cringe, the natural weapons of the otherwise defenceless, was like a person who has been long kept in a dark and silent room, suddenly exposed in some busy thoroughfare to the full glare of the midday sun; he was dazed by the fullness of life around him.

Misunderstandings and disappointments are inevitable. Tim buys some dormice as a present for Carol, who is angry and embarrassed at the anonymous and (he thinks) cheekily intended gift and hands it on to a fellow-fag of Tim's. Carol goes up and up in school glory, successful at football and cricket and finally in Pop; and the higher he rises the further he seems from Tim. But just before he leaves Eton, something brings them closer.

The big scenes in school stories often take place in chapel. Modern readers probably have little idea how much chapel-going went on in the public schools in the days of Tim and Carol. A suitable solemnity was generated by the ritual; building and atmosphere were right for emotion, not necessarily religious in the strict sense. From *Madame Bovary* at one end of the scale to many romantic novels at the other, religion and emotion – or, more crudely, religiosity and the erotic – have been linked, the glories and ecstacies of religious practice often suggesting the depths, heights and wonders of sensual feeling, the fervour and aesthetic satisfactions of religious ceremonial often seeming appropriate to the condition of being in love. When love between boys was being put forward for general acceptance, it was natural as well as tactful to give it ecclesiastical approval, the almost matrimonial blessing of a solemn occasion, a beautiful location, stained glass, organ music, fine singing and a mixture, familiar to readers of the time, of exotic feelings, reassuringly respectable even when most overwrought. Then there was the story of David and Jonathan, repeatedly used in the school story to give a biblical parallel to what was happening.

To quote Sturgis:

> It happened that morning that the first lesson was the beautiful lament of David over his dear friend Jonathan; and Tim, listening to the history of these two friends long ago, felt his love for his friend almost a religion to him. 'Thy love to me was wonderful,' said the voice of the reader, 'passing the love of women.' 'What woman could love him as I do?' thought Tim, as he looked naturally to the seat where Carol sat. At that moment a sunbeam from some hole high in the roof fell on the golden curly head, which seemed transfigured; and as Tim's hungry eyes rested on the face of his friend, he turned towards him and smiled upon him in his place.

When Carol leaves Eton the friendship is able to flourish again, free of the conventions of school life and its segregation according to age. The pair are no longer inhibited by the categories of older and younger, swell and nonentity. Tim becomes Carol's link with Eton, writing him splendid letters and, for his benefit, watching sports events he would otherwise not have bothered with. But in the meantime, Tim's father, still cold and unbending but longing jealously for his son's affection, asks Tim to give Carol up. At first Tim refuses, and becomes Carol's confidant in the first important emotional encounter of his (not, of course, of Tim's) life: he has met a girl, Violet. But the friends are being pulled apart, Tim by his father, Carol by Violet, both jealous of the friendship, and Tim falls seriously ill. In an effort to save Carol's relationship with Violet, Tim decides to give his friend up and Carol, who has never realised the depth of Tim's feelings, simply thinks Tim has grown tired of him. Tim's illness ('partly mental', according to his doctor) grows worse and when his father fetches him home from Eton, he is dying. Throughout the summer he waits for death and Carol. Understanding at last, his father suggests writing to him. When Carol comes, Tim explains why he gave him up, the pair are reconciled, and Tim waits – happily – for death.

Even in its own day *Tim* was thought sentimental. Even A. C. Benson, a close friend of Sturgis's, wrote: '*Tim* is an interesting book but reflects rather an abnormal point of view.' Elsewhere he said that the book 'hardly does him justice, owing to its preponderance of sentiment.' Sentimental to the point of hilarity it may be, but it is not unattractive. Its set pieces are visually vivid, its images suggesting others, as happens in the cinema. Carol's first appearance before the dazzled, injured Tim, an 'angel' to the child just recovering his senses, suggests other 'angelic' moments throughout the book and is an appropriate image since Tim is to die young; the deathbed scene, with its kiss between the friends, echoes the earlier scene in which Tim, as a child, was able without self-consciousness to ask for a goodbye kiss as he lay ill in bed. Was Sturgis perhaps influenced by hearing about Benson's dead schoolboy brother Martin?

An interesting psychological situation – unexplored, as it turns out, by Sturgis, but surely the compressed theme for a novel on its own – is Tim's father's feeling for Carol, the ideal boy he imagines to be, and for a moment loves as, his own son, who is then cruelly withdrawn and becomes an object of hatred, or at least rejection. At Tim's deathbed the two are reconciled and urged by Tim to love each other. One does not know (did Sturgis?) whether they do, or may come to do so. Sturgis was inclined to write half-novels, full of undeveloped good ideas. Later, in *Belchamber*, he wrote a novel about a man's devotion to a baby – his wife's, not his; yet officially his heir. Henry James criticised it severely to Sturgis himself and, in speaking to Benson, even more sternly called it 'a mere passage, a mere antechamber . . . [leading] to nothing.' As Leon Edel puts it, this was another instance among many of the Master's 'weighty foot treading on tender toes'.

3 *No being, perchance, is so distinct, none so beautiful or attractive as a noble English boy* J. E. C. Welldon

Welldon's *Gerald Eversley's Friendship* has achieved a little posthumous fame. Firstly, because of its badness, and secondly, because its author was no unknown hack when he wrote it, but headmaster of Harrow. Hugh Kingsmill took it as a parable of the public schools' experience during the second half of the nineteenth century, of the way in which brawn, beauty and birth superseded brains and virtue as the desirable qualities in life, above all the way in which the athletic had totally ousted the intellectual in the schools' esteem. Wodehouse took it for weepy rubbish, but since he got the plot completely wrong his knowledge of it seems to have been vague. Others mention it as a kind of sub-*Eric*, a mish-mash of pious nonsense. It gets my vote for the worst of the seriously intentioned school stories because there is nothing appealing about its badness. *Tim* is sentimental, as everyone has said, but pleasantly so; *Eric* is overheated and often absurd but dramatic and fiery; *The Hill* is snobbish and silly but enormously readable, and in its tremulous way dramatic too. But Welldon's book has almost nothing in its favour, so I will deal with it briefly. That he wrote so feebly, expressed himself so mawkishly, and understood human nature so little that he failed to realise how much his boys would laugh when they read him is strange when you consider his eminence at the time of its publication. He subtitled what can accurately be called his farrago of nonsense 'a study in real life'.

The story concerns two boys who arrive at St Anselm's, a great public school, together – Gerald Eversley, thin, pale, stooping, bespectacled, nervous, and sent on a scholarship; a poor clergyman's son with eight stepsisters younger than himself and a dreadful stepmother who is clearly, we are shown, no lady; and Harry Venniker, son and heir of a peer, from a 'stately ancestral seat and a house in Grosvenor Square', rich, handsome, confident,

> a splendid animal, healthy, vigorous, proud, elate . . . a type of generous, healthy English boyhood . . . lithe and stalwart, whose bright complexion and soft blue eyes were passports to favour, even without the radiant smile that played now and again, like a wandering sunbeam, on his mobile features.

With his dingy background and 'solitary sheltered life', what chance has poor clever Gerald when compared with this worldly paragon? Still, Harry befriends him and they move up the school together, Harry a blood almost from the start and Gerald a swot till the very last day:

> There had arisen in Gerald's mind a passionate admiration, a sentiment akin to hero-worship, for the boy, his inferior in intellect, but so brilliant, so

prominent in the ways of school life . . . To be near him was a delight. To be parted from him was a bereavement . . . To Gerald, Harry Venniker was all in all.

After many ups and downs, including a near-mortal illness (Harry's) and several religious crises (Gerald's), Gerald's love, with a noticeable drop in the emotional temperature, is transferred to Harry's sister Ethel, who dies three weeks before the wedding. Harry saves Gerald from jumping into the ancestral lake, and thirty years later we meet him again, still unmarried, still wearing a locket with Ethel's portrait in it. If the atmosphere of the book had had its way, the portrait in the locket would surely be Harry's; for, as Welldon puts it, 'No being, perchance, is so distinct, none so beautiful or attractive as a noble English boy,' and all that happens in the story illustrates this ingenuously expressed belief.

Everything is weighted in Harry's favour, yet the standards by which the two boys are judged are totally worldly and external. Looks, smartness and assurance are what count, and from descriptions of the fathers we know what their sons can expect. Lord Venniker is 'tall and strongly built', with 'the indescribably athletic air of an English country gentleman . . . showing easy temper, ample fortune and good breeding'. Of Mr Eversley we are told that 'his coat was a little threadbare at the elbow, and his clerical hat a little soiled about the brim'. When Lord Venniker gives his son advice at the start of his public-school career, it is clear that Squire Brown's views have not changed in half a century. 'You've not got to earn your living, you know, so you need not work your eyes out; I'd much rather you got into the Eleven,' he tells Harry; 'but do your duty like a Christian; don't swear, don't cheat, don't . . .' Here he runs out of prohibitions. 'Whatever you do,' he goes on, 'don't do anything unworthy of a gentleman – and a Venniker.' Gerald, with every moral and intellectual quality, gets nowhere at all in his early days at school, and without Harry's protection would be bullied and browbeaten. When the new boys are lined up and, as in a slave market, fags are chosen by the senior boys, presumably on their looks, Harry is picked by the captain of the house and Gerald is left humiliatingly unchosen. Thought 'awfully clever' but 'a dreadful sap', he is accused of sneaking, stealing an exam paper, cheating his way to academic success; as an outsider, he has no chance; for, as Welldon puts it, 'of the achievements of the intellect, if they stand alone, public school opinion is still, as it has always been, slightly contemptuous. But strength, speed, athletic skill, quickness of eye and hand,' he goes on, 'still command universal applause.' What is strange is not so much that he says this – obviously it was true – but that he seems, from the tone of the story and his whole attitude, to approve of it. What can two writers who were schoolboys under him, Churchill and Galsworthy, have thought of his preposterous school story, if they ever read it?

4 *You smiled at me, Caesar. It warmed me through and through*

H. A. Vachell

Horace Annesley Vachell wrote popular adult novels, one of which, *Brothers*, is about three men in love with the one girl. His school story, *The Hill*, is about two boys in love with the one boy. Both are 'romances' about a long amorous struggle that lasts for years and ends in death. Change a few names and circumstances in *The Hill*, shuffle the sexes, and you have the pattern of the melodramatic love-story of the day – a tale of frustration, jealousy, overtures, rejections, admissions, swappings, fulfilment; a tormenting seesaw of feeling as the beloved is lost or won; finally (just as happens in *Brothers*) lost physically in death but won spiritually in reconciliation. In *Brothers*, as someone puts it in the very last line, 'Betty died in order that the three men who loved her might live.' In *The Hill* the beloved dies because nothing can come of the love between the pair, an 'absolute' devotion like the hero's having no respectable outlet, as Vachell must have sensed, even if he did not admit it. And so, as the preacher puts it in the school chapel when the news of the beloved's death reaches Harrow,

> Better death, a thousand times, than the gradual decay of mind and spirit; better death than faithlessness, indifference and uncleanness. To you who are leaving Harrow, poised for flight into the great world of which this school is the microcosm, I commend the memory of Henry Desmond. It stands in our records for all we venerate and strive for: loyalty, honour, purity, strenuousness, and faithfulness in friendship.

Vachell was old-fashioned enough to be unselfconscious about the romantic pattern of *The Hill* and even sub-titled it 'A Romance of Friendship'. By the standards of 1905 he was, in fact, highly old-fashioned. Though his liking for the furbelows of rich living and the purple prose that goes with it are clearly Edwardian, his straightforward, unironic view of motive and feeling seems to come from several decades back, and he was in any case writing about Harrow thirty years earlier. Two attitudes run through *The Hill*, which might seem mutually exclusive but manage an uneasy coexistence: one of flaming romanticism, the other of flagrant snobbery. Sometimes one is in the ascendant, sometimes the other. And yet, for all Vachell's sentimentality, often verging on the maudlin, for all his exaggerations and even his psychological mistakes, he has a talent for description, for the vivid portrayal not of character, exactly, but of personality, of presence. This, I think, is what made *The Hill* so popular in its day, so well remembered for years. People still mention it with enthusiasm, when school stories are discussed. Its patterns, too, were recognisable and reassuring, even though readers may not have noticed that their familiarity came, quite clearly, from heterosexual love stories.

Its hero, John Verney, whose first recorded word in the book is 'Ra-ther' and who says hardly anything livelier throughout it, is stolid, dependable, husbandly, with an impeccable country-house background – though not too grand a one. Just as the school hero is not as a rule too tall or too handsome (whereas the beloved, or even the anti-hero, may be as tall or as handsome as you please), so the hero's circumstances, in Vachell as in nearly every other school story, are fair-to-middling in comparison with those of the rest. Central to John's life at Harrow is his friendship with Harry Desmond, known as Caesar because his second name is Julius, and his enmity with the Demon, his rival for Caesar's affections. John is all that a hero should be, less sunny and smiling than his idol but with finer qualities – above all, single-mindedness in love. Throughout their years at Harrow he never swerves from his initial infatuation, in spite of the claims of the prettiest, most girlish boy imaginable, the son of a duke. Caesar is much more magnetic than John: he affects his surroundings. Vachell describes him when he first appears as

> a curly-headed young gentleman of wonderfully prepossessing appearance, from whom emanated an air, an atmosphere of enjoyment that diffused itself. The bricks of the school buildings seemed redder and warmer, as if they were basking in his sunny smile.

The Demon* is fascinating too, but in a more sinister way. His name is Reginald Scaife, and Vachell describes him as being 'the most remarkable boy at Harrow, the Admirable Crichton who appears now and then in every decade'; by the last summer of his Harrow days 'Captain and epitome of the brains and muscle of the Eleven [who] had grown into a powerful man, with the mind, the tastes, the passions of manhood.' It is on this adult quality in Scaife – something quite unlike the approved 'manliness' – that Vachell dwells, with disapproval yet with interest.

* The Demon was said to be based on a boy called Vibart who, at the Eton and Harrow match in 1900, an occasion for anger, rioting and uproar, burst into the fight between the rival schools and cut open the face of one of the Etonians; who according to Shane Leslie, 'had to have his cheek sewn up with red meat-plaster'.

> [He] looked about a year older than John, but he had the air and manners of a man of the world – or so John thought. Also, he was very good-looking, handsomer than Desmond, and in striking contrast to that smiling, genial youth, being dark, almost swarthy of complexion, with strongly marked features.

Elsewhere we hear of his 'red, too-full lips', his 'rather coarse hands and feet'; yet even John, who comes to hate him, is 'captivated by his amazing grace, good looks and audacity.'

The Eton and Harrow match, at which he captains Harrow, sees him at the height of his glory. As he draws on his gloves to bat (Vachell leaps suddenly into an excited present tense)

> thousands of men and as many women are staring at his face and figure . . . Upon his face . . . the consciousness of power . . . As he warms to his work, he seems to expand. It is a Colossus batting, not a Harrow boy . . . Scaife has been transformed into a tremendous human machine, inexorably cutting and slicing, pulling and drawing – the embodied symbol of force, ruthlessly applied, indefatigable, omnipotent . . . Upon the tops of the coaches countesses, duchesses, ay, princesses – are cheering like fourth-form boys.

This mixture of lush prose and luscious living, suggesting strawberries and champagne for breakfast every day of the week, goes well with the voluptuous plot. Good but (as even the book's best friends' admit) dull John and the wicked, brilliant, reckless Demon, with his tremendous presence and sense of 'outsideness' – low birth and a disreputable background – struggle for the affections and finally for the soul of charming, lightweight Caesar. This is the central triangle; but a further emotional interest is provided by the girlish Fluff, Lord Esmé Kinloch of the 'delicately tinted face' and 'red quivering mouth'. 'John seemed to attract young Kinloch almost as magnetically as he himself was attracted to Caesar,' we hear. Fluff provides not only uncritical worship and a feminine personality but a home life of dazzling grandeur, a ducal carriage at Lord's, and a string of arrogant Etonian brothers with exotic names like Cosmo and Strathpeffer.

In the three school love stories I have looked at, the beloved is superior, in popular esteem, to the lover. In *The Hill*, as in the other two, he is a sportsman and a blood, charming, popular, sought after and above all handsome; while the lover is a much quieter figure, dogged, hard-working, unathletic, and not good-looking. *The Hill* varies the pattern by having a rival – almost a full-scale villain – who not only seeks the beloved's affections but almost takes over the reader's main interest. Scaife is known as the Demon because of his demonic personality, and today he might be called a super-cad; stylishly wicked and enticingly adult, he has a whiff, social as well as moral, of the great unknown outside world; social, because Scaife's caddishness is derived directly from the fact that his father is a self-made man, that his grandfather was a navvy. As soon as John hears these shocking facts, he understands why the Demon has 'no soul'.

For Vachell is not just the most misty-eyed of school-story writers, liable to be swept away by his own characters, but far and away the most snobbish. His snobbery is such that everything (every moral value, above all) is judged in relation to birth, pedigree, gentility. And it is of the bland, unblushing sort: quite simply, he loves a lord, and with the candour of a character from *The Young Visiters* ('I am very fond of fresh air and royalties'). The social life of his boys, all of it on the highest level, seems to have inspired N. Molesworth's view of school stories: 'Cads have always a grandmother who is the DUCHESS of BLANK hem hem. They are inclined to cheat at conkers having baked them for 300 years in the ancestral ovens.' Cads are not ducal in *The Hill*, though: an ancestral oven guarantees that you will win in the end at conkers or anything else, whatever the odds. To be a cad you must be lowly born. The lesser caddishness of a minor character, Beaumont-Greene, is derived from his family's occupation, which is slightly less lowly than Scaife's but still in Vachell's opinion pretty despicable: Beaumont-Greene's father has 'accumulated a large fortune in what was advertised in most of the public prints as the "Imperishable, Seamless, Whaleskin Boot",' and Vachell never misses a chance of sneering at this poor piece of footwear.

Vachell sees everything that happens at school as man-sized, fully formed, important not as preparation or training for life but *in itself*, in an ultimate, objective way. Harrow he sees as characterised by 'strenuousness and sentiment' – unobjectionable qualities in themselves but fatally misapplied when used by an adult to romanticise non-adult pursuits, in a world of boys. He appears to see his schoolboys not as adolescents but as equals, to envisage them without irony as heroic creatures engaged in glorious pursuits of almost national importance which are almost as far-reaching as adult activity (the fate of a school cricket match is likened to the fall of a government, or even exceeds it in importance: the cabinet minister cares *more* for what is happening at Lord's than for what is going on in the Cabinet). At the same time they seem like children rather than adolescents in the sense that they are sexless, incurious, cherubic, 'innocent', never having emerged from the pretty ways of childhood into the moody (never mind the sensual) ways of adolescence (except, that is, for the dreaded Scaife, and it is this – his masculinity as opposed to the good boys' manliness – that Vachell sees as a threat, but also as an attraction). A child perfectly in tune with his elders is credible: the 'nice' child who has been loved and given confidence. But the adolescent is finding his own music and almost invariably, and healthily, is out of tune with his elders' world and ideas.

Not Vachell's, though. His boys have no conflicts with their elders, no criticisms to make of distinguished visitors, no boredom or embarrassment or shuffling of feet during speeches or sermons supposedly expressing their views. Never do they cease to admire, be proud of, want to follow in the steps of their elders, to wave the flag and sing the school songs, quite straight, without blushing. Proudly, without any of the normal pinkness or spottiness of their age, they show their families round, introduce them to their friends, as unselfconscious as children or as adults, who have either never been through the pink and spotty stage or have outgrown it and are socially quite at ease. In every way they do what adults expect of them. When Caesar's father, the Cabinet Minister, asks John to work for him, John delightedly agrees (no question of any other ambitions, or of his political views). Caesar goes off to the Boer War in a flurry of patriotic excitement, ignorant of the issues and ready to accept whatever he is told. Nothing happens to disillusion him about war in general or that war in particular, and on the night he is killed – instantly, of course, presumably without pain – he writes to John:

> Over the veldt the stars are shining. It's so light that I can make out the hill on which, I hope, our flag will be waving within a few hours. The sight of this hill brings back our Hill . . . I have the absurd conviction strong in me that, tomorrow, I shall get up the hill here faster and easier than the other fellows because you and I have so often run up our Hill together.

This is pure Newbolt, linking school and battle, honour and sport.

Everything about Harrow strikes Vachell's boys in an almost mystical way, with a sense of awe and wonder. Vachell writes of John on his arrival:

> The boy glanced eagerly, ardently, up and down the panels. Ah, yes, here was his father's name, and here – his uncle's. And then out of the dull, finely grained oak, shone other names familiar to all who love the Hill and its traditions. John's heart grew warm again with pride . . . They were *Old Harrovians*.

Arnold Lunn's boys at Harrow feel no such awe. 'Who's that dowdy old gentleman there?', 'Who's that blighter with the tie?' they ask in *The Harrovians*, loud enough to be heard. Vachell's feel the same sort of awe for their friends' relations. 'John's eyes were popping out of his face,' Vachell says when his hero first sees Caesar's father. 'He had never seen any man like this resplendent, stately personage, smiling and nodding to the biggest fellows in the school.' It hardly seems the sort of figure to attract a boy's admiration, but John has all the right social reactions, including unlimited admiration for the official objects of it, Vachell-style – dukes, Cabinet ministers, bloods. Occasionally Vachell – and with him even John – is carried away by the swarthy, illicit attractions of the Demon, and the romantic outsider seems to be winning; but social glamour wins, as a rule, and with it go all the respectable and responsible virtues.

The Hill, as I have said, is a love story in the ordinary sense of the term, though Vachell preferred to call it a Romance. The Demon sneeringly calls John Jonathan, and Caesar affectionately takes up the idea. John's feelings are expressed at a Harrow concert, when the Harrow songs are sung and John himself sings a solo (for sheer religiosity it can be compared to a scene in the chapel):

John was singing like a lark, with a lark's spontaneous delight in singing, with an ease and self-abandonment which charmed eye almost as much as ear. Higher and higher rose the clear, sexless notes, till two of them met and mingled in a triumphant trill . . . At that moment Desmond loved the singer – the singer who called to him out of heaven, who summoned his friend to join him . . . John's eyes, which ascended, like his voice . . . met joyfully the eyes of Desmond. At last he was singing to his friend – *and his friend knew it.* John saw Desmond's radiant smile, and across that ocean of faces he smiled back. Then, knowing that he was nearer to his friend than he had ever been before, he gathered together his energies for the last line of the song . . . John had to sing three notes unsupported. He was smiling and staring at Desmond.

After the singing Desmond visits John:

'I felt odd when you were singing – quite weepsy, you know. You like me, old Jonathan, don't you?'

'Awfully,' said John.

'Why did you look at me when you sang the last verse? Did you know that you were looking at me?'

'Yes.'

'You looked at me because – well, because – bar chaff – you – liked – me?'

'Yes.'

'You – you like me better than any other fellow in the school?'

'Yes; better than any other fellow in the world.'

'Is it possible?'

'I have always felt the same since – yes – since the very first minute I saw you.'

'How rum! I've forgotten just where we did meet – for the first time.'

'I shall never forget,' said John, in the same slow, deliberate fashion, never taking his eyes from Desmond's face. Ever since he had sung, he had known that this moment was coming. 'I shall never forget it,' he repeated – 'never . . . You smiled at me, Caesar. It warmed me through and through.'

And so it goes on, this all-but-love scene, emotionally charged not just with John's fictional feelings for Caesar but with Vachell's own feelings for Harrow. He writes in *Brothers* of what his hero feels for Harrow:

> All school buildings, even the humblest, had a certain sanctity . . . The ancient Fourth Form room at Harrow was no battered mausoleum of dead names, but a glorious Campus Martius, where Byron, Peel and other immortal youths wrestled with their future, even as Jacob wrestled with the angel.

It is this emotionalism about Harrow and much else that makes Vachell's writing in its soupy way so readable. Humourless, snobbish, absurd as he is, he is nonetheless a good deal more readable than many more intelligent but less intense. His appeal, of course, is the ignoble and finally tooth-rotting one of too much sugar and cream and mush, of over-emphasis and unabashed excess. And logically enough (for at this level of feeling nothing can continue) his story has no development or ending in this world, just a full stop and the suggestion that it is better to die than to live on and (possibly, probably) be corrupted. The Headmaster cries in the chapel pulpit, remembering Caesar:

> To die young, clean, ardent, to die swiftly, in perfect health; to die saving others from death, or worse – disgrace – to die scaling heights; to die and to carry with you into the fuller, ampler life beyond, unattained hopes and aspirations, unembittered memories, all the freshness and gladness of May – is that not cause for joy rather than sorrow?

It sounds like a call for a new slaughter of the innocents. And so in a sense it was, though Vachell cannot have known or consciously meant it.

CHAPTER VIII

The school story as documentary: *The Oppidan, The Harrovians*

The field is still open to the Eton novel . . . Shane Leslie

A wish to put the record straight, to give an *exact* account of public-school life, was obvious in many seriously-intentioned school-story writers. But it was a hopeless wish when every school differed from every other, every house from every other house even in the same school, when fashions, attitudes and standards changed yearly, and even in the same place at the same time the atmosphere and outlook of one 'set' might be totally unfamiliar to another. The outlook, experiences and even expectations in (say) the Woodard Schools* in their early days would be very different from those of the 'great' schools. Human nature being varied and social organisations equally so, it was hardly surprising that even Tom Brown's Rugby was unknown country to some who had been his contemporaries there. Yet writers never ceased to say, from their own experience, '*This* is what public school is like,' and to put it all down in detail, tedious or fascinating, depending on one's view of it.

Most of the seriously-intentioned school stories are documentary to some extent – and the seriously-intentioned are not necessarily the

* Schools founded by the Rev. Nathaniel Woodard for what were then known as the middle classes, divided by him into three grades: 'The first for the sons of clergymen and other gentlemen; the second for the sons of substantial tradesmen, farmers, clerks and others of similar situation; and the third for the sons of petty shopkeepers, skilled mechanics, and others of very small means.' Lancing, Hurstpierpoint and Ardingly are the best-known Woodard schools.

best: the bad seriously-intentioned are duller than the bad lightly-intended, and when you find them at jumble sales it is the first category that is in good order, with a single name in the front, the second that is often falling to pieces with use. They are not merely novels about individuals but examiners and explainers of those individuals' surroundings, about the public pressures on their private selves, with plenty of facts, names and folklore. The 'greater' the school, the more the folklore accumulates around it and the more writers seem anxious to give it to a public they feel sure must be interested. So it is probably not a coincidence that the two most 'documentary' school stories deal in minute detail with life at Eton and Harrow. In them the school customs, slang, whole 'inner' life is presumed to be of interest to outsiders. Those who have been to minor schools do not generally presume that this kind of thing will fascinate outsiders. But there are shelf-loads not of fiction but of memoirs from Etonians and Harrovians, who have always been sure that the smallest particulars of their schools are of far-flung interest; which means that the names and places and special occasions, obscure rituals and arcane behaviour, are familiar from books to those who may have had no connection at all with the schools.

Eton has not done as well in fiction as its frequent appearance in memoirs might lead one to expect. Its two best fictional appearances are anonymous and adult: in Henry Green's *Pack my Bag* and Anthony Powell's *A Question of Upbringing* (the first of the *Dance to the Music of Time* sequence), where it is simply 'school' to the narrator, recognisable and undisguised but also unnamed.

Earlier stories from Eton exist, but few of them are memorable. *Ned Locksley, the Etonian*, a long anonymous novel from the 1860s, sounds like a school story but in fact merely shows by its title how Eton persists throughout a man's life; for although it sends its hero to Eton for a few pages at the beginning, it soon becomes an ordinary Victorian story of love, travel, war, adventure and high life. *The Etonian* by Alice and Claude Askew, prolific joint writers of popular novels, appeared soon after the turn of the century, a Vachell-like novel of high-minded romance with the hero's son at Eton rather than any particularly Etonian point to make. *Playing Fields,* by Eric Parker, appeared in 1922, one of those sadly forgotten books which are not without talent but somehow lack individuality, presence, or some other vital, memorable ingredient. Martin Wardon, an architect's son, goes to Eton as a King's Scholar, unprepared for the Oppidans' yells of 'Rotten tug! Dirty tug!' His progress through the school is described in detail, with every place-name, custom, pastime, expression, legend and piece of folk-lore.

Decent Fellows by John Heygate* takes a much more interesting look at Eton around the end of the First World War and the early twenties. It is dedicated to Henry Williamson, and was first published in 1930 by Gollancz, both of which suggest that something unexpected may be found in it. Mild though it now seems, like most once-shocking books, it nonetheless created some stir when first published and bookshops in Eton, I have been told by someone who, an Eton boy then, remembers the fuss and shock, refused to stock it. Probably the tone, rather than any particular incidents, was thought offensive, or at least alarming to authority and the status quo. A subterranean weariness and disgust – at times almost violent, and always extremely uncosy – comes across in a laconic style, with staccato sentences and throwaway descriptions, reeking of sour adolescence, ambiguous attitudes and momentary regrets, sharp retorts and sensual moments.

Denis, the hero, after three miserable years at Eton, is beginning to enjoy life and chucks his best friend Robin – his one-and-only, inseparable friend since he arrived – in order to 'mess' with an earl's son, Peter Ockley, Denis's family is poor by Eton standards and cannot afford to keep up with Peter's family, the Peritons; cannot even manage to send Denis to Scotland when they ask him to stay, and removes him from Eton, to send him to a crammers, when he fails to get the Kings scholarship he needs if he is to go to Cambridge. After which, without explanation, Denis writes rather shortly to Peter's mother refusing another much-wanted invitation to stay in London. The theme of snobbery – of the glamour of rank and riches yet of Denis's self-disgust because he finds them glamorous – runs through the story; which also touches on homosexual relationships at school, though not in any detail, and is highly exact on boy–girl friendships, chat among the young, social attitudes in general at the time. As a novel of character it is far more interesting than *The Oppidan,* but, presumably because the facts and folklore did not interest Heygate, it lacks *The Oppidan*'s documentary exactness.

Three years later Julian Hall's *The Senior Commoner,* which is clearly about Eton (called Ayrton College), used a similar staccato technique but less successfully. Heygate at times almost approaches Henry Green but Hall, though he has something of the same atmosphere of stylised flipness (as much a product of the time as of individual taste or mood), with similarly short sentences and an abrupt, laconic manner, has much less talent and force. As a documentary novel, his book has some interest. We are told all about 'Mob' (pre-

* Son of an Eton housemaster, brother of Elizabeth Heygate who wrote *A Girl at Eton*, he married, as his first wife, Evelyn Waugh's first wife, Evelyn. See Alec Waugh's *My Brother Evelyn and Other Profiles* (1967).

sumably Pop), about waistcoats and rolled umbrellas, privileges and peculiarities, visits from Middle-Eastern monarchs, orders of precedence among boys; once again it is presumed that the detail of Etonian life must fascinate outsiders.

But the leading Etonian school story, in the ordinary sense of the term, appeared in the early twenties, when Sir Shane Leslie wrote: 'The field is still open to the Eton novel . . . It was, and is, Eton's misfortune to miss description from a great literary artist.' His attempt to fill the gap is deliberately documentary, and *The Oppidan* is to Eton what Lunn's *The Harrovians*, seven years earlier, was to Harrow.

2 *The Eton spirit . . . all her athletic grace and speed, social contempt, self-centred freemasonry* A. C. Benson

Although there are plenty of differences between *The Oppidan* and *The Harrovian,* there are some odd similarities. Both heroes are called Peter, both are orphans, brought up in single-child loneliness by remote and/or unloved guardian uncles; both have fathers who, for the time and circumstances, had exotic occupations, Leslie's Peter's being an archaeologist, who died mysteriously in Egypt, Lunn's Peter's a mountaineer. Both boys are clever and hardworking and exert whatever influence they have through brains, not brawn; though both are well aware that brawn – athletic prowess, in other words – is much more desirable, particularly if it is combined with good looks and a grand background. Both know, in other words, that they will never make the grade as successful products of their school (swells or bloods), and a retrospective sadness, even bitterness, colours their view of things for that reason.

The Oppidan was written in 1922, but its subject is Eton at the turn of the century, when its author was there. In 1969 Leslie wrote a new preface to a new edition and gave the real names of many of the characters in it, among them A. C. Benson, who was a master in his time, and Ronald Knox, a boy contemporary. His preface to the first edition deals with school stories as a genre:

> In modern times all specialised spheres of life become subject to the novelist . . . Within the little world of England there are worlds within worlds, minute in time, unique in space. But to those who inhabit them they are the world, and to those who pass from them they remain sacred. The Eton world is such.

And, he maintained, since 'there could be nothing duller than a school novel true to life' and 'school life can be totally monotonous . . . the school novelist finds it necessary to caricature the worthy masters and to exaggerate the unworthy boys'; and also to telescope events, improvise plots and dramatise and intensify whatever there is to build on.

In this first preface Leslie shows for the first time, quite openly, the snobbery and anti-semitism that mar what otherwise, superficially, might seem an amiable novel. These take the socially naive brand of snobbery that consists in vehement opposition to everything un-English, a curious attitude from an Irishman with an American mother. Leslie's particular forms of snobbery are socially naive. It is not only Jews he objects to finding at Eton, but Catholics and what he calls 'Continentals.' Now, 'continental' boys at Eton around 1900 would be likely to belong to families more aristocratic than those of most Etonians, and the old Catholic families might reasonably be thought to belong to a pre-Tudor aristocracy, so could hardly be objected to on social grounds. What he calls the 'wealthy' Leslie also despises: presumably he means the *merely* rich, and would not turn down a duke on the grounds of his possessions.

Towards Jews, his attitude is plainly unpleasant. Anti-semitism was so widespread in this country in 1922, and expressed so openly in fiction, that it is not surprising to find it here. What is strange is that Leslie should not have been ashamed of it by 1969, when *The Oppidan* was reprinted, and should not only have allowed the anti-semitic sneers in the main text to remain, but have let the 1922 preface be included as well. Of the early years of the century he writes:

> The fine old yeoman and county family names outdating the Peerage grew scarce in the School Lists, while, unfortunately, financial finesse and Semitic snobbery have too often filled their place. It was perhaps inevitable that millionaires and magnates of industry, the social adventures, Orientals, and Continentals, should wish their offspring to share the enviable prestige built up by landed and leisured gentry . . . the pious hope may be permitted that Eton will one day prefer the children of poor tradesmen, and old-fashioned squires as of yore to Jews, who are ashamed of their race, or Catholics, who are ashamed of their own Schools.

Had Eton suddenly been crowded with 'poor tradesmen's' sons, Leslie's comments would have been worth hearing.

Ugly jibes also speckle the main text, too many to quote at length. Here are a few:

> Financial stability was only restored by the sons of an Indian Prince and of a Jewish Alderman then in the running for the London Mayoralty, whose mother's accent was large enough to attract an admiring crowd of Eton minnows during her visits to her son. The Alderman provided viands which were insultingly accepted by his son's fag masters;

> Mr Munfort . . . understood that good wine and good blood and, for that matter, a good House at Eton went together. Not that he was a snob . . . Mr

> Munfort had no room in his House for the nicest Jews or the best-born cosmopolites . . . An Indian Prince he could just abide as an Imperial curiosity. On the whole, he rejected aliens in religion or race.

And so on, nastily. Lunn has snobbish and Jew-baiting remarks in his school stories but does not appear to approve of them himself. He reports them (tastelessly, to modern taste) when others use them, whereas Leslie uses his in the narrative, which is his own view of things; he uses them with approval, as part of his build-up of approved characters. Mr Munfort's choice of excellence (in wine, in scholarship, in boys) involves a rejection of Jews and 'aliens' and Leslie clearly approves of it. Maxse's house ('derisively called "the Synagogue",' Leslie says) is obviously the worst of all the houses not just in Mr Munfort's opinion but in Leslie's.

The Oppidan not only shows approval of such attitudes, over and over again, but is coloured throughout by an unblushing worldliness. *The Hill* is *snobbish* in its affection for dukes and the old Harrovian families; but snobbishness is different from worldliness, more innocently silly, less hurtful and vicious. Much though he loves high living, Vachell never suggests that it is quite in order to drop your oldest friend if a duke comes along to replace him; whereas Leslie suggests that it is normal, natural, scarcely regrettable and certainly understandable to drop a close friend suddenly and completely when others, grander and socially better value, turn up. When Peter's best friend Socston, with whom he has 'messed' since their arrival together, achieves athletic success and is noticed by the school swells he drops Peter, gradually at first ('a slight but perceptible gulf already separated him from Peter. He had answered to the only test by which boy can judge boy, that of public athletic contest against his peers'), then, in direct proportion to his success, abruptly and finally ('His importance was immeasurable. He never spoke to Peter again in this world'). For this, Peter suffers. Cory's translation of the dirge for Heraclitus reminds him of his lost friendship. 'We were close friends at the beginning, and when he had no use for my friendship, I must have come to love him,' he tells a kindly master. 'Never mind,' the master says, with insensitive cheeriness. 'But I do mind,' says Peter, 'and I always will mind.' That Socston's behaviour is humanly horrible is never suggested, and he himself sees no reason to hide or even fudge it. When the Captain of the Boats greets him, Peter, who is walking with him, offers to move on. 'Yes, suppose you move on,' Socston says, and later returns to the house 'flushed with pride'. 'The swell school had seen his social rise,' says Leslie, 'and he took care that everyone in Morley's found out by the simple process of eschewing all conversation for forty-eight hours. "Gratters," murmured Peter. Absorbed in his future, Socston nodded and walked past.'

Leslie said that the novelist must 'exaggerate the unworthy boys'. But there is nonetheless a chilling acceptance that life, Etonian life anyway, is like that, and that Socston's values are normal ones. Admittedly he gets his deserts by being expelled (ironically, on account of Peter's sister), but he leaves in triumph, in a fly covered in flowers, rice and confetti, mobbed by dozens of cheering boys, and his sacking seems more like the climax of a successful career than an ignominious end to it. Other characters are arrogant with, it would seem, Leslie's approval, or at least to his amusement. For instance:

The bourgeois and the wealthy he [Mr Munford] could smell out like a false quantity, and he simply declined to enter their progeny in his book.

Or:

Socston's father had always thought the 'Varsity a poor place compared to Eton, and only endurable on account of the Old Etonians to be found in select and disgusted groups. 'Wait till you go there,' he informed his son, 'and have to herd with Harrow and Old Slops and Bedford Grammar.'*

Even in the fervour of Mafeking Night, when the spectators

devoted their remarks to compliment the silent boys marching through the streets, 'Three cheers for Florit [*sic*] Etona! Look at the rising generation, young 'eroes all o' them. Gawd bless them!' 'Cads all be damned!' was young Eton's comment.

Disgust is not too strong a word for the Etonians' attitude (according to Leslie, at least) to the non-Etonian world, and all the outside

* Like other writers of school stories, Leslie went on to at least one university novel. *The Cantab* (1926) takes a young man to King's College, Cambridge with similarly lively detail. The hero's Etonian brother, Julius, embodies many of Leslie's ideas, more explicitly expressed than they were in *The Oppidan*. 'Julius had felt the stress and strain of puberty as much as his keenness of body and health of mind permitted. He was vaguely satisfied by the adoration of his fags and hero-worshippers. Subconsciously their pink downless faces and baby blue eyes represented the other sex to him, and he allowed romance to colour his patronage. It flattered him to keep an album with the photograph of every pretty boy in the school . . . He did not feel complete in the eyes of the school without a swarm of good-looking satellites, and instinctively he chose them for their good looks, not caring if there was another criterion. Boys who came under his influence became smarter in their dress and cleaner of face and hands. They took themselves more seriously, and learnt that there was a code for gentlemen: that the first thing in life was to play games well and the second commandment was likewise. There was a third commandment to be good-looking . . . Julius was beyond instruction on any intellectual point. *Divus Julius!* Six foot, pure bronze, blue eyes, and a heart full of selfishness and honour.'

world's suspicion of the public schools' social exclusiveness is fully justified in *The Oppidan*. A. C. Benson, who appears as a housemaster, Mr Christopher, likes the words of 'The Eton Boating Song'. 'I do not say it is poetry,' he says, 'but it throws the Eton spirit into song, all her athletic grace and speed, social contempt, self-centred freemasonry.' This seems to be said with approval and affection, and Leslie's own brand of social contempt is not a pretty sight on the page.

3 *A comprehensive primer of information, a chronicle of historical detail, an architectural summary, and a treasury of tradition*

A reviewer

But there are prettier and much more intelligent things about *The Oppidan*. Peter, for one. He is a pleasant young hero, ingenuous, sweet-natured, and although on the first page we hear that he has 'dropped his nurse in Praed Street, to avoid any appearance of disgraceful company' on the platform at Paddington when he first takes the train to Eton, he is prepared to make a friend of a Colleger, the brilliant Ullathorne* (Knox), although he starts off with curious ideas about Collegers. He and three other boys arrive at Eton together. They identify themselves and then, Leslie writes:

> the fourth confessed with much shame that he was not an Oppidan, hardly a real Etonian, only a Colleger, and was not going to any House. His name was Ullathorne and he had taken a scholarship the previous year. Though he was excused the entrance examination, and passed direct into Fifth Form, all three felt that he was an object of intense pity.

When he sees the Collegers' dining room, Peter says to one of the masters, 'Do [they] really eat here? I thought they only had the remains of the food from the Oppidan Houses.' This is a sly joke of Leslie's, of course, but not too unbelievable if Eton was then at all like his picture of it. Strangely enough, in a 54-page chapter on Eton in his

* This was an odd name for Leslie to choose for his portrait of Ronald Knox (in the 1969 edition he acknowledged that it was a direct portrait), because it is that of an old north-country Catholic family, and the fictional Ullathorne is not a Catholic. Perhaps Leslie was deliberately making a 'Catholic' reference, since he wrote a long introduction to the autobiography of the Catholic Archbishop Ullathorne (the original draft was first published in 1941, although it was written for private circulation in 1868 and had appeared already in a number of bowdlerised versions), *From Cabin-boy to Archbishop*. This remarkable man (1806–1889), descendant of Sir Thomas More, prominent figure at the first Vatican Council, and good friend of Newman, was also chaplain at Botany Bay, a campaigner against the transportation of convicts, and widely experienced in the tough conditions of nineteenth-century Australia. Knox became a Catholic in 1922, five years before the publication of *The Oppidan,* and parallels between his conversion and Newman's may have occurred to Leslie.

autobiography[1] Leslie mentions Knox only once and briefly: 'There was one imperturbable little Colleger who always remained at the head of the class: the future Monsignor Ronald Knox, a purveyor of many good detective novels.' (In fact, Knox published only some half dozen.)

There is some pathos about Peter, with no one to love and mother him but the nurse he is ashamed to be seen with. His mother died giving birth to a sister he has never seen and scarcely heard of, a girl rejected rather oddly by his guardian (an uncle, so presumably hers as well) and left to grow up in some sort of international demi-monde ('drifting on the floating wave of white people who drift between the East and West'). Leslie introduces a preposterous sub-plot, in which this sister meets Socston, who has no idea who she is. She gives him half a jade charm found by her father in an Egyptian tomb, the other half of which, exactly matching it, belongs to Peter. Peter's 'dream sister' looks strangely familiar to Socston: 'He knew her and yet could not place her, those blue, rather wistful eyes and the serious, painstaking little mouth'; and he falls instantly in love.

This small diversion has little to do with the central story, though, which follows Peter through several hard-working years at Eton, years crowned with intellectual honours and prizes which do him little good in ways that count. The only time he is approached by the headmaster, thinking, with anxious joy, that he is at last to be spoken to and congratulated on his university exhibition, Dr Warre pauses merely to congratulate Socston on his rowing. In his autobiography, Leslie tells a similar tale of his own schooldays under Warre. 'It was a rare honour,' he writes of an occasion when he was sent to the headmaster.

> . . . The Head also doubted my merit, for when I handed him my two sets of Latin verses immaculately copper-plated on vellum he turned quite gruff. He refused to accept more than one and then insisted that the second copy was a hold-over from the previous half. I had been imagining a splendid scene worthy of the finale of *Eric or Little by Little*. I hoped to hear my headmaster's encomium and to feel the shake of his massive hand and be commended for all my work. It was the only time that I felt like swimming to the surface of the Eton pool. Alas, poor minnow! I was barely noticed and I retreated with choking grief.

A few days later, he adds, 'A blank stare was all I received from the Head on leaving.'[2]

Under Warre's headmastership, athletic success was paramount and intellectual distinction correspondingly undervalued. In this it followed the pattern of other schools and, although Leslie stresses its uniqueness, Eton in *The Oppidan* seems much like other school-story schools in that it is games-mad, ferociously competitive, contemptuous of all other schools, and with revered slang* and customs all its own. So Peter's progress takes him along a path to success parallel to the athletic, noticed by only a few sympathetic masters and a friend or two like Ullathorne. Early in his school career a master tells him that whom the gods love die young, and he longs romantically to die while at Eton. His wish is granted, painlessly: he is found dead, not burned but presumably overcome by fumes, after a fire at his house in the night.†

But his progress, the whole narrative, keeps being halted by slabs of information about the state of things at Eton, the ups and downs of houses, the games played, social customs, reputations, even work. When it first appeared a reviewer called it 'a comprehensive primer of information, a chronicle of historical detail, an architectural summary, and a treasury of tradition.' And so it is. Pretty well everything about the years 1898–1903 seems to be there, including Eton's reaction to public events – the Boer War, Queen Victoria's death and funeral, Mafeking Night – and their effect upon Eton. The fact that it was written twenty years later gave Leslie a certain degree of hindsight (he knew the generation he was writing about would be killed in the First World War), and ought to have given him a sense of the littleness and transience of much that he dealt with. But it does nothing of the sort. Leslie's eye-level throughout is that of an adult still persuaded by the boys' attitudes, still convinced of the importance of what they think important: notice from the swells, for instance, still seems to make him shiver with excitement, not smile with irony.

That the attitudes he deplored in Warre and his predecessors could not last for ever – attitudes he half-deplored, or by implication disapproved of – he did realise. He says at one point (Peter has been called pro-Boer because he reads the *Spectator*):

> Reaction was bound to come against the Philistine spirit prevailing. It was on its way, as a matter of fact, not through the masters but from the boys themselves. The old school of masters were impatient of religious or literary novelty. Warre and Hornby had suppressed anything connected with the Oxford Renaissance. The Head's idea of Heaven was based on a good military band transferred from the walls of Windsor to the celestial Jerusalem . . . They had banished Oscar Browning for his art's sake. Joynes had to leave for his sympathy with the Irish cause. Salt had left as a Humani-

* School slang still awaits its Partridge. It has not, I think, been collected systematically and is fast vanishing, so he/she should come forward soon.

† There was a real fire at Eton in 1903, in which two boys died.

tarian. 'It was the vegetarianism that did it,' had been Hornby's grim farewell. Reaction was certain.

Mr Christopher (A. C. Benson), 'who was a model housemaster', 'had reached the state of open criticism and secret disgust with the athleticism of the school,' Leslie writes. As 'his House was socially the best House at Eton', 'parents competed madly to place their boys at Christopher's'. A contributor to the *Yellow Book*, the author of many books of his own, 'he was the leader of the *literati*, and being approached, he believed, as to his policy should he be made Headmaster of Eton, he had let it be known that he was a reformer' (which clearly went against him). He and other masters at one point discuss Etonian writers, Etonian suicides, Etonian politicians and soldiers, Etonian distinction in every field. As one of the masters says:

> There is more variety in Eton deaths than lives. Etonians die deer-stalking in Scotland, or lion-hunting in Abyssinia. They are drowned in Hawaii, or murdered by Zulus, Afghans or Matabele. They have died riding in Portman Square, steeplechasing, or playing polo in the ends of the world. But all this variety points to one type. If only an Old Etonian sometimes died of absinthe in the Latin Quarter of Paris, or was poisoned as he entered a Papal Conclave, I should feel happier in my pupil-room.

In other chapters we hear of architectural innovations at the end of the nineteenth century, and the boys' preference for the uncomfortable but cosy warrens in which they used to live; about the religious ferments of the time, the link between philistine attitudes in general and philistinism in church practices, not just in the sermons ('My dear brethren, last Sunday I told you all about the Seraphim. This Sunday I will tell you all about the Cherubim'), but in the arrangement of the services and the use of music; about the aesthetic and literary movements of the time and how these seeped down to the boys. And so on and so on. Leslie is an amusing, occasionally even a witty writer, with a sense of irony that goes beyond anything in, say, Vachell. About life at Eton he seems to have total recall and can remember every detail of everyday life with a vividness that makes compelling reading. His potted history of Eton under its various headmasters, through its very varied periods, his portraits of real people under thin disguises or none at all, his often hardly credible but perhaps accurate quotations about aspects of life at Eton or society in general: these are worth having as social history, if nothing else. *The Oppidan* is not so much a novel as a record of an institution at a particular time, in a particular cultural climate.

Quotable comments abound, for the style is lively.

The standing of a House is more affected by its place in the Football Cup than by any other single event,

Leslie writes. Or:

In the Eton pool every fish sports and swims in awe of another minutely bigger or socially distinct.

Or:

Everybody was wildly interested in everybody and everything except in one subject which remained a matter of crushing indifference to the School, the new boys. They could be recognised by their slow, peering motions as they stood about uneasily watching their fellows and ludicrously grateful to anyone who treated them a little better than malodorous lepers.

Or:

It was necessary for the Eton system for the boys to feel, as a Head Master once explained to his King, that there could be nobody greater than himself.

Or:

'Is there nothing worse than a sap [hard worker]?' asked Peter. 'Yes, you might be a Tug [Colleger] and have to wear a beak's gown round your neck.' 'But what is worse still?' asked Peter, desirous to probe the depths of infamy. 'Well, you might be a cad and have to go to Harrow.'

If *The Oppidan* is hardly a novel, it is hardly a boys' book, either. Like *The Harrovians*, it has a misfit for hero, for, like Beetle (whom Leslie would surely have held in hideous contempt), like Gerald Eversley, Tim, and Peter O'Neil in *The Harrovians*, Peter Darley is the well-read, hardworking intellectual in a school of hearties he outshines but longs to be one of. Once again he provides the metaphor Kingsmill saw in *Gerald Eversley's Friendship*, an image of the way the public schools, since their early days of intellectual freedom and promise, had turned full circle against the intellectual life, against freedom of the spirit, to conformity, anti-intellectualism, and terrible competitiveness; and of how even the intellectual and the free-spirited conformed, by longing for approval from the conformists. This imagery is never explicit in Leslie, and was probably not deliberate. He is as much in love with success, with the bloods, with the sheer dazzle of being spoken to by the right people at the right place and time as ever Socston was. What is strange, pathetic, even a little contemptible to a modern reader is the fact that as an adult he still feels the glories of his late adolescence as piercingly as he must have felt them at seventeen.

And yet, in his autobiography, Leslie gives eloquent praise to the more lasting gifts Eton gave him:

But amid many wasted hours and a system which was often ridiculous I attained some of the most precious gifts that any system dares to promise. I learnt the wonder and beauty of the universe, the fascination of science, and the charm and power of literatures. Incredible as it seems, at Eton I learnt to love Greek . . . And I discerned the values and beauty latent in English writing . . . I played no games. I made few friends. I never won a colour, but I found pearls of great price. Eton left me a littérateur, desirous of letters and ready to appreciate the world of books . . . I could never be bored again throughout life. Magical keys had been thrust into my keeping. I bless the old school library. All miseries and loneliness and unpopularity were worth enduring for that.[3]

4 . . . *an unexplored theme which clamoured for translation into prose*

Arnold Lunn

Miseries and loneliness and unpopularity are part – some might say a large part – of *The Harrovians*, by Arnold Lunn,* but Lunn in his autobiography[4] is as anxious as Leslie was in his to balance his fictional portrait of school with his own 'real' feelings about it. It was published when he was twenty-five and was, as he put it 'enthusiastically praised and violently attacked'. Lunn insisted that it was written not as propaganda, but for purely artistic reasons.

I can never remember a time when I felt attracted to any other vocation than that of literature, and it was at the age of sixteen that I decided to write the first realistic school story. So I bought a diary and began to write down the conversation of my little friends . . . I wrote the book because creation is . . . essential to the born writer . . . because I had found an unexplored theme which clamoured for translation into prose . . . The older generation . . . read into it an attack on the school which was never intended. There was not the slightest reason why I should dislike Harrow. My career was not unsuccessful. I ended as a monitor and head of my House . . . And there is nothing in my book to suggest disapproval of Harrow in particular or the public schools in general. The trouble was, of course, that I had kept a careful record of the cynicism of Harrow youth rather than the sentiment of old Harrovians.[5]

The Harrovians (1913) was published only eight years after *The Hill* but seems to belong to a very different world. No wonder: for 'one of the many things which puzzled me in my youth' Lunn wrote, 'was the lack of realism in all the school stories which I read'. Vachell would have thought its characters cads and bounders, yet they apparently fill the same school as his high-minded, high-born lads. Of all the well-known school stories, it is the coolest; 'cool' in the sense of

* Son of Sir Henry Lunn (promoter of skiing, mountaineering and international understanding, founder of the travel agency that still bears his name). Sir Arnold Lunn was a prolific writer, prominent and vehement in controversies political and religious.

unexcited and also detached, knowing, 'smart'. It is hard to compare it with other school stories. Like *The Oppidan* it is a documentary novel, but with much less external detail and much more of its hero's inner life, of his moody outlook and his own temperament's effect on his surroundings. One feels Lunn inside him, as one does not feel Leslie inside *his* Peter.

In attitudes towards school it comes closest, I think, to *Stalky & Co.* In both books the unathletic, intellectual hero, unable to shine in the usual school way, nonetheless plunges into all the rivalries and conflicts of school life and uses his weapons of brain against those of brawn, successfully if not very likably. Peter O'Neil, like Stalky and Co., despises the image of the good schoolboy. Like them, he uses a mixture of ruthlessness and sharp practice to deal with others and has an open delight, high-spirited and unashamed, in settling old scores and seeing the discomfiture of his enemies. He too despises the uncritical acceptance of school *mores*, cheering at house matches, respecting the patriotic guff about the old school; longs for privacy and his own bolt-hole where he can escape from communal life; is too snide, sharp, clever and bouncy to do well officially, but in time gets respect of a kind from both masters and prefects for the sheer success of his tactics. Stalky and Co. show how dangerous it is to cross such boys, who can be avenged in subtle ways. Peter, like them, has a golden touch in dealing with opponents, using legal but secret methods of bringing them down. He fails to 'play the game' in the officially accepted way but has a certain rough morality of his own. Above all he loathes, as they did, adult sentimentalising of the central ideas of school life; but in Kipling anger at such adult ineptness suggests acceptance of the sacredness of these ideas and words, whereas in Lunn contempt merely suggests that they, as well as their upholders, may be ridiculous. When the Jelly-bellied Flag-flapper in *Stalky & Co.* talks of important things like Honour, the boys feel betrayed because it is something they care about. When Peter's aunt in *The Harrovians* carries on about football, or the visiting bishop uses slang and cricketing images, Peter merely despises them for bad form and phoniness, an altogether more light-hearted reason for disgust.

Lunn knew what he would get when he published *The Harrovians*, and made his boys in it forestall criticism. As one of them says:

> Unless you swear you had the time of your life here, people say, 'You were such a tick they booted you, that's why you don't love the old school.'

Or again:

> If anyone says anything against the Public Schools who hasn't been to one, everybody shouts, 'My dear man, what can you know about them? Nobody

but a Public School man can understand the fine old Public School spirit.' And if you have been to one, everybody says, 'You horrid cad, criticising your dear old Alma Mater. Where's your giddy patriotism?'

Four years after the publication of *The Harrovians*, Alec Waugh wrote *The Loom of Youth* and made the school chaplain rant against it in the pulpit, using the same terms that, very soon, were to be used against his own book. 'In the holidays,' he says, rousing the boys from their torpor, 'there appeared, as I am sorry to say, I expect some of you saw, a book pretending to deal with life at one of our largest Public Schools. I say, pretending, because the book contains hardly a word of truth . . .' 'The man's an utter fool,' snorts Gordon, Alec Waugh's hero, afterwards. 'When he is told the truth he won't believe it.' It must have been the general *tone* of *The Harrovians* rather than specific occasions and incidents that offended the strait-laced and the humourless; its brashness and genial send-ups, its questioning of old values and the whole truculent, self-confident, aggressive, enquiring, unsentimental treatment of things. Even the amiable Coke described Lunn as 'foul-smelling' in a letter to Alec Waugh's father.

A passage like this was strong stuff for 1913:

'"British grit," I suppose, the pluck that has made our England what it is' – Manson was gathering steam 'and then you have the blighters who come down and preach about the goodly heritage – Pah! – and what a splendid privilege it is to be a Public School boy, and that we're havin' the time of our little lives. If I thought *that* I'd shoot myself.'

Much more acceptable were the feelings of the hero about to leave school in Desmond Coke's *The Bending of a Twig*:

He must be worthy, now, of Shrewsbury! He must see that what the School gained from his name should be honour, not disgrace! His thoughts flew on through life – life, all so easy! – to success, valued not for itself nor for himself, but for the sake of Shrewsbury!

No wonder Coke's story was popular for years as a supposedly true picture of school. 'There's no doubt: you'll go where the good boys go, Marsh!' the bad boy sneers at the hero, about to leave. Of Lunn's hero, no one could ever say such a thing.

5 *A chiel's amang ye takin' notes, and, faith, he'll prent it . . .*

Robert Burns

There is a little story in *The Harrovians*, no dramatic sequence of events, no pattern of action or long-term conflict of character. It is a series of essays, or of incidents with a point to them, rather than a novel in the ordinary sense. Lunn has things to say about school and about boyhood, and each chapter illustrates these things. He writes unevenly and the narrative sometimes drags, but it is the work of a man who can observe, connect, set trifles in a larger context; and of a mind worth meeting. There are outbreaks of real wit here and there, and throughout the book a growling, often alarming humour; great energy and youthful bounce mixed with a certain adult sententiousness that turns up oddly in the context.

The Harrovians looks at life from an upper-middle-class point of view, certainly not an aristocratic one. Lunn's father was indeed far more 'self-made' than the despised Demon's, having started life – a grocer's son – as a grocer's apprentice, and Lunn and his brother Hugh Kingsmill describe the family's halfway position in Harrow society (they lived locally) between the Mupples (or upper-middle-class) and the Mipples (or mid-middle). Lunn does not suggest that dukes' sons are commonly found at Harrow, or that his boys, like Vachell's, are destined for brilliant futures in the smartest regiments or the Cabinet. A baronet's son with a country-house background who provides game for his friends is unusual enough to produce cupboard love and fawning. Lunn's boys expect to go to university and then into one of the professions, and lack both obvious snobbery and an obvious sympathy for 'the poor'. When the outside world touches theirs, their reaction is more convincing than that of Vachell's boys. John Verney's hero is Shaftesbury, and when he and Desmond come across 'the poor' it is in the dramatic, appealing form of a sick, perhaps dying child, a ragged, starving mother. Lunn's Peter appears at his most attractive to readers, and at the same time wholly convincing, when he grows angry with his school-fellows for calling the working classes 'the great unwashed'* and above all for jeering at a demonstration by a crowd of unemployed men. These men are not picturesque, pathetic and grateful; they are noisy, truculent, and, to the snug schoolboy world, alarming, a threat and a pointer to the future.

Lunn's epigraph is a quotation from Burns, 'A chiel's amang ye takin' notes, and, faith, he'll prent it,' and one of its chapters has at its head Samuel Butler's famous address to the unwary:

> O Schoolmasters – if any of you read this book – bear in mind when any particularly timid, drivelling urchin is brought by his papa into your study, and you treat him with the contempt he deserves – bear in mind that it is exactly in the disguise of such a boy that your future chronicler will appear.

Since Lunn himself had 'taken notes' at Harrow, his comments are a curious mixture of the immediate and the distanced, the childlike and

* Phrase used by various writers, including Thackeray, during the nineteenth century.

the adult. He dedicates it to a schoolfriend, claiming that it was 'based – to the sacrifice of form and cohesion – on a very careful diary which [he] kept as a Harrow boy' and recalling 'the many good things and bad jokes that [they] shared together.' Nothing very exciting happens throughout it, no 'adventure' in the usual schoolboy sense of the word and certainly none of what Vachell in *his* dedication calls 'the episodes of Drinking and Gambling', which abound in *The Hill.* Schoolboy sins of the sort would have seemed to Lunn too childish, as well as too unlikely, to write about; he would have thought them a cliché of fiction, not the stuff of life. But although no raffish *events* take place, the tone of *The Harrovians,* being so much more free-and-easy and more cynical than that of *The Hill,* suggests that Vachell's boys are laughably young both in their sins and in their priggishness about those sins, since everything takes place in a tight, unalterable framework of accepted morals and manners, and sin often appears as an infringement of the social as much as the moral code.

Lunn has a quotation at the beginning of each chapter: three from Machiavelli, two from Samuel Butler, one from Lord Chesterfield, and one which illustrates the rules of bushido, the ethical code of the Samurai. The chapter this heads is called 'More lessons in bushido', which suggests that Lunn thought Samurai-like conduct and responses particularly suited to public-school life: things like the concealment of pain, and the stoicism demanded by every detail of every day. Yet bushido, as seen by Lunn and the Samurai, seems not at all the same thing as the much drearier cult of 'good form'. That was mere convention, a fear of being unlike others, a mixture of self-consciousness, social nervousness, and all kinds of lack of confidence, hardened into rules and fiercely forbidding eccentricity. Lunn's boys care little for that sort of thing, Peter in particular being ready to stick his neck out, to do the odd or even the dislikable thing. This may have been characteristic of Harrow: L. P. Hartley, as I have said, remarked that eccentricity in his day, not very long after Lunn's, was not only tolerated but encouraged. (Eccentricity, of course, like many other abstract words, is subjective, and the kind tolerated in Lunn or Hartley's day was only very relatively eccentric. Social deviation of the sort that is common today would never have been envisaged, still less tolerated, by either the authorities or the boys. The whole question of 'revolution' – the real overturning instincts and ideas – in the public schools in their heyday has hardly been looked at. The efforts of boys like the Romilly brothers* in the thirties seem very mild

* Giles and Esmond Romilly, nephews of Sir Winston Churchill (their mother and Lady Churchill were sisters), started a magazine while they were at Wellington, in the middle thirties, called *Out of Bounds*. It was 'against Reaction, Militarism and Fascism

squibs today. Yet in their time the very idea of making them seemed daring.)

The Harrovians is not a 'total' school story, with the hero at public school from first page to last (like *The Oppidan* or *The Loom of Youth*). Peter is first shown at home, then at prep school, and in the last chapter he is at Oxford, and pays his old house at Harrow a visit. This is as it should be, because far from emphasising the life-long importance of school and its enormous presence in Peter's life, Lunn is at pains to play it down, to tell us that, except for fools, school is only the prelude to life, not its highest point of glory. From fag to head of house, we follow Peter's progress; from snivelling new boy, whose back is permanently curved to avoid kicks, to majestic tyrant determined to do down his ancient enemies – bloods, masters, or others he happens to dislike or owes a grudge. Ruthless, Machiavellian, unloving, he lacks a proper home-life (though the implications of this are not explored), despises the harmless but stupid uncle and aunt who have brought him up since his parents' death, seems incapable of any but superficial friendships and is not a particularly admirable or even likable hero. But he has the brains to win in a society where brains are supposed not to count, the courage to be disliked, and the humour to appear, at least, not to mind what is thought of him. The 'bushido' which appears to fascinate Lunn seems, in Peter, a mixture of one-upmanship and pride, a determination not to let anyone get the better of him under any circumstances, or see that he is hurt, physically or in his feelings. It is concerned, above all, with 'face' in the oriental sense, face that he must not lose before others or before himself. That a boy quite senior in the house should put on an extra pair of underpants when Peter canes him, like any small urchin, strikes Peter as losing him face. That Peter's uncle should grow publicly sentimental over the Harrow songs involves a loss of face not for Peter (who feels no loyalty towards him and has his friends' sympathy, anyway) as for adults in general (idiot uncles in particular) for forgetting what boys feel like and what it is decent or indecent to say.

---

in the Public Schools', contained contributions from public-school boys, and was sold wherever possible in the schools. Later they wrote a (joint) autobiography of their school days, also called *Out of Bounds* (1935), which was disappointingly dull. On Esmond Romilly, see Philip Toynbee's *Friends Apart* (1954) and Jessica Mitford's *Hons and Rebels* (1960). A less rosy view of him appears in T. C. Worsley's *Flannelled Fool* (1967). Worsley was teaching at Wellington where he found the fourteen-year-old Esmond 'not an attractive personality, a tough, ruthless, wholly unscrupulous, iron-hearted youth . . . a lone wolf with a wolf's bite for any hand that fed him, and a wolf's snarl for anyone who reasoned with him.' He was killed in the Second World War while serving with the Canadian Air Force.

School stories have prepared Peter for his prep school, Trollope House, but nothing runs quite true to form when he gets there. A Spaniard beats him in his first fight (after sneers about the Armada), and thereafter refers to him as 'the peeg'. Weeping in a corner, he hears someone shouting: 'Hallo, cry-baby, does oo want oo's mother?'. 'Curiously enough,' Lunn remarks, 'that is precisely what he did want.' This is as near as he can bring himself to the direct description of feeling, for Peter's mother has recently died. Then a ten-year-old dies at the school. The boys cry, whether or not they knew him well, Peter 'revelling in the sheer luxury of grief'.

A charmingly observed little scene shows Lunn at his best. A young stamp-dealer comes up to Peter and a friend of his:

> 'I say, you chaps, like to buy a complete set of Borneos surcharged Labuan?'
>
> 'Not *today,* thank you,' said Peter stiffly.
>
> 'We're not interested in stamps *today,*' added Morgan.

When Peter goes on from Trollope House to a house called 'The Oaks' at Harrow, he is greeted with 'Poor brute! Poor brute! What on earth made you come to this horrid hole? It's the worst house in the school.' Peter is astounded. Loyalty to the house seems non-existent, hatred of football almost universal. As one of the boys says:

> You have the ol' women in the hols who tell you how nice it is to be goin' back to footer – all boys love footer – Silly old ganders. Why do people think a small man likes bargin' into a big man?

'Oh Lord! Footer!' says another. 'Makes me sick to think of it. And then you have those glorious Harrow songs, as my aunt calls 'em. All about the glory of playin' up and all that tosh. How's it go?

> 'Who cares a jot, I should like to know,
> Whether the game be toilsome or no.
> Play up, you fellows, play up!'

A third says, more rationally:

> It's not footer I loathe, footer's a good enough game if it's decently run. But why should I be expected to like a game in which I never get a chance; in which I get run off my legs from beginnin' to end, in which I'm barged over by some hefty brute, twice my size, when I do get near the ball; in which I'm cursed at whenever I touch the ball, and cursed at whenever I miss the ball; in which I get whopped for slacking when I've simply sweated – why the hell should I like it?

All this talk about games has its point, for with a good deal of shrewdness and a certain retrospective bitterness to give it edge,

Lunn insists on one thing above all, the precocious 'greatness' of the schoolboy when he reaches the top, the enormity and absurdity of a blood's prestige. Being unathletic, Peter has no chance of ever becoming a blood, though success at work takes him up the school fast and then his brains successfully keep him there. The blood, as Lunn sees him, is a mixture of politician, pop star and totalitarian policeman, dispensing justice under strictly undemocratic conditions. 'Boooooooooooooo . . . oOY!' Lunn makes him yell across a whole page and no less than seventeen vowels, to emphasise his majesty.

> What old Harrovian can hear this imperious summons as it floats across the road without a moment's regret for lost power? Never again will he be so great. Menials may do his bidding, but they will do it for money and they will give notice if unsatisfied. There was a day when he had but to lift his voice and an unpaid attendant sprang to do him service. This attendant could not give notice, but he could be whopped. There is no Trade Union of fags.

The blood's prestige can scarcely be measured (or, in our day, believed). He patronises, and is fawned upon by, not only the younger boys or the non-bloods of his own age or older, but the masters, their wives and daughters, the old boys, anyone connected with the school. Masters are proud if they are noticed by him; it raises their prestige to be seen talking to him in public. Again and again Lunn contrasts this ridiculous eminence with the bathos that 'real life' will produce later on. Non-bloods may console themselves (as clearly Lunn was doing, retrospectively) by thinking of the dreary fate that lies ahead of a blood – living on past triumphs, retelling old tales, trudging back for each match to be patronised by each new generation of youngsters. Since athletes are so dull, what can they possibly become but duller once they cease to be young and athletic? Whereas, the corollary says, imaginative fellows like Peter can only mature and improve with the years, can only find life more rewarding once the childish preliminaries of school are done with. Yet Lunn's preoccupation with school, for all his efforts to shrug it off, is obvious: his obsession with the bloods, with the silliness of the system, is that of one secretly humiliated.

What is left for the boy thus humiliated? If he can reach it, power. If he gets to the right stage of his school career, even the unathletic boy can savour, if not the glory of prestige, at least the sweetness of power. Lunn is frank in describing its effects, and as always he contrasts it with the relative powerlessness of later life, with the pathetic anti-climax which everything else is likely to be to the boy who takes himself too seriously at school. Lunn may laugh or sneer at the system that puts almost absolute power over their fellows for a few months or a year or two into the hands of a few adolescents. But he does not despise its fruits. Naked power, without apology or excuse, is a plaything temporarily handed to each generation, prized and adored very briefly, then lost forever.

For the non-blood, there is always a kind of retrospective revenge or a chance of vicarious glory. If he is a Lunn, he can write about his schooldays. Then the past can be explained, glorified, enlarged, enlivened; brains beat brawn there, the failure finds belated success or at least notoriety. But the writer's attitude to his own success or failure colours his view of schooldays. The main difference between those two subversive school stories, *Stalky & Co.* and *The Harrovians,* may be found, I think, in the fact that, although Kipling looked back with many of the same attitudes and sneered at many similar things about school, he saw his schooldays with the affectionate irony made possible by the sense of having made a success of them. In a strange (because unathletic) way, Kipling was something of a blood. Lunn, whatever he may say in his autobiography, was not; or so it would seem from his book, for he looks back on school without irony (though with shrewdness and wit), and with something of a scratchy sense of having failed there. The world may have compensated him for it, one feels, his book may avenge him for it, later life may be brighter and more rewarding by contrast with it, but the fact remains that, among his schoolfellows, he seems never to have tasted glory.

CHAPTER IX

Apprentice genius at work: Wodehouse

The average public schoolboy likes *his school . . . but as for any passionate, deep-seated love of the place, he would think it rather bad form than otherwise* P. G. Wodehouse

When, by the turn of the century, the school story was properly established, any young fiction-writer with little experience behind him except that of school had a genre ready and waiting. P. G. Wodehouse and Hugh Walpole both used it at the beginning of their writing careers, Walpole (rather oddly, considering the laughable degree of difference between them) being directly inspired by Wodehouse's school stories. Late in life, Wodehouse disparaged his own. Richard Usborne wrote:

> I knew [he] thought I'd paid inordinate attention to his school stories. He reckoned that he had been an amateur when he wrote them and that my praise of them had been uncritical and my criticism a waste of time.[1]

Amateur or not, the books which appeared between 1902 and 1907 still read well: *The Pothunters, A Prefect's Uncle* (my favourite of this early lot: about the embarrassment of having a very small uncle at school, when you are high among the prefects; uncle and nephew addressing each other, in these curious circumstances, no doubt realistically by their surnames); *Tales of St Austin's, The Gold Bat, The Head of Kays,* and *The White Feather. The Little Nugget,* set in a prep school and featuring a horrendous young American millionaire and a plot to kidnap him, came later, in 1913, and is an adult novel in Wodehouse's later style rather than a school story proper. Between it and the early stories, in 1909, came the best of them all,

Mike, first published in serial form in *The Captain,* though brought out in book form the same year. It divided neatly into two, so in 1935 the second half was published separately as *Enter Psmith,* and later still, in 1953, the whole thing was reissued in two volumes as *Mike at Wrykyn* and *Mike and Psmith.* Like Hughes, Farrar, E. F. Benson, Turley and no doubt others, Wodehouse wrote a sequel to his school story, taking the two main characters a year or so ahead. This was *Psmith in the City,* and, unlike the others' sequels, it went splendidly and is still in print.

Wodehouse was a comic writer of genius and if *Mike* was prentice work it nonetheless shows all kinds of qualities he was to develop further – not the least of them fun and charm. Not many funny writers have written school stories, not many school stories are funny. And not many, above all, are as good-natured as Wodehouse's, as free of obsessions and resentments or of the overemphasis and heartiness that grow out of them, the embarrassing imbalance that characterises most of them. Wodehouse's balance seems just about right: he is not too fond or too nostalgic, yet amiably involved enough, pleasantly boyish without the over-mateyness that so often mars writing about school. Can that intelligent, balanced headmaster of his, Gilkes of Dulwich, perhaps have some of the credit for his mixture of enthusiasm and detachment? Even when recalling the grisly prep school in which Bertie Wooster and some of his friends languished, where the headmaster, the Reverend Aubrey Upjohn, is remembered as a cross between Simon Legree* and Captain Bligh, the tone is friendly, relaxed and forgiving. Indeed, in all Wodehouse wrote, the simplest thing was forgiving. Indeed, in all Wodehouse wrote, the simplest thing was coloured by this amiability, this lack of indignation. Throughout his life he seems to have returned good for evil – or, if that sounds too pious for such a man, cheerfulness for what some might call injury. His spirit seems to have been innately sunny (though he was not a jokey or gregarious man), and as it allowed him to get over the horrors of his middle age and write on in the old spirit for another three decades, so it allowed him to get over, in fact to seem perfectly content with, the sort of childhood that left others as emotional cripples.

He was a classic case of the child educated in England mostly among strangers and aunts, while his parents were abroad. What seemed to warp or at least mildly disfigure the spirit of Saki, Kipling and innumerable silent others appears to have done nothing injurious to Wodehouse, who seems like someone cushioned by the early security one feels he cannot have had. He loved his (generally absent) parents, his schooldays, his country's way of life, its literature (good

* The cruel slave-owner in *Uncle Tom's Cabin.*

and bad), he laughed at aunts (whom Saki loathed and Kenneth Grahame sneered at), and seems to have regarded school not as a rock to cling to or a stepmother to hate but merely as something to look back on with affection and enjoyment. But the easy-going amiability that suited the school story was totally inadequate for the situation he found himself in during the Second World War, when the Nazis by whom he had been interned offered him the chance to broadcast from Berlin and send – as he thought – a non-political wave to his friends and fans on the other side. His very good-nature, his lack of spleen and anger (righteous or not), as well as amazing naivety, must surely have made him drop this clanger in an otherwise blamelessly respectable life, reverberations from which affected the rest of it (he never returned to England). It is hard to understand quite how he could have made the broadcasts, and easy to see the rage they aroused; but few people can have suffered more for lack of political awareness, for a brief misjudgement.

When he began writing, it was natural enough for Wodehouse to use the school story. At twenty, he had known little apart from school, and like the hero of *Mike* had gone straight from school to languish in a bank. Unusually (for those days) he had chosen his own school. He was destined for the navy, but, after visiting an older brother at Dulwich, persuaded his father to send him there instead. So he had an advantage over the boy who had merely been dumped in the school chosen for him; perhaps even a sense of autonomy. Throughout his life he kept in friendly touch with Dulwich, but there was no excessive sentiment about his memories of it, nothing like Alec Waugh's obsession with Sherborne or Kipling's retrospective excitement when he wrote about 'the Coll.'; nor was he an almost excessively generous benefactor, like Walpole or Maugham at the school where they had both been wretched. In *Mike* he wrote:

> The average public schoolboy *likes* his school. He hopes it will beat Bedford at footer or Malvern at cricket, but he rather bets it won't. He is sorry to leave, and he likes going back at the end of the holidays, but as for any passionate, deep-seated love of the place, he would think it rather bad form than otherwise. If anybody came up to him, slapped him on the back and cried: 'Come along, Jenkins, my boy! Play up for the old school, Jenkins! The dear old School! the old place you love so!' he would feel seriously ill.

Orwell in a well-intentioned but patronising essay on Wodehouse, whose quality as a writer he almost entirely failed to appreciate, wrote: 'It is clear that for many years he remained "fixated" on his old school.'[2] But like many of the remarks in the essay, this one is a little askew. Wodehouse was too equable for fixations, too humorous for exaggerations of the kind.

To him, public school, though a world in itself, was loosely and usefully attached to other worlds that came after it; it was broad-based and, within its own sphere and limitations, quite unsnobbish. Even in 1909 there is no overt suggestion that Sedleigh, where Mike and Psmith are sent in their last year, is *socially* deplorable; simply that its cricket is appalling in comparison with that of their previous schools. The nasty exclusiveness of Leslie, or Vachell's idiotic sense of grandeur, have no place at all in Wodehouse; just as the aggressiveness, the social insensitivity, the racialist sneers and open snobbery that mar so many writers in the period are totally absent. One is not retrospectively embarassed by him, or shocked at an attitude that now seems unacceptable, even though he accepted the *mores* of his youth and never seems to have updated them. On this, Orwell is askew again: 'A harmless old-fashioned snobbishness is perceptible all through his work . . . Wodehouse's real sin has been to present the English upper classes as much nicer than they are.'[3] Orwell writes as if a *class* can be nice or not, as if it is not composed of varied individuals; which is the same as making sweeping statements about blacks or Catholics or the bourgeoisie. And he shows a touch of snobbishness himself in his attitude to Wodehouse's school. 'Wrykyn, Wodehouse's imaginary public school,' he says, 'is a school of a more fashionable type than Dulwich', remarking too that Wodehouse 'loathed the unromantic job and the lower-middle-class surroundings in which he found himself' after leaving school. Once again he got things wrong. Wodehouse's father, a judge in Hong Kong, meant his son to be sent out there by the Hong Kong and Shanghai Bank after a training period at its London branch. Though bored by his job and determined to avoid a lifetime in banking, Wodehouse was certainly not plunged into social dinginess on account of it. The idea that he wrote about smart schools and later about smart goings-on out of school to compensate for social chips on his shoulder is nonsense. Orwell himself ('a poor boy at Eton, an Etonian among the poor,' in Francis Hope's words) had so many social chips of his own that he seemed determined to find them in others, and to attribute snobbery and social uneasiness where they did not exist. Wodehouse wrote about public schools as if they were all much of a muchness, socially speaking. As his frequent references to real schools show, he put them in no particular social pecking order. In his stories (as in those of Hughes, Farrar, Reed, Kipling and indeed almost any other mainstream school story writer) they were places people went to in the normal way. He was writing, after all, for people who assumed this. Not that all readers of *Chums* or *The Captain* or *The Public School Magazine* were at public school themselves, but that, for purposes of circulation, it was assumed that they were, or wished they were and identified with those who were.

School is important in Wodehouse's work as a way of life, the formative first stage that brings together friends and enemies, lifelong associates who speak the same language and understand one another's ways; but no more important than it was for most others in his day, and a good deal less so than it was for many. Dulwich was mainly a day school, after all, and in London; therefore much more in touch with the outside world than most public schools at the time. In Wodehouse's later books the patterns laid down at school are echoed, though not exactly repeated, in adult life; but because irony colours everything he wrote (a fact that seems to escape Orwell entirely), these parts are evocative one of another, flow into one another, suggest other things. The circular references to this and that, the echoes – sometimes the merest bat-squeaks – and reverberations can, with care and affection, be endlessly picked up and enjoyed. Richard Usborne, writing about Wodehouse's best-known hero, asks:

> What does authority mean to someone with a family, social and educational background such as Bertie's? I think it is based on the public school system. In public school, both of fiction and of fact, headmasters, housemasters and their lackeys, the prefects, represent Authority in a highly undemocratic state. The serfs and proles of the Lower and Middle Schools have no say in who bosses them. Authority is always elected from above. Prefects are not, in any schools that I know of, chosen from an electorate of juniors saying 'Please govern us'. The housemaster nominates the prefects, the headmaster nominates the housemaster, and the Governing Body nominates the Headmaster.[4]

(A corollary of this, spiralling downwards rather than upwards, can be found in Busby of Westminster's explanation of his own power: 'The fathers govern the nation; the mothers govern the fathers; but the boys govern the mothers, and I govern the boys.') Thus Wodehouse wove his school experience into adult life (he never wasted anything), but lightly and suggestively, without being dogged by it or excessively involved.

In his school stories – that is, in his earliest, almost schoolboy work – he was already sending up the conventions of past school stories, threading the language of present-day slang with phrases familiar from Victorian school fiction and, more importantly, using the plots of the school story (all of them already familiar to a wide public) with new twists and ironies, an unpretentious originality. 'Are you the Bully, the Pride of the School, or the Boy who takes to drink and is led astray in Chapter Sixteen?' Psmith asks Mike on arriving at Sedleigh. With such genial send-ups of a world he knew well (school stories as well as school), Wodehouse began his writing career; to go on to higher sendups in which school was, to some extent, always present.

2 *If you ever have occasion to write to me, would you mind sticking a P at the beginning of my name? P-s-m-i-t-h. See?* P. G. Wodehouse

Orwell almost damned *Mike* with faint praise. It 'must be one of the best "light" school stories in English,' he wrote.[5] *Mike* is about a cricketing genius. There have been rather too many cricketing geniuses in school stories but, as I have said, the school story can repeat its characters. In fact, in one aimed at a popular audience (not a 'serious' story in the sense that most of those I have discussed so far have been) it is almost obligatory for the hero to be instantly recognisable, at least to fall within certain limitations. Mike's limitations are obvious. His whole reason for living, like that of his whole family (not only parents and Mike but Joe and Reggie, Frank and Bob, Marjery, Phyllis, Ella and Gladys in her high chair) is cricket. He starts as a rather elderly prep-school boy (aged fifteen), about to go off to Wrykyn, where all his brothers have been cricket stars and where, if the professional who comes up to coach them each summer is anything to go by, he will be starrier than any of them.

So off he goes, and the whole first half of the book is concerned with his cricketing rise and triumphs at Wrykyn. That Wodehouse was a real writer is shown as early as *Mike* by the fact that even the cricket matches, with plenty of technical detail, are readable; not just the ancillary parts of the cricketing mania but the matches themselves, their long-winded ritual. The Jacksons' belief that nothing, positively nothing counts as much or as absolutely as cricket is on a par with Lord Emsworth's passion for his prize pig, a psychological quirk, a ruling passion. Any writer can produce drama out of particular strokes, out of the single dramatic moment; but Wodehouse can communicate a more general excitement and interest, can carry the reader along with him. He even communicates a sense of the mystery of young genius, the way in which a child may seem to have been chosen from conception for supreme performance and nothing can stop it appearing, so that at an immature stage he has already gone far beyond his elders. Mike outstrips Bob early in their joint days at Wrykyn and Bob, though wry about it, shows no serious resentment.

Another family connection at Wrykyn is the one between Wyatt, Mike's special friend, and his step-father, Wain, who is also his and Mike's housemaster. Here family life overlaps uneasily with school life. School stories tend to suggest that it won't do, although Reed, perhaps characteristically, seems to find few problems in the fact that one of his boys at St Dominic's is the headmaster's son. Only when his father asks him a *direct* question about things in the school does communication dry up between them. The Wyatt/Wain relationship is handled rather limply by Wodehouse, as if in some embarrassment. Perhaps the whole thing loomed too large in his general plan for *Mike*; if taken to heart at all, it might threaten to take over the story. Wyatt and Wain address each other as 'Father' and 'James' in private, as 'Sir' and 'Wyatt' in public. Wyatt climbs out of his dormitory at night by removing the bars of the window, which brings him disgrace and expulsion, and the threat of life at some desk-bound city job; until Mike rescues him with help from his father, whose connections in the Argentine get him a splendid time with cattle, rustlers and other delights on the pampas. Almost Stalky-like news of his adventures comes back to an almost wistful Mike. Meantime, at Wrykyn, Mike has gone up and up in the school hierarchy and become as starry a blood as it is possible, in their terms, to be.

But hubris awaits the starry in the middle (if not at the end) of school stories. The second half of *Mike* begins at Chapter XXX. Two years have gone by, Mike's school reports have grown steadily worse and his father at last decides to remove him from Wrykyn (where he has just become captain of cricket) and send him to Sedleigh, a school where boys work hard and the local vicar's son has just got a Balliol scholarship. As Wodehouse said:

> Mike's outlook on life was that of a cricketer, pure and simple. What had Sedleigh ever done? What were they ever likely to do? Whom did they play? What Old Sedleighan had ever done anything in cricket? Perhaps they didn't even *play* cricket!

But they do. Not only do they play but they have another enthusiast in command. Adair is captain of cricket and much else besides. He is 'that rare type, the natural leader . . . the sort that comes to the top by sheer force of character and determination.' Adair seems to have strayed into Wodehouse's world from another, where different values count. Dogged, humourless, idealistic, he is not the sort of person his creator really likes or understands, but he sets him down vividly and tries to explain him. Wodehouse says of him:

> He had that passionate fondness for his school which every boy is popularly supposed to have, but which really is implanted in about one in a thousand. To Adair, Sedleigh was almost a religion.

Why this is so, he tries to explain by probing into the past rather more than is usual with him.

> Both his parents were dead; his guardian, with whom he spent the holidays,

was a man with neuralgia at one end of him and gout at the other; and the only really pleasant times Adair had had, as far back as he could remember, he owed to Sedleigh. The place had grown on him, absorbed him. Where Mike, violently transplanted from Wrykyn, saw only a wretched little hole not to be mentioned in the same breath with Wrykyn, Adair, dreaming of the future, saw a colossal establishment, a public school among public schools, a lump of human radium, shooting out Blues and Balliol scholars year after year without ceasing.

Between Mike who cares nothing for Sedleigh and Adair to whom it means everything there is bound to be trouble, especially when cricket is involved. Mike refuses to play for the school and joins a local village team instead. Adair discovers what sort of a cricketer he has – or ought to have – in Mike. Eventually, they fight. Wodehouse recalls Tom Brown's fight with Slogger Williams, and other famous school-story fights brood over the scene. Adair is knocked out, injures his wrist, and is unable to play against the MCC. But all bad feeling is punched out of their relationship and when someone says that Adair is 'not a bad cove' Mike is able to reply shortly: 'He's all right'.

The pair achieve a grudging respect for each other, and when Mike discovers what Sedleigh means to Adair, and, on his own account, finds it is not such a wretched little hole as he first thought it, he arranges a match between Sedleigh and Wrykyn. This, Sedleigh has no hope of winning, Wrykyn being used to playing the MCC and other such giants. But with Mike in the team and some cunning tactics, Sedleigh wins. Which is just as it should be, since, in school stories, the side the reader wants to win wins. Enemies who turn into friendly allies are another familiar ingredient.

More of a surprise – the happiest of surprises, carried on into later books with no sense of anti-climax – is Psmith. When introducing him Wodehouse writes:

A very long, thin youth, with a solemn face and immaculate clothes, was leaning against the mantelpiece. As Mike entered, he fumbled in his top left waistcoat pocket, produced an eyeglass attached to a cord, and fixed it in his right eye . . .

Now Mike, a fairly stolid youth with his mind on little but cricket, might be expected to take against such a dandy, rather as Turley's hero took against Japanese fans. But not a bit of it. The pair become friends at once when they both arrive at Sedleigh together, fed up at the loss of their past schools and likely to feel lost (this part of the serial was in fact called 'The Lost Lambs' when it appeared in *The Captain*). It seems rather too much of a coincidence that they both come from near Bridgnorth in Shropshire; but that was Wodehouse's great good place, where his parents lived when they came to England, and therefore Lord Emsworth had to live later,* and the Empress of Blandings; a rural paradise, an unchanging never-never land.

Psmith's name is one of Wodehouse's masterstrokes. It is a joke of orthography, mislaid (rather than lost) when spoken; and there is a certain ambiguity in its use both on the page and off it whenever the character is mentioned. When Psmith appears in the narrative, he is given his extra, silent, P; but when someone addresses him, he reverts (on the page) to plain Smith. It is clear that Wodehouse never meant the P to be sounded, but wanted it simply to remain offstage in the mind, a visual rather than an aural curlicue to that plainest of names. ' "My name," he added pensively, "is Smith." ' Thus does Wodehouse introduce him, disguised and unrecognisable in the unfamiliar spelling. But he goes on almost at once:

> 'If you ever have occasion to write to me, would you mind sticking a P at the beginning of my name? P-s-m-i-t-h. See? There are too many Smiths, and I don't care for Smythe. My father's content to worry along in the old-fashioned way, but I've decided to strike out a fresh line. I shall found a new dynasty . . . In conversation you may address me as Rupert (though I hope you won't), or simply Smith, the P not being sounded. Cp. [*sic*] the name Zbysco, in which the Z is given a similar miss-in-baulk. See?'

It is something of a teaser. One never thinks of Psmith, envisages him in any way, as anything but Psmith. The mental image of him involves six letters, an upper-case P and a lower-case S, and insofar as the written word counts in one's feeling for a person – his atmosphere and aura, his size and shape – then Psmith is a very different character from Smith. (To a lesser degree all spelling variants with the same pronunciation involve this kind of mental adjustment.) Yet he is not to be *called* (aloud) anything but Smith, undifferentiated from the thousands of other Smiths, and complicated mental acrobatics are needed to switch from the *sight* (even the inward eyesight) of Psmith to the *sound* of Smith. As Wodehouse must have realised. The idea must surely have come to him in a flash, as it did to Psmith. 'The resolve came to me unexpectedly this morning, as I was buying a simple penn'orth of butterscotch out of the automatic machine at Paddington,' he tells Mike. It is not the kind of thing that could be brooded over or calculated. Wodehouse pushed private jokes into his writing wherever they would go, without explanation, like a builder putting coins that may never be discovered into a wall cavity or under

* Although, according to Alec Waugh, Blandings Castle itself was based on Corsham Court in Wiltshire, seen (from the outside only) by Wodehouse on a brief visit to the neighbourhood. Other houses have been suggested as influences, too.

a floor. When asked at Wrykyn where he has come from, for instance, Mike says: 'A private school in Hampshire. King-Hall's. At a place called Emsworth.' One can imagine his friends the King-Halls with whom he stayed in Hampshire smiling at this small literary bow to their prep school. Later Emsworth, where they lived, became the best joke of them all, and, incidentally, the house he stayed at was called Threepwood Grange. As I said, he never wasted a thing.

The dandy, of which Psmith is so good an example, is not as rare in school fiction as might be expected. Or, if not the dandy in appearance, then the verbosely brilliant in conversation, the drawly, articulate, adult-seeming young man who makes the others seem like inky fags. Pembury in *The Fifth Form at St Dominic's* is one, crippled and therefore able to make his influence felt only through words. The Caterpillar in *The Hill* is another, a stickler for form, a pedant on school customs. The monocled ninnies of the pop school stories are in the same tradition, though without the supposed underlying cleverness. In popular fiction outside the school story the best known examples are probably Sir Percy Blakeney, the Scarlet Pimpernel, and Lord Peter Wimsey, languorous silly asses on the surface, brains well camouflaged but in first-rate order. The dandy appears in serious fiction too: Anthony Blanche in *Brideshead Revisited* is an obvious case.

Psmith, boy wonder and cheerer of every glum situation, with his alleged socialism and his way of addressing everyone as Comrade, is something of a Stalky when it comes to getting his own way. His first act on arriving at Sedleigh is to bag a study which a boy called Spiller has his eye on and believes is to be his. By a mixture of brains and brawn (mostly brains, in his tackling of the housemaster) Psmith gets it and outwits the angry Spiller. He and Mike settle happily in. ' "There are few pleasures," said Psmith, as he resumed his favourite position against the mantelpiece and surveyed the commandeered study with the pride of a householder, "keener to the reflective mind than sitting under one's own rooftree. This place would have been wasted on Spiller." ' It recalls Stalky and Co. in their cliff-top hide, totally content and at home, all their domesticising instincts concentrated on the single small private place; and many other studies and hideouts in many other school stories, where the cosy fug and sausages round the fire are, to outsiders, part of the school glamour, to insiders part of its best memories. *Mike* was Wodehouse's last public-school story and a worthy one to end on.

CHAPTER X

The school story as novel of character: Hugh Walpole

. . . *the iron prison of some hideous dream* . . . Hugh Walpole

Two years after *Mike* appeared, Hugh Walpole published his second novel, a school story called *Mr Perrin and Mr Traill* (1911), which turned out to be the most lastingly successful novel of a lifetime filled with more ephemeral successes. To compare his reputation with Wodehouse's in their early years and then today is a lesson in the vagaries of human judgement. Most people writing on the novel in the twenties and thirties – Henry James among them – put Walpole among those to be seriously discussed, a candidate for immortality. Wodehouse, except with his (mainly non-literary) fans, came nowhere in those early stakes. Later the quality of his writing came to be recognised by literary people (Hilaire Belloc, Evelyn Waugh, L. A. G. Strong and Gilbert Murray among them) but the general public certainly did not consider him one of the potentially great, the big names. Yet today Walpole is almost forgotten and Wodehouse, at all levels of appreciation, lives on, many of his books either permanently in print or snapped up wherever they are available second-hand. The only novel of Walpole's that is now remembered (apart from the Jeremy stories, which are still read, I am told, in prep schools) is his adult school story, of all his novels the one based most directly on his own experience.

Walpole admitted that it was 'almost a literal transcription of events that occurred to [him], seen of course in the light of [his] own character and personality',[1] and in his diary he called it 'my truest novel'. Certainly a first edition which I was lent by the man who preceded Walpole in his teaching job at Epsom College, on which the book is based, and claimed to be the model for Mr Traill, had a number of names, presumably of Epsom characters, pencilled in beside those of their fictional counterparts, as well as gleeful remarks of approval and recognition, underlinings and exclamations, beside certain phrases which were presumably recognisable. The boys at Epsom, as has happened in the case of many other school stories set in recognisable schools (*The Harrovians, The Loom of Youth, Frost in May, Schoolboy Rising*), were delighted, the authorities angry. Only later, when he was famous and knighted, was Walpole invited back and asked to give the school prizes. (The same sort of thing happened at Durham School.)

Mr Perrin and Mr Traill was highly praised when it first appeared and still reads, on the whole, rather better than his other fiction. Like many writers with a single early work that overshadows the rest, Walpole was put out by its continuing success. 'I will frankly confess that I have some irritation with regard to it, an irritation that every author feels when an early book of his is steadily preferred to later ones,' he wrote.[2] A modern view, from Angus Ross, finds it 'his best book, a short but powerfully realistic story'.[3] At the time of its publication Robert Ross wrote that 'the character of Perrin [was] a masterpiece of observation, invention and imagination'.[4] Charles Marriott, a Cornish novelist whose work Walpole admired, called it '*miles* above anything [he had] done before . . . really first-hand stuff, developed with sympathy and insight.'[5] And Henry James, taking it very seriously, as he took the work of his friends, even when treading on tender toes, wrote:

> I think the book represents a very marked advance on its predecessors . . . It has life and beauty and reality, and is more closely *done* than the others, with its immense advantage, clearly, of resting on the known and felt thing.[6]

They were right, it *was* 'first-hand stuff', 'resting on the known and felt thing'. This is undoubtedly why it is the best of Walpole's novels, since he was not inventive or imaginative enough to write about what he had not directly experienced. His insights into human nature were superficial, and his main failure, in his own life as in his novels, was in the vital sphere of human relations. Yet early success (through the publication of his school story) meant that he became a full-time writer before he had managed to fit much else into his life, and never acquired the background of colleagues, jobs and what in general might be called ordinary living. His homosexuality, unacknowledged in any public context and inadmissible even by implication in respectable fiction at the time, must also have severely handicapped a writer as prolific, as careless, as ingenuous. Walpole was, quite simply, not the man to be burdened with so heavy a secret. He had no ordinary domesticity to draw upon, never marrying or having an acknowledged partner with whom he shared a home; as his childhood was disrupted and lonely, without security or continuity, he had no strong, fertile background of settled memories, either; and as, except for the year's teaching at Epsom and some short spells of tutoring in private families,* he had no experience of working with others, he had little of the solid social knowledge which the second-rate writer as a rule relies upon. Such limitations have little importance to a real writer, of course: he has enough and to spare within him, and no need of the rough-and-ready knowledge of the world known as 'experience'.

But Walpole probably needed exact knowledge, personal experience, to do his best; which accounts for the (artistic as well as popular) success of his photographically exact representation of Epsom life. Yet he wrote with what seems craven dishonesty about the place he disliked and disapproved of: 'Epsom College is a splendid school with a grand history and has supplied for the world many of its finest doctors.'[7] Perhaps, when he gave away the prizes there and at Durham, his speeches rivalled in hypocrisy that of his fictional headmaster at the prize-giving in *Mr Perrin and Mr Traill.* The trouble was that Walpole had what he himself described as 'a passionate desire to be liked, a longing for approval, and a frantic reaction to anybody's geniality',[8] all of which made for (at least social) dishonesty.

Unlike Wodehouse, he was wretched at school; or rather wretched, whether at school or out of it, during childhood, adolescence, and young manhood. To start with he was a failure – 'discontented, ugly, abnormally sensitive and excessively conceited',[9] as he described himself. The story of the ugly duckling can seldom have been so dramatically played out in real life, for quite suddenly he became successful, lionised, taken up by the great (including James), famous beyond not just his wildest dreams but his (very modest) deserts. Posterity has got its own back by forgetting him, but in his lifetime he did brilliantly by the standards of the incompetent schoolboy who scraped into Cambridge and there, though he worked hard, scraped a third. On the surface, at least, he even became quite suddenly cheerful and self-confident, but the 'frantic reaction' must still have been waiting not far below it. Maugham put him recognisably into *Cakes and Ale* as the contemptible Alroy Keir, the bland literary climber

* The main one was that of the Baroness von Arnim, the 'Elizabeth' of *Elizabeth and her German Garden*, who remained a lifelong friend.

who crept into the good graces of the establishment with flattery and fawning.* You can call it flattery and fawning, or just his own confessed 'longing for approval', which the disastrous childhood helps to explain.

School was a large presence in his life, so it was not surprising that he used it as a setting for an early novel and that his school story turned out so well. Like all children without a settled home, he must have expected too much of school, drawn too much upon it in his early years. And he was bullied and terrified at his prep school.

> I have never, after those days, thank God, known continuous terror night and day . . . Some of the small boys (I was always one) were made to stand on their heads, hang on to the gas and swing slowly round, fight one another with hair brushes, and jump from the top of the school lockers to the ground.[10]

These horrors were followed by five terms at the King's School, Canterbury, where according to his biographer, Sir Rupert Hart-Davis, 'he was not particularly happy . . . and certainly no more successful than he was at other schools.'[11] 'I'm longing to leave,' he wrote to his parents just before leaving, '. . . I can't bear this place now I don't know why .' Yet ever afterwards he claimed it as his own, and even today reference books give it as his one and only school. By lavish presents he made sure of his position as an Old Boy, paying for elaborate improvements and for years collecting the manuscripts and rare books that today form the Walpole Collection. Only Somerset Maugham gave equally lavishly to the school at about the same time (he too had been fairly wretched there, as *Of Human Bondage*, autobiographical in the early chapters, shows), and the two men probably competed in generosity. Walpole then spent seven adolescent years as a day-boy at Durham School, since his father had been made principal of Bede College in Durham. This school he seems to have disliked and despised. 'I learnt nothing whatever,' he wrote of his time there. '. . . nothing of any sort or kind. I am therefore today one of the most ignorant human beings in the world.'[12] A poor excuse, of course, especially for a day-boy, with plenty of time outside school to become less ignorant, and three years at Cambridge to catch up.

Was it snobbery that made him reject Durham and cling so tenaciously to King's? King's was certainly the smarter school and Walpole was undoubtedly a snob; even in a snobbish age well-known and noticed for the unblushing way in which he would cancel an acceptance if something grander came along, or drop a friend in favour of

* See Alec Waugh: *My Brother Evelyn and Other Profiles* (1967), where he maintains that this broke Walpole completely in the last years of his life, humiliating him in his relations with others and inhibiting his behaviour at every turn.

someone smarter. Then there is the odd fact that, whatever the horrors of boarding school, the social horror of being a day-boy was, at the time of Walpole's schooldays, by many considered worse. By snobs in particular. Alec Waugh said: 'At most boarding schools the day boy is looked down upon; for some obscure reason [he] always seems to be inferior to the boarder . . . At six o'clock, when the bell rings for tea and the intimate life of the day begins, he . . . passes into another life.'[13] 'The man was only a beastly Home-bug,' Lunn's hero remarks of someone in *The Harrovians*, astonished to find he has done well at Oxford. 'Being a miserable day-boy,' Wodehouse wrote of one of his characters in *The Pothunters*, 'he had no experience of the inner life of a boarding house, which is the real life of a Public School.' Yet Wodehouse himself, though he boarded some of his time at Dulwich, was in a school consisting mainly of day-boys. Compton Mackenzie's hero, in *Sinister Street*, Michael Fane, feels the same about his own time at St Paul's (known in the book as St James's). The 'Home-bug', or whatever else he was rudely called, was not envied his freedom but pitied for what he missed. He might also be poorer than the boarders and still share the privilege of being at the same school. Marguerite Steen wrote, describing Walpole's schooldays at Durham:

> To the aristocracy – that is to say, the boarding pupils – the social position of the day-boy is a cross between that of the boots and the dustman; no matter what your scholastic attainments . . . you are in outer darkness, as far as the inner life of the school is concerned.[14]

And Walpole had no scholastic attainments, either.

To Epsom College, a minor public school which specialised in medical families, he went to teach because it was a public school; whereas the other job he was offered by Gabbitas Thring, the scholastic agency which found jobs for so many aspiring literary men, was at Bristol Grammar School, a lively place by the sound of it at the time but (Walpole would have thought), like Home-bugs, in outer darkness. When he wrote his school story he called Epsom 'Moffatts' and set it in Cornwall instead of Surrey; but – dingy, narrow, petty, miserable, cramping the spirits of masters and boys, horribly overcrowded, uncomfortable and uncivilised, the very opposite of a free society of educated men training boys in the way they should go, 'the iron prison of some hideous dream', as it seems to Archie Traill – it was immediately recognisable.

Not that it really matters whether it was Epsom that inspired this or that episode. The book is a novel of character set in an institution. This happens to be a public school, but it might almost as well be a prison, an asylum or a remote hospital. What counts is the rubbing of personality against personality in narrow circumstances, the jealousies, rivalries and tensions when things are harsh, dispiriting and tyrannical, when there is bullying from above and pettiness among equals. As so often happens at any such institution, there is a strong sense of difference from the outside world, a feeling of enclosure, of each man's imprisonment not just in the place but in himself, crowded but lonely, jostled but single, alone. From the moment term starts a curtain seems to fall round Moffatts, enveloping everything in it, masters and boys and the masters' families when they have them, cutting the 'real' world out entirely. In one of his moments of fantasy, rare in his early books, more frequent later, Walpole makes the heroine, Isabel Desart, sum it up like this:

> Her present feeling was something akin to Alice's sensation at the croquet party when the mallets (being flamingoes) would walk away and climb up trees, and the balls (being hedgehogs) would wander off the ground. They were all flamingoes and hedgehogs at Moffatts.

Between the flamingoes and hedgehogs inside and ordinary people outside there seems an unbridgeable gap, which as the term proceeds grows wider. Masters are as much in prison as boys; probably more so, in fact, in 1911, when chances of advancement or even alternatives for untalented masters from minor public schools were few. After a time the sense of unreality in relation to the world outside affects even the least imaginative of masters. Towards the end of the book Perrin begins to see visions and even the phlegmatic Traill finds himself flying into rages over trifles, snapping at the boys, and calling one of the other masters a 'damned counter-jumper'. There is a sense of total enclosure, of pent-up feeling: in 1911 public schools did not, as they try to do now, mix with the local community.

2 *There is a great vogue in these introspective days for outspokenness upon intimate matters* Ian Hay

Mr Perrin and Mr Traill is a study of conflict, frustration and temperamental contrast. Vincent Perrin is a dried-up middle-aged pedant, an unlovable Chips with a rough moustache, shabby clothes and a pompous manner. Returning to Moffatts for the autumn term he feels buoyed up by the fact that he has fallen in love with a girl who stays with one of the other master's families, and means to ask her to marry him. Full of hope and confidence, he is determined that this term is at last going to be different. And so, in an unexpected way, it is, because, presenting an obvious and painful contrast to Perrin, is a new master, Archie Traill, fresh from Cambridge.

Clearly Walpole meant his readers to see Traill as a golden boy, clean, fresh, attractive, a likeable contrast to the decrepit, indeed rather repulsive, Perrin. On the contrast between the two the book hangs, and Walpole himself took it very seriously. 'While the young, buoyant, vital Mr Traill was what I would have liked to be, the tortured, half-maddened Mr Perrin was what I thought I was,' he wrote.[15] But Henry James saw Traill in a very different light. He wrote to Walpole:

I don't quite understand why, positing the situation as also a part of the experience of Mr Traill, you yet take such pains to demonstrate that Mr Traill was, as a vessel of experience, absolutely *nil* – recognising, feeling, knowing, understanding, appreciating, that is, absolutely nothing that happened to him. Experience – reported – is interesting, is *recorded* to us, according to some vessel (the capacity and quality of such) that contains it, and I don't make out Mr Traill's capacity at all.

The reader today will probably agree. Traill epitomises all the thick-headed, thickset and finally thick-souled qualities that produced school heroes; utterly without imagination, the embodiment of the soggy philistinism to which Tom Brown's high spirits had sunk.

Of course it is hard to make the reader sympathise with a bright lucky fellow who has everything on his side, when he is contrasted with a more life-scarred figure who has nothing to recommend him, no social graces at all. One's instinctive sympathy is with the underdog, and Perrin is a sometimes pathetic and generally credible figure, with a forceful, vivid presence. At an incomparably higher level, the situation is similar in *The Mayor of Casterbridge*, where even Hardy cannot make much of the trim, up-and-coming Farfrae, contrasted with the sullen Henchard, tragically on the skids. But Perrin is no tragic hero, nor was Walpole capable of writing a tragedy. A curious reversal of feeling took place in him, though, as the book went ahead, rather as it did with Galsworthy and Soames Forsyte as the years and the books went by. Walpole seems to have come round more and more to his Perrin and, inevitably in matters of emotional commitment, correspondingly to lose interest in Traill. This is particularly so in the quite different version of the book which Walpole wrote for the American market, in which Perrin becomes a noble, heroic figure and Traill diminishes into someone quite negligible.

The two men are contrasted in every way. Both are in love with the same girl, and Traill wins her. In 1911, they could hardly be rivals over one of the boys, but Walpole does the next best thing and makes her physically as much like a boy as possible:

> With her rather short brown hair that curled about her head, her straight eyes, her firm mouth, her vigorous, unerring movements, the swing of her arms as she walked . . . to most people she was a delightful boy – splendidly healthy, direct, uncompromising.

Traill is immediately popular with the boys, especially because, like the bloods in school stories, he is outstandingly good at games. His youth gives him the future, and it is obvious that he is pausing at Moffatts on his way to something better; whereas Perrin has been stuck there for twenty years and nothing else is ever coming his way. These large differences are reflected in small ones. A row over an umbrella flares up, and has the pair of them scrabbling on the floor (Walpole's original title for the book was in fact *The Umbrella*). At a dinner-party Perrin's shabby clothes are a contrast to Traill's smart ones. At the end-of-term celebrations, when the masters are clapped or ignored by the boys, Traill gets thunderous applause and Perrin silence. His bitterness is increased by the defection of his favourite among the boys, Garden Minimus.

Minor dramas go on in the background. The masters' efforts to stand up to the headmaster, a sadistic bully, are always unsuccessful. The Combers, with whom the heroine Isabel is staying, are wretchedly unhappy: he because of frustration and fury with life in general, with the school and his wife in particular; she because she cannot 'manage' properly – the shopping or the maids, their poverty, the entertaining – because she is stupid and pathetic and unloved, even by her three loutish sons, and the school wives and matrons sneer at her. Realistically regarded, Isabel's visits to the Combers, lasting for many weeks, seem unlikely. Freddie Comber is antagonistic to her, the atmosphere is explosively miserable, a long-term guest in a hard-up household would surely be a financial as well as an emotional burden (the boys being away at another school, Isabel is alone with the Comber parents), and she is said to lead a full, rich, happy life in London, surrounded by friends. But Walpole never seemed to notice that such things were, realistically regarded, unconvincing.

Perrin's reaction to the news of Traill's engagement to Isabel is one of the best things in the book. In his mind he accuses her, at first, of betraying him, although there has been nothing between them, she knows nothing of his feelings. Traill's triumph over him, or what Perrin sees as malicious one-upmanship, culminating in the winning away of Isabel, maddens him, and he writes a suicide letter to his mother (touching and exact), meaning to kill first Traill and then himself. But when he threatens Traill on the cliff-edge, Traill slips, is injured, loses consciousness, and is threatened by the incoming tide; and then, quite suddenly, Perrin is overwhelmed by a new feeling –

that, whatever happens, he must save Traill. He does so, by sacrificing himself and drowning. Just before he abandons himself to the sea, he seizes Traill's hand and kisses it; and this farewell kiss, so outlandish within the context of school – even more, of school-story – behaviour, suggests not tenderness so much as overtly homosexual feeling; not deliberately in Perrin, but unrealisingly in Walpole: not characterisation but self-revelation.

Mr Perrin and Mr Traill was not a school story in the sense that it was written for boys, about schoolboy life. It was the first successful novel about adults in a public school. In its day it was thought not only adult but 'unpleasant'. Ian Hay said that while it was 'a very able book', it was not one to recommend to 'schoolmasters while recovering, let us say, from influenza'. And immediately after that he went on to deplore 'a very insistent and rather discordant note of realism – the sort of realism which leaves nothing unphotographed,' in the school stories of the day. He went on severely:

> There is a tendency . . . to discuss matters which are better not discussed, at any rate in a work of fiction. There is a great vogue in these introspective days for outspokenness upon intimate matters. We are told that such matters should not be excluded from the text, because it is 'true to life'. So are the police reports in the Sunday newspapers.[16]

It was surely (at least in part) Walpole's effect that he was deploring. Some certainly thought that *Mr Perrin and Mr Traill* heralded a new kind of school fiction, harsh, realistic, outspoken, an earlier version of 'kitchen sink' writing. Today its realism seems mild, its manner almost prissy; yet school with its narrow confines and violent emotions concentrated Walpole's talent as few other things were to do.

3 *We are afraid that Mr Walpole is writing with too great facility . . .*

The *Westminster Gazette*

In the Fitzwilliam Museum in Cambridge and at the King's School, Canterbury, I made two discoveries about *Mr Perrin and Mr Traill*. These, to me at least, were exciting, because both were new to me. The manuscript in the Fitzwilliam, an almost perfectly correct copy of the novel in Walpole's handwriting, shows that a character who was clearly important to him was completely cut out of it in the published version. This was an old man met in the woods by both Traill and Isabel, embodying a spirit of nature, a pan-like force, anarchical and free, loving and wise. His name is Garrick, an obvious theatrical reference, but Walpole refers to him as Punch, for he carries a box theatre on his back with a Punch and Judy show in it, and roams the countryside, presumably giving shows, with two small dogs for company. Walpole dedicated the book, to Henry James's annoyance and slight jealousy, to someone he called Punch. This was Percy Anderson, aged nearly sixty when the novel appeared, and a candidate – one among many – for the role of Walpole's 'ideal friend'. He was a designer of stage costumes, who dressed the original Gilbert and Sullivan operas from *The Yeomen of the Guard* onwards, Beerbohm Tree's Shakespeare productions, and James's ill-fated play *Guy Domville*. (In his fiction Walpole used the names of people he had known in real life: his one and only friend in his unhappy prep-school days was called Jumbo, for instance, and he gave the name to Jeremy's faithful chum at Crale; he used the name Pomfret-Walpole for a boy Marguerite Steen regarded as his own schoolboy *persona*, and then changed it, in the American version of his book, to Somerset-Walpole, which, without the hyphen, was his father's name.)

The rustic sage, Punch, was cut out before publication, and his 'poetic' Mummerset – showing Walpole at his worst – is mercifully lost. His philosophising is much like the opening of Walpole's novel *Fortitude*: 'T'isn't life that matters! 'Tis the courage you bring to it!'* Punch disapproves of school. 'In these brown Autumn days when the air hangs tight about yer like drawn silk and the sun fades away into darkness before yer sight it's not teachin' boys Algebra in gaslight that yer ought to be doin',' he tells Traill, adding darkly: 'I'd burn all the schools down if I 'ad my chance'. Pyromaniac fantasies do not deter Isabel from making friends with him and she confides in him about her engagement and the school. He takes on an almost mystical quality: 'Sometimes she thought he was not real at all; sometimes she fancied that if she did not love Archie the little man would disappear altogether.' They discuss Perrin, too. 'Perrin became, as Punch talked to her, a heroic figure fighting out his own salvation,' Walpole writes, reflecting his own growing sympathy for him. In the last chapter, it is Punch who saves Traill, left on the cliffside by Perrin, now dead. When Isabel thanks him, he tells her how much he admires and loves her. 'There's nothing in earth or 'eaven like your lovely eyes,' he says, and asks for a keepsake; she gives him a silver chain, and he kisses her hand. But editorial fingers presumably snuffed him out. He occupies many pages of neat manuscript, though.

The manuscript's neatness is the most striking thing about it. Of course it may have been a fair copy, taken from others more messy or revised, but from what I have seen of other manuscripts of Walpole's, and heard about his treatment of his own finished work, I doubt it. Lack of corrections does not necessarily indicate a careless writer, or a

* Surely echoed in Bertie Wooster's 'In this life it is not aunts that matter, but the courage that one brings to them.'

thick fuzz of corrections (like Tolstoy's, or Proust's) a good one; but in Walpole's case, since almost every phrase shows him to have been careless, it does suggest either laziness or complacency; or both. That he valued even very poor work of his own is clear from the manuscripts he bequeathed to the King's School, handsomely and unsuitably bound in leather. That he failed to correct when he had a chance to is even odder. In a passage cut from *The House of Macmillan* when it was published but later quoted from the manuscript by Lovat Dickson in *The House of Words*, Charles Morgan revealed that in the last years of his life Walpole did not even read the proofs of his own books:

> It is astonishing that Walpole . . . who knew that he was by nature too fluent a writer, should not have availed himself of his chance, in a series of galley proofs, to apply stringent criticism to what he had written. He did not, and many of his faults are the consequence.

The *Westminster Gazette* had taken him to task for carelessness in his earliest days. 'We are afraid that Mr Walpole is writing with too great facility,' it said of *Mr Perrin and Mr Traill*, in severe, schoolmasterly style, 'and we think that if he would take greater pains he might do much better.' Walpole's casual attitude extended not just to his style but to everything he used in his books. Even the most ordinary of Latin tags, for instance, he was liable to get wrong ('*Saevus indignatio*' is the heading for one of his chapters in the manuscript).

In the Walpole Collection at the King's School, I found a book called *The Gods and Mr Perrin*. I had never heard of it, and found it was the American edition of *Mr Perrin and Mr Traill*. There were few changes in the text until the last three chapters, which were completely rewritten, thus altering the book's tone and emphasis. The idea is obviously to give not only a happy ending but one more vigorous, positive, forward-looking and optimistic. At the prize-giving, instead of merely glaring at the presenter of prizes, who is rambling on about public schools in general and the fine spirit of Moffatts in particular, Perrin leaps up. He shrieks at the astounded governors, staff and boys:

> 'It's all lies! It's lies, all lies! . . . We are unhappy here, all of us. We are downtrodden by that man – we are not paid enough – we are not considered at all – never considered – everything is wrong – we all hate each other – we hate *him* – he hates *us* – we are unhappy – it is all hell . . . hell!'

The outburst makes him see that his hatred of Traill is unimportant.

> It was not Traill that he was going to kill; it was something larger, greater, more sweeping – a system . . . He was elated, he was triumphant.

Later, Traill visits him and asks him to shake hands; they make up their differences, but none of this matters to Perrin, who is determined to kill himself. Leaving the suicide note to his mother in a prominent position, he goes out to the cliffs at daybreak. At a place where the sea opens out below, he meets Isabel, who has followed him down (as so often happens, Walpole posits something unlikely: that she should be up and about at daybreak and so happen to see him). They talk, and in the new scene Walpole makes Perrin replace Traill, emotionally, as he never does in the English version. Isabel tells him how much she admired his outburst at the prize-giving, and asks him to be her friend before they part. He bursts into sobs and tells her:

> 'I've seen that I'm a complete failure in every possible sense of the word . . . we are at opposite ends of the world, you and I . . . but you have been everything to one useless creature.' Curiously, in the growing light, with that strange, uncouth figure holding her hand, she felt more strongly moved than she had ever been before – yes, even Archie Traill's wooing had not touched her as this did. As he looked at her he knew that he might kiss her and that she would not have drawn back.

(The enormous social and sexual importance of a kiss between social equals at that time has to be borne in mind here: to them both, it would have meant commitment to marriage, as fiction of the time often shows, or else the grossest disloyalty to Traill.) Isabel begs Perrin to go back to Moffatts and fight for what he believes in: 'The new day shone about their heads.' Later she tells Mrs Comber that Perrin is 'coming back like a hero. Why, when I think of Archie and myself and our lives,' she goes on, '. . . and then I think of all the awkward, bad-mannered, stiff, jolty people who are heroes every day of their lives, I'm ashamed!' With this, even Traill is made to join the unadventurous, the unheroic.

What Walpole thought of this other version of his most successful book, and of changes in it so basic that it becomes almost another work, we cannot know. Was he committed to the new Perrin, or did he alter the emphasis merely because he was asked to do so for the American market? Certainly he gave Perrin a new, heroic dimension, even considering him a possible sexual rival to Traill, too honourable to press his advantage but capable, at least momentarily, of winning Isabel. Perhaps he began the new chapters in a pot-boiling spirit, admitting that alterations could be made, and then, as he wrote, finding himself persuaded by them. He seems not to have discussed the new version with others; James, as far as I know, knew nothing about it; so perhaps, considering how well documented most of his writing is, he did not like what he had done.

4 . . . *broad in the back, thick and short in the leg* Hugh Walpole

Walpole wrote an ordinary school story as well, boy-centred and boy-level, and it too proved one of his most lasting successes, much liked by the young, at least until recently and perhaps still. *Jeremy at Crale* (1927) is the third of a trilogy of books about a boy called Jeremy Cole whose father is a clergyman in the cathedral city of Polchester, the centre of Walpole's imaginary county where most of his characters turn up and intertwine across the years. Jeremy, like the others, wanders in and out of other books as a minor character, turning up as an adult later on. In *Jeremy at Crale*, which covers a single school term, he is fifteen and at a famous public school, a junior version of Archie Traill, thick-set, bullet-headed, short-legged (Walpole had curious taste when it came to his heroes' physique), brilliant at football but without any idea – when he is mentioned – who Keats is. (This alone throws an odd light on the teaching of the time.) His friends call him Stocky, his enemies the Farmer; his best friend is an even thicker-headed lad called Jumbo Payne, and his enemy a slender aristocratic boy called Staire – an effective name for one so disdainful – who goes abroad for holidays or else lives grandly in Leicestershire, where his father is an MFH. Walpole, who cared about such things, made a good deal of the plain social snobbery of school life. Jeremy's talent for games, though important, never makes up for his modest clerical background. Crale is one of the 'great' schools, not a socially dingy one like Epsom/Moffatts; and it is hard not to think that some of Walpole's approval and disapproval of things at the former and the latter was due to his sense of their social standing. The three books about him, *Jeremy, Jeremy and Hamlet*, and *Jeremy at Crale*, are reputed to have popularised Jeremy's name, as Barrie popularised Peter, and Farrar, Eric.

Most of what is found in the stock school story is found in *Jeremy at Crale*: football match, fight between the hero and his enemy with predictable but dramatic victory, bullying, running away, house supper with favourite visitor and frantic singing of the ritual songs, romantic attachment. More is made of the romantic attachment than is usual in school stories – it runs through the plot, suggesting 'otherness', the world of the imagination, non-school values – but it is very much on an idealised, 'best friend' level, nothing like as definite as the romantic friendships of *Tim* or *The Hill*. The homosexual atmosphere, though, is strong; less explicitly considered than in E. F. Benson's *David Blaize*, where it occupies a central moral position, but quite as pervasive.

On the whole we get a cheerful view of school life. If you are a boy like Jeremy, Walpole seems to be saying, sociable, equable, able to hold your own, a good games player and a natural leader, then all is well. Jeremy loves the rough-and-tumble, the noise and companionableness of it all. Occasionally he has twinges of longing for higher things, moments when he watches a sunset or some such irrelevance, which Jumbo cannot possibly understand. The boy he adores from a distance, Ridley, to whom he has never spoken – it is the simplest case of love at first sight – will be the answer to these moments, if he can only get to know him. On the last page he does and life seems to alter dramatically. After swapping a few sentences with him, Jeremy is 'happier than he had ever been in all his life before'.

If, on the other hand, you are *not* like Jeremy, if you are new, small, trustful, tender, and a natural prey to bullies, like Walpole in his prep school days or the small Charles Morgan* who idolises Jeremy and suffers for it, then you had best stay away from even a good public school like Crale. Like Charlie Evson in *St Winifred's*, Morgan, known as the Dormouse, is tormented, terrified, altered and almost destroyed. At last he makes a bolt for it but is brought back, alive and more or less kicking, to start again on a new footing, mysteriously confident and improved. Presumably he justifies Walpole's belief in the efficacy of the public school in making anyone fit for anything. Of course, protected by someone stronger, the frailest boy can find a comfortable niche. Walpole describes the sort of domestic arrangement that makes this possible. A boy called Llewellyn, he says,

> was a little as Jeremy might be, three years from now, broad in the back, thick and short in the leg. He'd had his nose broken, boxing . . . he cared for nothing but football, boxing, his dogs at home and his friend Corner, who shared a study with him. Corner was the exact opposite of Llewellyn, being slender, wistful and musical. Rather like a girl and known as Alice by his enemies, Llewellyn [*sic*] adored him and thought everything he did was wonderful.

Later, Llewellyn seems attracted by Jeremy (a little surprisingly, since physically Jeremy is like himself, not at all like Alice Corner). He 'drew Jeremy to him, putting an arm round his shoulder . . . "Look here, will you come in a lot to our Study next term?"' But Jeremy, thinking of Alice's jealousy, says no.

* The 'real' names which turn up in school stories are a source of innocent fun. Charles Morgan was not writing by 1911, but he wrote about Walpole later. Other recognisable names (sometimes 'misspelt') turn up to amuse those with long memories. Anyone who remembers a great American scandal some years back will be delighted to find the heroine of Angela Brazil's *The Nicest Girl in the School* is called Patty Hirst [*sic*]. My own favourites in this game of retrospective coincidence are the rival cricket captains in *Mike*, who are called Burgess and [*sic*] Maclain.

So the fights and sing-songs and house matches are threaded on a story of emotional ups and downs, or, if you look at it another way, as perhaps the child reader was meant to, the emotional parts are punctuation marks in a story of fights and sing-songs and house matches; in other words in the usual stuff of school stories, rather more skilfully (but also rather more pretentiously) handled than most. Walpole was a mediocre writer who thought himself, and was thought by many, a good one, perhaps even a great one. In fact he was not, even at the simplest level, a competent one (his elementary grammatical mistake in the Llewellyn piece was typical), let alone a competent analyst of the human heart or of human society. But his school stories show him at his best, *Mr Perrin and Mr Traill* because he really knew the background and had imaginative sympathy with what was going on, and *Jeremy at Crale* because he was writing simply and with enjoyment; not, I think, about his own boyhood but about what he would have liked it to be.

CHAPTER XI

The school story as allegory: *The Lanchester Tradition*

He had often experienced an absurd sensation of being considered morally, as well as socially, inferior to the more fortunate alumni of the great public schools G. F. Bradby

If a story is to be more than an anecdote it must have a meaning outside itself, must reflect and connect, make points which are more than anecdotal. The parable is a simple example of metaphor in action. A stands for B, X for Y, and so on; A's action gives an insight into B's behaviour and motives, and so on. The three school love stories I dealt with showed, in personal terms, what happened when mind and body – or brains and athleticism – became too sharply divided: on the one hand, the weedy intellectual, worthy, high-minded, dull in appearance and personality; on the other, the golden-haired athlete, beautiful, sensual, a little giddy. A parable dealing with a fairly but not exactly similar division in more powerful, less personal, terms was G. F. Bradby's *The Lanchester Tradition* (1913).

Apart from this book, Bradby's novels were all inconspicuous and are now entirely forgotten. A schoolmaster himself (he taught at Rugby) he wrote one other school story, of (by comparison) astonishing feebleness, *The Chronicles of Dawnhope*, and several novels in the grey area (much trodden by minor novelists early in the century) between adult and children's fiction, one about a Nesbit-like family of children in a village, another about a gang of good-hearted street-boys in an industrial town, another about a man retiring to an old Norfolk farmhouse to write, with mild rural adventure thrown in. *The Lanchester Tradition* is incomparably better than anything else he wrote, and some people have actually claimed it is the best school story of all.

This large claim has been made for plenty of others, but it does have a special place among school stories. It does not, like the love stories, *personify* attitudes, but it shows events, circumstances, attitudes and changes in *action*, in what takes place in a school across several months.

Using a situation familiar, even conventional, in the school story – that of an outsider coming in with new ideas to change an unchanging milieu – it tells the much wider story of the schools' change of spirit and emphasis from Arnold's day until the early years of the twentieth century. (It appeared in 1913, when good school stories were coming thick and fast.) Narrowly, and perhaps even in Bradby's own conscious intention, it reflected recognisable events in his own time at Rugby, when an ineffective headmaster was followed by a dynamic one. But there was much more to it than that, a much more widely applicable meaning. In the detail of a particular school, it showed how Arnold's ideas had been twisted into something he never intended or dreamed of; how athleticism dominated the scene, how learning, intelligence and even Christian morality were undervalued, and how the idealised athlete, far from being an inspiring master or a golden boy, had often become a pompous bore or a spoiled brat. If metaphor is what counts in any work of art (the ability to make connections, to send out echoes and soundings, ripples, comparisons), and the school story has any artistic pretensions, then *The Lanchester Tradition*, the most metaphorical of them all, the least narrow in its application and episodic in its form, certainly deserves a close look.

Chiltern, its fictional school, is an amalgam of a number of schools, real or fictional, and, since Bradby likes his little joke, 'the only institution of its kind about which nobody has yet written a school story'. Clearly it is one of the 'great' schools, although, when the story opens, it has been in a state of decline for some years. 'When Abraham Lanchester became headmaster at the end of the eighteenth century,' we are told, 'he found the place little more than a country grammar school; he left it an institution of National, almost Imperial, importance.' Inspired by what it believes to be his spirit, the school carries on without change or development. Bradby writes:

Chiltern has lived ever since on the memory of Dr Lanchester. The Lanchester tradition permeates the place like an atmosphere, invisible but stimulating. It is difficult to analyse, for, like all great truths, it states itself in different terms to different minds and has a special message for each. To the general public it stands for the Classics and faith in the educational value of Latin verse. To the masters it means a firm belief in the efficacy of the methods, or absence of method, to which they have become attached through long habit. To the Old Chiltonians it embodies the social ideas and customs with which they grew up; and to the boys themselves, if it means anything more than a name, it represents a certain immutability and fixity of things, an as-it-was-in-the-beginning-is-now-and-ever-shall-be attitude towards life that appeals to their best conservative instincts. Any change in the hour of a lesson or the colour of a ribbon is regarded as an outrage on the Lanchester tradition, and is popularly supposed to make the dead hero turn in his grave.

For twenty-four years the school has slithered along these well-worn tracks under the colourless rule of an amiable, weak headmaster, Dr Gussy, backed by the Reverend Henry Chowdler, 'the strong man of Chiltern'. Chowdler is Bradby's best-drawn character, a man he regards with fascination and distaste:

Narrow but concentrated, with an aggressive will and a brusque intolerance of all who differed from him, he was a fighter who loved fighting for its own sake and who triumphed through the sheer exhaustion of his enemies. . . . A tall man, with broad shoulders, round head, thin sandy hair and full lips, he caught the eye in whatever company he might be, and his resonant voice attracted attention . . . his confident manner impressed parents, and his was considered *the* house at Chiltern.

From that description and others that come later he seems almost weirdly like Archie Traill, twenty or thirty years on; or Walpole's Jeremy, in middle age. Of his personal life, we know only that he has a fluttering, devoted wife, and gather that like many schoolmasters at the time he has few private interests outside the school.

When Dr Gussy's somnolent reign is over and a new headmaster is sought, the School Council finds itself unable to agree between the two obvious choices and falls back on a compromise candidate, the Reverend Septimus Flaggon. He is an outsider, as famous and successful headmasters have sometimes been (Sanderson was considered one at Oundle; Norwood – nicknamed 'Boots' because he wore them – was also one at Marlborough when he went there from Bristol Grammar School, to be greeted with snobbish sneers by the boys). 'Fellow of an obscure college, tutor to a foreign prince, and subsequently president of some educational institution in Wales, his youth and inexperience ruled him out of serious consideration,' Bradby writes. Yet he is not only considered but elected the new headmaster.

Chiltern is outraged. Cox, a 75-year-old master given to resigning and then withdrawing his resignation, hands in his notice once too often and to his chagrin finds it accepted. The new choice is discussed eagerly by everyone except Chowdler, who is holding his fire. Flaggon arrives to look round the school and is confronted, most obviously and aggressively, by Chowdler. Bradby writes:

Antipathies are often physical as well as moral and the two men suddenly became conscious of a kind of physical distaste for one another. In Chowdler's fleshy limbs, broad shoulders, bullet head and aggressive manner, Mr Flaggon saw for a moment the personification of that narrow but confident prejudice which blocks progress and strangles reform; while Mr Chowdler realised acutely that 'the man Flaggon' would easily get on his nerves.

Flaggon, an unsuitably named non-drinker and a non-smoker in the days when all good schoolmasters smoked pipes, is shy and uncommunicative. The son of a vicar in Cumberland, he has no public-school experience, having been to a provincial grammar school from which he won a classical exhibition to a small Oxford college. At Oxford, we hear,

he had often experienced an absurd sensation of being considered morally, as well as socially, inferior to the more fortunate alumni of the great public schools . . . Of public schools he knew nothing from the inside and he had few opportunities of studying public school men at his own small college. In such as he came across he noted a certain self-sufficiency and polite lack of interest in things intellectual, which he put down to the narrowness of their training.

Flaggon's withdrawn manner, his youth, his lack of inches (he is 'rather below middle height'), perhaps – though Bradby does not mention it as a disadvantage – his bachelor status, are all against him. But he has his points:

With a clear-cut face and intellectual forehead, his most striking feature was his eyes – fearless, grey, receptive eyes which looked out on the world with a quiet but penetrating interest.

He has strong views on education, too:

He knew what [it] ought to be, what it had been to himself – an individual renaissance, a quickening of the highest faculties of mind and spirit, and he knew that that was precisely what public school education was *not* . . . In his mind's eye he saw the boys as hungry sheep who looked up and were not fed. He had not yet become acquainted with that particular brand of sheep that is born without an appetite.

On Flaggon's visit to Chiltern before taking up the headmastership, Chowdler tries to needle him with talk of the Lanchester tradition. 'Aren't you forgetting that Dr Lanchester was always considered a radical?' Flaggon asks; as indeed Arnold was in his day. On a walk round the school he is struck by a curious air among some of the boys, a mixture of snideness, knowingness and social contempt. Later, in chapel, he notes that

there was an air of insolence and swagger about the way in which the bigger boys strolled in last and lounged, instead of kneeling, during prayers . . . Here were no hungry sheep looking up to be fed, but indifference, inertia, and an unknown something that was probably worse than either and possibly the cause of both.

The sermons he and Chowdler give when he takes over the following term fire the first shots. Everyone now knows that it is war between them. Flaggon's sermon is full of new ideas; Chowdler's text is: 'Hold fast to that which is good.' A new broom who cares nothing for the static Lanchester tradition, Flaggon goes about things in a totally new way, to the outrage of the boys and the indignation of some of the masters. The first master he appoints is an 'aesthete' who thinks *The Picture of Dorian Gray* a great work of art (further outrage). The views of parents (of all people) are invited on changes in the curriculum. Motor-bikes are forbidden. Discipline improves. The drunken porter, past whom it has always been easy to slip, is dismissed, and a new, efficient one installed in his place. A parents' committee is set up to improve standards, a daring innovation in those days.

Two masters go for walks together, discuss what is happening, and reflect on the state of play. The unfortunately-named Bent, Bradby's mouthpiece, discovers Dr Lanchester's long-forgotten letters. 'Lanchester was a much finer fellow than I realised,' he tells his friend Plummer; but the school, far from following him in his modernity, has traduced him. 'I wasn't crabbing the *real* Lanchester,' says Bent. 'It's only his ghost that annoys me.' With his ghost still stalking the school the masters sway this way and that in their feelings about Flaggon and his reforms.

To Chowdler, a boy of the 'right type' (that is, his own type) can get away with a good deal. To Flaggon, all boys are equal and equally responsible for their actions. When le Willows, head of Chowdler's house, is caught smoking, Flaggon deprives him permanently of his praetorship (that is, demotes him from being head of house) and school prefectship. Chowdler defends the boy, furiously but without success (and it does seem a severe punishment, to a modern reader). Then le Willows is caught cribbing, and Flaggon expels him at the end of term (again, the punishment seems excessive, especially at a time when cribbing was so widespread). le Willows is a fine cricketer, socially well connected; his parents are incredulous, his grandfather writes to the chairman of the Council to complain, and Lord Chalvey, a prospective parent, withdraws his son's name. Unmoved by all this, Flaggon picks a boy called Dennison, whom Chowdler detests, as head of Chowdler's house. Dennison tells Flaggon that the house is morally bad, and one of the boys involved there is one of the insolent trio Flaggon noticed on his first visit to the school. When accused, he denies everything and defies Flaggon, who threatens him with the police. In another house, three prominent boys are expelled for 'moral' reasons (presumably homosexual acts; Bradby is extremely vague but readers are expected to know or guess). An explosive staff meeting, at which a new time-table is put forward, finds Chowdler at breaking point and he refuses to accept it. Flaggon is forced to ask for his resignation; Chowdler refuses it, and appeals to the School Council.

It is now Chowdler against Flaggon in the Council, the reforming against the conservative spirit. Unless it supports him, Flaggon says, he will resign. Staff and boys are now coming round to Flaggon's views, to admiration for his reforms; and so, to some extent, is the Council. By the narrowest of majorities – the chairman's casting vote – Flaggon wins its support and Chowdler has to go. He stays until the end of term, unable to understand what has happened. Then, as often happens in school stories, pent-up emotion suddenly breaks through with dramatic effect, and Bradby has his big scene of surrender and pathos. Again, as so often happens, it takes place in the school chapel:

> Mr Chowdler was suddenly overcome by his emotions and his broad shoulders shook with the sobs he was powerless to control. It was not remorse; it was not even regret for what he had done. Something there was of the bitterness of defeat, and something of the grief of a sanguine man who has lost an only child. Mr Chowdler had loved Chiltern with all the strength of a robust and unimaginative nature . . . The Headmaster saw and understood.'

2 *Indifference, inertia, and an unknown something that was probably worse than either and possibly the cause of both* G. F. Bradby

The underlying meaning of this quite simple action is clear. *The Lanchester Tradition* is not a ragbag of anecdotes like so many school stories, but the image of an idea, worked out in action. Dr Lanchester (Arnold) was a reformer, an innovator in education, a radical and 'intensely modern'. Since his day, pious tradition has embalmed him, making him an image not of what he was but of what his successors like to think he was. Since his day Chiltern (the public schools) has lost its original impetus, its intellectual vigour and even interests, its candour and liberal values, its curiosity and courtesy, in fact all that distinguished it as a force for good in its earlier days. Sports worship and snobbery rule. Blinkered men like Chowdler, feeble men like Gussy, are now in command. And under the surface lie, as Flaggon had noted, 'indifference, inertia, and an unknown something that [is] probably worse than either and possibly the cause of both.' Like all school-story writers of his day, Bradby was unable to name or even to hint too obviously at what that 'unknown something' might be. Four years later Alec Waugh said rather more clearly that it was homosexual feeling and behaviour, and that these were inevitable in a single-sex community up to the age of nineteen. There were yelps of outrage, for no one had actually admitted it so clearly before. But Bradby, like everyone else connected with the public schools, knew what he knew and dropped the sort of hints that those in the know like himself would surely have been able to pick up.

For all its mildness of tone, *The Lanchester Tradition* is more sweepingly critical of the current public schools than any other school story of the time. *The Harrovians,* published in the same year, was scratchy and critical of a great deal and caused much more offence, but it made no fundamental criticisms, like Bradby's. His suggested reform was radical: get in an outsider, who will turn the system upside down. Flaggon acts untrammelled by the public-school tradition, against all the established prejudices of Bradby's readers. He is against the bloods, the worship of games and sportsmen, the forgiving of certain things in a boy because he is particularly good at certain others; he is against the complementary disparagement of learning and intellectual interests, and against snobbery, the subtle as well as the overt snobbery of the school system of his time, which could suggest, as was suggested to him at Oxford, that there was something morally as well as socially reprehensible about not having been to a public school, and could forgive all kinds of things in a boy like le Willows because he was well-connected, a good games-player, the 'right sort'. There was a strong feeling at the time that a boy was or was not the 'right type' or the 'right sort', depending mainly not on his character but on his social background and ability to look and sound right, to play the right games, wear the right clothes, do the right thing, above all 'fit in'. Flaggon is even against the idea that a boy does not sneak to a master (Dennison sneaks with devastating results about the goings-on in his house), and that public schools are independent of the outside world and its laws, keeping their own secrets (he is prepared to call in the police when defied by a boy). Worst of all (I should have thought), he takes away the housemaster's autonomy, his right to rule under his own roof, by putting in a boy Chowdler hates as head of Chowdler's house.

Bradby deplores what has happened in every way to the liberal, intellectual, high-minded and keen-spirited public schools as they used to be, as they might have been, as Arnold would have wanted them. Snobbery and anti-intellectualism, conformity and a kind of loutishness peculiar, around Bradby's time, to many products of the public schools whose sense of social superiority to everyone else had been drummed into them for years: these he saw and attacked and it is easy to sympathise with him, because they are just what modern readers most deplore. How right he was, they feel, how clear-sighted to see it!

And yet, as an embodiment of reform and modernity, Flaggon is not really up to his position. He is the book's main weakness. An admirable character he may be, but his personality is no more impressive than his outlandish name, and it is hard not to wonder, like some of those in the story, how on earth he got the headmastership in the first place. The simple, peppery Chowdler, who is rather like Bullard, the tough games master in *The Loom of Youth,* with his equally explosive rages and frustrating inability to see what's what around him, is a good deal more credible and interesting; another loser with whom the modern world is catching up. The year of *The Lanchester Tradition* – 1913 – was the final year of the old world, the true end of the nineteenth century and of the public-school world at its confident height. In his allegory in realistic dress, Bradby seems – almost in spite of himself and his limitations – prophetic, even visionary, about some aspects of the modern world.

CHAPTER XII

The schoolboy's school story: *The Loom of Youth*

Devilish, sensual, unthinkable, destructive of and mocking at all ideals, battening on profanity . . . 'God save England', if these are her Gods Montague Rendall, headmaster of Winchester

I thought of putting *The Loom of Youth* among the 'documentary' school stories, because, as the most painstakingly detailed and accurate-seeming of them all, it seemed to fit there. I thought of combining it with other school stories written during or after the First World War, and considering how its spirit matched theirs. But it seemed to belong on its own, to fit nowhere exactly; perhaps because, as I said earlier, it is the only major school story written by a boy.

Alec Waugh was seventeen when he wrote it – fast, in two months; not quite a schoolboy, but nearly one, because he had only just left Sherborne to go into the army, in 1916. And because he was then in what now seems an extraordinary (but in those days seems to have been quite a normal) state of 'homesickness' for his school, it is very much an 'inside' novel, passionate and committed – though inevitably with a pinch of the critical detachment afforded by distance. The most factual novel about life in one of the most mainstream public schools at the moment when they had reached their peak of self-confidence, when Arnold's ideas had been coarsened almost out of all recognition, it is one of the school-story enthusiast's most useful sources. After the war this self-confidence was to wane, and questions were to be asked (many of them inspired by it) about the function of the public schools and their place in a world greatly altered. Never again would it be possible to take them quite so straight, quite so much at their own valuation.

Alec Waugh's own interest in the public-school world was intense but not, for its time, unusual. His father felt exactly as he did – not merely interested but involved and committed – and telegrams were sent home from Sherborne after every match or exam, giving scores and marks. Arthur Waugh wrote in his autobiography:

> During the next four years I must have been the youngest man of my age in London. When once I was free of the office, all my thoughts and interests were absorbed in my two schoolboys*. I might almost be said to have lived at Sherborne in my imagination . . . It was so easy to slip into a train at Waterloo on a Friday evening, and arrive at Sherborne in time to see the lights still shining in the School House studies. Then there was the full weekend to enjoy, with a house match on Saturday afternoon, a dinner party of boys at the Digby Hotel in the evening, with a game of coon-can afterwards.[1]

Although Evelyn Waugh called his father's interest in Sherborne 'obsessive', this involvement of an adult in school affairs was not thought particularly odd. The relationship worked both ways. Outstanding schoolboys were occasionally known among adults of their class; a boy of unusual academic promise might be known well beyond his school, and in one of his adult books Alec Waugh mentions hearing of a well-known public-school cricketer even in his prisoner-of-war camp in Germany. A small circle in one way, in others the public-school world was far-flung and tentacular.†

The Loom of Youth is interesting for its subjects and the circumstances in which it was written, and because it caught a doomed set of people and way of life at a particular moment with ingenuous realism. This gives it the fly-in-amber quality that is so artless at the time, so valuable later. It does not suggest its author was a prodigy, or even a boy of special promise. As the work of a seventeen-year-old it is remarkably competent, even its length – 335 pages of small print in the early editions – suggesting an unusual degree of staying power and fluency for a boy that age. But it has little literary merit, little sense of language and no apparent pleasure in or skill with words. Its philosophising, like its imagery, is both naive and dull; often it has the flat-footedness rather than the freshness of youth. Yet it has that curious thing, 'personality', rather as *Tom Brown's Schooldays* has, a dynamic quality that seems to go with boyishness of spirit, and keeps

* Evelyn Waugh, five years younger than his brother, was then at a day prep school in Hampstead, called Heath Mount.

† As any number of memoirs and biographies will confirm, the same names turn up over and over again, not necessarily in school contexts, the same people's lives overlapping. This gave, indeed still gives, a cohesiveness to the whole of the upper middle class (not merely to a small aristocracy) which often amazed and even today continues to surprise foreigners.

you listening as you would to an enthusiastic talker, prosy but spirited, and with the sort of presence to arouse sympathy and a response from the heart.

This, I think, must have been what its first readers responded to; and its author's belief that they would listen. Its scandalous interest meant that it was overpraised at the beginning, and the fury it aroused in some people probably made its supporters warmer in their praise than they might have been if it had dealt with a neutral subject. At Sherborne itself, the authorities gradually worked themselves up into hysterical denunciations. 'Alec Waugh, one of the worst specimens ever turned out by Sherborne,' one of the masters wrote of this amiable, popular, school-loving young man, of whom no one who knew him outside the context of school seemed able to speak ill. The headmaster of Winchester* wrote in a letter:

> Amazingly clever and well-written for a lad of 17 but devilish, sensual, unthinkable, destructive of and mocking at all ideals, battening on profanity, Baudelaire and bawd – not liberty but licence. To my thinking it is incredibly untrue and yet it is clearly a photograph! 'God save England', if these are her Gods.

'Uniformly dull, occasionally unpleasant, and, in my judgement at least, almost wholly untrue,' Canon Edward Lyttelton wrote in the *Contemporary Review*.

Frank and complete for its time, *The Loom of Youth* seemed to cover most aspects of school life. Even the author's own ordinariness – the way he was both athletic and academically able, and could see both sides of every question – made it appear fresh and convincing. His intellectual interests were middlebrow, his critical comments reassuringly banal. Had he been sharper, more ruthless, more rebellious, or more unattractive, had his ideas been more radical or more snidely expressed, he would have been less successful. As it was, he became every liberal's favourite liberal, threatening no one as he bravely bared his teeth. H. W. Massingham wrote of *The Loom of Youth* at the time:

> It seems to me a revolutionary work. If only the parents of England will read it and having read it, act on it. If they do the one without the other, it is on their consciences that they risk the ruin of their children's characters and minds.[2]

At this distance it seems amazing that a book as conventional and as mild could ever have been thought revolutionary, that criticisms as gently formulated could ever have produced such dismay and delight, such a pother of excitement. In the middle of the most terrible war anyone had ever known or envisaged, there was still time and energy to dispute long and vehemently the question of the public schools. No

* Montague Rendall (1862–1950).

one yet seemed to realise that the war was killing off, not just their young products, but the world they were made for. Nothing quite like *The Loom of Youth* had been seen before, nothing as central or as generally applicable; hence the excitement. Nothing, above all, so typical of a great *many* schools.

The best-known school stories had so far been relevant to a single school, and whether they applied as much to the rest the general reader had no way of telling. *Tom Brown's Schooldays* belonged almost to the pre-history of the modern public school; *Stalky & Co.* was about a very special place, very much a one-class, almost a one-sect school preparing its boys for a similar sort of future; *The Hill* and *The Harrovians* were too exactly about Harrow to apply elsewhere; the pop stories were not taken seriously. But *The Loom of Youth,* because it stood dead centre, seemed to apply almost anywhere within the system. Neither the author nor the school was too clever or too smart or in any way eccentric. The very flatness of style, the dogged, unadventurous narrative, must have carried conviction.

Sherborne, which in the novel was called Fernhurst and transferred from Dorset to Derbyshire, was one of the old grammar schools which had 'come on' in Victorian times to become known as public schools. In 1850 it had forty boys, two of them boarders, the rest local boys who were taken free, and a single master; by 1877 there were 278 boys, only thirty of them day boys, and eighteen masters. By Alec Waugh's day it was as 'typical' a place of the sort as you could find, although, as I have said, no public school could really be called typical of the rest. Sherborne was, at any rate, the outsider's idea of such a place, the story-book school come true. (Its buildings were in fact used in the most recent film of *Goodbye, Mr Chips*.) Set in a charming small town, surrounded by the splendid Dorset countryside, with beautiful, very old buildings of its own, sports-mad but not cruelly so (as some called Marlborough, for instance), tough, as they all were at the time, but without the harsh reputation of, say, Wellington; solidly middle-class, middle-income and middlingly intellectual, it was as much the quintessential public school as Alec Waugh was (in his own view) the quintessential public schoolboy:

> I loved school life. I might well have seemed the boy for whom the public school system was designed – gregarious, sociable, as keen on his work in form as on his prowess in the field, a boy for whom the fifteen hours of the day seemed too narrow a casket for all it contained.[3]

All went well at Sherborne from the start. 'Nearly all boys enjoy their last term at a public school,' he wrote, 'but I had a good time from the start. I enjoyed every aspect of its life.'[4]

Four years earlier *The Harrovians* had caused a stir. But Harrow, with its own atmosphere and *mores*, cannot have seemed as familiar to the middle-class readers who felt at home with Sherborne/Fernhurst. Alec Waugh admired *The Harrovians* enormously. His hero called it 'the finest school story I have ever read'. In *The Loom of Youth* he described its exhilarating effect on public schoolboys at the time, and the sense of outrage among adults that things had been made public which should have been kept inside the walls of the school or at least of the public school system and class. Closing ranks was then an almost automatic reaction to any disclosure or criticism of bourgeois life. This conspiracy of silence was so tight and powerful in public-school matters that only today, forty or fifty years from their prime, are memoirs, letters and outspoken autobiographies telling a wider public what must have been widely known inside the system. Loyalty, shame, secrecy, an almost Mafia-like sense of *omertà*, until very recently involved those who had been to public schools in all kinds of double standards of honesty, and in see-saw emotional attitudes of love and hatred.

What Alec Waugh disliked and what he loved about the system and his own school it is often hard to disentangle. *Odi et amo* – as he admitted, that was his retrospective trouble. Sherborne, he said, was like 'the mistress whom he still [adored] but nonetheless [held] largely responsible for the rupture.'[5] The rupture came when he was asked to leave (not quite officially expelled), a much graver matter in those days than it is now; for Arthur Waugh's son, it must have been grave indeed. His hero in the novel has a last evening of poignant school songs, ending with 'Auld Lang Syne' and 'God Save the King', then leaves next morning with handclasps and fluttering handkerchiefs at the station. 'He wanted to keep in his mind the memory of Fernhurst as he had last seen it, silver and beautiful in the morning sun,' Alec Waugh writes. His own last days at Sherborne must have been very different, his own last night more sombre. And so came *The Loom of Youth*. 'It was in part a nostalgic book,' he said in his autobiography; 'and yet at the same time tinged with resentment . . . I was impelled by the need to explain and justify myself.'[6]

2 *I was excited by the atmosphere of competition. I was ambitious and now, at Sherborne, I was in the arena* Alec Waugh

For all Alec Waugh's criticisms, one aspect of public-school life entirely escaped his censure, an aspect most people at the time – and presumably he himself – took as natural, not reprehensible. This was its competitiveness. Day after day there was open, encouraged confrontation between boy and boy, competition for marks, scores, places in class or team, positions of authority; more subtly, there was competition for popularity and prestige, for the privilege and sweetness and triumph of being a blood. An outsize figure in school stories, standing on the pinnacle of achievement and fame, the blood as a rule had an official position, at least in athletics; but not necessarily. Age and position gave him physical power over the younger boys, the power to chastise them; but this was not what mattered. His authority was based on admiration from below, nearly always on the worship (since he was almost invariably an athlete) of athletics, and of what almost invariably went with it – the right manner, the power to impress. With these, too, went the small but much-prized privileges which allowed him to do the things forbidden to his inferiors, who were thus hedged and irritated every moment of their lives; things prized far beyond their intrinsic value, as symbols of authority and importance.

Thomas Seccombe's rather turgid introduction to *The Loom of Youth* (for which Alec Waugh found a publisher after six rejections) suggests that its main theme is the 'Tyranny of the Bloods'. In fact, it is rather more about their triumph. For the hero ends as very much a blood himself and Waugh, though critical of detail, clearly failed to find much wrong with the system that put the bloods where they were. He criticised the criteria used in putting them there, but not the way the whole system worked. And the public-school system as a whole was involved here, its entire ethical basis. But Alec Waugh never saw this, never seems to have noticed that the system reflected the adult world at its harshest. H. G. Wells wrote that the public schools

> sought a human motive [in urging the boys to work] in vanity and competition; they turned to rewards, distinctions and competitions . . . The class-list with its pitiless relegation of two-thirds of the class to self-conscious mediocrity and dufferdom was the symbol [of their method of teaching] . . . An aristocracy of leading boys made the pace and the rest of the school found its compensation in games or misbehaviour.[7]

This was so not just in the public-school years, but from childhood, from the age of eight or even earlier. For the prep school was highly competitive too, since competitiveness was an essential part of getting into public school at all, and a high degree of it was needed by some small boys from an early age if their only chance of public school – or at least of one of the leading ones – lay in scholarships.

This competitiveness may have been an effective rough-and-ready sieve for imperial functionaries and army officers. The constant scramble not to fall through its holes may have produced, in most, the required degree of self-reliance, toughness, ability to keep one's counsel and one's end up, and the kind of lonely pride that allowed men to live, if necessary, in conditions of comfortless isolation. It may be an old joke, but it seems likely to be true, that the public-school product survived better than most in prison. Writing of prisoners-of-war in Italy during the Second World War, Stuart Hood remarked on 'those whose lives were adjusted to an orderly and not unpleasant routine in the prison camp such as they had known before in prep or public school'.[8] But it was a system which involved trampling over others in the scramble, moral ruthlessness and possibly moral sharp practice; at its mildest, it meant playing for popularity, influence and prestige.

Though it grew up gradually, without the implications always being considered, it was all quite deliberately the exact opposite of home. At home, if he is lucky in his parents, the child feels 'single' as well as one of a group, specially, uniquely cherished, himself and no one else. Parents try to give him a sense of this uniqueness, of the qualities that belong to him alone. The prep and public schools of Alec Waugh's boyhood did exactly the opposite. Both officially and unofficially, the boy was pounded in with the others as soon as he arrived there, stirred into an amorphous mass from which he could emerge only when he had in some way proved himself. 'The function of the preparatory school,' as Alec Waugh wrote and I quoted earlier, 'is to iron out the idiosyncrasies of the home, so that a standardised product may be presented to the public school.' His suppressed individuality could later emerge through his own efforts. If there was none so formless and unrecognisable as the new boy, there was none so individual and noticeable as the blood. To this glory, through the competitive system, the newest boy could aspire, and the sooner he realised this the better able he was to lay his plans, know the right people, do the right things. There were even 'bloodlets' – future bloods, hangers-on or obvious contenders, spotted early, groomed for stardom, possibly taken up by their elders on the one hand, sometimes disliked for it by their equals on the other. The Caterpillar in *The Hill* is one such boy. Vachell describes him as

> a dandy, the understudy . . . of one of the 'Bloods', a 'Junior Blood' or 'Would-be', a tremendous authority on 'swagger', a stickler for tradition, who had been nearly three years at the school.

All school stories, *The Loom of Youth* among them, show how the new boy arriving at public school was made to feel as unremarkable as possible, as indistinguishable as could be from the rest; his distinctiveness blurred, his sense of uniqueness and even, to some extent, his sense of his own identity removed. In this way he was taken down a peg after what might have been a triumphant last phase at his prep school and taught (it was obscurely felt) that anything remarkable was not inherent in him, a quality of his own spirit and personality, but something that must be fought for and won. After that, distinction might come quickly; indeed, it was often forced: from fag to prefect, as Alec Waugh said, in a matter of months. This meant that from nobody to blood, from nonentity to hero, the rise could be swift and dazzling. It favoured, of course, the extrovert and the showman, the pusher and the show-off, some might also say the creeper and the crawler.

To restore the sense of selfhood which was stripped away at the beginning meant pushing up out of the mass – inevitably at other people's expense. Alec Waugh loved it, the scramble for power and place. He seems not to have seen it as a moral issue of any kind, but simply to have responded to the challenge and the drama. 'I was excited by the atmosphere of competition,' he wrote of his first days at Sherborne. '. . . I [was] ambitious and now, at Sherborne, I was in the arena.'[9] His hero feels the same at Fernhurst: 'He longed with a wild longing for power and popularity.' In schoolboy terms Alec Waugh's arena was a large one, since it included work as well as games. His main criticism of the system was not that boys were set against one another like gladiators but simply that the field in which they competed was too small. If games were absurdly over-valued, then all values became lop-sided, he felt, and the intellect was correspondingly despised.

'Every term offered its own prize for the winning, a promotion in form, a cap upon the field . . . The life of a public school is essentially dramatic: there are the rivalries of individual boys and of the various houses . . . The crowd is silent or applauds. Every incident is dramatised, and there is so much that is dramatic in school life. The weekly orders in form; the prize-givings on the last day of term; the anxieties and rewards of the struggle for a place in the house or school.'[10]

He loved the battle, and even while he was writing the novel still thought it worth fighting; its triumphs still stirred him, its failures still hurt. Hughes had used martial imagery and thought of life in general and school life in particular as a battle, but the fight was for moral victory, not self-aggrandisement. 'Games don't win battles, but brains do, and brains aren't trained on the footer field,' says Waugh's hero; but he does not ask where competitiveness, the bigger problem, is leading or what it implies.

As Shane Leslie puts it succinctly in The *Oppidan*: 'Captaincy, athletic success, pocket money, brilliance of mind, good looks': in the public school system, whatever Farrar might say or Hughes more winningly imply, these, as the century progressed, counted more than the moral qualities, and, as the school story progressed as well, they counted more in fiction too. Cyril Connolly was honest (if a little depressing) when he wrote of public-school life, not unenthusiastically:

> What matters is getting popular and winning colours, tasting the joys of power for the first time, acquiring knowledge and avoiding punishment.[11]

And when 'getting popular and winning colours' were all-important, the exterior qualities mattered more and more, the inner qualities prized by Arnold and Gilkes less and less. These outer qualities included those of birth, rank, wealth and status, parents' position, family home and whole way of life. No one in *Tom Brown's Schooldays* is put down or thought less of because his parents or grandparents are lowly; no one even considers it. But by 1905, in *The Hill*, the 'top drawer' is mentioned on the very first page, and throughout the book (as in many others), social distinctions are always emphasised, colouring conduct and moral worth at every turn. Social snobbery was not the only or even the most important criterion in judging school importance, although, as the century of school stories moved on, it came to colour all aspects of school life. In a school story less successful than *The Harrovians*, Lunn takes a different view of snobbery at school level:

> Few boys are snobs in the narrower sense of the word, for it is only the small and unimportant minority that will cultivate the scion of a noble house . . . Snobbery, however, interpreted in a wider sense, is common enough. The schoolboy snob cultivates the local aristocracy, an aristocracy not of birth but of muscle. He devotes his energy to getting into 'Society' as 'Society' is understood at school, and he derives the same thrill from the friendship of a cricket 'blood' as he will extract a few years later from the companionship of a peer. School life has its social ladder, and the social aspirant selects his friends from the boys who may be expected ultimately to get the School Colours.

So, it may not have been social snobbery that counted most; but qualities that could not be acquired any more than a place in Debrett, arbitrary gifts of fortune, always took precedence over those immeasurable gifts – the unique qualities of the individual. All the external qualities, which after all were a matter of luck or chance, mattered much more than those hidden qualities and even much more than the more measurable ones of virtue.

The Flashmans of fact or fiction might be put down (or sacked), and wickedness might not flourish. But neither did goodness unadorned. The bloods who swagger through school stories and memoirs, admired, fawned upon, fêted, all-powerful, much more influential than the masters, much grander than they seem likely to be in later life, unconstitutional rulers in an oligarchy where their particular qualities, and above all their assurance, are what count, are not the best or the wisest but the most successful, those with enough of the talent that counts; and with the foresight and ambition to lay plans, the patience to carry them through, and the ruthlessness to cut out any dead-wood friends on the way.

The talent was generally athletic, as nearly every school story makes wearisomely clear. In Desmond Coke's *The Worst House at Sherborough* the hero, Dick Hunter, is brought in from another house to become head of Wilson's and pull it up from disgrace. He is a 'good' boy, admittedly, with a strong personality and plenty of that quality indispensable in good schoolboys, keenness. But the real, in fact the admitted, reason why he is called in to put things right is the fact that he is the school's best athlete and will make the house win cups for games. Its prestige will then rise, it will acquire keenness and proper spirit and all will be well. The two things go together: athletically successful (or at any rate 'keen') = morally worthy; unathletic = morally poor. The fact that no cups have been won lately means that Wilson's is a 'bad' house in every other way. Other houses despise it, so it lacks pride in itself, and so has become undisciplined, riotous, in every way 'slack'. The only way out of this moral slough is not through goodness pure and simple or even through an improvement in discipline, pride and the rest of it. It is possible *only* through athletic success in the first place, which will then bring discipline, pride and the rest in its wake.

One after another, the school stories hammer home this point. Alec Waugh is explicit about it:

> Gordon went to Fernhurst determined to succeed and at once was brought face to face with the fact that success lay in a blind worship at the shrine of the god of Athleticism. Honesty, virtue, moral determination – these mattered not at all.

By the early years of this century, plain virtue was nowhere in the system; even Arnold's 'gentlemanly conduct' had little place there, for gentlemanliness is not competitive; and as for the *Christian* gentlemen he had hoped to form, they had long been superseded by what someone with Hughes's brand of muscular Christianity in mind called 'lovable Goths'.

The moral implications of all this must have struck any thoughtful schoolboy. The contrast between theory and practice, between the ostensible desire for virtue and the actual worship of athleticism (even at the official level, even in the chapel pulpit) must have jolted the feelings of anyone who looked squarely at it. Lunn puts it into religious terms in *The Harrovians*. Peter, he says,

could not find much contact between the Christ of the Gospels and the Christ who was vaguely supposed to be the authority for the schoolmaster and schoolboy code. What did the teaching of the School pulpit amount to? 'Consider the lilies of the field' – hardly! Rather, 'Blessed are those who work hard and play hard, for Solomon in all his glory was not arrayed like a flannel at Lord's or a monitor on Speech Day.' 'Blessed are the meek.' No, rather 'Blessed are those who have a decent self-respect and take a proper place among their fellows. Blessed are those who have a proper sense of their importance' . . .

Well, it still applies, of course; all this, or something much like it, can be said today, quite outside the public schools. But the contrast between theory and practice, since they were supposedly Christian institutions, with headmasters generally in orders and clergymen plentiful among the rest of the staff, was even more glaring there. In the world, even the pushy Edwardian and early Georgian world, there was room, though schoolboys may not have suspected it, for the uncompetitive, the man unable or unwilling to shove; which is what made it, as Forster found, so delightful and so kind compared with school. Alec Waugh found it easy to see the absurdity of games-worship. What he did not see were the much wider implications of the whole system. And so his criticisms were not much more than affectionate suggestions, unsystematic swipes of high-spirited annoyance at this or that detail. Deeply embedded in the system, in the womb-like snugness of its middle layers, where he was exactly placed by birth and sympathy, by talents and home life and even aspirations (you cannot imagine him regretting that he had not been to another school), clever and athletic enough to do well in it himself, he had ideas for change but only for changes of emphasis, nothing more.

3 *And now Fernhurst, that has made me what I am, turns round and says, 'You are not fit to be a member of this great school' and I have to go. Oh, it's fair, isn't it?* Alec Waugh

Alec Waugh's hero was called Caruthers. That was before the name had become a joke, but when it is linked with the slang of the period ('gratters, Caruther!' or 'By jove, Caruthers!') it is hard not to smile. His first name, Gordon, today has a more robust, proletarian quality than it probably had then.

The first two sentences of *The Loom of Youth* show how dismally little feeling the boy who wrote it had for the English language. Every word is slightly askew, awkwardly set beside the others. A cobbled mixture of aphorism and cliché, over which (presumably, since it opens the book) its author must have sweated, it is hard to imagine a more depressing first sentence: 'There comes some time an end to all things, to the good and to the bad.' This is followed by a more informative one, again full of misplaced, ill-fitting words: 'And at last Gordon Caruthers' first day at school, which had so combined excitement and depression as to make it unforgettable, ended also.' Here, clearly, is no natural stylist.

Gordon, aged thirteen, has arrived at Fernhurst with his parents. 'Seldom had he felt such a supreme happiness as when he stepped out at Fernhurst station,' we hear. 'Supreme happiness' seems odd for a nervous newcomer; perhaps excitement, a sense of anticipation, is meant. Waugh goes on:

> There are few schools in England more surrounded by the glamour of medieval England than Fernhurst. Founded in the eighth century by a Saxon saint, it was the abode of monks until the Dissolution of the Monasteries . . . The Abbey and the School House studies stand as they stood seven hundred years ago. To a boy of any imagination, such a place could not but waken a wonderful sense of the beautiful.

Perhaps; yet C. Day-Lewis, surely an imaginative boy, wrote of Sherborne: 'To the beauty and antiquity of the place I was for years almost blind.'[12] Whatever the boys' reaction to it, what Alec Waugh describes as the 'great grey Abbey', the 'grey, ivy-clad studies' and the 'magnificent oak-panelled room, where generations of men have cut their names' with 'a large statue of Edward VI looking down on the tables', would certainly have been most readers' idea of a public school.

Gordon learns his first lessons very quickly. On the first night he gathers, uncomfortably but confusedly, that someone has misbehaved with someone else, but that since the culprit is in the First XV, nobody minds. Lesson one: 'For those who wore a blue and gold ribbon laws ceased to exist . . . To the athlete all things are forgiven.' Lesson two: 'It's obvious a blood must be a bit of a rip,' he is told later. What being a rip exactly means is not spelled out (Lunn uses the word in the same sense in *The Harrovians*). 'Is it impossible for a blood to be a decent fellow?' Gordon asks timidly, and is given his first lesson in schoolboy double-think (bearing in mind the fact that homosexuality was thought heinous): 'Decent fellow? Who on earth said they were anything else: Johnson's a simply glorious man. Only a bit fast; and that doesn't matter much,' he is told. Words like 'fast', 'rip', 'morality', 'broadmindedness', 'wildness', and 'accepted customs' suggest not just that homosexuality is general but (far more shocking to the average parent) that it is the 'best' boys – the bloods, the great athletes, those petted and praised by authority – who are most inclined to practise it and, having most power and influence, to get their way with the younger boys. In other words it is not a sign of weakness or degeneracy but of energy, strength and physical fitness. Rugger leads to it more surely than Swinburne, and the Pride of the School is likely to get the pick of the boys.

Nor is there any stigma attached to it, at school; in fact it is almost an accepted part of being a blood, certainly a background to the cult of physical prowess, and produced by muscularity, not feebleness. The very casualness with which the subject is treated suggests that it is so normal that only a few, nature's loners and bachelors, the cold or the unattractive or the unsuccessful, can avoid it, and that those occasionally caught deserve punishment far less than the many who escape; certainly far less than the influential bloods, who are presumably much harder for the younger boys to refuse. Gordon himself is pursued by an amorous blood in his first term, and tells him 'in polite language to go to the "devil".' A friend urges caution. 'If Meredith gets fed up with you he could give you a hell of a time.' 'Damn it all,' says the still ingenuous Gordon, 'the man is a gentleman.' 'Of course he is,' the friend says darkly, 'but all the same he is a blood, and it pays to keep on good terms with them.'

This worldly-wise friend is himself expelled when *his* relationship with another boy is discovered. In angry self-justification he bursts out to his friends:

> Who made me what I am but Fernhurst? Two years ago I came here as innocent as Caruthers there; never knew anything. Fernhurst taught me everything; Fernhurst made me worship games, and think that they alone mattered, and everything else could go to the deuce. I heard men say about bloods whose lives were an open scandal, 'Oh, it's all right, they can play football.' I thought it was all right too. Fernhurst made me think it was. And now Fernhurst, that has made me what I am, turns round and says, 'You are not fit to be a member of this great school' and I have to go. Oh, it's fair, isn't it?

Soon afterwards, Gordon shares a study with a boy who, every now and then, asks him to clear out for a while because another boy is visiting him. 'You quite understand, don't you?' Soon Gordon is asking *him* to move out for a while: 'I've often cleared out for you, you know.' 'Of course, that's quite all right, my dear fellow. Any time you like, I understand!' says the other, and goes out smiling. This kind of thing keeps happening, fairly lightly treated, and it was surely the hint of homosexuality (not much more than a hint, but suggesting its commonness and pervasiveness) that mainly shocked readers. No other school story had been so explicit about it. Apart from a mention of 'beastliness' there is scarcely a word about it in *Stalky & Co.*; and books openly describing romantic friendships between boys, like *The Hill*, were too ingenuous as a rule to suggest further meanings in what they were saying. It takes a more wide-awake reader than Hugh Walpole's average contemporary to read a homosexual meaning even into *Mr Perrin and Mr Traill* or *Jeremy at Crale*. Alec Waugh put down what he knew very reticently and obliquely, but not quite reticently or obliquely enough to avoid offending his age.

Other shocks came from the language used by the boys. By modern standards it seems tame but by those of the age it was evidently rather rough. Gordon is 'immensely shocked' to hear 'Damn your eyes' and 'You blasted idiot' on his first morning in the bathroom at Fernhurst, but is soon saying 'Damn' and 'Hell' with the best of them. Even an occasional 'bloody' slips in, and is probably what the headmaster is referring to when he speaks of 'language that would disgrace a costermonger'. Alec Waugh gives a clumsy version of the proverb: 'When one is in Rome,' he says more than once, 'one does as Rome does', and suggests that it sums up the public schoolboy's attitude. He arrives from his prep school green, innocent, truthful and with high ideals. All that is soon over:

> Parsons and godmothers will, of course, protest that, if you found yourself among a crowd of robbers and drunkards, you would not copy *them*! And yet this is precisely what the average individual will do.

School life, in other words, is a long period of accommodation, of compromise with other people's standards:

> The code of a Public School boy's honour is very elastic. Masters are regarded as common enemies; and it is never necessary to tell them the truth. Expediency is the golden rule;
>
> Everything except money is public property;
>
> Boys do what they know is wrong; then invent a theory to prove it is right; and finally persuade themselves that black is white;
>
> As soon as we begin to look on a thing as ordinary and natural, we also begin to think it is right. After a little Gordon ceased to wonder whether such things were right or wrong. It was silly to quarrel with existing conditions.

With remarks like these what seems an accurate and not too cynical a picture of a middling schoolboy's mind and outlook is built up.

Alec Waugh's aphorisms are often clumsy and long-winded, but it is mainly for them that one relishes *The Loom of Youth*. Though muddled and contradictory, they are an honest boy's effort to explain an often muddled and contradictory situation to himself and to others, to sort out feelings shaken by each mood and each new experience. Often they read like parody:

Death is an anti-climax. The heart that once loved, and was as grass before the winds of passion, has grown cold amid a world of commonplace. But at school there was no dragging out of triumphs. All too soon the six short years fly past, and we stand on the threshold of life in the very flush of our pride.

Shift a word or two, and it might be Wodehouse on the world of the Woosters. Or this, from Alec Waugh:

The Freemasonry of a Public School is amazing. No man who has been through a good school can be an outsider. He may hang round the Empire bar, he may cheat at business; but you can be certain of one thing, he will never let you down. Very few Public School men ever do a mean thing to their friends. And for a system that produces such a spirit there is something to be said after all.

Did his brother Evelyn lift whole sentences intact? It is the authentic voice of Captain Grimes:*

I'm a public school man. That means everything. There is a blessed equity in the English school system that ensures the public school man against starvation . . . They may kick you out, but they never let you down . . . Someone always turns up and says 'I can't see a public-school man down and out. Let me see you on your feet again.'

Never could anyone, after reading *Decline and Fall*, use the words 'public school man' again, straight-faced; though it was published only a decade after *The Loom of Youth*.

Yet for all its corny philosophy, its clichés, its purple passages, its inept quotations, its clumsiness, *The Loom of Youth* is in a sense marvellously true to life, to corny, clumsy, inept, purple-hearted adolescence. Just because the adolescent writing it is unaware of his oddities and limitations he is touchingly sincere, betraying himself at every point. 'He himself was so volatile, so open to the influence of the minute,' Waugh says of his hero; 'and yet he had no standards by which to tell the jewel from the paste.' To himself this applies just as well. Incapable of telling the jewel from the paste in language, he nonetheless often gets a feeling right, a moment pinned down exactly. The naivety, even for a seventeen-year-old, is extreme. But there is probably nothing more exactly true to life as seen by a seventeen-year-old of his class and time.

Alec Waugh was no Chatterton, no Radiguet; but Chatterton and Radiguet had not led his totally conventional life, and did not have his totally middling outlook and mediocre talents; so that they could not have understood and enjoyed, as he did, the conventional excitements of his age and class. His very limitations, in this case, stood him in good stead.

* In *Decline and Fall*.

CHAPTER XIII

Girls' school stories

We were terribly, terribly keen on games E. Arnot Robertson

Girls have so far been (perhaps noticeably) absent from this book. Occasionally they have a small part in one of the boys' school stories: Dr Grimstone's young daughter Dulcie in *Vice Versa*, for instance, or Iris, the housemaster's daughter in *The Hill*, whose schoolboy admirer growls that she is sure to marry an Etonian ('"Never!" cries Miss Iris'). There are sisters in the background, of course; Gerald Eversley's eight and Mike Jackson's more moderate four. But on the whole feminine influence is small. Girls have always read boys' books, though, and no doubt knew all about the doings of Tom Brown and Eric for generations. Soon after the turn of the century they began to get school stories of their own, but these never achieved the status of the boys' books.

There have been brilliant adult novels set in girls' schools – from Antonia White's *Frost in May* to Dorothy Bussy's *Olivia* – but these do not really belong to the genre. Among writers of school stories for girls (as opposed to adult stories about girls at school) there was no one anywhere near the level of Kipling or Wodehouse, or even of Reed, Walpole or Turley. Like every other form of fiction, girls's school stories have a sociological interest, telling us a great deal about their time and its attitudes; but it is very hard to consider them as more than (occasionally charming) kitsch. If any more imaginative, more ironic writer had turned up to write about girls at school, their status might have changed; but it is impossible to imagine irony or even imagination in them, so fettered is one's ideal of them by the treatment they have had. As it was, they never achieved recognition as anything more interesting than (say) pony books, another popular genre among girls, never considered as serious writing.

'Run, girls, run!' the girls at Sherborne were told when E. Arnot Robertson[1] was there about 1920, the idea being that if they ran like boys they would have no energy left to think *about* boys, or any other such disconcerting subject. Because some schools slavishly copied the methods of boys' schools and tried to make girls as boyish as possible, it is tempting to assume that girls' school stories are just boys' school stories in skirts. But they differ as much as the schools differed from the boys' schools and from one another. By girls' schools I mean the sort of school written about in school stories; the social equivalent of boys' public schools and of the schools written about in boys' school stories. But they were never quite equivalent. You cannot set them side by side and find that this sort of boys' school had its exact counterpart in that sort of girls' school. The difference is partly historical: girls' schools, in any widespread and serious sense, were much the more recent. When Arnold was at Rugby there were girls' schools in existence, even girls' boarding schools (where the young Brontës starved and two of them died, for instance), but they were not so well known or so widely scattered that enough young readers could be found to identify with them; so school stories about them could not exist in any popular form.

Then, while boys' schools were well established in certain patterns, girls' schools were still trying to find patterns of their own. And their social habits differed. Upper-class girls continued to be educated at home for about two centuries longer than their brothers. So girls' public schools on the whole were more middle-class than the leading boys' schools. Girls were more likely to be sent to day schools, and a strongly democratic day-school movement descended from Miss Buss's North London Collegiate School, the first successful, influential day school. A very large number of small private schools, some boarding, some day and some a mixture of the two, varied enormously in quality and academic standards; and then there were schools with no male equivalent, the 'silly' schools much despised by the girls' public schools, which were (and still are) openly unacademic and, by a sort of fashionable osmosis (girls went there because other girls went there because other girls . . .), socially smart. And there were convents, much less like other girls' schools than boys' public schools run by monks were like other public schools.

Among the girls' public schools, there were always variations as great as those within the boys'. Cheltenham Ladies' College, the first and probably still the best known, founded by Miss Beale in the eighteen-sixties, was not the establisher of girls' heartiness and tough games. St Leonard's at St Andrews seems to have been the first of the real boy-copiers. Games were the thing there, as they were at all the heartier girls' public schools; and if in the boys' schools they were taken to ridiculous lengths, in the girls' they seem even more ridiculously, artificially imposed. As E. Arnot Robertson wrote:

> It is very difficult to convey the atmosphere of an English public school for girls to anyone who has the good fortune not to have been sent to one. They are – or at least this one was in my time – run on a male system imperfectly adapted to female needs. We were terribly, terribly keen on games. A carefully fostered and almost entirely spurious interest in house matches was our main subject of conversation. Girls at boarding school age are suggestible almost beyond belief . . . Now I do not believe that sporting conjecture of this kind comes natural to one girl in twenty; but this was the tradition of the place (officially described as the High Moral Tone of the School), and so this was how we talked, even when we were alone.[2]

It was from this sort of school that the wilder fantasies of St Trinian's mushroomed: the image of the schoolgirl as guerrilla, black-stockinged, gym-tunicked, shock-haired, machine gun under the dormitory pillow, butcher's cleaver at the ready when Mamzelle came into the form-room. Angela Brazil would no more have recognised St Trinian's than Arnold would have found much that was familiar in turn-of the-century Marlborough.

So, as schools varied for boys, they varied enormously for girls; and because school was less general among girls, perhaps school stories had more influence on them than they had on boys. The mopey 'only' child, if a girl, might read about boarding school larks and long to share them. The mopey 'only' boy would be thrown among them anyway.

2 *It's too absolutely, perfectly, deliciously scrumshus!* One of Angela Brazil's characters

The only well-known name among school-story writers for girls is that of Angela Brazil (which I continue to pronounce like the country, for so all her family pronounced it until, in 1911, she and her brother decided it sounded grander as Brazzle). Although she was no feminist, and seemed to take little notice of the movements of life around her, she wrote her early stories at a time that was seething with feminism, with dreams of education, with daughters yearning to open windows on to a wider world. She does not often deal with ideas of university and professional training (though occasionally they are referred to, as part of school success in general, like Balliol scholarships in boys' stories), but they were there, and school was the first step on the way to fulfilling them. In 1906 when she published her first school story, *The Fortunes of Philippa*, feminism was awake and something of it, if only an undefined longing for a more spirited outlook, for greater autonomy than could be found at home, was filtering down into girls' fiction.

Angela Brazil seems almost like a fictional character herself, so closely does she conform to type. A novelist creating a writer of bad children's books might be tempted to take her for a model, almost too obvious to be credible. She liked to think of herself as, and to be thought, 'a chronic child', never married and seems to have had no relationships with men apart from her brothers, father and nephew; she lived in a world of exciting fantasy in which everything she experienced or remembered was recycled at a girlish level of fun; she believed in – or at least talked a lot about – fairies, pixies, and 'little people', seemed genuinely fond of the company, the chatter, the letters of schoolgirls and the memory of her own schooldays, and gave children's parties, with games and rich, sweet food, not just to children but to (sometimes disgruntled) adults. A narcissistic, posey child who happened to grow up and grow old but never lost the self-admiring attitudes that made her see herself, idealised, in her own heroines, she was, as her biographer Gillian Freeman puts it, 'an unflagging seeker of "jolly times" '.[3] Jolly times, yes; jolly hockey-sticks, no. She never advocated a hearty attitude in her schoolgirls, although she believed in games and missed them in her own school-days. The schools in her books were not public schools or generally large; they were middle-sized or small, as a rule, homely, private places with motherly, if extremely lady-like, headmistresses, often named after the house where they happened to be found; like 'The Hollies' in *The Fortunes of Philippa*, which was based on her own school, Ellerslie, in a Manchester suburb.

She seems to have been only slightly more likable than Enid Blyton (who wrote much more and much worse). Snobbish, self-regarding, fey, self-centred and self-willed, at once wildly romantic and a tough businesswoman with a touch of meanness, she was born at Preston in 1869, second daughter and fourth child of an Irish father (a sculptor manqué, manager of a cotton mill), and his half-Scottish, half-Spanish wife, born Angelica McKinnell, whose first ten years were spent (suitably, considering her married name) in her birthplace, Rio de Janeiro, and whose father owned the first shipping line to ply between Liverpool and Rio. Angela adored her mother and her fictional mothers or mother-substitutes are always warm, wise, loving and totally satisfactory. It was on her mother's experiences as a child that she based her first and to my mind best, though by no means most typical, school story, *The Fortunes of Philippa*, in which an English girl reared in a South American country is sent to school in England for five years, where she has many ups and downs, is 'taken in' by her best friend's family, the Winstanleys, and spends happy holidays with them, thinks she has lost her father in a shipwreck and then finds he was rescued, so that they are at last reunited – permanently – in England.

Like many of her contemporaries, Angela Brazil added a little glamour when she looked back on her suburban mid-middle-class life (just as later in life she referred to her cottage in Polperro as her Cornish 'estate'). As a child she was imaginative and self-conscious, and put herself into her first book as the lovable Peggy, all curls and cuteness. She went to five schools in all, particularly enjoying the last one, Ellerslie, where she boarded happily in her last year (midnight feasts and the bed full of lingering crumbs); but she always regretted that the girls had few non-academic outlets or interests. She would have liked games and school plays, concerts, societies and a lending library; and when she came to write her books, by which time she was in her late thirties and all these things had arrived at her old school, she put in plenty of them for her schoolgirls to enjoy, and had them forever getting up tableaux and concerts, dressing up, organising events. Although no games fanatic, she thought it important for girls to develop every side of their nature, and games helped to achieve the informality she liked to see in schools. In 1924 she wrote:

> The introduction of games is no doubt largely responsible for the removal of the old-fashioned barrier which used to exist between governess and pupil. We should no more have dreamt of our dignified headmistress indulging in hockey than (forgive the simile [*sic*]) we should have expected to see St Peter, halo, keys and all, engaged in a tustle at football. It was simply unthinkable.

Quite unlike Sherborne, in fact. There was no question of 'Run, girls, run!' in Angela Brazil. The thought of boys simply failed to cross her schoolgirls' minds (except on a few rather special, untypical occasions).

For over forty years she turned out books for schoolgirls at a spanking pace. They were long, and quite carefully plotted. *The Nicest Girl in the School* was the most successful. Her books sold all over the world, in India and America and most European countries, and she had fan letters from them all, which (this shows her at her best) she answered herself, carefully and personally, often enclosing a photograph. (*For the Sake of the School* is dedicated 'To the

SCHOOLGIRL READERS who have sent me such Nice Letters.') But schools on the whole disliked her – presumably for her silliness, her inadequacy. The headmistress of St Paul's in 1936 declared that she would like to burn all her books. At my own school they – indeed, all schoolgirl stories – were strictly forbidden. Yet the moral tone of the books was always high. As her biographer puts it, she felt 'a sense of duty to impart a code of honourable behaviour to British girls, while acknowledging that this often meant an inner struggle with the baser self.'[4] Non-headmistresses often paid tribute to her good influence, readers wrote, almost as they had written to Farrar, to thank her for advice and guidance. Recently Lord Goodman, in a broadcast on the influence of books read in childhood, said that whatever he had become he owed to Angela Brazil.

Perhaps headmistresses and schools in general were less innocent than she was in their attitude to 'crushes' and passionate friendships. Even when the passionate friends were called, of all things, Lesbia and Regina (in *Loyal to the School*), it was all at an unselfconsciously soulful level, for she was a great believer in the passionate intertwining of souls. 'Occasionally in our lives we meet with people whose whole electric atmosphere seems to merge and blend with our own,' she wrote. 'We feel we are not so much making a new acquaintance as picking up the threads of some former soul-friendship.' Yet Regina loves Lesbia 'much as a boy would, for her pretty hair, her dainty movements and the general Celtic glamour that hung about her; she behaved indeed more like a youth in love than an ordinary schoolgirl.' In one of her later books, Angela Brazil introduced a close friendship between a young girl and a middle-aged woman, seeing herself as 'the Lavender Lady', a vision of beauty, understanding and friendship in fluffy mauve (rather as another Angela – Mrs Thirkell – saw herself in several of her books as the older woman with whom all the young men were chastely in love; a sometimes witty novelist rather more astringent and less lavender than her namesake, though). The fact that she was equally unselfconscious about kisses and squeezes and even the occasional shared bed may have raised some suspicious school eyebrows. If so, it was unfair to her, for it was all very lightly suggested, very innocently done.

Like better writers than herself, Angela Brazil believed in the ability of a school – of the whole experience of being there, particularly as a boarder – to teach lessons in living, to serve as a pattern for much else. She wrote, in *The Leader of the Lower School*:

A large school is a state in miniature. Quite apart from the mistresses, it has its own particular institutions and its own system of self-government. In their special domain its officers are of quite as much importance as Members of

Parliament, comparable to that of Cabinet Ministers. Tyrannies, struggles for freedom, minor corruptions and hot debates have their place there as well as in the wider world of politics.

Sensible and true; but her theory was better than her practice. She referred to her books grandly as The Works, but nothing about them justifies it. Their eye-level is that of adolescence, yet they are the work of a middle-aged woman, then of an old woman, a real-life Peter Pan. And although they have a good deal of presence and fire, they are inescapably silly, childish and insubstantial.

One can point to their merits. In the best days, her first twenty-five years as a writer, they were not written to a formula, and the plots, though no better, are no worse, than those of other school stories. The stories are taken from a number of points of view, they vary in tone and emphasis, too, and are not even too closely confined to school, or to schools of a particular kind; some of them are set very closely within the context of their time (*A Patriotic Schoolgirl* in the First World War, for instance); some are set in schools abroad (*The School in the South* in Italy; *Nesta's new School* in Switzerland). The dated Christian names, as in any period piece, make one smile at this distance, but that is hardly her fault. What is limiting and wrong and absurd is not the set-up of the stories but the outlook that produced them, the total lack of irony that can say: ' "I still can't quite, quite believe it – it's too absolutely, perfectly, deliciously scrumshus!" bleated Gwen hysterically', and expect the reader to take it quite straight. Whether she was the best (or at least the most energetic) of a bad lot, or whether she killed the girls' school story stone dead before anyone else could get at it, it is hard to say. Certainly obscurer writers of girls' school stories tended to write in much the same way, and to be taken in the same spirit by their readers – seriously, perhaps, in adolescence, satirically later. Arthur Marshall seems to have done the only thing possible with them. His take-offs and reviews of schoolgirl stories are funnier, and almost more affectionate, than they deserve.

Angela Brazil lived until 1947, when she died in her sleep in the Coventry house she had shared for almost a lifetime with a brother and sister. Neighbours remember Walter Brazil going to another church the Sunday after Coventry cathedral was bombed, sister Amy on one arm, sister Angela on the other, as always. By the 1930s, Lord Berners was able to satirise Angela Brazil in a privately printed book called *The Girls of Radcliffe Hall* by Adela Quebec. Already her writing was well known enough to be parodied and for people to understand what was meant. Almost without exaggeration Lord Berners caught the tone, the mixture of romance and good cheer and gentle absurdity. 'It was a merry scene, all those fresh young faces glowing in the firelight,' he says at one point; 'a scene that Raphael or Botticelli would have loved to paint.' At another he writes, perhaps even better: 'Miss Carfax sat alone before a dying fire. Memories grave and gay fluttered like autumn leaves across her brain.' This is not unkind parody; it is almost affectionate imitation.

3 *I'm glad I'm not pretty* Quoted by E. Arnot Robertson

Geoffrey Trease called Angela Brazil the Talbot Baines Reed of the girls' school story.[5] Certainly she was its populariser, its central figure, famous (as a name, at least) outside school-story circles. Its Kipling was still to come, Trease wrote in the forties, when boys' school stories, except at a very pop level, were fading out but girls' school stories were still vigorous; much read, it seems, even by girls at work in factories (a girl could leave school on her fourteenth birthday then, so state-school leavers were often barely adolescent). The early writers of girls' school stories were, like Angela Brazil, soulful, earnest, high-minded, generally very lively but, even when writing of 'madcaps', unshakably lady-like. Bessie Marchant, Kathlyn Rhodes, May Wynne, Christine Chaundler, Ethel Talbot, Evelyn Smith, Doris Pocock, Winifred Darch, Dorita Fairlie Bruce and many, many others turned out schoolgirl stories by the dozen; no better, on the whole, though occasionally a good deal worse, than Angela Brazil's. Certainly no Kipling turned up among them.

'Honour' was a concept much discussed and taken to heart in these books, as is shown by titles like Bessie Marchant's *By Honour Bound*, Kathlyn Rhodes's *Schoolgirl Honour*, or Winifred Darch's *For the Honour of the House*; not, of course, in the old sense of the word, connected with chastity, but in the portmanteau meaning of 'fair play', honesty, high standards. High spirits might produce harmless pranks, but where it really mattered 'honour' was invoked, and girls were put 'on their honour' not to do this or that. Within the schools, in the early books, romantic friendships were common; outside the school world, less so, though occasionally a pretty young mistress or a more daunting middle-aged one would, in the last chapter, marry the heroine's widowed father. This happens in a book that embodies many of the changing social attitudes and stands very much on the crest of the wave (social and sexual) that was breaking in the twenties, *Miss Pike and her Pupils*, by Mabel L. Tyrrell. Its plot is like that of certain Hollywood films in which the heroine whisks off her glasses and unalluring cardigan to reveal a beauty underneath. Miss Pike runs a small school at just the time, in the mid-twenties, when female clothes were changing from the long, baggy styles with soft, feminine hair, still worn by older women, to the brief flapper skirts and shingled hair of young girls. Dowdy Miss Pike goes in for the elderly look so that parents will think her a suitable age to run a school and the girls will respect her, and only at the very end does she take off the disguising hat and specs, put on modern dress and marry her pupil's father.

There seems to be a parable of sorts here, almost parallel with the process of toughening and games-playing in the boys' public schools half a century earlier. As time went on and skirts and shingles grew shorter, the girls gave up their affectionate, Brazil-like ways and became progressively more androgynous, even being given boys' names at times or hermaphroditic nicknames. School stories from the twenties and thirties are full of girls called Freddie and Bill or else with half-playful, half-insulting, sexless nicknames like Twerp or Midge or Smudge. The mistresses they admire (like the heroines of much adult fiction) are boyish hoydens with Eton crops, sometimes lacrosse internationals or famous county players at hockey. Curly hair, interest in clothes or domesticity, frilliness or softness of any kind, are thought 'soppy' and soon become quite unmentionable. 'I'm glad I'm not pretty,' E. Arnot Robertson was told by a Sherborne girl ('who certainly had much to be thankful for'),[6] and this kind of attitude marches on with increasing vehemence through the girls' stories. (Nor was it confined to school stories, of course. Arthur Ransome's girls, in their early or mid-teens, loathe nothing so scornfully as pretty clothes.) I remember, from long ago, a story called 'Curls in the Fourth', about an unfortunate girl with long curly hair, considered a disgrace to the Fourth Form until, badgered beyond endurance, she has it cut to a 'neat, boyish shingle' and becomes popular and accepted. It turns out that she has been longing to have this done for ages, and is therefore not guilty, as the Fourth Formers have thought, but that her parents refused to allow it.

Girl guiding, a tough occupation in those days, is sometimes combined with a school story (*The guides of Fairley*, by Diana Pares; *The Guides of North Cliff* by S. B. Owsley), and writers between the wars began to look outside the usual formula, the ordinary locations. Elinor M. Brent-Dyer set the enormous Chalet School series in the Austrian Tyrol, and went back there after the Second World War, bringing in Old Girls' children and covering a positively Proustian range of ages and memories (as Angela Thirkell did in her Barsetshire novels when she really got going). Postwar schoolgirls went even further, in all senses: into space and up to the moon and heaven knows where else, but this hardly concerns us. Their stories lasted longer than the boys', but they had started later and were always nearer the pop level, on which such larks continued well into the fifties and sixties. The almost-pop range was dominated by Enid Blyton, much loved by many children, much hated by many adults, who found her style flavourless, her manner boring, and some of her ideas distasteful. Efforts by more serious writers like Antonia Forrest, Mary Harris or Elfrida Vipont to treat school as an adjunct of 'real life', not a peculiar condition isolated from it, were praiseworthy but not influential. The schools in which school stories flourished had changed and the vintage situations, whether sensibly or nonsensically treated, were no longer effective. With St Trinian's the girls' school story took off into pure farce and has never come down again.

CHAPTER XIV

The once-famous: E. F. Benson, Desmond Coke, Ian Hay, Charles Turley

Lads in the springtime of hope and promise E. F. Benson

While the stories I have dealt with in detail were setting the pace, minor ones were appearing in large numbers, a now-forgotten background to the genre. There were also school stories which, in their day, were as well known as those I have considered and thought quite as likely to last; talented books which have sunk not entirely without trace (there are still enthusiasts who remember them) but with little lasting effect. Some of them are well worth another look. It is perhaps no coincidence that most of the writers of these better-than-most but now neglected books were very much 'insiders', men who really knew the public schools (or at least one of them), who had grown up in the system and had sometimes taught in it as well, and had plenty of friends and connections there to appreciate the authenticity of what they wrote. I have called them the once-famous because that was just what, in school-story terms, they were. When the school story is discussed by their contemporaries they are mentioned as central and lasting examples of the genre.

Best-known was probably E. F. Benson, whose Mapp and Lucia books (high comedy about 'cultured' provincial life) still have an enthusiastic following. It seems inevitable that one of the Benson family, at least, should have turned out a school story, because the whole family was so deeply embedded in the system that members of it turn up in other people's memoirs of school over and over again across nearly a century: Edward White Benson, the father, later

Archbishop of Canterbury, as headmaster of Wellington (the energetic flogger I mentioned earlier), and the three sons, A. C., E. F., and R. H. (like Wodehouse's cricketing Jacksons, they were generally known by initials, but domestically they answered to Arthur, Fred and Hugh) as the authors of nearly two hundred books between them, many on the fringes of school life.

A. C., 'Mr Christopher' in *The Oppidan*, was the most prolific writer of the three, whose diary alone ran to 180 manuscript volumes; but although he wrote a book called *The Schoolmaster*, the words of 'Land of Hope and Glory', and much, much else, he never turned out a school story. R. H. or Robert Hugh, the youngest, was an aggressively enthusiastic convert to Roman Catholicism who became a Monsignor and wrote novels little read today except, perhaps, by dedicated recusants. E. F. or Fred, who lived in Henry James's Lamb House at Rye for many years after James's death, was the one who wrote a school story, *David Blaize*, which was followed by an undergraduate novel with the same hero and some of his same friends, *David at King's*.

But although only a single school story came out of this enormous output, all the Bensons' work was steeped in the atmosphere of the public schools (although this may have gone a little awry in books by the Catholic Hugh). The Benson parents were second cousins, Mrs Benson a sister of Henry Sidgwick, chosen when she was only eleven by her future husband, who waited until she was seventeen and then married her. It was a curious union, unVictorianly described in Mrs Benson's diaries (she too was a prolific, though private, writer); and the five surviving children – two daughters as well as the three literary sons – all seem to have been, like her, homosexually inclined, if not practising. None of them married and there were no descendants, so they failed to spread their influence downwards and sideways, as so many of these – much intermarried – school families often did; sons, sons-in-law and nephews all being taken back into the system as masters, to become the pattern-formers of the next generation.*

As a piece of writing, *David Blaize* compares favourably with most other school stories, because Benson was a much more accomplished writer than most who used the school story, with a light touch and a neat use of irony; but it is more sentimental than his satirical novels and, perhaps therefore, less effective. In content and in its treatment of the subject it is an adult novel rather than a book for boys; though no doubt many of the young once read it at another level of understanding. It was published shortly before *The Loom of Youth* but

* For details of some of the intermarried public-school families, see T. W. Bamford, *The Rise of the Public Schools*, 1967.

caused no similar shock among adults, though at times it is rather more outspoken. A clergyman who lent me *David at King's* found the copy in a prep school, rather to his dismay; but prep schools are very much the kind of place in which such half-forgotten works are likely to be found. David Blaize's own early schooldays are spent in a prep school which may, I think, be based on Temple Grove, almost the oldest prep school in the country, where the Benson boys were sent when it was near Richmond in Surrey (it is now near Uckfield in Sussex); its location, at least, is the same as Temple Grove's, for the headmaster mentions boys 'having shirked into Richmond and devoured more than sufficiency of Maids of Honour' (cakes which set it firmly in Surrey and not, with the other Richmond, in Yorkshire). David then goes on to his public school, called by Benson, 'Marchester', where, in the wake of his great and grand friend Hughes (who later goes to the bad and is sacked, though he and David have drifted apart by then), and his even older and grander friend Maddox, he goes into Mr Adams's house, followed by his rather humble friend Bags who at prep school worships him and is treated by him in rather lordly fashion.

Some of the best parts are concerned with David's father's gaffes when he visits the prep school. An archdeacon who writes learned books, he wears gaiters and a shovel hat and – worse – a brown flannel shirt in which he bowls, with a long-sleeved Jaeger vest clearly visible at the wrists. Worse still, he bathes in a striped garment to his knees in full view of the school, and dives a terrible belly-flopper. He also shows an unselfconscious friendliness towards everyone, taking an interest in things he knows nothing about, such as cricket, and asking ignorant questions. A sense of acute embarrassment mixed with warm affection comes across, David being really fond and sometimes even proud of his (by schoolboy standards) eccentric parent, yet hating to be called 'David' loudly on the cricket field and to have to sit through long sermons by his father in which the boys are addressed as 'lads in the springtime of hope and promise'. Other good things are the headmaster's daughters, Miss Edith and Miss Mabel, otherwise Goggles and Carrots, surely distant relations of Evelyn Waugh's Dingy and Flossie, Dr Fagan's daughters at Llanabba Castle, and of Ian Hay's housemaster's daughters Spot and Plain.

Two themes touched upon in many school stories are the main ones in *David Blaize*: homosexuality and cribbing. The first is dealt with mainly in the relationship between David and Maddox, several years older than himself; but it runs through the narrative as something just below the surface, never quite mentioned yet always obliquely suggested (an older boy sits on David's bed, is chased away angrily by

Maddox when found there, etc.). The book is sometimes said to be a school story 'about' homosexuality. It is not. Like several others, it is a school story steeped in homosexual *feeling*, which is a little different; in which the homosexual patterns are clearer than they are in most school stories, more openly admitted yet not so explicit as to offend anyone who does not want to notice. David's 'white innocence, his utter want of curiosity about all that was filthy' moves the not very innocent Maddox to mend his ways. Totally unaware of any lustful thoughts in his friend, David is startled to find him staring at his nakedness after a bath. In Benson's words:

> There was Maddox only looking at him, only smiling. But instantly he had some sense of choking discomfort. He looked back at him, frowning and puzzled, and his sense of discomfort hugely increased. He merely wanted to get away.

Seeing how David feels, Maddox is ashamed, and their relationship thereafter is warm but unlustful (or so we are meant to assume). But the sum of human happiness in those years is to be together, to spend days at the sea and enjoy sunshine, bathing, silence, communion. There is a sense of total joy in proximity, and of repletion, as in a love affair.

Cribbing, the more discussable moral problem, occupies quite a central position in *David Blaize*, as it does in nearly every school story with any pretension to seriousness. To crib or not to crib? This question, more discussable than emotional passions, closer to life than stealing exam papers or habitual drunkenness, may seem a small one to the outsider today but to the scrupulous or even the ordinarily conscientious boy at the time it was often an intense one, ruffling the daily pursuit of virtue (if that was what he was pursuing) in the most unavoidable way. What was a boy to do? When everyone else used cribs for preparing his work, then any work done without them was lost in competition with the cribbers (who could not, of course, be denounced) and in any case there was never time enough, with all those games to play and the practice they demanded, to fit in the necessary hours of preparation. Unless cribbing could be stopped altogether, which of course it could not, it seemed hard on the middlingly honest (or middlingly dishonest) boy to expect him to do without it. The problem never seems to have been solved satisfactorily in any school story I know, no doubt because the system made life impossible for any but the brilliant or the most dedicated swots. Of course exams and even unseens eventually sorted our good boys and malefactors but they were distant solutions. Day-to-day survival demanded help and cribs were there to give it. In a system where

Greek and Latin were the central subjects and few boys were ever able to achieve even a small degree of proficiency in them – never mind pleasure – cribbing seems to have remained an unresolved, indeed insoluble, moral problem. As with much else in the schools, it was the system that was at fault.

Benson, though not a schoolmaster, was so closely connected with the school world that he understood its pressures, what mattered and what could be taken lightly. More than almost any other writer he gives a sense of the school world as something which involved – if it did not quite include – the whole of life, certainly the whole of social life, all one's friends and relations and the friends and relations of everyone in it too. He is so much inside it that there is hardly a sense of 'innerness' at all: that, like so much else, is taken for granted.

2 *I dislike those school stories, because they read men's notions into boyish actions. Boys get hold of them and get fanciful ideas*

Desmond Coke

The most mysteriously once-famous is (to me) Desmond Coke, who in his day – he died in 1931 – had what now seems a curiously high reputation for his school stories, in particular for the best known of them, *The Bending of a Twig*. Ian Hay said that it was 'perhaps the best of all in this class [the undramatic realists] . . . an absolutely faithful picture drawn with unerring instinct and refreshing humour'.[1] C. A. Alington called it 'brilliant'; 'there is a touch of real genius in the picture,' he wrote. Others said much the same sort of thing, and other school stories of his – *The Worm, The Worst House at Sherborough* – were also praised for their realism and lightness of touch.

The Bending of a Twig – which has mnemonic disadvantages, lacking a title that at once proclaims it a school story – is based on a single idea, not used, as far as I know, in any other school story. This is the idea that a school story can be written about the falsity of other school stories. Other writers had made jibes about other school stories but none, I think, had based a book of his own on disapproval of them. 'Its modest aim,' Coke wrote, 'is, in fact, to level destructive satire at the conventional school story, and on its ruin to erect a structure rather nearer to real life.'[2] Hardly a modest aim: Coke was actually saying that what he wrote about school was true, what others wrote was false, or at least unreliable and exaggerated. The four school stories he uses as training manuals for his hero, about to set off for public school – *Tom Brown's Schooldays, Eric, Stalky & Co.* and *The Hill* – are presumably meant to be examples of this falsity. But for 'destructive satire' Coke was far too mild and ineffective a writer.

The Bending of a Twig is about young Lycidas Marsh, brought up by dotty parents in total isolation; never having met other boys, certainly never having been inside a school. They send him for his interview at Shrewsbury, aged thirteen, in a velvet suit which gets him christened Lord Fauntleroy, and so ignorant of school matters that he has no idea whether the sixth form is at the top of the school or the bottom, or how Shrewsbury is pronounced. His mother's idea of preparing him for school is to give him the four well-known school stories and another – a 'pop' story of the time, low-brow fun and frolics about a headmaster who turns out to be Jack the Ripper. So Lycidas goes off with all sorts of romantic ideas about honour and friendship, about fighting the bully and making dramatic gestures; none of which does him any good, so that at last he admits that, as sources of information and guides to school behaviour, school stories are useless. 'Lycidas was still the prey of the dramatic impulse,' writes Coke, 'still somewhat pleased with himself, still a little of a prig; but never again would he go to these books, in the old simple way, for help.' And his kind, wise housemaster, who is presumably Coke's mouthpiece, when confessed to about the secret influence in Lycidas's early school days, says: 'I dislike these school stories, because they read men's notions into boyish actions. Boys get hold of them and get fanciful ideas.'

If Coke had stuck to his school story idea and ended the tale with Lycidas's disillusion, his book might have been a good deal better. But he lost all shape and purpose by continuing it as an ordinary story about Lycidas's progress up the school, a good boy but unnoticed because he is no athlete. Coke writes:

> Lycidas saw that everything came back to that. To be popular, to have influence, one must be good at games . . . Why was he no good at games? . . . perhaps, now, he would never be an athlete. Probably it would be against him all his life.

Russell, the boy he most admires, is of course an athlete, with the arrogance to match his talents and the self-confidence to make Lycidas feel inferior. So the romantic friendships of the school stories are not for him, and he forms sober relationships with dull boys like himself.

'Real life' was Coke's avowed intention. 'With this last end in view, it seemed to me wiser to take as background a school which I knew and loved,' he wrote; 'and having taken it, to call it Shrewsbury, not Harbury or Shrewstow.'[3] He was determined to be accurate, to look at school steadily, without letting sentiment get in the way; but his efforts to do this were hampered by his parallel wish to make psychological patterns, to use a plot in which events and characters were nicely balanced: the good boy and the bad, the worthy and the attractive, the muff at games and the athlete. So *The Bending of a Twig* is the old, old story out of school stories, though it claims to be sending them up. The end of his schooldays (by which time he must be close on twenty, having been at school six years) finds Lycidas as reluctant to leave as Tom Brown was, with the sight of boys who will be back next term producing 'a great envy in his heart'. When he finally leaves, it is with his housemaster's advice to make school and university into 'a kind of minor religion' and with the determination that whatever he achieves will be 'valued not for itself nor for himself, but for the sake of Shrewsbury'. Coke had promised himself and his readers sobriety and accuracy in his portrayal of school life. Was this, then, the sober truth, the kind of thing a housemaster would suggest, a departing boy accept? Perhaps at the time it was (incredibly to us) perfectly credible.

3 *If this be mediocrity, who would soar?* Ian Hay

Major-General John Hay Beith, CBE, MC, educated at Fettes and St John's College, Cambridge, where he read classics and was captain of the College Boat Club, had a distinguished record in the First World War, about which he wrote a good deal, was director of Public Relations at the War Office in the Second, and also wrote a good deal about school, with which he was involved, and by which he was conditioned, almost as much as the Bensons. Though an often witty user of school imagery, he was not obsessed by school; rather, he was an example of the way in which it was part and parcel of the life of people like himself; memoirs of schooldays or of schoolmastering, of this or that aspect of school life, references to school customs and institutions, attitudes, slang and much else, *Punch* articles, Fourth Leaders in *The Times,* all assuming that their readers were familiar with what they were talking about.

As Ian Hay, he is perhaps the most 'central' figure of his day who wrote about school, observed what was happening there, read the school stories, and gave away (sometimes deliberately, sometimes unconsciously) a great deal about current attitudes: the class system, the particular humour of the day, the complacency, the admired characteristics. His books are period pieces in the best – and sometimes the worst – sense; deeply embedded in their time, deeply dated (therefore sometimes embarrassing at a later date), sometimes charming, sometimes arch; often like Milne's in attitude but less lastingly right in tone. One's teeth are set on edge, now and then; yet he is funny as well, and (one feels) almost inexhaustibly nice. As we draw further away from him, what maddened those who came immediately after him becomes more acceptable, a case of period idiosyncrasy rather than something to arouse personal irritation. Hay, who often seems sentimental and obvious, has not lost a reputation, like Hugh Walpole (partly because his reputation never stood as high); but his appeal has somehow drained away. Yet he is one of the best sources of information about school life in his day, and even more about school attitudes, in a broad sense school feeling.

Pip (1913) subtitled 'A Romance of Youth', shows him at his coyest in his treatment of the young. Four early chapters deal with school and one of these is set in the sort of kindergarten known grandly, even today, as a 'pre-prep' school. Here he uses the phonetically spelt baby-talk then much in vogue with middlebrow writers and presumably enjoyed by their readers, though no modern English writer would dare to use it. Two further chapters develop the theme of Pip the cricketing genius, and Pip the peculiarly placed orphan who, pathetically, has never read a book apart from school ones. A kindly master takes him in hand with Sherlock Holmes, *Treasure Island* and *Vice Versa*. We then jump ahead to Pip at eighteen, still a cricketing genius but for technical reasons unable to captain the team; and to meet his friend/enemy Linklater, who goes through a bad patch (bullying a younger boy with a red-hot poker, which seems extreme), and is saved from serious trouble by Pip at the cost of a broken collar-bone and concussion (reconciliation scene at the bedside). It is slyly, neatly clever and quotable and naturally presumes on its readers' familiarity with what is described or discussed. 'Until one is a "blood", or a "dook", or a "bug" (or whatever they call it at your school, sir)', Hay writes at one point. He also describes what has been described in very similar terms in other school stories:

> That aristocracy – the most exclusive aristocracy in the world – in which brains, as such, count for nothing, birth has no part, and wealth is simply disregarded; where genuine ability occasionally gains a precarious footing, and then only by disguising itself as something else, but to which muscle, swiftness of foot, and general ability to manipulate a ball with greater dexterity than one's neighbour is received unquestioningly, joyfully, proudly.

This kind of thing had by Hay's time been said so often that it makes one, like much else in his work, impatient. 'The most exclusive aristocracy in the world,' in the sense he uses it, could describe any playground gang, after all.

The Lighter Side of School Life was Hay's compendium of public school information, immensely popular from its publication in 1913 and reprinted seven times in the next decade. In a determinedly unpretentious way, as its title suggests, it has things to say about masters and boys, about work, about family visits, about school stories, and about the men finally produced from the schoolboys described. It is in the last chapter, admiringly describing the public-school product, that the gap between then and now yawns widest. In 1913 the schools were mainly aiming to turn out the administrative class for the Empire, and Hay seems to accept the stereotypes without trouble or criticism. The public school man is, he says:

> a type, not an individual; and when the daily, hourly business of a nation is to govern others, perhaps it is as well to do so through the medium of men who, by merging their own individuality in a common stock, have evolved a standard of Character and Manners which, while never meteoric, seldom brilliant, too often hopelessly dull, is always conscientious, generally efficient, and never, never tyrannical or corrupt. If this be mediocrity, who would soar?

I am reminded here of Welldon's not-too-critically intended remark in *Gerald Eversley's Friendship* that at a public school 'mediocrity sits upon her throne'.

But what strikes the reader most forcibly today is not so much the gap between ideas then and now as its opposite – the recognisably modern tone of a great deal of what Hay says. Anyone who thinks of 1913 as a socially monolithic, unchanging period, particularly in the public schools, is in for a surprise when reading of the 'new race of parents, men who avow, modestly but firmly, that they have been made not by the Classics but by themselves'. The 'Self-Made Man, and Proud of it' tells the headmaster:

> Learn him to be a scholar, and I'll pay any bill you like to send in. I've got the dibs. He's not a bad lad, as lads go, but he wants his jacket dusted now and then. My father dusted mine regular every Saturday night for fifteen years . . .

And Hay actually suggests (in 1913!) that

> if [the headmaster] decides that the exuberance of his papa has not been inherited to an ineradicable extent, he accepts the cowering youth and does his best for him. As a rule he is justified in his judgement.

Then, just as there is today,

> there is our old friend the Man in the Street, who, through the medium of his favourite mouthpiece, the halfpenny press, asks the Headmaster very sternly what he means by turning out 'scholars' who are incapable of writing an invoice in commercial Spanish and to whom double entry is Double Dutch.

Modern again are the parents who, when their son is expelled, stir up trouble in the popular press, which 'leads to a discussion as to whether the public schools shall or shall not be abolished'.

Modern, too, is the idea that a headmaster needs to be a good administrator, skilled in public relations. This is something often said today, as if it had just struck the speaker as something original and new. A scholar in command of a public school is wasted, Hay says:

As well appoint an Astronomer Royal to command an ocean liner. He may be on terms of easy familiarity with the movements of the heavenly bodies, yet fail to understand the right way of dealing with refractory stokers . . . Nowadays in the great public schools the Head . . . devotes his energies to such trifling details as the organisation of school routine, the supervision of the cook, the administration of justice, the diplomatic handling of the Governing Body, and the suppression of parents.

A 'majestic' presence, he suggests, is not hard to achieve when boys are so impressionable, so ready to expect majesty. 'More than one King Log has left a name behind him, through standing still in the limelight and keeping his mouth shut.' All this sounds oddly modern. More dated, or perhaps more unselfconsciously expressed than it could be today, is the general conclusion:

On the whole we may say of the public schoolboy throughout the ages that *plus que l'on le change, plus c'est la même chose.* Schoolboy gods have not altered. Strength, fleetness of foot, physical beauty, loyalty to one's House and one's School – youth still worships these things.

Hay's single complete school story is *Housemaster,* which appeared in 1936. Like almost every product of that (at least partly hideous) decade, it has about it today an air half-repulsive and half-appealing. Hay belonged not just to the public-school world he knew so well but to a wider social scene, that of the theatre and review, of light literary larks of all kinds; so in writing about school he lacked the earnest narrowness of, say, a school-master like Coke and was able to write larkily about the sort of 'outrage' that was perfectly acceptable to the readers of his day, who liked to think themselves unconventional enough to take to their hearts the unconventional and the larky.

The outrage in *Housemaster* is the invasion in term-time of a sedate bachelor housemaster's house at an old-fashioned public school by three teenage sisters and their aunt, who unexpectedly turn up there and ask to stay. Known as the Girls' Friendly Society for obvious but quite innocent reasons, Rosemary, Chris and Button are girls of a kind adored by readers and theatre-goers of the time, descendants of the flappers and bright young things of the twenties but less brittle, more familiar, and therefore more acceptable. They are noisy, scatter-brained, extrovert and articulate, and plainly meant to be pretty and delicious as well; they shriek a lot and call the crusty old housemaster 'Charles' (long ago he was in love with their mother, so forgives them everything); they swoop about kissing and hugging, dancing and laughing, play havoc with the school rules and with some, at least of the boys' and young masters' hearts, and almost bring about poor Charles's resignation. But at the very end, by a stroke of luck and deviousness that is quite incredible, the tiresome headmaster is kicked upstairs to a bishopric and Mr Donkin (the long-suffering Charles) is made headmaster in his place.

Realistically, of course, it is all quite absurd; but absurdities are needed to get three girls and their aunt inside a boys' public school in the thirties, which is the point of the exercise. Two marriages tie up the ends for them as neatly as Sir Berkeley Nightingale, the convenient cabinet-minister uncle of Donkin's house-captain, ties up the ends for Donkin. Hay uses many of the school-story conventions while turning the conventional school story a little (not entirely) upside down with the conventional unconventionality he always used.

His description of Marbledown, the public school in the story, might come from any of a hundred school stories, nearly all of which start with one just like it. Marbledown is

> a good solid foundation of the old-fashioned type. Two hundred years ago it was, and has been from time immemorial, the ancient Grammar School of a small market town – a single building in the Market Square . . . In the middle of Queen Victoria's reign it had hopelessly outgrown its accommodation . . . The School achieved its present shape and constitution in the early seventies, that period of educational awakening and reform all round.

The new headmaster, too, might come from almost any story. Donkin describes him: 'A very brilliant man . . . a magnificent organiser; the routine goes on oiled wheels since he came here. He's a profound theologian, a genuine scholar, a brilliant teacher . . .' 'And he hasn't the faintest beginning of an idea what goes on inside a boy's head!' interrupts his friend Beamish. Hay later on says: 'The Head was all cold dignity and clear, flawless exposition. Since his arrival at Marbledown he had organised the Sixth Form into a perfectly functioning machine for the acquisition of Open Scholarships.' He does dreadful things, though, like forbidding the school to take part in the town regatta and carnival, and planning to phase out rowing among the school sports (Hay, as I mentioned, was captain of rowing in his college).

There are the familiar (but pleasant) school-story jokes. As I mentioned, a housemaster's daughters are known as Spot and Plain. A society flourishes known as the MMM (Marbledown Mass Murderers). Donkin is known as The Moke. Button has a twin at the school, a boy called Bimbo; they were christened Gerald and Geraldine. Aunt Barbara, whom they plan to marry off to Donkin, turns out to have been engaged for the past thirty-two years to another of the masters. And so on. Hay's main point seems to be that what counts in a housemaster, in a schoolmaster of any sort, is personal qualities and an understanding of boys.

Hay belonged to his time and when the time moved ahead he never moved along with it; which, whatever its literary limitations, makes his writing valuable as social history. He belonged to the upper level of talent in the school-story-and-connected scene, with Wodehouse and Stephen King-Hall, with whom he collaborated, with Turley, whom he admired. *Housemaster* is as good a lesson in social attitudes around 1936 as an afternoon spent with bound copies of *Punch,* and not very different in effect.

4 *The very nicest sort of public schoolboy, and at the same time the simplest and most delightful English gentleman* A. A. Milne

To me, the most appealing of the once-famous is Charles Turley (1869–1940). If only he had had a publisher perspicacious, ruthless and frank enough to make him cut a third or even half of what he wrote, he might have been the first-rate professional writer of school stories who never appeared. He was not in the class of Kipling or Wodehouse, but they hardly count as 'professional' school-story writers. Although Turley wrote books on explorers – Scott, Amundsen and Nansen – school stands at the centre of his work and everything else is on the fringes. Good-humoured and good-natured, amusing and attractive, credible yet idiosyncratic, with plots that work and above all excellent characterisation; 'founded upon the bed-rock of human nature,' as someone put it, 'which does not change, though literary fashions come and go'; why are his books not remembered? Turley is funny and sometimes moving, racy and readable; even in attitude he has dated little – and quite pleasantly – for he totally lacks the ugly characteristics that appear in so many of his contemporaries. A kind of approval of philistinism (implied, anyway) is all you can accuse him of; but it may be that he was merely smiling at it, and was not quite skilful enough to let you know if he liked it, or merely lumped it, in his heroes. Even the almost impossible feat of writing as a boy in the first person he manages without being ridiculous. Yet all his gifts are lost because of a fatal flaw in his writing. Every one of his books is far too long.

Yet the first dip into one of them is a surprise and delight. Ian Hay asked of them:

What quality keeps them alive and readable? The answer is quite simple. The characters . . . Over and over again we say as we read: 'I know that boy; I was in the Lower Fourth with him once!'[4]

Exactly (one feels); Turley gets his eye-level right, and takes his tricky subject both seriously and lightly; seriously in that he cares about it, lightly in that he is never heavy-handed. An admirer once called him 'Jane Austen in trousers' – hardly the soundest criticism, but an attempted tribute to his deftness and grace.

Ian Hay wrote:

When writing school fiction you must never try to stimulate the interest of your readers by introducing into your plot sensational happenings or unusual events; because if you do your story will immediately cease to be a genuine school story. In other words, schoolboy interests are small interests . . . School and school routine contain within them all the necessary material for an absorbing novel of school life; but to make your tale ring true you must possess the art of transmuting small change into pure gold.[5]

Exactly again (one feels), and at moments Turley possessed this art. But when it failed him he wrote pages and whole chapters that ought to have been scrapped, he rambled and repeated. Without Wodehouse's gifts, which could make much out of little, he seems to have worked rather too hard on the same small patch.

His personal popularity may have been partly to blame. He was clearly much loved. When he died a book of tributes by his friends appeared, *Dear Turley,* which makes it clear how people found in him the old-fashioned virtues without any old-fashioned stuffiness, simplicity without simple-mindedness, brain and brawn nicely balanced. There must have been more complexity than that about him, which the biography that will now never be written might have brought out. But at the level of intimacy he achieved with, among others, J. M. Barrie, Hugh Walpole and A. A. Milne, he seems to have been a man of transparent goodness. 'Sir James always spoke of you as the most lovable of English gentlemen,' Barrie's manservant* wrote to him after his master's death. Similar expressions turn up in all that was said of him. Milne wrote:

* Frank Thurston, a Jeeves-like character of vast culture, described by several of Barrie's friends. See Lady Cynthia Asquith's essay in *Dear Turley* (1942): as '. . . Barrie's incomparable manservant, famous both for his extreme erudition and for his unfailing tact. There was no missing quotation he could not supply while he filled your glass; no undesired visitor, however importunate, he could not exclude without being uncivil.'

He remained all his life the very nicest sort of public schoolboy, and at the same time the simplest and most delightful English gentleman . . . If you can imagine a man who had all the simple Christian virtues without any awareness of having them; who combined, as they are so rarely combined, an innocent goodness of heart with a keen sense of humour, and intelligence with a boyish devotion to games; and if you add to this the most completely irresistible laugh – well then, perhaps, you will understand why he had so many friends and why he was so loved by them.[6]

Much of this attractiveness comes across in what he wrote.

He was born Charles Turley Smith in 1869 and went to Cheltenham, one of the new public schools, in its toughest, most ebullient period, the eighteen-eighties. An excellent sportsman, he understood, though with tongue often pleasantly in cheek, the manic enthusiasms of sportsmen. His own interest in cricket produced, in the happy days of cheap telegrams, telegraphed messages from Barrie in London to Turley in Cornwall on what was happening at Lord's or the Oval. 'PALSIED EXCITEMENT. X AWAITING HIS INNINGS IN HYSTERIA' or 'DREADFUL DELAY. FIELDING SUPERB', Barrie would signal throughout the summer. In 1926, the march of science put an end to this agreeable extravagance. 'Do you get wireless news now or can I still have the fun of telegraphing?' Barrie asked. Alas, the wireless had arrived, but the weekly letters between the two men continued.

Godfrey Marten, Schoolboy, Turley's portrait of Cheltenham in his own time there, is his best-known book, first published in 1902, and reprinted for the Cheltenham centenary celebrations in 1939, a year before his death. Fougasse's illustrations in this edition show the new boy as a very diminutive insect, a tiny creature at a desk the size and shape of a Wurlitzer organ, then growing gradually into a young man on the threshold of undergraduate life. *Godfrey Marten, Undergraduate* (1904) predictably failed, like the other sequels of school stories, but its failures are interesting. 'Be a man, Godfrey,' the hero's father tells him as he starts university life, 'and don't forget that the first step towards becoming one is to behave like a gentleman.' This kind of thing makes people smile today, but does not make one like Turley any the less.

Godfrey Marten, Schoolboy shows Cheltenham just as Turley knew it. 'I can answer for the vivid truth of it ten years later,' says the

---

In her *Portrait of Barrie* (1954), in which, very oddly, although there is almost a chapter about him, Thurston does not appear in the index, she says that Barrie's last letter when he was dying was written to his servant: 'I want you besides the monetary bequest to pick yourself a hundred of my books,' he wrote. 'Few persons who have entered that loved flat have done more to honour books.'

foreword to the centenary edition. 'The essential truth and interest still remain [in 1939] because the boys in it are boys, not pigmy geniuses or dwarf grown-ups.'[7] Barrie gave a copy of it to every schoolboy he knew, Ian Hay wrote of 'the quality which [it] shares with the other school classics. We know the characters, we have met them; we have been there.' Godfrey himself, the narrator, is both clever and a sportsman; he has a scholarship, and is good at football and cricket. Hay describes him as

the perfect type of the happy-go-lucky English boy – plucky, bumptious, self-confident, impulsive, loyal; bone-idle, utterly irresponsible and ripe for any mischief; yet right-minded and perfectly acquiescent when just retribution falls on him.

This is all very well, but it makes him sound like Tom Brown's twin, and he is really rather more interesting. For one thing he is more humorous, and more inclined to brood about this or that, to move from the particular to the general, to draw conclusions. Deep they may not be: ('I hate saying it, but it does seem to me that when a boy is a brute he is a far greater one than any other human being . . . When a boy is cruel, he has a most horrible way of going on'), but they give the book a certain moral dimension, without overt preaching. Then, for his time and the sort of book it is, Turley makes him almost startlingly realistic at times. Here is Godfrey, having lost the money with which he intended to pay for a meal:

'That's a pretty lie!' she said, pushing her disagreeable face into mine.

'You shut up!' I roared back at her, our noses nearly meeting. 'It is neither pretty nor a lie, but a most awful nuisance. You keep a civil tongue in your head!'

And then Turley had not just a sense of fun but a sense of humour, and was good at putting his own into a form that might credibly be found in a boy. Here is Godfrey describing his first meeting with his headmaster:

I smiled. I suppose I oughtn't to have done it, and it would by most people be considered a great want of respect on my part, though, as a matter of fact, I smiled because I couldn't help it, and not with any idea of putting this very powerful gentleman at his ease. But when anyone looks over the top of his spectacles, I am always compelled to laugh, for some reason which I cannot explain or justify. The head spotted my smile all right, and his face, which I had thought benevolent, took a sudden change for the worse. He was either angry or wanted to smile back.

Godfrey, probably like most of his contemporaries at Cheltenham at the time, and possibly with Turley's approval, is a fair young philistine too. He hates 'abroad' as Turley's other hero hates Japanese fans (see Chapter III, Section 5):

> I had to spend my Christmas holidays at Mentone . . . I simply hated the place . . . My advice to any fellow whose people want to carry him off to the South of France for his holidays is to raise a friend, or even a maiden aunt, who will keep him in England. I am sure he would have a better time feeding cats, or whatever it is that maiden aunts are supposed to take delight in, than pottering around in Mentone.

But whether this is Turley's own view, or Godfrey's view approved by Turley, or Godfrey's view merely smiled at by Turley, it is impossible to tell; a difficulty one meets quite often in Turley's books, and one which shows up his limitations as a writer.

He wrote about the upper-middle layer of the public schools – not the intellectually distinguished, not the socially smart, but not the dingy or the obscure ones, either. He invented a number of schools, and although they vary in age and background they are all much like Cheltenham, with boys of similar background, tastes and customs, whether they happen to be called Cliborough or Bradminster, Rossborough or Granby, Minvern or Lexham or Crayford. Unlike many writers of school stories, Turley brings no whiffs of the great world into his schools; there are no titles or great estates in the background. But in their way his boys are supremely sure of themselves, as the English professional classes were in the days when the world seemed to belong to them; not just the world immediately around them but that quarter of the globe painted red.

Though not particularly strong on plots, Turley introduced conflict of character into most of his school stories. There is the conflict between the keen, determined character and the loutish boys and weak housemaster he has to deal with; or the conflict between school and the boy from an adventurous background with none of the received public-school ideas, who can laugh at the self-importance of the bloods and the absurdity of sports mania. There is the contrast within a family between fanatical cricketers and the youngest boy, who is interested in other things; or between twins, one a fine athlete, the other lame; or between the manly, democratic hero and his supercilious rival. Turley has a moral rather than a social view of gentlemanliness and shows in action just what he means. As in the following exchange, in *The Lefthander*:

> 'My name is Pedder. I'm the Boss's butler; and you will be Mr Gresham,' he said.
>
> 'Bang right, first pop,' Jack answered and held out his hand.

'Some of you,' Pedder continued, 'shake hands with me at first sight, and some of you don't.'

One cannot imagine the boys of Vachell, Lunn or Leslie shaking hands with the butler on arrival; still less using slangy talk when addressing him. It is part of the Turley charm that he makes his boys do both. So, too, is this kind of exchange:

'For heaven's sake, sit down, and don't stand there like an ape with epilepsy.'

To this ungracious remark I replied:

'Look here, Dobson, what we want to know is, are you or are you not going to leave me alone?'

'Oh, that's it, is it?' was his answer, and he relapsed into silence and food.

Not many school story writers use zeugma, either. It too is a part of Turley's charm. In a metaphorical sense he used it throughout his books, those long-winded half-successes; he combined the solid and the abstract, the literal and the figurative, things like silence and food. He is one of the most attractive of school-story writers, yet one of the least remembered.

CHAPTER XV

The school story at war: *Tell England, Prelude*

For officers, Britain turned to her public schools Ian Hay

The First World War saw the apotheosis of the public schools. Everything they had been teaching seemed to come into its own, and their products, almost an entire generation, were killed. An extension of the prefect system put boys in their late teens in command of seasoned men and once they were at the front gave them, on average, three weeks to live. In courage and unblinking obedience to the authorities and the system that put them there, they justified their training. The sixth-formers of the school stories became the subalterns of the trenches. Writers of memoirs have recalled that they made no plans for a future after school, knowing they would almost certainly die soon after leaving it.

Ian Hay wrote in 1922:

> For officers, Britain turned to her public schools. Each of these schools possessed a purely voluntary Officers' Training Corps Unit, maintaining a precarious existence against the superior attractions of cricket and football. When the great call came, these young Armies of ours were officered, without difficulty, by many thousand competent cadets furnished by this system. They were pathetically young; but they possessed two priceless qualifications: they knew their job, and they played the game. They never asked men to go where they would not go themselves. So, children though they were, their men followed them everywhere. There are not many of them left now.[1]

The school myth and the school stories that popularised and perpetuated it were at their height. The flood of school stories – many of the best, certainly of the most 'serious' – in the early years of the century were not dealing with war or even prophesying war but preaching the attitudes that made people prepared to go into it with blind, absurd, heroic enthusiasm. And by a terrible artistic rightness the schoolboy hero of fiction, who had no future to equal his school greatness, could realistically be killed at Gallipoli or on the Somme, thus embodying the idea of youth as perfection, and of school as a life-in-itself (with a three-week coda). If in adult life the blood could never achieve the glory he had known at school, then death was the perfect solution: heroic, absolute, it combined artistic and emotional rightness. Vachell had suggested this at the end of *The Hill*, but with a single death: the next generation could be more sweepingly slaughtered.

Death looms large in the school story. It loomed large in society in general, of course, striking at the young as well as everyone else with fearful suddenness. Illness then was what the road accident is today: everyone knew someone who had been struck, families who had lost not just their elders but their young and active. In the school story, though, death is more than a random event: it ties up loose ends, settles psychological impossibilities, leaves friends free to make other, less passionate relationships in the world outside, to marry and procreate; even takes its revenge for the sins of youth. All in all, it was a tempting alternative to the outside world. When someone dies young, perhaps the only consolation is that the horrors of old age, the deterioration of physical if not moral life in general, are avoided. How much more tempting to feel this at a time when adolescence and schooldays were thought the prime of life, when school glory made all later glories seem unimportant. Rather than face the anti-climax of the world, the deflation of school-centred loves and enthusiasms, the heroes of school stories often had to die.

And violent, honourable death was in the wings. For boys in *The Hill*, there was the Boer War to provide it; for boys in *Stalky & Co.*, the outposts of the Empire. A few years earlier than these the Prince Imperial, son of the exiled Napoleon III, had been the perfect symbol of young glory-in-death, much identified with by admiring English schoolboys, as contemporary fiction shows. By dying (heroically at the hand of Zulus, in war as a volunteer) he became for ever the *possible* Emperor, not the emperor-manqué he would probably have been, the failed claimant, the pathetic middle-aged pretender; going out in a blaze of glory, never to become dull and paunchy and unathletic.

And underlying the theme of death-as-amber, pickling the perfect specimen at his moment of perfection, was the complementary theme of death rather than dishonour. In the moral language of the time, that included sexual dishonour, which included the admission of homosexual feeling. Rather than face their own sexual feelings, or rather than allow their creators to admit such feelings existed, some of these young heroes had to die. The First World War brought death to a whole generation, which took away its glamour and meant that the public schools, like the country, would never be the same again.

By 1914, we are often told, the nineteenth century and a way of life that to the leisured classes had seemed eternal, came to an end. Even if outwardly this way of life continued into the twenties and thirties, and the great divisions between the classes showed few signs of being broken down until after the Second World War, after 1918 the atmosphere could never be the same again, in either the schools or the school stories. An innocence had gone, the uncritical, unquestioning loyalty, the boyish self-importance, even the sense of total involvement in, and of belonging to, a school and the society it reflected. But school stories kept being written and death gave them a neat, satisfying and, in the circumstances, all too credible ending. The fact that they were inadequate to reflect the vastness, horror and even beauty of what had happened did not entirely vitiate their poignancy.

2 . . . *the dead schoolboys of your generation* From *Tell England by Ernest Raymond*

The one really successful school story written during the war, *The Loom of Youth*, said nothing about it. Quite deliberately, it was not a war story, not set in the context of a war. And yet the schools must have been linked very closely and emotionally with what was happening. As each year's intake of boys went off to the front the next year's boys must have held their breath – enviously at first, then, perhaps, more warily. Memorial services for the dead boys, attended by parents and relations, were frequently held at the schools. Memoirs recall the sadness of middle-aged masters left behind while dozens of boys they knew went off to the war, and few returned.

Soon after the war, Ernest Raymond and Beverley Nichols both produced first novels which started with school and ended, credibly enough, with death. Both find death fitting, even beautiful, in their pitifully young heroes. This may have been an old-fashioned attitude to take by then, but both writers were exponents of already old-fashioned attitudes towards school, the family, society in general, and the war.

Tell England (1922) was one of the most popular of all school stories, and of all war stories too; but as it was only half a school story, it is not generally considered one. Still, I propose to consider it. Exactly half of it is set in school, and as it is a long book this makes the school part into a fair-sized novel on its own. Ernest Raymond, back from Gallipoli and out of the Anglican church where he had been a clergyman and found he had lost his faith, sub-titled it 'A study in a generation'. Its arresting, succinct and memorable title, pretentious and dated today but exactly right for its time, must have had something to do with its immediate, remarkable success. No other book of Raymond's, though he wrote on for another sixty years, ever came near it in fame or popularity.

Like Talbot Baines Reed, Raymond went to a London day school (St Paul's), but set his book in a boarding school far from London; and like most school-story writers he jacked it up a little in glamour and smartness. At Kensingtowe ('the finest school in England') and Bramhall ('its best house') Rupert Ray, the narrator, and his friends Archie Pennybet ('dark and dictatorial') and Edgar Gray Doe ('fair and enthusiastic') spend five great years after five earlier years in 'the Nursery', Kensingtowe's prep school. Rupert, known as 'the Gem' because (he overhears someone saying) his eyes are 'something between a diamond and a turquoise', is innocently in love with Doe and both boys are equally innocently in love with Radley, a cricketing master who canes hard and then says: 'You're two plucky boys' ('his little ration of gentleness'). But their housemaster, Carpet Slippers, they hate. 'How I hated Carpet Slippers, and was happy in my hate!' cries Rupert. 'I hated the silkiness of his chestnut beard; I hated the sheen of his pink cranium; I hated his soft rotundity and his little curvilinear features; I hated, above all, his poisonous speeches.' There is a good deal of whacking at Kensingtowe, by masters and prefects, on hands and bottoms; and the headmaster keeps telling boys to take off their spectacles so that he can smack their faces. Rupert, though frequently whacked, is something of a prefects' pet and his eye-level is constantly changing in regard to them and his own self as he writes, in dug-outs, a few years ahead. 'Were Stanley alive now,' he muses, 'instead of lying beneath the sea at Gallipoli, he would be twenty-seven years of age, very junior in his profession, and therefore much younger than when he was a house-captain of nineteen.'

It is while the school cricket team is playing 'The Masters' that the Archduke is assassinated at Sarajevo, and Rupert, like the others knowing nothing of what is involved or what is to come, cries: 'Oh, what fun! We'll give 'em no end of a thrashing!' When he hears of boys just ahead of him at school who will soon be in France he groans:

'Lucky beggars!' and Pennybet, lucky beggar, is soon among them, killed at Neuve Chapelle even before Rupert and Edgar have got going for Gallipoli. The colonel in Rupert's grandfather's regiment gives them a remarkable harangue when they call to see him:

Eighteen, by Jove! You've timed your lives wonderfully, my boys. To be eighteen in 1914 is to be the best thing in England. England's wealth used to consist in other things. Nowadays you boys are the richest thing she's got . . . Eighteen years ago you were born for this day. Through the last eighteen years you've been educated for it. Your birth and breeding were given you that you might officer England's youth in this hour. And now you enter upon your inheritance. Just as this is *the* day in the history of the world so yours is *the* generation. No other generation has been called to such grand things, to such crowded, glorious living . . .

The strange thing is that Raymond, even after the war, and specifically after going through Gallipoli, one of its most terrible battlefields, still seemed to take this straight, to be persuaded by the rhetoric. For when some of the officers laugh at him Rupert says:

Yet the Colonel was right, and the scoffers wrong. The Colonel was a poet who could listen and hear how the heart of the world was beating; the scoffers were very prosaic cattle who scarcely knew that the world had a heart at all.

No wonder *Tell England* appealed to post-war readers: it tells of the war in what seems a pre-war spirit. Sunny, youthful, idealistic, with an air of extraordinary ingenuousness and optimism, with all its ideas still intact on patriotism and valour, on the need for sacrifice and the worthiness of the cause, it must have taken people back to an earlier view of things, giving them the feeling so many must have lost, that it was, after all, worth while. Nothing he had seen and lived through seems to have quenched Raymond's enthusiasm for life, or his basic sweetness of spirit. *Tell England* is full of the old decencies, the old innocence (sexual as well as otherwise), the lost atmosphere of pre-1914 middle-class life, in which inequalities were expected but courage and courtesy demanded in return for privilege.

Not that Raymond was exactly privileged; his background must have been, at the very least, confusing. Supposedly an orphan, he was brought up against an apparently conventional suburban background in a group of half-brothers and the 'aunts' who had borne them by the same man; and he discovered which 'aunt' was his mother only on the eve of his departure for Gallipoli. In *Tell England* he shows an attitude towards women, family life and motherhood that comes strangely from a man who had scarcely known normal family life or mothering: an attitude at once sentimental and genuinely tender, without irony and certainly with no bitterness. His autobiography[2] tells his strange story in an accepting, unresentful way, just as *Tell England* shows none of the bitterness and weariness, the harshness and even cynicism of so much post-war writing, but keeps to the old pattern of belief and feeling that seemed so appropriate in 1914. The first half of the book naturally lays the foundations for the second. School trains the young for the war that is to swallow them up, and Raymond seems not to resent the great maw that is to do this, just as he seems somehow generous towards luckier, more admissible, more conventional fates than his own.

Rupert is dead by the time his book appears, killed in the last days of the war, aged twenty-two, leaving the manuscript of a book his Gallipoli friend, Padre Monty, suggested he should write: '"Tell England" – you must write a book and tell 'em, Rupert, about the dead schoolboys of your generation.' Three years later, in the autumn of 1918, Rupert writes the final chapter before going 'over the top' next morning. 'I thought I would add a paragraph or two, in case I go down in the morning. If I come through all right, I shall wipe these paragraphs out.' Since they are still there, Rupert is dead. The three friends who first met aged six, six and eight are all dead by the end of the war; but Rupert has set down their vivid presences for survivors to be reassured that this is just how the young were, just how the war looked. Of their last days in England before setting off for the war, he wrote:

> What young bucks we were, Doe and I! We bought motor-bicycles and raced over the countryside, Doe, ever a preacher of Life, calling out 'This is Life, isn't it?' I remember our bowling along a deserted country road and shouting for a lark: 'Sing of joy, sing of bliss, it was never like this, Yip-i-addy-i-ay!' . . . I see the figure of Doe standing breathless by his bicycle after a breakneck run, his hair blown into disorder by the wind, and the white dust of England round his eyes and on his cheeks, and saying: 'My godfathers, this is Life!'

What is strange is that all this should have been written *after* the war, after the experiences that scarred and maimed so many spirits, as well as bodies. On his last night alive, Rupert writes from his trench: 'As Monty used to say, we are given now and then moments of surpassing joy which outweigh decades of grief. I think I knew such a moment when I won the swimming cup for Bramhall [his house at school].' It is easy to mock at this kind of thing, and *Tell England*, like every period piece, has had its share of mockery in later periods. But Raymond was not writing from the inexperienced safety of home: he, like Rupert, had been through it. Yet he could still express (and, I am sure, feel, for he was a man of transparent decency and truthfulness) the idea which was possibly all that the dead men's families could cling to – that of aesthetic and moral perfection in a very young man's death. He says – or at least makes Rupert say:

> I feel that the old Colonel was right when he saw nothing unlovely in Penny's death, and that Monty was right when he said that Doe had done a perfect thing at the last, and so grasped the Grail. And I have the strange idea that very likely I, too, shall find beauty in the morning.

Tell England is a period piece with none of the specific nastiness of its time. Its school life is bathed in sunshine, like the home-life of its three young heroes, and it is perhaps significant that, just as he never had such a home-life, Raymond never had such a school-life, either. The most loving pictures of boarding-school have often been painted by day-boys. But there was more to it than that. Raymond, like Wodehouse – but with more cause for resentments than Wodehouse seems to have had – returned good for evil. That its expression was sometimes sentimental does not diminish the oddity, the interest, almost the heroism of his attitudes. If forgiveness cancels out injury, then Raymond must have been one of the most uninjured of men: he managed to forgive not just his own circumstances but the war and what it did to his generation of schoolboys.

3 *Here, I recognised with surprise, relief, and the joy of recognition, are characters who feel and think as I do* Geoffrey Trease

Beverley Nichols's *Prelude* (1920) is not, like *Tell England*, half a school story and half a war story. It is a school story with a few pages at the end that take its hero out to France and to his death. In callowness, it is often like *The Loom of Youth*, which is not surprising since both books were written very soon after their authors left school – in Nichols's case, Marlborough. But far from admiring Alec Waugh's book, Nichols attacked it vehemently. 'The man who wrote *The Loom of Youth* could criticise as much as he liked, because he obviously must have loathed school and had a beastly time there,' one of the boys in *Prelude* remarks, curiously misreading what seems a transparently loving memoir of schooldays. Although a more accomplished stylist than the young Alec Waugh, Nichols was liable to make the sort of sweeping generalisation that might have come straight out of *The Loom of Youth*:

> A public school is a place of paradox. It is a hotbed of romance, a desert of materialism. In it the angels and the brutes flourish together; all that is stupid and base, all that is lofty and ideal . . . It is a pilgrimage – one enters its gates alone, shy, empty-handed and afraid, and one comes out laughing, shouting

and with glad eyes, the centre of a group of friends; with one's arms full of the flowers of five great years.

And so it is with his hero, Paul. He starts off at Martinsell (Marlborough) miserably enough, never having left his home or his mother before, therefore totally unprepared for public school; friendless, wretched and forlorn, not quite bullied but ignored, teased and kicked about. Then gradually he makes friends and adjustments and comes to love it; until, from his trench in France, he can write:

It's Martinsell, Martinsell, Martinsell, that I long for, Martinsell that, somehow – I don't know how – has given me strength and power and has made me love. I don't know whether its system be right or wrong, but it is Martinsell that has made me come here and fight, and has guided me right, all along . . . Goodbye till we see each other again – oh God – if it were at Martinsell, and in the Spring!

Like Ernest Raymond, Nichols had a bad time in childhood, but whereas Raymond's childhood seems to have lacked warmth and a sense of home and family, Nichols's was all too claustrophobically domestic. Like Raymond, too, he described it in an autobiography. This, in Nichols's case, was a horrifying book called *Father Figure* in which (quite unlike Raymond) he got his own back on everything that went wrong. What went mainly wrong was the drunken father he loathed and several times tried to kill, whose alcoholism had to be kept secret from the neighbours and so precluded any social life at all. Penned up together, they vented their spleen and viciousness on each other and school at Marlborough must have proved a happy escape.

Prelude gets its own back in another way, by eliminating the father altogether. Paul's father is dead and he can enjoy his mother's doting presence and shopping expeditions all on his own. He also compensates for the drab social circumstances of his childhood by wild fantasies of grandeur. Paul seems to be a self-portrait and his mother a portrait of Nichols's mother, to whom the book is dedicated; but their way of life has been enormously smartened up. No retired-solicitor-in-Torquay life for them, as for the real-life Nichols, but a Mayfair house with a Veronese in a mere spare bedroom, a house in Devon with 'old stone balustrades' and music room and a French butler who dotes on 'Monsieur Paul', and school holidays that are a whirl of Claridge's and the Café Royal, of seeing Nijinsky and shopping with his mother for her luxurious clothes and amazing hats. The *Young Visiters* atmosphere even extends to school, where 'three dozen large hot-house peaches' or 'a large case of claret and liqueurs' may suddenly turn up and at 'little parties [for] select members of House' they drink Château Lafitte 1877 and at 'choir supper' have 'turtle soup and salmon, drowned in quantities of delicious mayonnaise'. No bangers and mash in the young Nichols's day-dreams, in which his mother visits him at school 'looking elusively beautiful in a frock of French grey . . . and a delicate black hat crowned with white ospreys' or fades 'softly out of the room in a cloud of sable and lavender'.

Like the young Nichols, the hero of *Prelude* is clearly an unusual schoolboy, since 'there was nothing Paul hated more', Nichols says, 'than appearing an ordinary boy'. Now, since this was the exact opposite of most boys' attitudes at school, at least on arrival, it might have made an interesting book. But Nichols is painfully self-indulgent and wallows throughout, if not in literal self-portraiture, at least in fanciful self-adornment. Paul, a musical prodigy, is portrayed (in chapters with titles like 'Stray chords', 'Broken melodies', 'Interlude', 'Pastorale', 'Coda') as a boy thought lovable by his creator but likely, I think, to set most readers' teeth on edge:

At home he had always danced before going to bed; he had danced like a mad thing. He had dressed up and acted, and stood very still in some strange pose in front of a flickering candle. When his voice was still unbroken it had been of exceptional beauty, and he had sung all day long, songs out of French and Italian opera, improvising accompaniments as he sang.

Or:

He would start to sing in a high treble of a curious and almost metallic sweetness, making up words which sounded like Italian, accompanying himself in the dark. And there was always an invisible audience that he sang to, so that elaborate bows to the dark and empty corners of the salon were necessary.

Or:

There are various forms of seeking exercise: dancing in the moonlight round an old pond of lilies, cool and closed hours past, was Paul's.

It is easy to laugh at it all at this distance, to imagine what Wodehouse (not to mention Kipling) would have done with him if Paul had strayed into one of his books, to shudder over the gruesome 'sophistication' of his talk of clothes with his mother's dressmakers or his friends' mothers. But nearer its own day *Prelude* actually seems to have been thought something of a 'liberating' school story, a breaker of conventions and taboos. The mere idea of having an epicene young hero whose idea of exercise is to dance round a lily pond by moonlight, and who yet manages to love a tough games-mad school like Martinsell/Marlborough, to make friends and to fit in with a good many school conventions, apparently operated in its day among some people as a powerful eye-opener and soul-stirrer. Geoffrey Trease wrote:

I remember how I was moved by Beverley Nichols' first precocious novel, *Prelude*. Here, I realised with surprise, relief, and the joy of recognition, are characters who feel and think as I do. The first book which does that for a boy or girl is not a milestone but a bridge, carrying them over from the love of romance to the appreciation of reality. From *Prelude* I went on to *Sinister Street*.[3]

It is odd to think of *Prelude*, much of which now seems shrill and over-written, as an introduction to reality, but not surprising to hear of it leading on to Compton Mackenzie's *Sinister Street*, another example of the kind of rather old-hat 'decadence' that has a powerful appeal for adolescents.

It is not easy to see (as it is with *Tell England*) that *Prelude* has much to say about the attitudes that took boys from school into the war not reluctantly but (at least at the beginning) with delight, with wild enthusiasm. There seems little connection between Paul's Café Royal parties and salmon suppers with the choir and his sudden transfer to life in the trenches and honourable death, loved by his men and his colonel. But Nichols has, like Raymond, kept to the pre-war attitudes, to the idea that young death in war is beautiful, not wasteful; that Paul had died at his peak, gallant, unspoiled, unsullied.

CHAPTER XVI

The pop school story: Greyfriars and Co.

Needless to say, these stories are fantastically unlike life at a real public school George Orwell

The accepted and acknowledged school stories and myths all had their effect on the 'upper' levels of school life. Below them lay other myth-makers. C. Day-Lewis, as I have said, called school itself an 'invisible compost'. Another compost, steamier and hotter and more generally enticing, nourishing its readers' imaginative rather than real-life world, was the mythical school story for boys who had never been to, and were never going anywhere near, the sort of school they dealt with. It was hardly surprising that a man who was taken from his home at eight and kept in what were then the isolated conditions of prep-school and then public-school life for the next ten years should have plenty to feel and sometimes to say about it. What is odd is that the mystique of this system filtered through to those who had never experienced it. On the surface it was diffused by the peculiarly English mixture of idealism and snobbery, high-mindedness and self-interest, shown in memoirs and talk of school, and by a few approved school stories. But what probably spread it most widely was the underground, scarcely acknowledged cult of the popular school story.

By what I shall call the 'pop' school story I do not mean the more or less seriously intentioned stories of Reed and his immediate followers, but the baroque imaginings of – mainly – Frank Richards, who built up Greyfriars and, under other pseudonyms, others like it to become the apotheosis of the public school: a cloud-cuckoo-land, an all-purpose repository of dreams for those who had never been there. This kind of thing was much odder than the memoirs of school-obsessed Old Boys or the weird loyalties of, for example, Baden-Powell, who went about Mafeking in the middle of the siege looking for an Old Carthusian with whom to celebrate Founder's Day. Much odder than the school magazines for initiates were publicly-intentioned magazines like *The Captain*, which make it plain that the public school was not just a part of youthful fantasy through the school story, but that the *real* public schools and their affairs were actively 'followed', in a fan-club kind of way, by all sorts of people besides Old Boys.

In other words, the public school was, by the end of the century, an object of interest to those who had nothing to do with it, a symbol of romance, as Hollywood and film stars used to be, as pop stars and footballers are today. Articles would appear on, for instance, cricket in a number of public schools, with photographs of captains and teams and plenty of space and detail. That Old Boys turned up to cheer at matches may make us smile today; but even people without public-school experience felt involved in their doings, and the public-school world had a hold on some of the pop-readership of its day. If the Old Boy was a rum figure, the Old Boy manqué was even rummer. Orwell wrote as recently as 1940:

> It is quite clear that there are tens and scores of thousands to whom every detail of life at a 'posh' public school is wildly thrilling and romantic. They happen to be outside the mystic world of quadrangles and house colours, but they yearn after it, day-dream about it, live mentally in it for hours at a stretch.[1]

With other mythologies and other dreams (of army, empire, pioneering, exploration), public-school feeling – above all the self-confidence that arouses confidence in others – was at its height from about 1880 to 1914. Frank Richards carried it on, at a popular level, for another three decades or so. Strangely enough (when you consider how large a place school had in the lives of public-school boys, and, increasingly, their sisters) approved writing – 'bourgeois' writing – for the young did not often deal with school. Approved writers for the young were writing for what we should now call an almost exclusively middle-class audience about almost exclusively middle-class doings; or at least for an audience that approved of these writers' outlook, and wanted to identify with it. Yet they nearly always avoided the most important single factor in most middle-class children's lives: school. A few school stories were approved but on the whole approved writers for boys (such as Rider Haggard, Henty, Ballantyne, Marryat,

Brereton and their imitators) had either adult heroes or else boy heroes who might still be of school age but were in fact following some late-Victorian dream of soldiering or trading or pioneering, whatever period of history they happened to be set in.

At first sight it seems odd to have school ignored in most fiction written for the young of a class which was kept at school most of the time. Even in books with a modern setting, things generally took place in the holidays, on islands of adventure, spot-lit and special occasions. Because 'real life' in the sense that most people would now consider it (normal family life domestically lived in the ordinary world) for the children of professional and administrative parents upwards really did not exist. For two-thirds of the year they were in the wholly 'manufactured' conditions of school, and this meant three months on end, not divided by the weekends at home and long half-terms, the frequent visits outside school or visits at school from outsiders, which boarding schools have today. For the remaining third, they were in the hardly less artificial conditions of a home geared for their short-term presence or, if the parents were on the move or posted abroad, in make-shift conditions of all kinds – with relations, in lodgings. Even the idyllic holidays spent by Arthur Ransome's Swallows in the Lake District, envied by every child who read about them in the twenties, thirties and forties, were not spent in a home of their own or as a complete family. Their naval father was at the other end of the earth and they merely lodged in a farmhouse.

Until school was over, which then meant the age of eighteen or nineteen, everything to do with ordinary life was kept at a distance: not just domesticity but money, managing, the general arrangement of life (except within the context of school, where a good deal of administrative ability was called for: but of a political or proconsular kind, the sort required in the civil service rather than a home); as well as the most obvious thing of all, heterosexual feeling or experience, even the companionship of women. Evelyn Waugh wrote of his time at Lancing:

> The exclusion of feminine influence and domestic life was absolute. We never entered a human dwelling or saw a shop; to a boy like myself, coming straight from home, the experience was chilling.[2]

Over and over again, the same sort of point is made. In *Prelude* one of the boys bursts out indignantly (the time is 1915):

> Here, when we're the very people who'll have to be among what you call the governing classes after this ruddy war, we're being taught not a thing about the conditions of the country . . . we ought to be learning about what the socialists are saying, what Henderson and Macdonald are thinking – and it

wouldn't be a bad idea if occasionally we thought what we were fighting about. You ask the average person in the school if he knows anything about the Alsace-Lorraine question and he'll look at you as though he'd been bitten by a large cow. Ask them about the Living Wage, the standard of life, Poland, Ireland, Shaw, if they ever read the *Herald*, life, life, life – what people are saying and doing and suffering – God – they don't know. We're shut out from it all, it's all kept from us. That's the tragedy of the whole thing . . . We don't know how they live, what they think, what their wives and children think and eat . . .

And much later, in 1940, T. C. Worsley wrote that boys from eight to eighteen were

quite out of contact with the larger community life – with adults earning their living, marrying, having babies, dying, going on strike, voting, discussing, visiting the cinema, dancing.[3]

Elderly men remember how ashamed they were, while at school, of having sisters, and how they kept quiet about them if they could. Forster, at an early age, found it was thought shameful even to have a mother. This bias against home continued long after Forster's school-days, or Waugh's. 'One famous headmaster to whom I spoke the other day assured me that in his opinion no parent was really qualified to bring up his son,' John Rodgers wrote as recently as 1938.[4] Even today, schools that take day-boys often expect them to put in such long hours, even at weekends, that they go home only to sleep; the implication being that time spent at school is always better employed than time spent elsewhere.

In the central years of the public schools, many boys came to expect this monastic, spartan, bachelor state of affairs. Beetle says:

I've met chaps in the holidays who've got married housemasters. It's perfectly awful! They have babies and teething and measles and all that sort of thing right bung *in* the school; and the master's wives give tea-parties – tea-parties, padre! – and ask the chaps to breakfast.

This was no twelve-year-old determined to be tough, but a Beetle of sixteen, the age of marriage, certainly of courtship, for plenty of working-class boys today. Boys in the public-school heyday were kept in a state of barrack-like toughness until adult life: no wonder some of them never left it.

It was a circular, self-perpetuating process, this 'abnormalising' of life. In the early days of the public schools, school was seen as part of the process of growing up, inside and outside the school, and *Tom Brown's Schooldays*, heartfelt if sentimental, ends with a summing-up of current attitudes:

For it is only through our mysterious human relationships, through the love and tenderness and purity of mothers, and sisters, and wives, through the strength and courage and wisdom of fathers and brothers and teachers, that we can come to some knowledge of Him, in whom alone the love, and the tenderness, and the purity, and the strength, and the courage, and the wisdom of all these dwell together in perfect fullness.

Mothers and sisters – even wives – are acknowledged as influences, fathers and brothers mentioned before teachers; and a word like 'tenderness' is so alien to the world of the later public schools and to a book like *Stalky & Co.* that its very use in the context shows the distance travelled in fifty years.

At Arnold's Rugby the hard division between home and school, the outer and the inner worlds, a boy's feeling for his family and what he felt for his school friends, had yet to come. So had the packed timetable, physical isolation from the rest of the world, uniform, compulsory games, military training, the whole concentrating, hardening process that came later. Gradually, as the century advanced, school became not just more enclosed, more box-like and monolithic but, as a corollary of this, more secret, more unknown to outsiders. It was something that could hardly be treated at child-level, when the official and the unofficial views of it differed as widely as they did. Quite apart from the sexuality which writers like Alec Waugh hinted at, school life showed a deviousness, snobbery and what used to be called worldliness that was clearly not a fit subject for the Victorian or Edwardian young. Real school life was unchildlike, even unboyish if boys were thought to be like Tom Brown. It was jungly and political, responsible and competitive, sensual and secret, it was everything the child or adolescent was supposed not to be; unfaceably 'adult' in the primitive but not innocent way shown by William Golding (once a schoolmaster) in *Lord of the Flies*. It could not be used 'straight' in fiction for the young, but the central situation could be given mythic encrustations.

So the pop school story grew up in spite of, not because of, the reality of the public schools. It grew up unconsidered by adults, and even banned at some schools, burrowing deeper and deeper into fantasy until it became surrealistic and self-perpetuating. Through it, the public schools were given a new life of their own, something quite beyond reality and the facts. 'Needless to say,' Orwell wrote of Frank Richards' stories, 'these stories are fantastically unlike life at a real public school.'[5] 'Fantastically' was the right word, for they were fantasies and, like the American West or Sherlock Holmes's London, their world was vividly familiar to people who had never been there, giving a generalised, outsider's view of what such a place ought to be.

Although school stories written from the inside differed among themselves as much as public schools did, when the school story became a popular genre the schools took on an undifferentiated, essential quality, as distinctive a style as that of Byzantine saints. Whether its name was Greyfriars or Northolme Academy or Manor House School, it was always much the same, an amalgam of public and prep school, full of fierce loyalties and hoary japes, of mortar-boards and Indian princes, of cricket scores, and snobberies, and cream buns.

2 . . *all those swanky words like Wham, Ouch, Yaroosh, Oof and Jolly Well* Sean O'Faolain

To many people today the school story means the pop school story, and if fed the words 'school story' they will answer 'Billy Bunter'. In other words, they are thinking of the magazine school stories which flourished for about thirty years, from about 1910 to about 1940, and the books and television series that grew out of them later. Ironically, the serious and once well-considered novel-length school story has been largely forgotten, while the despised imitations that tagged along behind it still have a devoted following, are still remembered as a central part of the public-school myth. They appeared in the boys' magazines of the late Victorian, Edwardian and (most importantly) inter-war years, many of which had originally set out to counter the influence of what were then known (rather oddly, when you think of the other meaning of the word, in school stories) as 'bloods' – by which was meant the 'blood-and-thunder' papers or 'penny dreadfuls' dealing with violence, murder and terror of all sorts and bearing titles enticing to the young, such as *Joskin the Body Snatcher* or *Three-Fingered Jack, the Terror of the Antilles*. Victorian adults were loud in their condemnation of these much-loved rags.

Samuel Beeton (whose wife was to become better known for her cookery than he was for his publishing) in 1855 set out to offer an alternative to the penny dreadfuls in a monthly called the *Boy's Own Magazine*, which in seven years achieved a circulation of 40,000 and dealt with the sort of thing later popularised much more successfully in the *Boy's Own Paper* – manly exercises, physical skills, nature study, simple science, adventure and historical stories. Between 1866 and the end of the century W. L. Emmett, Edwin J. Brett and Charles Fox published a large number of papers from *Chatterbox* and *Boys of England* to the *Boy's Comic Journal* and the *Boy's Standard*. Their rivalry was obvious: when Emmett brought out the *Young Gentleman's Journal* in '67, Brett replied with *Young Men of Great Britain* the following year, and Emmett's *Sons of Britannia* was followed by

Brett's *Boy's of the Empire*. One year, 1872, they managed to produce *Rover's Log* (Emmett) and *Rovers of the Sea* (Brett) simultaneously. Their stories had heroes with names like Frank Fearnot and Tom Tearaway, and when they were school stories the masters had names like Bircham, Scarum, Wagjaw and Hackchild. The best known of these stories were the Jack Harkaway tales in Brett's *Boys of England*, quickly pirated in America, which began with 'Jack Harkaway's Schooldays' at Pomona House School and then took him off round the world on adventures E. S. Turner has called 'likable, fearless and full-blooded',[6] much loved in childhood by H. G. Wells, Havelock Ellis and many less famous others.

The Emmett, Brett, and Fox publications, though more highbrow than the penny dreadfuls, were not of a kind to appeal to middle-class parents; nor, in intention or result, were the Amalgamated Press magazines for boys founded in the eighties and nineties by Alfred Harmsworth (later Lord Northcliffe), of whom A. A. Milne wrote that it was he 'who killed the penny dreadful by the simple process of producing a halfpenny dreadfuller': *Answers*, *Comic Cuts*, *Chips*, the *Halfpenny Wonder* and the *Halfpenny Marvel*, the *Union Jack* (in which the Sexton Blake detective stories appeared), *Pluck* and the *Boy's Friend* (which ran for thirty-two years and published *Bob Redding's Schooldays*).

School stories were published in penny instalments by the Aldine Press and appeared, in crude and jolly forms, in many of these magazines, but it was with the founding of the *Boy's Own Paper* in 1879 that the whole genre of middlebrow and popular school fiction had really begun, with Reed's stories as their model. The *Boy's Own Paper*, published by The Religious Tract Society, was the most long-lasting of the magazines, carrying on in its tough but 'decent' way until 1967; and its early contributors included many of the main writers for boys at the time – Ballantyne, Henty, Algernon Blackwood, Conan Doyle, W. H. G. Kingston, Gunby Hadath, H. de Vere Stacpoole and Jules Verne (*20,000 Leagues under the Sea* was serialised in it). Its real (as opposed to its nominal) editor from the beginning until his death in 1912 was G. A. Hutchison, a friend of Talbot Baines Reed, and from the start it was enormously successful. Within three years it warranted a neat take-off in *Punch*:

'Wet Bob, or The Adventures of a Little Eton Boy Among the Hotwhata Cannibals' by the Author of 'The Three Young Benchers and How They All Got the Woolsack', 'From Bench to Yard Arm', etc.

Chums, which appeared in 1892, edited by Max Pemberton, was the second of the 'respectable' boys' magazines (it first published – not too successfully – *Treasure Island*); and *The Captain*, edited by R. S. Warren Bell, first out in 1899, the third. Of these *The Captain*, in particular, dealt in fact – as well as fiction – about the public schools, suggesting that by then plenty of people felt involved in their doings. This was something that had been growing as the century advanced. The dedicated Old Boy was a product of its second half, and the supporter who might not even be an Old Boy was at his height at the turn of the century, when *The Captain* first appeared. Today, *The Captain*'s main claim to fame is the fact that it published Wodehouse's early school stories.

The Gem and *The Magnet*, in which the pop school story really took off, appeared a little later, respectively in 1907 and 1908; running on until, respectively, 1939 and 1940, when they were abruptly closed down.

They dominated the pop school scene until the Second World War, but other papers had their pop school stories. In 1922 the Amalgamated Press put out the *Champion*, edited by F. Addington Symonds, and two years later *Triumph*; and, also in 1922, D. C. Thomson and Co. of Dundee started what were known as its 'Big Five', *Rover*, *Wizard*, *Skipper*, *Hotspur*, and *Adventure*, which – *Hotspur* in particular – published, among others, stories about tough boarding schools without the aristocratic connections affected by Greyfriars. All of these spread the word about public school and made it a place of fantasy to the working class, 'the first real and acceptable mythology that those small boys ever encountered', as John Arlott put it in a broadcast.

Sean O'Faolain, referring to some Irish lads , miles away, spiritually as well as physically, from a public school, wrote:

> They saw him as the typical school-captain they read about in English boys' papers like *The Gem* and *The Magnet*, *The Boy's Own Paper*, *The Captain* and *Chums*, which was where they got all those swanky words like Wham, Ouch, Yaroosh, Oof and Jolly Well. He was their Tom Brown, their Bob Cherry, their Tom Merry, those heroes who were always leading Greyfriars School or Blackfriars School to victory on the cricket field amid the cap-tossing huzzas of the juniors and admiring smiles of visiting parents. It never occurred to them that *The Magnet* and *The Gem* would have seen all four of them as perfect models for some such story as *The Cads of Greyfriars* or *The Bounders of Blackfriars* . . . a quartet of rotters fated to be caned ceremoniously in the last chapter before the entire awestruck school, and then whistled off at dead of night back to their heartbroken fathers and mothers.[7]

Many boys who came closer to public school than they had been before turned up expecting the glamour of Greyfriars, only to be disillusioned. As H. E. Bates wrote of his arrival at Kettering Grammar School:

> The first day was a great shock . . . The school was newly built, of fresh red brick, not at all beautiful, and stood in a large asphalt playground. It was a little grander, but not much, than the school I had left. There were no quadrangles and no playing fields of lovely grass with avenues of quiet elms.[8]

'Heard melodies are sweet but those unheard/Are sweeter': illusion, as so often happens, was very much better than reality. The illusions fostered by the pop school stories were in a broad sense social, political, even spiritual: the stories envisaged a world of a certain kind, and the outlook it made possible. Because that world has gone, the pop school story has died; and so, at a deeper level, has the public school that was its excuse, though not very directly its model.

3 *Everything is safe, solid and unquestionable. Everything will be the same for ever and ever* George Orwell

It seems inadequate to deal in a few pages with a man who claimed to have written over sixty million school-story words, a number equivalent to a thousand novels.

Charles Hamilton, the most prolific, the best known and probably the most amiable of the pop-story writers, first appeared with a school story in *Pluck* in 1906, under his own name, then, under his pseudonym of Martin Clifford, in the third number of *The Gem*, in 1907. The following year he was asked to turn out a similar series of stories for the new *Magnet*, and for over thirty years, mainly as Frank Richards, he produced his million and a half annual words, and often more. Occasionally his stories were written by stand-ins, and some of the old ones were reprinted, but his output was astonishing, nonetheless. His many names and his own liking for mystery and jokey confusion made it hard for readers to keep up with him, and he even went into *Who's Who* under his pseudonym of Frank Richards. Apart from that name, and Martin Clifford in *The Gem*, he was Owen Conquest in the *Boy's Friend*, Hilda Richards in girls' papers where Cliff House School was the female equivalent of Greyfriars, and dozens of others elsewhere. After the war he wrote complete books about Billy Bunter and, later, television scripts for him. His *Who's Who* entry mentions these, not *The Gem* and *The Magnet* stories, as his main work.

Frank Richards was a one-man factory, and bibliographically *The Gem*, *The Magnet*, the full-length Bunter stories and Richards' other writings are much too complicated to be treated briefly. The Charles

Hamilton Collection which began to appear in 1972, published by enthusiasts, or J. S. Butcher's *Greyfriars School, a Prospectus*, which appeared in 1965, nibble at the edges of the phenomenon and presumably further enthusiasm will bite further into it as time goes on. Charles Hamilton was something of a mystery, a lonely, intensely busy, serious man who never married, had few friends (though innumerable distant admirers) and, though he wrote an *Autobiography of Frank Richards*, gave away almost nothing about himself. John Arlott described him as 'this little neat, rather birdlike man, with the bright busy eyes and the slightly fussy manner' and went on:

He talked seriously about his work, with illuminating enthusiasm. It was clear that every one of his characters was real to him . . . He had the pride of the creator, in this respect, and he referred to them with friendly familiarity . . . I asked him if he had ever been to a public school, but he was very evasive on this point . . . I came away with the impression that, like so many of his boyish admirers, he had never been to [one] and that he wished that he had and perhaps indeed really believed that he had in his heart and mind, after all those years of writing.[9]

Elsewhere Arlott says:

My word, how we lapped him up! When we were boys in Hampshire elementary school, forty years ago. I suppose there was an element of snobbery in it and I wonder if public school boys ever read his stuff? But we did. These were the things we would like to have done, magnified to something more than life-size. All his characters were more good, more brilliant, more athletic, or more wicked, fat, unscrupulous or strong than we could ever hope to be. This was our language inflated to giant standards and surely we remember it with gratitude.[10]

And Denzil Batchelor wrote:

The astonishing thing is that today, in middle age, I would prefer to be stranded before a smoky fire in a lonely inn with a copy of *The Magnet* rather than with, say, Gibbon's *Decline and Fall* or even *Pendennis* . . . because Frank Richards had the Homeric gift of characterisation . . . Oh, the bliss of surrendering oneself to such deft hands![11]

But on the other side there is Arthur Marshall, no fan at all of Greyfriars:

Generally speaking Richards' stories were never read by public schoolboys. They were in a different class, in two senses, from the *Boy's Own Paper* and *The Captain* and would have been considered ludicrously false and feeble. To their gullible juvenile readers they gave a markedly unreal picture of public schools and did a hearty disservice both to fact and to fiction. The wearisome repetitions, the implausibility, the tastelessness, the Ho! Ho! Ho! and Ha! Ha! Ha! are over. To borrow a phrase, He! He! He!

Bunter he clearly loathes. As he wrote when the final Bunter book appeared in 1965:

> At long last it is the end of the road for the monstrous Billy Bunter, the revolting, chortling fatty in the tightest trousers in Greyfriars and the permanently straitened circumstances, despite a rich stockbroker pater at Bunter Villa, Reigate. Obese and, one suspects, impotent, he is like no schoolboy that ever was and seems in character and person to have more in common with a gin-swilling, petty-cash fiddling, perspiring middle-aged businessman, endlessly swapping dirty stories with the lads and chatting up Miss Loosely in the snug.[12]

Whatever the secret of their original appeal, or whoever they originally appealed to, it is hard, today, to disentangle contemporary and nostalgic enjoyment of the stories. A psychiatrist, I see, has suggested that what to Arthur Marshall are 'wearisome repetitions' are in fact a device (not, perhaps, consciously employed by Richards, but used skilfully nonetheless) for hypnotising the reader. Admirers have confessed to using the books at bedtime to induce, with absolute certainty, sleep at a particular stage in the story. The triggering of familiar memories, the lulling repetition of particular phrases, the rhythm of expected events, circumstances, episodes, dialogue and slang, the whole unsurprisingness of it all – these are not unlike the means used by the hypnotist to put his subject into a trance. This explanation may work for adults, but it is unlikely that schoolboys would have found themselves comatose over the adventures of the Famous Five, Harry Wharton and Co: on the contrary, they seem to have found them stimulating, exciting and (as Arlott said) outsize.

Talking of which, Bunter in the early days was the butt and buffoon of Greyfriars, nothing more. The central figures were Harry Wharton and, at St Jim's, Tom Merry, stock-sized boys both spiritually and physically. But gradually the Fat Owl of the Remove took over from the rest, and by 1960 many hardcover books had appeared, in which what Arthur Marshall calls 'the deplorable dumpling' held the centre of the stage, and his school chums, once so contemptuous of him, were relegated to walking-on parts. When *The Gem* and *The Magnet* closed down at the beginning of the Second World War, Hamilton/Richards was deprived overnight not just of an excellent livelihood but of the characters with whom he had spent the past three decades and more in intimate companionship. But when he took to writing about them again, it was Billy Bunter whom people best remembered, and in more than thirty books and forty-five television plays Bunter joined the few physically unmistakable characters of English fiction.

Orwell was probably his first intellectual admirer. In an article in

Horizon in 1940, he said that *The Magnet*, in which the Greyfriars stories appeared, had always had the edge over *The Gem* (St Jim's) because it had 'a really first-rate character in the fat boy, Billy Bunter'. This was before Bunter's real rise to fame, with a public above schoolboy age that could instantly recognise him. In the vast acreage of Frank Richards' never-never-land, it was the despised outsider, who never became accepted as part of anyone's cosy study life at Greyfriars, who took over. Orwell's essay called 'Boys' Weeklies' was probably the first to take serious notice of the magazines. Frank Richards was given space to reply in *Horizon* and although his answer was marred by some silly jibes at what he considered highbrow, it was very effective in a manly, no-nonsense way. Considering what a persuasive polemicist Orwell was, Richards' reply was remarkable in that it almost persuades one that he, and not Orwell, came out of the contest the winner. Partly it was a defence of his attitudes and partly a plea to Orwell to come off it and stop taking things too heavily; and several times it caught Orwell on the raw and made him, rather than the stories, look silly. Richards took his work seriously; he was hurt when he thought it was being sneered at or misunderstood, and occasionally he sensed sneering or misapprehension in Orwell. *Horizon* readers thought Orwell eccentric for being interested enough in boys' weeklies to look into them and write at length about them, and if in places he was careless and patronising he also paid them the compliment of serious attention. His main point was that the stories pickled the attitudes of a world which was old-fashioned even before the First World War, and perpetuated ideas of class, society and politics, and attitudes towards foreigners and the rest of the world, which had no place in 1940. Above all, he caught the simplistic snobbery of the originals:

The year is 1910 or 1940, but it is all the same. You are at Greyfriars, a rosy-cheeked boy of fourteen in posh, tailor-made clothes, sitting down to tea in your study on the Remove passage after an exciting game of football which was won by an odd goal in the last half-minute. There is a cosy fire in the study, and outside the wind is whistling. The ivy clusters thickly round the old grey stones. The King is on his throne and the pound is worth a pound. Over in Europe the comic foreigners are jabbering and gesticulating, but the grim grey battleships of the British Fleet are steaming up the Channel and at the outposts of Empire the monocled Englishmen are holding the niggers at bay . . . Everything is safe, solid and unquestionable. Everything will be the same for ever and ever.[13]

CHAPTER XVII

The decline and fall of the school story

Crikey! Katharine Hull and Pamela Whitlock

It was not, of course. Nothing was ever the same again. It had not been the same, if that meant the rock-like world of security and above all confidence, since the end of the First World War. But the twenties and thirties, ugly decades for the dispossessed and even for those in possession uneasy and menacing, were marking time, pretending while pretence was still possible, whistling in the dark.

The public schools whistled as loudly as anyone. School stories abounded, but at a low level. Those who knew about these things knew it was all over, and even those who knew little felt it was so in their bones. Hence loud emotional criticism of the atmosphere and spirit of the public schools, even when the system was not attacked on an intellectual level. On the one hand, in the thirties, Auden:

> The best reason I have for opposing Fascism is that at school I lived in a Fascist state.[1]

On the other, writing at the same time, Harold Nicolson:

> The public schools in the pre-war period were designed to provide a large number of young men fitted for the conquest, administration and retention of a vast Oriental Empire. There are now no more areas to be conquered; the opportunities for administration will be increasingly restricted; and the prospects of retention, momentarily at least, seem insecure.[2]

At both levels, the emotional and the intellectual, the political basis of the public schools – their *raison d'être* by that time – was being questioned.

Like the world they were made for, the public schools were then in the final phase of the way they had been for nearly a century. Yet it seemed, not an Indian summer, mellow and perhaps nostalgic for former glories, but a tense, unyielding, unattractive season. It was not just the very poor, feeling the full ferocity of the depression, who suffered from the thundery climate, the air of precariousness. The public-school class, though few then noticed, was also strung uneasily between the end of an age and the beginning of a new one. And the philistines were firmly in charge. This was clearly reflected at the junior levels of school and children's books. In an intelligent one published in the late thirties, aimed at the sort of child being educated in the public-school system, a mere mention of Brahms elicits a startled 'Crikey!'[3]

The old patterns were crumbling. Of course they are always crumbling, indefinitely slithery, just as one age is always turning into another; but in the thirties they were crumbling at a dramatic rate, like Dunwich falling, almost visibly, into the sea. Social life, not knowing how to take it, often lacked warmth, as if the need to keep up a front of dignity and formality before inferiors had overflowed into relationships with equals, with everyone; even in families. The school habit of slapping down the young had spread into family life, and books about the middle-class young of the time are full of examples of it: vanity was the worst of sins, uppishness and swank its expression, so children must never be pampered or made 'special'; indeed, they were often assured that they were no better than anyone else (except, of course, socially, where they knew from babyhood that they were). The memsahibs at home seemed to be doing their best to keep the natives in their place and in so doing to avoid all spontaneity, all that flowed directly from heart or spirit, all that might be called intuitive or instinctive. Maugham portrayed such people brilliantly – their aggressive philistinism, unjustified self-confidence, ugly arrogance, overweening national as well as social attitudes. What we should now call humanity or warmth seems to have been curiously avoided. It was a time when a stranger did not easily catch another's eye, exchange a smiling look for no reason, pass the time of day unintroduced. The rest of the world not surprisingly believed in the stiffness and coldness of the English, who cordially despised the rest of the world for not sharing their limitations.

In my chapter on girls' school stories I mentioned how, in this interwar period, girls became progressively more boyish, less feminine. So the domestic (as well as what is vaguely called the cultural) was undervalued. Not surprisingly, perhaps, since it was the last period in which the employer class did not have to keep the wheels of everyday life turning by its own physical efforts (there were servants). But whatever the reason, girls often grew up without domestic skills, without the female talents for handwork and crafts, without the pleasures of creative, non-intellectual pursuits. The schools had a hand in this. Women teachers who had grown up in the ardour of the suffragette movement and had reacted against the femininity of their own backgrounds, most of them spinsters by necessity since the middle-class men they might have married had been killed in large numbers in the war, were often quite unable to fend for themselves domestically, and had sternly rejected the traditional skills like sewing, cooking, household management. Their prejudices were passed on to their pupils, who in turn became as helpless and scornful as contemporary bachelors in the face of these skills. The feminine was as underrated, as heartily despised, as the clothes and prettiness so contemptuously treated in the later school stories.

All these limitations were clearest in and around the public schools. Less relaxed, less comfortable and therefore I think less kind than many of their equivalents are today, uncertainly placed between Victorian attitudes familiar from their own childhood and a new world they had not yet absorbed, public-school parents of the time were often deeply ignorant of their children's needs. The average parent of the sort did not expect to communicate to the young child a cultural pattern in any broad sense, or an interest in things of the mind, in books or the arts or the world in general, since it was the custom – so generally observed that exceptions were surprising – to hand children over from infancy largely to the care and company of servants. Nannies might be emotionally as well equipped as many mothers to deal with young children but their cultural patterns were their own, not the mothers'; or else their own patterns had been lost through living in an alien culture, that of their employers. After early childhood (those vital first seven years) came boarding school to make the cultural patterns, and even during the holidays the parents' company might still be something rarely known. School stories of the time mention the 'upheavals' of home life, its lack of continuity and stability, its restlessness, the fact that families often spent the few weeks free of school not in the familiar surroundings of home but all over the place – in hotels, on holidays here or there. Whole families even *lived* in hotels for years on end. And all this refers to families whose parents lived *in the same country* as their children. Many lived at opposite ends of the earth, often for years at a stretch, when travel was slow and difficult and the barbarity of long separations within families seems not to have been noticed.

Philip Toynbee makes one of the masters in *A School in Private* discuss some of these points in his diary:

> The parents' day was interesting. Not one of the boys looked pleased to see his mother or father. This is odd, even allowing for their embarrassment, their inability to live in two worlds at the same time. At this age, how much do they really feel about their parents? They see them for less than a third of the year, and they must realise that their parents' lives are developing more and more away from their own. For the first eight or nine years of these boys' lives, their mothers are necessarily preoccupied with them. The life of the family caters for them, even if it's not centred on them. But sending children to a boarding school is a gesture of release for the majority of parents. In effect the parents say: 'Now, perhaps, we can go back to our honeymoons, to the time when we could live our own adult lives without interference.' In the holidays they have to make concessions. They take their sons to matinées, to the seaside. But everybody must know that a deliberate effort is being made. And so the boys feel worse in the holidays than ever they do in term. Here at least they are the most important people, and the adults exist only for them.

The inadequacies of adult life were of course reflected in the schools, just as the attitudes of the schools were, deliberately or not, reflected in the books inspired by them. In the isolated communities of boarding school masters might be penned for more years than their pupils in conditions they disliked but for which there was no alternative, celibate not from choice but because they could not afford to be otherwise, the daily grind often totally unrelieved by other activities or outlets or even local involvements. Poverty and precariousness combined to make them put up with what now seem appalling conditions. Out of these came a number of school stories, some of them novels for adults, some rather uneasily combining the genre of school story with that of adult fiction.

2 *It's wrong to blame the Public Schools for what is actually the nature of boys* Arthur Calder-Marshall

One of the most interesting of these realistic school stories was Arthur Calder-Marshall's *Dead Centre* (1934), an adult novel about a middle-of-the-road public school called Richbury, which shows very clearly the dreariness of such places in this period. The difference between it and the straightforward school story, adult or child's, is that it has no single narrator or hero, no centre of gravity or any single eye-level, but about sixty separate ones. Most of these narrators are boys or masters, but a few of them are people connected with the school – maid, porter, matron, master's wife. In nearly seventy short chapters (some of the characters speak more than once) each person speaks for himself. Names and ages, nothing more, are given at the head of each chapter.

I say each person 'speaks' rather than 'writes' because Calder-Marshall makes no attempt to reproduce the likely *written* style of any of his characters, and so makes the pieces sound more like tape recordings than written narratives. Even as spoken narrative they occasionally jar, the younger boys, in particular, being too literary and too visually observant, describing things rather than taking them for granted, and using other people's direct speech. This is probably unavoidable with such a method, which cannot attempt strict realism. Moravia said that in *The Woman of Rome* he wrote not as a Roman prostitute would in fact express herself but as she would if she could. He was aiming at a kind of supra-realism, in fact, and this is what, to a lesser degree, Calder-Marshall is aiming at in *Dead Centre*. In each case he seems to reproduce a voice rather than a literary style, and more a tone of voice than the exact words each voice might use. (A very original writer may sometimes manage these things more realistically while using a non-realistic method: Henry Green in *Pack My Bag*, for instance.)

Technically, Calder-Marshall does two things. First, he paints about sixty portraits – sketches, but vivid enough to interest the reader right away, to conjure a figure; second, he takes the action ahead, involving as many of the characters as possible, sometimes advancing a single person separately from the rest, sometimes linking several. His method, choppy rather than fluid, recalls not a film but slides on a screen, still and momentary: click, a certain character appears; click, he vanishes and another appears. The boys vary in age from thirteen to eighteen, from little fellows who wonder on arrival if school will be like the Billy Bunter stories, to a young man who, believing he has got one of the maids pregnant, steals and sells some watches belonging to other boys to pay for an abortion. A boy will speak for himself, then in the next chapter be spoken of by another boy or by a master. Small Arley, for instance, is Potts's fag and enjoys being swept up off the floor by him, then swooped down again. One wonders (though Arley does not) about all this physical effusiveness. The next chapter, written by Potts, confirms the suspicion of his sexual feelings for Arley. Or there is Green, who resents being pushed to work hard at maths by his housemaster, Biddles (not surprisingly known as Piddles). In Biddles's own chapter we discover his warm feelings for Green and how he is planning to take him on a bicycling holiday. And so on.

In the crowded common-room the masters quarrel, half-violent, half-waspish. Most of them are unmarried – unable to afford it, unable to find a wife, homosexually inclined, emotionally dried up, or fiercely frustrated. The few existing women at the school are no help. 'A pack of hags,' Burroughs, aged twenty-five, calls the other masters' wives. 'It gets me down,' he goes on, 'so that I think any woman with a nose, two eyes and her own teeth is a beauty, and any woman who can hold her tongue a wit.' Another young master, Joliffe, has actually managed to marry while still in his twenties, but he has got the wrong wife and she nags him, cannot bear the social isolation, and is losing him whatever friends he once had. A middle-aged master, Richie, partly paralysed and crippled, is dismissed after twenty-seven years to economise on staff salaries. He and his wife will be desperately poor and hope to set up some kind of tutorial establishment in London.

There is little plot. In one of the book's rare dramatic moments a handsome, popular boy is killed in an accident. As he lies on the ground, unconscious, perhaps nearly dead, the others watch helplessly as his legs shoot back and forth, 'as if there was something inside him struggling to get out'. Then school life carries on, vivid and drab. One has the impression of a place that is above all harsh and dull, well-meaning but repressive, with much pain and ugliness in it but not entirely to be condemned, since there are reasons and excuses for its faults and failures, to be found, not least, in the outside world. Jarrell, one of the most sympathetic of the masters, says:

> It's wrong to blame the Public Schools for what is actually the nature of boys. It's false to isolate the influence of the school from the previous and present domestic relations of each boy. I notice changes, while they are here, some for better, some for worse, but I can't say the extent to which they are produced by the school and the extent to which they are a part of the evolution of the boy's nature.

3 *At school I lived in a Fascist state* W. H. Auden

Another off-beat public-school story is Reginald Turnor's *Bring Them Up Alive*, which ought, by the sound of what happens, to be one of the most interesting. This long, detailed novel, published in 1938, is not obviously an adult one, like Calder-Marshall's, because it has a teenage hero from whose point of view everything is seen. Indeed, reading it as an adult one tends to take a rather different attitude to what happens from that of its hero. It shows a close knowledge of two sorts of school at the time: the public school of a rigid, old-fashioned kind, and the coeducational progressive school, with nude teenage mixed bathing, and other things unlikely in other schools of the period. It also draws parallels between school and the outside world, between attitudes inside the school and the rise of fascism in Europe. All this ought, one feels, to throw light on Auden's gnomic remark: 'at school I lived in a Fascist state'. But it throws little light on anything. The author writes dully, with little style and no presence, and in colourless, laundry-list prose his people are unconvincing; the hero, in particular, comes across as a sententious young prig with whom it is hard to sympathise, although clearly the reader is meant to. Still, it has documentary value as a detailed account of public-school life in the late thirties, and its politically-minded hero's awareness of the fascist element in school life, of the menace of Hitler, the likelihood of war, and of intolerance and prejudice in general – all things almost untouched in school stories of the time – makes it something of a curiosity.

John Luttrell is fifteen and at a coeducational, progressive boarding school when his father, one of the school's main moral supporters and financial backers, suddenly dies and John is removed by his uncle and sent to Craigleith, 'one of the rigider and more famous public schools'. Everything there is bewildering – manners, customs, spirit and ritual, the hierarchical system, the ragging, bullying and unfriendliness, beatings, fagging, petty rules, suspiciousness and dirty-mindedness, the philistinic attitude towards books, the arts and school work, the prurience which involves lavatories without doors, giggles at dirty postcards and gossip when John takes his housemaster's daughter for a walk or is seen talking to the pretty young wife of another of the masters. When things come to a climax in his house and a boy commits suicide, John leads a strike against the prefects, in which almost everyone joins.

Outraged, the school authorities find themselves helpless. They cannot expel everyone, and if the ringleaders are expelled the rest (they threaten) will run away *en masse*. They cannot be involved in the publicity that calling for help or telling parents would bring. The strikers are sober, well-disciplined and respectful; they simply refuse to watch or play games unless they want to, attend compulsory chapel, write lines for the masters or be caned by the prefects. They also want a change in the innumerable rules, most of them boy-invented and boy-maintained, which govern their everyday lives. In the end they get what they want, agree to tell no one outside the school, so that nobody need lose face, change the whole atmosphere of the school and manage to make the authorities, especially the headmaster, feel they have not really climbed down but merely undertaken necessary reforms. John turns out to be no revolutionary. In fact, to his uncle's delight, he is made a prefect. 'I think you'll agree,' says Uncle Mervyn, 'that it was a pretty good move, my sending you to Craigleith.' 'I think perhaps it was,' says the poacher turned gamekeeper, savouring the irony of it.

4 . . . *dinner, call-over, prep and lights out* James Hilton

Probably the best-known full-length school story of all – at least with the best-known title – appeared in this decade of the declining school story; to me a symbol of the genre's decadence and its inability to say anything of value to its time. James Hilton's *Goodbye, Mr Chips* appeared in 1934 and strangely, considering its late appearance, the name Chips has become almost a part of our language, a schoolmaster of his sort sometimes being called a Mr Chips, in the certainty that everyone will know what is meant. Like many proper names in school stories, its sound has associations of a suitable sort. According to the *Shorter Oxford English Dictionary*, an old meaning of 'chip' is 'anything . . . without flavour, innutritious, dried up'; but the American 'chipper' means 'lively, cheerful, chirpy'. So Mr Chips comes somewhere between the two. His real name is in fact Chipping and he has no Christian name, since even his wife rather horribly calls him by his school nickname of Chips.

Based, it has been said, partly on Balgarnie of the Leys School, Cambridge, and partly on Hilton's father, headmaster of an elementary school, the person of Mr Chips is better known through films, a film musical and hearsay than through the book itself, a volume both slight and slim (126 pages of large print, widely spaced, in the edition I am using). I say his 'person' rather than anything else because Mr Chips has a figure, a recognisable exterior, a personality easily transmitted by an actor, rather than any soul, mind, inner life or real character of his own. A bunch of mannerisms and clichés, the handsome forms of Robert Donat and, later, of Peter O'Toole, made him known to the film-going public, and his story, much extended, has been dramatised for radio as well. His image is that of the old-fashioned schoolmaster, a kindly, bumbling fellow with a few dry jokes and much-repeated stories, whose life has been spent at a single school, whose interests are all centred upon it, who retires as near to it as possible, knows everything and everyone connected with it, remembers things further back and with more zealous interest than anyone else and has become what is known as a legend in his lifetime.

Hilton regards him with a soft, indeed a sentimental eye, without any but the most superficial and affectionate irony. He seems to respect what Chips is supposed to stand for, to admire what he is supposed to have done. There is none of the rich eyebrow-raising with which Waugh regards his Scott-King, or even of the ambivalent attitude of Hugh Walpole towards Mr Perrin, or of Terence Rattigan towards Crocker-Harris in *The Browning Version* – dislike and pity together, a mixed sense of revulsion and pathos, a noting of missed opportunities, failed idealism. 'I became a schoolmaster partly out of ambition and partly from incompetence,' says Mr Jarrell in Arthur Calder-Marshall's *Dead Centre*. Nothing like that in Chips.

The book's form may have suggested it to the film-makers, since it uses the long flashback so dear to the cinema. An octogenarian Chips, retired more than ten years earlier, is living out his last years in a room at Mrs Wickett's, 'just across the road from the school', Brookfield, measuring out his days by 'dinner, call-over, prep and lights out'. After the last school bell at night he winds up his clock and goes to bed. Mrs Wickett was once in charge of the school linen-room, so together they mull over old times. 'Cheeky, 'e was to me, gener'ly,' she says, in the patois of the fictional lower orders. 'But we never 'ad no bad words between us. Just cheeky-like.' 'Dear me, I remember Collingwood very well,' says Mr Chips. 'I once thrashed him – umph – for climbing on to the gymnasium roof.' Such reminiscences sweeten his days. 'A pleasant, placid life at Mrs Wickett's,' Hilton calls it, in a room crammed with sporting trophies and photographs, fixture cards and books, where new masters and boys come regularly to visit him, and Mr Chips mixes the tea out of several caddies, fussily, to their amusement. 'A typical old bachelor, if ever there was one,' they say.

Then comes the flashback, to show how wrong they are. Long ago, in 1896, on a climbing holiday in the Lake District when he is nearly fifty, Chips meets a girl young enough to be his daughter – Katherine of the 'blue, flashing eyes and freckled cheeks and smooth, straw-coloured hair'. They fall in love and are engaged within the week; suitably she is a governess who likes boys and believes idealistically in the importance of Chips's work. So they are married and for two years –

> a warm and vivid patch in his life, casting a radiance that glowed in a thousand recollections –

Chips blossoms and expands.

> She made him, to all appearances, a new man; though most of the newness was really a warming to life of things that were old, imprisoned and unguessed . . . She broadened his views and opinions, also, giving him an outlook far beyond the roofs and turrets of Brookfield, so that he saw his country as something deep and gracious to which Brookfield was but one of many feeding

streams . . . Her young idealism worked upon his maturity to produce an amalgam very gentle and wise.

(Gentleness and wisdom do not exclude snobbishness, however, and at one point an anti-semitic sneer that, particularly in an atmosphere as soft and self-indulgent, comes as a shock.) Then Katherine dies in childbirth and the child dies too, and Chips lapses back into the familiar bachelor life, growing gradually more set in his ways and jokes, saying 'umph' between phrases and able to recite chunks of old School Lists from the days when he took call-over, chanting them like a litany, presumably for reassurance and pleasure: 'Ainsworth, Attwood, Avonmore, Babcock, Baggs, Barnard, Bassenthwaite, Battersby, Beccles, Bedford-Marshall, Bentley, Best . . .'

Thus Mr Chips is given the advantage of both schoolmasterly situations: that of the charming but absurd old pedant, wrapped up in his small school world, and that of the warm, wise man who has known love and sorrow, etc., etc. In school stories these situations and characters are often contrasted, implicitly if not explicitly. The fictional schoolmaster has often been celibate not so much because, as Evelyn Waugh suggested, 'most good schoolteachers . . . are homosexual by inclination'[4] (the school story could hardly be expected to examine *that*), as because the school has become his religion and his whole life and there is no room or energy for other interests and affections; and because a lifetime among schoolboys and in a school atmosphere has made him unfitted for the adult world, unable to talk anyone else's language. Even on holiday he is often available for activities connected with school – camping, walking or bicycling with his favourites or spending time at their homes; or else he goes climbing with a colleague, or on a trip down the Rhine in a schoolmasterly group, never, apparently, having 'outside' friends. He has the half-comic, half-pathetic mannerisms that celibacy and this atmosphere are supposed to encourage, and the untidy domestic arrangements that go with them and arouse pity of a not unaffectionate sort in those more comfortably placed. A slightly patronising warmth is what readers seem meant to feel for him, the kind felt for teddy bears and discarded books, the attics of childhood and adolescence; and, to the adult reader at least, this fictional schoolmaster seems the inhabitant of a lost world, enthusiast for a suppressed culture, toppled by time from his perch yet still wearing his chalky finery. All this, Mr Chips embodies in his tea-caddy routine, his jokiness, his prosy reminiscences, his winding up of the clock to the sound of the school bell.

But Hilton is not content to make him merely a figure of fun, an affectionate caricature. He wants him 'real' as well, normal and domesticated, husband and father, attractive and heterosexual; a man of the 'real world' with a mind that goes beyond batting averages and the ancient glories of his school. So Katherine is not just an ordinary wife but a beauty, a glorious creature any other man would envy him, 'this astonishing girl-wife whom nobody had expected, least of all Chips himself'. Nearly twenty years after meeting her a man who, as an East End cockney boy, met her on a single occasion, asks Chips eagerly for news of her, and on hearing of her death says: 'I'm really sorry to 'ear that, sir. There's two or three o' my pals, anyhow, who remember 'er as clear as anything, though we only did see 'er that wunst. Yes, we remember 'er, all right.' See (Hilton is saying) what a woman Chips managed to attract! What hidden fires, what unknown depths, there must have been under that dingy exterior!

When he loses her, Chips reverts to his dry-stick role, disliking all innovation, proud that his lessons have not changed since 1870. Having shown his ability to get out of them, he slips back (rather to Hilton's relief, it is hard not to feel) into more familiar surroundings. But the romantic interlude and the fact that he managed to get a girl like Katherine to love him makes it clear that, however bumbling he may have become in old age, in his prime he was not only attractive as (beneath the whiskers) the actors chosen to play him were, but an inhabitant of the 'real world'. Chips wins on both counts, or would do if Hilton had been able to write a book that in any way carried conviction, or to paint anyone but a chocolate-box schoolmaster.

5 *The End*

There were a great many other books, of course, including plenty of school stories for the young, and a good deal of miscellaneous writing about school in general and about particular schools, factually or in fiction. Some, like Ian Hay's *Housemaster*, viewed it all cosily, treating school with the affection and warmth and approval of those who like things as they are and see no reason to change them. The only school story I can think of in this period conjuring an atmosphere of pleasantness at school is D. Wynne-Willson's *Early Closing* (1931) which deals with a small country school and lacks, on the one hand, the bitterness, cynicism and psychological tenseness of so many school stories of the time, and, on the other, the rather smug self-confidence of Ian Hay and writers less good but with similar attitudes towards school. Others took a sharper look. Lionel Birch's novels set in school, for instance, are curiously outspoken for their time (the early thirties) and regard it with quizzical irony. One, called *The System*, uses an epigraph from Auden (as Roy Fuller was to do in a school story twenty-five years later): he speaks of those who 'justified the system'. Whether this meant the wider system of which the public schools were a part, or the system within the schools themselves, hardly matters. The two were intertwined. But by the thirties even firm upholders of the system were becoming deeply confused. Liberal views, or even illiberal but anxious views, no longer married with the old certainties; after 1918, unquestioning loyalty was no longer the virtue it had once seemed.

In Winifred Holtby's *South Riding* (1936) the heroine, a headmistress, exhorts her girls, when they sing 'I vow to thee my country' (the hymn which includes the famous line about 'the love that asks no question'), never to love without questioning, always to examine the rights and wrongs of everything. *South Riding*, despite its heroine, was not a school story (although school came into it a good deal), but, like much middlebrow fiction, it showed the way the wind was blowing. Desmond Coke, who had celebrated his own and young Lycidas's love for Shrewsbury so fervently in *The Bending of a Twig*, by the early thirties seemed thoroughly confused about what he expected from a school, and was certainly no longer looking for one like Shrewsbury. His *Stanton* (1931) is a chronicle of turbulent questioning within the established school-story framework. By the time he wrote it Coke had been vice-master, i.e. No. 2, for some years in a school then thought progressive, whose founder he had much admired (Clayesmore in Dorset). His fictional school, Stanton, also founded with ideals and ideas quite unlike those of conventional schools, is gradually altered by a new headmaster into a copy of an old-style public school, acquiring a successful reputation but losing its soul on the way. Coke questions everything about the system – competitiveness, formality, compulsory games, the O.T.C., toughness, autocratic methods, suspiciousness of the relations between boys of different ages, the impossibility of having time or hobbies or uncompetitive, unuseful interests or even mooning about with nothing in particular to show for it. The first half has its boy hero going up through the school, the second has the same character some years later, asked by the ageing headmaster to take the school over. All this gives the garrulous, imprecise Coke a chance to air his views and hesitations and alarms, which must have been shared by many questioning liberals, worried parents, ruffled youngsters. Soon after writing *Stanton* he died, presumably with his innumerable ideas still unsorted.

No wonder writers of school stories, those reflectors of what was happening in the school world, were confused. No wonder people kept putting the record straight, as they saw it, by giving their views and versions a fictional form. And no wonder those who kept writing straight school stories for the young were not particularly good. For decades they had been told that the public schools were training men to administer an overseas empire. Not all their products were involved in this administration, but for nearly a century the system had been built up, and with it a belief in the men who would go anywhere and do whatever was expected of them. The First World War seemed to justify that belief. They did exactly what was expected of them and most of them died. Then came the pause, a new generation of schoolboys and an atmosphere altogether different. This might involve what Christopher Hollis, writing of Eton, referred to as antinomianism; it might be mere Bolshieness and kicking over the traces; or it might be what, at my school, was known as 'bad spirit', which meant a failure to support enthusiastically whatever authority put forward. It might even be a questioning, as opposed to an unquestioning, love. Whatever it was, the system that had begun with idealistic fervour ended in rhetoric and emptiness, in the inanities and whimsies of Mr Chips.

It had prepared boys to give up their private lives for public service. In many cultures the supposedly privileged have been expected to suffer for their privilege (Chinese girls' bound feet, for instance). Similarly, through the public-school system, certain ordinary affections and emotional needs were removed and the (to some extent) psychically crippled product was exactly what was wanted. A man who was taken from his family at seven or eight would tend not to have much feeling for family life, or even much ability to produce it later for his own family. He would then be able to detach himself (as, in public service, he often had to) from his own children. And so it would go on, if his children were similarly trained. Domestic affections were replaced by a feeling for the group, heterosexual feeling by a more vivid appreciation of male company; and it was not just domestic affections that were weakened but the sense of home and base and personal territory, the love of what was settled, familiar, deep-rooted, long-used.

The imperial functionary or the soldier gave up much that most people value – his country, the landscape of childhood, a familiar way of life, his cultural patterns, much ordinary family life and the chance to see his children grow up. When he retired it was as a stranger to his own land, among people he did not know, to a way of life he had forgotten, lost the taste for, or never really known in the first place. In relation to his family, the schoolboy was similarly placed. Less absolutely and starkly, but still to a great extent, he became an outsider at home, an exile in the sense that he had little contact with the locals, little feeling for home unless it was an exceptionally strong and settled one, and as a rule few friendships outside school, since there was little time or chance to develop them. School established a pattern for the adult way of life by removing him from what was familiar and individual.

In both cases there was a similar reward – prestige and power, the homage of inferiors, even physical service from them; a sense of responsible, adult achievement in ruling, for their own good, irresponsible, childish others. The schoolboy was trained for leadership, his 'greatness' at the height of his school career preparing him for the lonely eminence he might later enjoy. His fags would become native servants, the whole hierarchy of school could be translated into terms of imperial or service life. That was the pattern for both adult and boy, more or less rigidly imposed, more or less generally accepted, and reflected clearly, even if innocently and unrecognised, in the school stories. Without an outside world to demand their products, to need their skills and limitations, even to accept the sacrifices they were ready to make, there was little point in the particular form the schools had taken.

People must have sensed that the world was changing but, in writing about school, they seldom made any radical suggestions. Often they were still fascinated by it as an entity and an influence; or as a survival from the past, a thing to react against. Yet however critical of public school they might be, one suspects that writers might later send their children there as automatically as they had been sent by their parents (there seemed no other social choice). Any criticism was directed at the detailed organisation of the schools, not at the original concept of them. Boarding, selection by class or price, the training given – these were seldom questioned in any basic way.

At schoolboy level the books had, by the thirties, sunk almost entirely to the pop level, to the outsize absurdities of Greyfriars and others less goodnatured, more pretentious. When they were taken straight, the atmosphere was often unpleasant with snobbery and xenophobia. The Empire, like the school story, was grinding to an end. For a few more years the forms remained but the spirit had gone out of them. What had made the school story not merely popular but influential was mainly the sense of continuity and certainty, the ritual and repetition, and a feeling that it reflected, if only remotely, something real, some ideas that mattered. When the reality behind the ritual was clearly crumbling and the ideas no longer mattered, it seemed empty, ridiculous, almost tasteless.

During and after the war came a number of adult school novels set in public or prep schools, still a good setting for a concentrated study of personality, of clash and rivalry, politics and power. Two excellent realistic prep-school stories – reflecting their authors' schooldays some years earlier – appeared early in the war: Philip Toynbee's *A school in Private* (1941) and J. T. C. Pember's *Not Me, Sir* (1942). Although written from the boys' point of view (Toynbee taking a number of boys, Pember a single central figure, with glimpses of his home life as well), these were clearly for adults, not children; documentary works of some sharpness reflecting the extraordinary conditions, attitudes and organisation of the inter-war prep schools. *George Brown's Schooldays*, by Bruce Marshall (1946), set in a public school in 1912, was another harshly adult look at a single boy's experiences, sufferings and occasional glories; Roy Fuller's *The Ruined Boys* (1959) dealt, also realistically but in a more adult, more elegiac way, with a boarding school that aped the manners and attitudes of the public schools in the twenties; Michael Campbell's *Lord Dismiss Us* (1967) made school seem a richer, more agreeable place in many ways, and harked back to the pre-war stories that took things there fairly straight.

Occasionally a novel might be set in a school which was shown from the point of view of masters and their wives, not the boys: Iris Murdoch's *The Sandcastle* (1957), for instance, set in a public school, or Pamela Hansford Johnson's *The Honours Board* (1970), set in a prep school that was very recognisably contemporary and therefore of particular documentary interest, since it showed what such schools were like, not in the twenties or thirties, but as recently as the sixties, with attitudes much modified but some things (competitiveness, for one) almost unchanged. Adult novels criticising named, recognisable schools, such as David Benedictus's *The Fourth of June* (1962, Eton) or Nigel Foxell's *Schoolboy Rising* (1973, Aldenham), which years earlier would have raised indignant protests and rejoinders, still raised some but much less noisily (the general public no longer cared). In some novels about schoolboys, surface manners and attitudes and talk might be chillingly familiar while their actions took to their logical conclusions the long-learned lessons of aggression and competitiveness: William Golding's *Lord of the Flies* (1954) and John Rae's *The Custard Boys* (1960), both of which ended in the killing of a boy by his schoolfellows, threw light on the nature of boyhood rather than of school (though of boyhood fed with public-school dreams), although, or perhaps because, both were written by schoolmasters.

At child-level, some good writers used school in books for the young, but a different sort of school, another sort of child or adolescent: C. Day-Lewis's swarming detectives in a small town day-school in *The Otterbury Incident* (1948), for instance, or William Mayne's choristers and others at schools of various kinds. Several more good writers whom I mentioned in my chapter on girls' stories wrote about girls at school as far as possible realistically and within the context of home and family and the outside world. Among pop school stories, Billy Bunter ruled undisputed (except by Enid Blyton, who took them 'straight'), taking them to further excesses so that no one, not even the once passionate fan, could take them seriously. Like St Trinian's or the Nigel Molesworth books, they became pure farce.

The genre was finished. It had relied on readers with ideas in common, shared experiences, above all a coherent attitude to the world around it; and schools now differed, writers differed, above all readers differed – from one another, and from what they had been before. In the genre of school story, what counted was certainty and self-confidence, insularity, cheerfulness, and acceptance of the accepted; and in a world grown so much more self-conscious and uncertain, so much more international, gloomy, and self-questioning, with schools that were changing almost out of all recognition, it was impossible to keep it going.

At the beginning of this book I made an arboreal image, and can now do with another: there was never a neat family tree, showing how this school story descended from that and generated another; rather, a general unorganised sprouting from slips of the first formless thickets: an undergrowth of undifferentiated pop stories, a fair number of seriously intentioned and seriously received stories now forgotten, a very few still remembered, one or two forgotten but worth reviving, the vilified *Stalky & Co.,* the almost juvenile writings of Wodehouse, Walpole, Alec Waugh and Nichols. My choice of what to look at and what to leave out has necessarily been personal, even arbitrary. Where, for instance, is the most memorable school of them all, Llanabba Castle in *Decline and Fall?* Not, I felt, within the school story genre. Where is Miss Minchin's cruel academy for poor little rich girls in *Sara Crewe, or A Little Princess?* Not, I felt again, in the genre made her own by Angela Brazil. Many novelists have touched on school and at first I thought of including most of them. But there were too many. On the pop school stories alone volumes can be – and even have been – written. The school story flourished while the public schools, in their nineteenth-century form, flourished. When they joined the modern world the school story died.

Notes

CHAPTER I

1 C. Day-Lewis. *The Buried Day*, 1960

2 R. M. Ogilvie. *Latin and Greek: A History of the Influence of the Classics on English life from 1600–1918*, 1967

3 J. R. de S. Honey. *Tom Brown's Universe: the Development of the Victorian Public Schools*, 1977

4 Graham Greene. Essay in *The Old School*. Essays by divers hands, ed. Graham Greene, 1934

5 Cyril Connolly. *Enemies of Promise*, 1938

6 Alec Waugh, *Early Years*, 1962

7 Waugh, *ibid.*

8 Graham Greene. 'The Burden of Childhood', *The Lost Childhood and other essays*, 1951

9 Alec Waugh. *Public School Life*, 1922

10 Mark Girouard. *Life in the English Country House*, 1978

11 Harold Nicolson. *Good Behaviour*, 1955

12 T. C. Worsley. *Barbarians and Philistines; Democracy and the Public Schools*, 1940

13 John Atkins. *George Orwell*, 1954

14 Anthony Sampson. *New Anatomy of Britain*, 1971

15 Vivian Ogilvie. *The English Public School*, 1957

16 A. F. Leach. *A History of Winchester College*, 1899

17 Brian Gardner. *The Public Schools*, 1973

18 Joshua Fitch. *Thomas and Matthew Arnold and their Influence on English Education*, 1897

19 George Orwell. 'My Country Right or Left', *New Writing*, 1940

20 George Orwell. Review of Galsworthy's *Glimpses and Reflections*, *New Statesman and Nation*, 12 March 1938

21 Robin Davis. *The Grammar School*, 1967

22 Robin Maugham. *The Link*, 1969

23 George Orwell. 'Inside the Whale', *New Directions in Prose and Poetry*, 1940

24 Evelyn Waugh. *Ronald Knox*, 1959

25 Alec Waugh. *Public School Life*, 1922

26 Alec Waugh. *Early Years*, 1962

27 Ronald Knox. *A Spiritual Aenead,* 1918
28 George Orwell. 'Such, such were the joys', written in May 1947, *Partisan Review,* September–October 1952
29 Jocelyn Brooke. *The Military Orchid,* 1948
30 Christopher Hollis. *Eton,* 1960
31 Rupert Wilkinson. *The Prefects: British Leadership and the Public School Tradition,* 1964
32 Edward C. Mack and W. H. G. Armytage. *Thomas Hughes,* 1952
33 W. Vincent. *A Defence of Public Education,* 1801
34 Oscar Browning. *An Introduction to the History of Educational Theories,* 1881
35 T. W. Bamford. *The Rise of the Public Schools,* 1967
36 L. E. O. Charlton. *Charlton,* 1938
37 George Orwell. 'Such, such were the joys'
38 Christopher Hollis. *A Study of George Orwell,* 1956
39 Alec Waugh. *Public School Life,* 1922
40 Cyril Connolly. Review of *Antony* by the Earl of Lytton, 1935, reprinted in *The Condemned Playground,* 1945
41 Waugh. *op. cit.*
42 Philip L. Masters. *Preparatory Schools Today,* 1966
43 Osbert Sitwell. *The Scarlet Tree,* 1946
44 George Orwell. Letter to Cyril Connolly, *Encounter,* January 1962
45 James Lees-Milne. *Another Self,* 1970
46 Edward Lucie-Smith. *The Burnt Child,* 1975
47 Worsley. *op. cit.*

CHAPTER II

1 Lionel Trilling. *Matthew Arnold,* 1939
2 Hugh Kingsmill. *Matthew Arnold,* 1928
3 A. P. Stanley. *Life and Correspondence of Thomas Arnold,* 1844
4 Reginald Farrar. *Life of F. W. Farrar,* 1905
5 Trilling. *op. cit.*
6 Charles Lamb. 'The Old and New Schoolmaster,' *Essays of Elia*, 1823
7 W. H. Auden. Essay in *The Old School,* 1934
8 Harold Nicolson. Essay in *The Old School,* 1934
9 Howard Foster Lowrey. Introduction to his edition of Matthew Arnold's *Letters to Clough,* 1932
10 G. G. Coulton. *A Victorian Schoolmaster,* 1923
11 Bernard Darwin. *The English Public School,* 1929
12 Hugh Kingsmill. 'From Shakespeare to Dean Farrar', *After Puritanism,* 1929
13 Trilling. *op. cit.*
14 Lytton Strachey. Essay on Thomas Arnold in *Eminent Victorians,* 1918
15 Rex Warner. *English Public Schools,* 1946
16 Joshua Fitch. *Thomas and Matthew Arnold and their Influence on English Education,* 1897

17 A. C. Swinburne. 'Matthew Arnold's New Poems', *Essays and Studies,* 1875
18 Stanley. *op. cit.*
19 George Orwell. From his column, 'As I please', *Tribune,* July 7, 1944
20 Ian Hay. *The Lighter Side of School Life,* 1914
21 A. H. Gilkes. Preface to *Boys and Masters,* 1887
22 W. R. M. Leake and others. *Gilkes and Dulwich,* 1938
23 A. H. Gilkes. Introduction to his *School Lectures on the Electra of Sophocles and Macbeth,* 1880

CHAPTER III

1 Derek Verschoyle. Essay in *The Old School,* 1934
2 Anthony Powell. Essay in *The Old School,* 1934
3 Louis MacNeice. *The Strings are False,* 1965
4 Rupert Wilkinson. *op. cit.*
5 H. J. Bruce. *Silken Dalliance,* 1947
6 Noel Annan. 'Kipling's Place in the History of Ideas', *Kipling's Mind and Art,* ed. Andrew Rutherford, 1964
7 Edward S. Mack and W. H. G. Armytage. *Thomas Hughes,* 1952
8 Fitch. *op. cit.*
9 Quoted by Mack and Armytage, *op. cit.*
10 Mack and Armytage. *op. cit.*
11 C. Day-Lewis. *The Buried Day*, 1960
12 Harold Nicolson. Essay in *The Old School,* 1934
13 T. C. Worsley. *Flannelled Fool,* 1967
14 Leonard Woolf. *Sowing,* 1960
15 William Plomer. Essay in *The Old School,* 1934
16 L. P. Hartley. Essay in *The Old School,* 1934
17 John Gale. *Clean Young Englishman,* 1965
18 Fitch. *op. cit.*
19 Mack and Armytage, *op. cit.*
20 Lord Elton. Introduction to the World's Classics edn. of *Tom Brown's Schooldays,* 1953
21 C. S. Lewis. *Surprised by Joy,* 1955
22 Thomas Arnold (son of Dr Arnold). *Passages in a Wandering Life,* 1900
23 Fitch. *op. cit.*
24 Strachey. *op. cit.*
25 Hugh Kingsmill. *Matthew Arnold,* 1928
26 P. G. Wodehouse. Essay on school stories in the *Public School Magazine,* published anonymously but identified as Wodehouse's by Richard Usborne, quoted in *Wodehouse at Work,* 1961
27 Ian Hay, *op. cit.*
28 Hugh Kingsmill. 'From Shakespeare to Dean Farrar', *After Puritanism,* 1929
29 Harold Nicolson. *op. cit.*

CHAPTER IV

1 Stanley Morison. *Talbot Baines Reed,* 1960
2 Brian Alderson. Introduction to the 1971 edn. of *The Fifth Form at St Dominic's,* first published in volume form in 1887
3 Stanley Morison. *op. cit.*
4 Frank Eyre. *British Children's Books of the Twentieth Century,* 1952
5 Mrs G. Forsyth Grant. *The Beresford Boys.* 1906
6 Rupert Brooke. Article on 'The School Novel' in *The Phoenix,* a supplement to the Rugby School magazine, 1904
7 S. P. B. Mais. *A Schoolmaster's Diary,* 1918
8 H. G. Wells. *The Story of a Great Schoolmaster: being a plain account of the life and ideas of Sanderson of Oundle,* 1924
9 Sir Ian Hamilton. Introduction to *The Making of Wellington College,* compiled by J. L. Bevir, 1920
10 H. E. Bates. Essay in *The Old School,* 1934
11 Talbot Baines Reed. *The Fifth Form at St Dominic's*, 1887 (in volume form).

CHAPTER V

1 C. S. Lewis. *op. cit.*
2 Louis MacNeice. *The Strings are False,* 1965

CHAPTER VI

1 Edmund Wilson. 'The Kipling Nobody Read', *Kipling's Mind and Art,* ed. Andrew Rutherford, 1964
2 Richard Usborne. *Wodehouse at Work,* 1961
3 Louis L. Cornell. *Kipling in India,* 1966
4 Bonamy Dobrée. *The Lamp and the Lute,* 1964
5 George Orwell. 'Rudyard Kipling', *Horizon,* February 1942
6 Lionel Trilling. Essay on Kipling in *The Liberal Imagination,* 1940
7 Rudyard Kipling. *Something of Myself,* 1937
8 An article in an American paper, *The Youth's Companion,* 1893
9 Charles Carrington. *Rudyard Kipling, His Life and Work,* 1955
10 Carrington. *ibid.*
11 Andrew Rutherford. ed., *Kipling's Mind and Art,* 1964
12 Philip Mason. *Kipling, the Glass, the Shadow and the Fire*, 1975
13 Janet Adam Smith. 'Boy of Letters', *Rudyard Kipling,* ed. John Gross, 1972
14 Carrington, *op. cit.*
15 H. G. Wells. *An Outline of History,* 1920
16 Steven Marcus. Essay on *Stalky & Co.,* 1962, published in *Representations: Essays on Literature and Society,* 1976

CHAPTER VII

1 Robert Graves. *Goodbye to All That,* 1929
2 John Lehmann. *In the Purely Pagan Sense,* 1976

CHAPTER VIII

1 Shane Leslie. *The Film of Memory,* 1938
2 Shane Leslie. *ibid.*
3 Shane Leslie. *ibid.*
4 Arnold Lunn. *Memory to Memory,* 1956
5 Arnold Lunn. *ibid.*

CHAPTER IX

1 Richard Usborne. *Wodehouse at Work to the End,* 1976
2 George Orwell. 'In Defence of P. G. Wodehouse', *Windmill,* No. 2, 1945
3 George Orwell, *ibid.*
4 Usborne. *op. cit.*
5 George Orwell. *ibid.*

CHAPTER X

1 Hugh Walpole. Preface to the Dent edn. of *Mr Perrin and Mr Traill,* 1935
2 Hugh Walpole, *ibid.*
3 Angus Ross. Entry on Walpole in *The Penguin Companion to English Literature,* Vol. 1, 1971
4 Robert Ross. Letter to Walpole, 1911
5 Charles Marriott. Letter to Walpole, 1911
6 Henry James. Letter to Walpole, 1911
7 Hugh Walpole. *op. cit.*
8 Hugh Walpole. *The Crystal Box,* 1924
9 Hugh Walpole. *ibid.*
10 Hugh Walpole. *ibid.*
11 Rupert Hart-Davis. *Hugh Walpole,* 1952
12 Hugh Walpole. *The Crystal Box,* 1924
13 Alec Waugh. *Public School Life,* 1922
14 Marguerite Steen. *Hugh Walpole: a study,* 1933
15 Hugh Walpole. Preface to the Dent edn. of *Mr Perrin and Mr Traill,* 1935
16 Ian Hay. *op. cit.*

CHAPTER XII

1 Arthur Waugh. *One Man's Road,* 1932
2 H. W. Massingham. His 'Wayfarer' column in the *Nation,* which he edited, 1917

3 Alec Waugh. *Early Years,* 1962
4 Waugh. *ibid.*
5 Waugh. *ibid.*
6 Waugh. *ibid.*
7 H. G. Wells. *Outline of History,* 1920
8 Stuart Hood. *Pebbles from My Skull,* 1963
9 Alec Waugh. *op. cit.*
10 Alec Waugh. *op. cit.*
11 Cyril Connolly. Review of *Antony* by the Earl of Lytton (1935), reprinted in *The Condemned Playground,* 1945
12 C. Day-Lewis. *The Buried Day,* 1960

CHAPTER XIII

1 E. Arnot Robertson. Essay in *The Old School,* 1934
2 E. Arnot Robertson. *ibid.*
3 Gillian Freeman. *The Schoolgirl Ethic: the Life and Work of Angela Brazil,* 1976
4 Gillian Freeman. *ibid.*
5 Geoffrey Trease. *Tales out of School,* 1948
6 E. Arnot Robertson. *op. cit.*

CHAPTER XIV

1 Ian Hay, *The Lighter Side of School Life,* 1914
2 Desmond Coke. Preface to *The Bending of a Twig,* 1906
3 Desmond Coke. *ibid.*
4 Ian Hay. Introduction to *Godfrey Marten, Schoolboy,* edn. published for the centenary of Cheltenham College, 1940
5 Ian Hay. *ibid.*
6 A. A. Milne. Essay in *Dear Turley,* ed. Eleanor Adlard, 1942
7 Ian Hay. *op cit.*

CHAPTER XV

1 Ian Hay. *The Lighter Side of School Life,* 1922 edn.
2 Ernest Raymond. *The Story of My Days: an autobiography 1888–1922,* 1968
3 Geoffrey Trease. *op. cit.*

CHAPTER XVI

1 George Orwell. 'Boys' Weeklies', *Horizon,* March 1940
2 Evelyn Waugh. *A Little Learning,* 1964
3 T. C. Worsley. *Barbarians and Philistines,* 1940
4 John Rodgers. *The Old Public Schools of England,* 1938
5 *Orwell. op cit.*

6 E. S. Turner. *Boys will be Boys,* 1948
7 Sean O'Faolain. Title story in *The Talking Trees,* 1971
8 H. E. Bates. Essay in *The Old School,* 1934
9 John Arlott. *The Charles Hamilton Collection,* 1972
10 Arlott. *ibid.*
11 Denzil Batchelor. *The Charles Hamilton Collection*, 1972
12 Arthur Marshall. Review of *Bunter's Last Fling,* 1965, reprinted in *Girls will be Girls,* 1974
13 Orwell. *op. cit.*

CHAPTER XVII

1 W. H. Auden. Essay in *The Old School,* 1934
2 Harold Nicolson. Essay in *The Old School,* 1934
3 Katharine Hull and Pamela Whitlock. *The Far-Distant Oxus,* 1938
4 Evelyn Waugh. *op. cit.*

Bibliography

If it is not to stretch across far too many pages, the bibliography of a book like this must be strictly selected. For behind its subject stands the whole history of this country and its Empire from the eighteenth century (or earlier) until the mid-twentieth: political, social, economic, even personal and affective. The school story may seem a mouse born from so great a mountain, but it cannot be understood without reference to it. So readers must include in an ideal bibliography innumerable volumes of history, philosophy, biography, travel, memoirs and diaries, poetry and fiction, to give them a cultural familiarity with the period and its attitudes; as well as the vast number of schools memoirs, school histories and the biographies and autobiographies of almost everyone belonging to the educated (or at least the ruling) classes of the period, nearly all of which have, not surprisingly, things to say about school, or indirect light to throw on it. The school stories themselves which have not been mentioned in the text cannot be listed: there are too many.

On the history of public schools in general, there are (among others) the following:

Bernard Darwin, *The English Public School*. Longman, Green and Co., 1929

John Rodgers, *The Old Public Schools of England*. Batsford, 1938

Vivian Ogilvie, *The English Public School*. Batsford, 1957

T. W. Bamford, *The Rise of the Public School*. Nelson, 1967

Felicia Lamb and Helen Pickthorn, *Locked-up Daughters*. Hodder & Stoughton, 1968

Brian Heeney, *Mission to the Middle Classes. The Woodard Schools, 1848–1891*. Published for the Church Historical Society in association with the University of Alberta Press by SPCK, 1969

Alicia C. Percival, *The Origins of the Headmasters' Conference*. Murray, 1969

Brian Gardner, *The Public Schools*. Hamish Hamilton, 1973

J. R. de S. Honey, *Tom Brown's Universe, the Development of the Victorian Public School*. Millington, 1977

Jonathan Gathorne-Hardy, *The Public School Phenomenon*. Hodder & Stoughton, 1977

George Macdonald Fraser (ed.), *The World of the Public School* (essays). Weidenfeld & Nicolson, 1977

Noel Annan's *Roxburgh of Stowe*, Longman, 1965, contains one of the best summaries I know of the public schools' history and ethos up to the twenties and thirties.

The schools themselves nearly all have published histories; the main schools have several, as well as bound volumes of school lists, volumes of essays to celebrate centenaries, and so on. In its library Eton has many shelf-loads of books about itself, and eighty years ago L. V. Harcourt's *An Eton Bibliography* already ran to 132 pages. Among the livelier and better written of the school histories are:

David Newsome, *A History of Wellington College, 1859–1959*. Murray, 1959

Christopher Hollis, *Eton*. Hollis & Carter, 1960

Christopher Dilke, *Dr Moberly's Mint-Mark: a Study of Winchester College*. Heinemann, 1965

Volumes of essays on particular schools at particular times are valuable (if often repetitive and trivial) to anyone interested in the subject. For example:

Graham Greene (ed.), *The Old School*. Cape, 1934

Brian Inglis (ed.), *John Bull's Schooldays*. Hutchinson, 1961

On particular aspects of public-school life, making this or that point, there are so many books that again it is impossible to list them all. As the Headmaster of Marlborough put it, at the start of his, in 1963: 'One trembles to lay before the public yet another book on the public schools.'

Here are a few examples:

Alec Waugh, *Public School Life*. Collins, 1922

T. C. Worsley, *Barbarians and Philistines: Democracy and the Public Schools*. Robert Hale, 1940

J. C. Dancy, *The Public Schools and the Future*. Faber, 1963

Graham Kalton, *The Public Schools: a Factual Survey*. Longman, Green, 1966

Royston Lambert, John Hipkin, Susan Stagg, *New Wine in Old Bottles? Studies in Integration within the Public Schools*. Bell, 1968

T. E. B. Howarth, *Culture, Anarchy and the Public Schools*. Cassell, 1969

John Wakeford, *The Cloistered Elite: a Sociological Analysis of the English Public School*. Macmillan, 1969

John Rae, *The Public School Revolution: Britain's Independent Schools 1964–79*. Faber, 1981

J. A. Mangan, *Athleticism in Victorian and Edwardian Public Schools*. Cambridge University Press, 1981

Headmasters have often been written about, even when they are now forgotten, and many for reasons other than the schoolmasterly (they went on, sometimes, to other things: bishoprics, quite often). A few books which deal with them are:

A. P. Stanley, *Life and Correspondence of Dr. Arnold*. Ward Lock, 1844
G. R. Parkin, *Life and Letters of Edward Thring* (of Uppingham). Macmillan, 1898
F. D. How, *Six Great Schoolmasters*. Methuen, 1904
H. G. Wells, *The Story of a Great Schoolmaster* (Sanderson of Oundle). Chatto & Windus, 1924
Arnold Whitridge (Arnold's great-grandson), *Dr. Arnold of Rugby*. Cassell, 1929
W. R. M. Leake and others, *Gilkes and Dulwich*. Alleyn Club, 1938
N. G. Wymer, *Dr. Arnold of Rugby*. Robert Hale, 1953
T. W. Bamford, *Thomas Arnold*. Cresset Press, 1960
Noel Annan, *Roxburgh of Stowe*. Longman, 1965
Betty Askwith, *Two Victorian Families* (one of them is the Bensons). Chatto & Windus, 1971
——— *The Lytteltons*. Chatto & Windus, 1975
Alicia C. Percival, *Very Superior Men: some early Public-School Headmasters and their Achievements*. Charles Knight, 1973

Headmasters also appear in so many memoirs that even when there is no single biography a composite portrait can be built up from a number of sources; and they often turn up in family histories, too, as members of academically distinguished families.

The writers of school stories are often too obscure for full biographies or even a place in the *DNB*. Here, however, are a few biographies:

Reginald Farrar, *Life of Frederick William Farrar*. James Nisbet and Co., 1904
Eleanor Adlard (ed.), *Dear Turley*. Tributes from friends. Frederick Muller, 1942
Edward C. Mack and W. H. G. Armytage, *Thomas Hughes*. Benn, 1952
Stanley Morison, *Talbot Baines Reed, Author, Bibliographer, Typefounder*. Cambridge University Press, 1968
Rupert Hart-Davis, *Hugh Walpole*. Macmillan, 1952
Gillian Freeman, *The Schoolgirl Ethic: the Life and Work of Angela Brazil*. Allen Lane, 1976

Leslie, Lunn, Vachell, Benson, Kipling, Wodehouse, Raymond, Nichols and Frank Richards wrote their memoirs.

On Kipling and Wodehouse there are, of course, many books. Here is a selection.

On Kipling:

Charles Carrington, *Rudyard Kipling*. Macmillan, 1955. Rev. edn.
J. M. S. Tompkins, *The Art of Rudyard Kipling*. Methuen, 1959
Andrew Rutherford (ed.), *Kipling's Mind and Art*. Essays. Oliver & Boyd, 1964
C. A. Bodelsen, *Aspects of Kipling's Art*. Manchester University Press, 1964
Roger Lancelyn Green, *Kipling and the Children*. Elek Books, 1965
J. I. M. Stewart, *Rudyard Kipling*. Gollancz, 1966

Louis L. Cornell, *Kipling in India*. Macmillan, 1966

Bonamy Dobrée, *Rudyard Kipling, Realist and Fabulist*. Oxford University Press, 1967

T. R. Henn, *Kipling*. Oliver & Boyd, 1967

John Gross (ed.), *Rudyard Kipling* (essays). Weidenfeld & Nicolson, 1972

Roger Lancelyn Green (ed.), *Kipling: the Critical Heritage*. Critical writings on Kipling. Routledge & Kegan Paul, 1971

Philip Mason, *Kipling, the Glass, the Shadow and the Fire*. Cape, 1975

Lord Birkenhead, *Rudyard Kipling*. Weidenfeld & Nicolson, 1978

Angus Wilson, *The Strange Ride of Rudyard Kipling: his Life and Works*. Secker & Warburg, 1977

There are also influential essays on him by T. S. Eliot in *A Choice of Kipling's Verse*. Faber, 1941, and C. S. Lewis in *They Asked for a Paper*, Geoffrey Bles, 1962. *Something of Myself* (1937) is Kipling's autobiography.

On Wodehouse:

Richard Usborne, *Wodehouse at Work*. Herbert Jenkins, 1961. Revised as *Wodehouse at Work to the End*. Barrie & Jenkins, 1976

R. B. D. French, *P. G. Wodehouse*. Oliver & Boyd, 1966

Thelma Cazalet-Keir (ed.), *Homage to P. G. Wodehouse*. Essays. Barrie & Jenkins, 1973

David A. Jason, *P. G. Wodehouse: a Portrait of a Master*. Garnstone Press, 1975

Owen Dudley Edwards, *P. G. Wodehouse: a Critical and Historical Essay*. Martin Brian & O'Keeffe, 1977

Performing Flea (1953) and *Over Seventy* (1957) are Wodehouse's autobiographies, and a number of books about him and his work appeared in 1981, for the centenary of his birth.

Finally, there are many unclassifiable books which anyone interested in the school story, the period, or the public school as 'imaginative country' should not fail to look at. For instance:

Edward C. Mack, *Public Schools and British Opinion, 1780–1860*. Methuen, 1938

J. F. C. Harrison, *A History of the Working Men's College, 1854–1954*. Routledge & Kegan Paul, 1954. (Much about Hughes, Maurice and the Christian Socialists.)

E. S. Turner, *Boys Will be Boys*. Michael Joseph, 1948. New and rev. edn. 1957

David Newsome, *Godliness and Good Learning*. Murray, 1961

R. M. Ogilvie, *Latin and Greek: a History of the Influence of the Classics on English Life from 1600 to 1918*. Routledge & Kegan Paul, 1964

And, of course, Samuel Butler's *The Way of All Flesh*, Robert Graves's *Goodbye to All That* . . .

It is hard to know where to draw the line, because the subject leads one not just on and on, but round and round; into detailed examination of all sorts of things, or broad speculation of quite another kind.

Acknowledgements

Grateful thanks are due to the following for their kind permission to reproduce copyright material:
The Hamlyn Publishing Group for permission to reproduce Gareth Floyd's illustration to *The Naughtiest Girl is a Monitor* by Enid Blyton; Howard Baker (The Greyfriars Press) Ltd, London and Amalgamated Press Ltd, London, for Greyfriars illustrations; the National Trust, Macmillan & Co. of London and Doubleday & Co. Inc., New York, for excerpts from *Stalky & Co.* by Rudyard Kipling; John Murray Ltd for excerpts from *The Hill* by H. A. Vachell and *The Lanchester Tradition* by G. F. Bradby; A. D. Peters & Co. Ltd for excerpts from *The Loom of Youth* by Alec Waugh.

Index